Consulting For Dummies®

Using the Internet to Market Yourself

Without a doubt, the Internet offers an exciting new opportunity to market yourself and the consulting services that you offer. And though obtaining an Internet e-mail address is the minimum price of admission for starting your online marketing efforts, you can get your message to your target population of prospects in a variety of other ways — all at a fairly low cost:

- Create and publish a Web page.
- Get noticed by Internet search engines.
- Build and trade hypertext links to your site with other Web sites.
- Do targeted e-mail mass mailings.
- Get involved in bulletin boards and newsgroups.
- Advertise your Internet address every-where.
- Establish your own Web domain name.
- Become a system operator for an online service forum.
- Affiliate with an online consultant referral service.
- Set up an Internet mailing list.

Building Business with Your Current Clients

It's easy to throw a *lot* of money at marketing your business while forgetting your best and most reliable source of new business: your current clients. An effective marketing campaign starts with making sure that your current clients are your biggest fans and supporters. Here are some proven techniques for doing so:

- Be on time and within budget.
- Anticipate your clients' needs (and be ready with suggestions to address them).
- Be easy to work with.
- Keep in touch with your clients.
- Be honest and ethical.
- Give a little more than you promise.
- Ask your clients for testimonials and referrals.
- Offer financial incentives for continuing to do business with you.
- Educate your clients about all the services that you offer.
- Do great work.

Building Your Own Consulting Code of Ethics

Ethics are particularly important for consultants because of the high level of trust that clients grant them and because of the access that many consultants have to the confidential and inner workings of the organizations that employ them. Consider building your own consulting code of ethics out of these building blocks:

- Account for your time accurately and honestly.
- Don't make promises that you can't keep.
- Don't recommend products or services that your clients don't need.
- Be candid and give your honest opinion.
- Protect your clients' confidentiality.
- Follow through on your promises.
- Disclose conflicts of interest.
- Don't use inside information to your advantage.
- Don't break the law.

For Dummies: Bestselling Book Series for Beginners

Consulting For Dummies®

Cheat Sheet

Ten Secrets of Better Consulting

Though there are many ways to become a more effective consultant, if you make the following ten techniques a part of your standard operating procedure, you'll be *way* ahead of your competition:

- **Listen to your clients.** To determine the best solutions for your clients, you must listen to them. Make it a point to listen to your clients more than you talk.

- **Quickly establish rapport with your clients.** Consulting is very much a one-to-one, person-to-person kind of business. Establishing rapport with your clients builds a bridge that enables trust to grow.

- **Keep your ego on a short leash.** Though it's okay to be self-confident, it's *not* okay to let your ego get in the way of your common sense and your ability to listen to what your clients are telling you.

- **Be flexible and responsive.** Flexibility is one of the main reasons why people hire consultants. If you can't respond to your clients' needs immediately, someone else will.

- **Don't overprice your services.** The higher your price, the less demand there will be for your services. If your prices are significantly higher than average, be prepared to explain why you deserve to be paid more than your competition.

- **Don't underprice your services.** If your price is too low, you won't make money and will be flooded with unprofitable business. Don't forget: No client will ever tell you that you aren't charging enough!

- **Have more than one primary client.** Putting all your eggs in one basket is never a good policy. Work toward securing a number of clients in a variety of fields instead of just one, even if your main client keeps you busy full-time.

- **Accept as much work as you can without compromising quality.** Small jobs may lead to big jobs. Never turn down work unless doing so will cause the quality of your work to suffer.

- **Treat your current clients like gold.** Not only do your current clients pay your bills, but they are your best source for referral business. Don't forget your most important clients: your *current* clients.

- **Constantly market to bring in future business.** Although your current clients pay your bills now, you need a constant stream of future clients to grow your business and pay your future bills. Set aside one-third to one-half of your time prospecting for future clients.

For Dummies: Bestselling Book Series for Beginners

Praise Praise Praise For Consulting For Dummies

"*Consulting For Dummies* is the perfect combination of practical advice and profitable tips that can help anyone succeed. I'm going to add it to the very short list of books that I use to build my consulting business. My advice? Get it!"

> — Bill Eastman, President, Applied Innovations Group, Gloucester, Virginia

"Refreshingly irreverent and lucidly written: Only a dummy would deny him or herself the practical advice this book offers. Go for it, whether you're a wannabe or an old pro!"

> — James H. Kennedy, Founder, *Consultants News*, Fitzwilliam, New Hampshire

"Whether you are a novice consultant or a pro, *Consulting For Dummies* coaches you to outstanding success. It is crammed with practical, proven tips and techniques to attract clients and to deliver a quality project profitably while having fun."

> — Bradley Zehner II, Ph.D., Professor, Pepperdine University, and Founder, Zetec, Strategy and Marketing Consulting

"This book is a revelation — and a must read."

> — Ken Shelton, Editor, *Executive Excellence*

Praise Praise Praise For Nelson and Economy's Managing For Dummies

". . . *Managing For Dummies* . . . provides easily digestible sound bites on popular management topics. It's good for new managers and as a refresher."

> — *Computerworld Magazine*

". . . a fun and information-packed read . . . their advice is solid and up-to-date."

> — *Quality Digest*

"This is the one handbook that I keep close by as a reference for daily work problems. It serves as both guide and refresher for a myriad of situations that arise at work."

> — Sam Steinhardt, Vice President and CFO, Context Integration, Inc.

"This book recognizes that it is a new world of management out there. But it takes the best of proven, older principles to apply to the new workplace."

> — Dr. Rick Crandall, Speaker and Author, *Marketing Your Service: For People Who HATE to Sell;* Publisher and Editor of *Executive Edge* newsletter

"This is a valuable book for any manager or any aspiring manager. It provides a useful, easy-to-read description of the tools that an effective manager must draw from. I like its breadth and diversity of topics, from interviewing to budgeting, from technology to teambuilding, from coaching to compensation. They're put together in a practical package that'll make sense to anyone in the world of business."

> — Oren Harari, Contributor, Management Review and Professor, McLaren School of Busiess, University of San Francisco

Other Books by Bob Nelson and Peter Economy

Managing For Dummies
Better Business Meetings

Other Books by Bob Nelson

1001 Ways to Reward Employees
1001 Ways to Energize Employees
Motivating Today's Employees
Empowering Employees Through Delegation
Delegation: The Power of Letting Go
Decision Point: A Business Game Book
Exploring the World of Business (with Ken Blanchard, Charles Shewe, and Alex Hiam)
The Perfect Letter (with Patricia Westheimer)
We Have to Start Meeting Like This: A Guide to Successful Meeting Management (with Roger Mosvick)
The Presentation Primer: Getting Your Point Across (with Jennifer Wallick)
Making More Effective Presentations
Louder and Funnier: A Practical Guide to Overcoming Stage Fright in Speechmaking
The Supervisor's Guide to Controlling Absenteeism
The Job Hunt: The Biggest Job You'll Ever Have

. . . and as a Series Editor

The New Manager's Handbook, by Brad Thompson
Straight Answers to People Problems, by Fred Jandt
Rewarding and Recognizing Employees, by Joan Klubnik
Listen for Success: A Guide to Effective Listening, by Arthur Robertson
Managing Stress: Keeping Calm Under Fire, by Barbara Braham
Managing Your Priorities: From Start to Success, by Bill Bond
The Berkeley Guide to Employment for New College Graduates, by James Briggs
Strategic Planning: Selected Readings, by J. William Pfeiffer
Odiorne on Management, by George S. Odiorne

Other Books by Peter Economy

Business Negotiating Basics
Negotiating to Win

Consulting
FOR
DUMMIES®

by Bob Nelson and Peter Economy

Wiley Publishing, Inc.

Consulting For Dummies®

Published by
Wiley Publishing, Inc.
909 Third Avenue
New York, NY 10022
www.wiley.com

Copyright © 1997 by Wiley Publishing, Inc., Indianapolis, Indiana

Published simultaneously in Canada

For general information on our other products and services or to obtain technical support, please contact our Customer Care Department within the U.S. at 800-762-2974, outside the U.S. at 317-572-3993, or fax 317-572-4002.

Wiley also publishes its books in a variety of electronic formats. Some content that appears in print may not be available in electronic books.

Library of Congress Cataloging-in-Publication Data:

Library of Congress Catalog Card No.: 97-71815

ISBN: 0-7645-5034-9

Manufactured in the United States of America

20 19 18 17 16 15

1B/QT/QZ/QS/IN

About the Authors

Bob Nelson (San Diego, CA) is founder of Nelson Motivation, Inc., and former vice president of Blanchard Training and Development, Inc., in San Diego. At Blanchard Training, Bob's responsibilities have included management of product development, customized products, assessments, and publications. He also has served on the company's strategic planning group and was formerly chief of staff for Dr. Ken Blanchard, coauthor of *The One Minute Manager*. Prior to joining Blanchard, Bob was a management trainer for Control Data Corporation and Norwest Banks.

Bob has published 17 books on business and management and has been featured extensively in the media: on CNN, PBS, and CNBC; and *The New York Times, The Wall Street Journal,* and *Inc.* magazine, among other publications. He publishes a monthly newsletter entitled *Rewarding Employees* and advises a variety of clients on how to motivate and energize their workforces. Bob holds a master's degree in business administration from UC Berkeley and is currently a doctoral candidate in the Executive Management Program at the Claremont Graduate University in Los Angeles.

For more information on products and services offered by Nelson Motivation, Inc., including speaking or consulting services, call 800-575-5521. *Rewarding Employees* newsletter is available by writing 1001 Rewards, P. O. Box 500872, San Diego, CA 92150-9973, or faxing 619-673-9031. Bob's e-mail address is BobRewards@aol.com and his Web site is at http://www.nelson-motivation.com.

Peter Economy (Pacific Beach, CA) is a business consultant and freelance business writer who is the coauthor of *Managing For Dummies* and *Better Business Meetings* with Bob Nelson and the author of numerous books and articles on a wide variety of business topics. Peter combines his consulting and writing expertise with more than 15 years of management experience to provide his clients and readers with solid, hands-on information. He received his bachelor's degree in economics from Stanford University and is pursuing his MBA. Peter can be reached via e-mail at bizzwriter@alumni.stanford.org.

Dedication

To the many unsung consultants who quietly dedicate their working lives to helping others reach their goals.

Authors' Acknowledgments

We would like to give our sincere thanks to all the consultants whose personal stories and experiences helped bring this book to life, including Stephen Crow, Steve Dente, Bill Eastman, Jim Harris, W. Lee Hill, Cindy Kazan, Douglas Poretz, Evan Rose, Janice Seto, Richard Vaaler, and Jamie Zebrowski.

Many thanks to Bill VanCanagan for his expert legal advice on the manuscript and to Bill Brooks for his quick response to our questions early in the writing process.

Bob and Peter are especially appreciative of all the talented folks at Hungry Minds, Inc., especially Kathy Welton, Mark Butler, Stacy Collins, and Pam Mourouzis for their infinite wisdom, guidance, and support on this project.

On the personal side, Bob would like to acknowledge the ongoing love and support of his father Edward, his wife Jennifer, and his children Daniel and Michelle. Peter acknowledges his mother Betty Economy Gritis, his wife Jan, and his children Peter J and Skylar for love everlasting. *May the circle be unbroken.*

Publisher's Acknowledgments

We're proud of this book; please register your comments through our online registration form located at www.dummies.com/register.

Some of the people who helped bring this book to market include the following:

Acquisitions, Development, and Editorial

Senior Project Editor: Pamela Mourouzis

Acquisitions Editor: Mark Butler

Copy Editors: Tina Sims, Michael Simsic

General Reviewers: Brad Zehner, Ph.D.;
Bill Eastman

Editorial Manager: Leah P. Cameron

Editorial Assistant: Chris H. Collins

Special Help

Mary C. Corder, Editorial Manager;
Steven H. Hayes, Editorial Assistant;
Stephanie Koutek, Proof Editor; Kelly Oliver,
Project Editor; Diane Graves Steele,
Vice President and Associate Publisher

Production

Associate Project Coordinator:
E. Shawn Aylsworth

Layout and Graphics: Brett Black,
Linda M. Boyer, Elizabeth Cárdenas-Nelson,
Angela F. Hunckler, Todd Klemme,
Drew R. Moore, Mark C. Owens,
Brent Savage, Renee L. Schmith,
Deirdre Smith, Dan Whetstine

Proofreaders: Betty Kish, Kelli Botta,
Melissa D. Buddendeck, Nancy Price, Dwight
Ramsey, Robert Springer

Indexer: Anne Leach

Publishing and Editorial for Consumer Dummies
   Diane Graves Steele, Vice President and Publisher, Consumer Dummies
   Joyce Pepple, Acquisitions Director, Consumer Dummies
   Kristin A. Cocks, Product Development Director, Consumer Dummies
   Michael Spring, Vice President and Publisher, Travel
   Brice Gosnell, Publishing Director, Travel
   Suzanne Jannetta, Editorial Director, Travel

Publishing for Technology Dummies
   Richard Swadley, Vice President and Executive Group Publisher
   Andy Cummings, Vice President and Publisher

Composition Services
   Gerry Fahey, Vice President of Production Services
   Debbie Stailey, Director of Composition Services

Contents at a Glance

Table of Contents

Introduction

*T*here are many reasons for becoming a consultant. Perhaps you've worked at your job for a number of years and you dream of striking out on your own — being your own boss and getting paid well for the expertise that you have developed during your career. Maybe you've been recently downsized, rightsized, or reengineered (or you're concerned that you're next on the list), and you're looking for a way to help pay your rent or to buy some measure of independence from the avarice of your company's management. Or perhaps you simply relish the thought of diving into a variety of problems with a variety of clients rather than being wedded to one firm.

Whatever the reason, consulting can be an exciting and rewarding profession — and not just in a financial sense. Whenever a problem beyond the capability of your client arises, all it takes is a single phone call, and expert opinion stands ready to serve. No muss, no fuss.

Of course, in the real world, consulting involves much more than tapping your client's head with a magic wand and watching all the problems go away. To be a consultant, you have to

- Be an expert (or at least *appear* to be an expert) on some topic
- Know how and when to listen to your clients
- Be perceptive yet diplomatic
- Know how to make your business thrive

Consulting For Dummies is perfect for both new and experienced consultants, and consultants-to-be. New consultants and consultants-to-be can find everything that they need to know to be successful and popular beyond their wildest beliefs. Experienced consultants are challenged to shift their perspectives and to take a fresh look at their philosophies and techniques — what's working for them and what's not, and how to get more of the former.

About This Book

Consulting For Dummies is full of useful information, tips, and checklists that any consultant or consultant-to-be can use right away. Whether you are just thinking about becoming a consultant or you are already a seasoned pro, you can find everything you need to make consulting both fun and profitable for yourself and your clients.

The good news is that the information you find within the covers of this book is firmly grounded in the real world. This book is *not* an abstract collection of theoretical mumbo-jumbo that sounds good but that doesn't work when you put it to the test. We have culled the *best* information, the *best* strategies, and the *best* techniques for consulting from people who already do it for a living. This book is a toolbox full of road-tested solutions to your every question and problem.

And although *Consulting For Dummies* is overflowing with useful advice and information, it is presented in a fun, easy-to-access format.

First, this book is *fun,* which reflects our strong belief and experience that consulting can be both profitable and fun, too. Nobody said that you can't get your work done while making sure that both you and your clients enjoy yourselves in the process. We even help you to maintain a sense of humor in the face of upcoming deadlines and seemingly insurmountable challenges that all consultants have to deal with from time to time. Some days, you *will* be challenged to your limit or beyond. However, on many more days, the satisfaction of resolving a production bottleneck, recommending a new accounting system, or installing a new client-server computer network will bring you a sense of fulfillment that you never could have imagined possible.

Second, the material in this book is easy to access. What good is all the information in the world if you can't get to it quickly and easily? Have no fear; we have designed this book with you, the reader, in mind. Here's how to get to the precise information you seek:

- ✔ If you want to find out about a specific area, such as gathering data or setting up a home office, you can flip to that chapter and get your answers quickly. Faster than you can say "The check's in the mail," you have your answer.

- ✔ If you want a crash course in consulting, read this book from cover to cover. Forget spending lots of money on high-priced seminars and videos. Forget learning by trial and error. Forget spending countless nights poring over some fly-by-night correspondence course. Everything you need to know about consulting is right here. Really.

We know from personal experience that consulting can be an intimidating job. Consultants — especially ones who are just learning the ropes — are often at a loss as to what they need to do and when they need to do it. Don't worry. Relax. Help is at your fingertips. A prominent feature of *Consulting For Dummies* is the advice that we have gathered from interviews with consultants in various fields and areas of expertise. You don't find any filler here — just practical solutions to everyday problems.

Foolish Assumptions

While we were writing this book, we made a few assumptions about you. For example, we assume that you have at least a passing interest in consulting. Maybe you're already a consultant, or perhaps consulting is something that you might like to try. We also assume that you have a skill or expertise that your friends, relatives, or clients will be willing to pay you for. This expertise may be providing your advice on anything from postage stamp collections to Internet consulting to aerospace engineering services. One more thing: We assume that you don't already know everything that there is to know about consulting and that you are eager to acquire some new perspectives on the topic.

How This Book Is Organized

Consulting For Dummies is divided into six parts. The chapters within each part cover specific topics in detail. Because we have organized the book this way, you can find the topic you're looking for — quickly and easily. Simply look up your general area of interest and then find the chapter that concerns your particular needs. Whatever the topic, it's sure to be covered someplace!

Each part addresses a major area of the business of consulting. Following is a summary of what you can find in each part.

Part I: What's a Consultant?

Consultants are many things to many people. This part considers what consultants are, what they do, and *why* they do what they do. We explore some ways for you to assess your own skills and abilities, understand the different roles that consultants play, and define the kind of consulting that you want to do.

Part II: The Consulting Process

There is a right way and a wrong way to consult. In this part, we explain the *right* way. We explain how to clearly diagnose the client's problem, collect data effectively, and analyze it quickly and efficiently. Finally, we talk about how to give feedback to your clients and ensure that your advice gets implemented.

Part III: Key Consulting Skills

Although almost everyone is an expert in *something,* not everyone can be a consultant. If you want to be a successful consultant, you have to develop a variety of key skills. This part addresses the skills that are most important to running a successful consultant practice, including preparing reports, organizing your time, communicating effectively, holding client meetings, giving presentations, and using the latest technology to your advantage.

Part IV: Setting Up Your Business

A consulting business involves more than just consulting — you have to set up and run the business, too. In this part, we consider the critical issue of setting fees, negotiating and drafting contracts, tracking your time, paying your bills, and using support services. You also can find information about the advantages and disadvantages of home offices versus more conventional alternatives.

Part V: Marketing Your Business

Spreading the word about your business is key to your success as a consultant. Here you can find out about public relations, advertising, and building business with new clients and through referrals. Use your success to create even greater success!

Part VI: The Part of Tens

Here, in a concise and lively set of short chapters, you can find tips that can really launch your consulting practice into orbit. In these chapters, we address using the Internet and other publicity tools to market your services, avoiding consulting mistakes, writing proposals, negotiating contracts, and building business with existing clients.

Icons Used in This Book

To guide you along the way and point out the information you really need to know about consulting, this book uses icons along its left margins. You see the following icons in this book:

This icon points you to tips and tricks to make consulting easier.

Watch out! If you don't heed the advice next to these icons, the whole situation may blow up in your face.

Remember these important points of information, and you'll be a much better consultant.

These real-life anecdotes from Bob and Peter and other consultants show you the right — and occasionally wrong — way to be a consultant.

Following the advice next to these icons will make you stand out from the consultant crowd.

This icon points out wise sayings and other kernels of wisdom that you can take with you on your journey to becoming a better consultant.

Where to Go from Here

Although a book such as this, especially one with so many pages that just *happen* to make great kindling for the logs in your fireplace, can be used in many different ways, we suggest the best way to use this book is to *read* it. *How* you read it is up to you.

If you are a new or aspiring consultant, you may want to start at the beginning of this book and work your way through to the end. A wealth of information and practical advice awaits you. Simply turn the page and you're on your way!

If you're already a consultant and you're short of time (and what consultant *isn't* short of time?), you may want to turn to a particular topic to address a specific need or question. If that's the case, the Table of Contents gives a chapter-by-chapter description of all the topics in this book, and the thorough index can help you find exactly what you're looking for.

If you're *really* short of time, simply place this book under your pillow at night. You're sure to pick up a concept or two!

Regardless of how you find your way around *Consulting For Dummies,* we're sure that you'll enjoy getting there. If you have specific questions or comments, please feel free to write us in care of IDG Books Worldwide (check out the *great* Dummies Press Web site at http://www.dummies.com), or drop us a line at BobRewards@aol.com (Bob) or bizzwriter@alumni.stanford.org (Peter). We love to hear your personal anecdotes and suggestions for improving future revisions of this book, and we promise to take every one of them to heart.

Here's to your success!

Part I

What's a Consultant?

The 5th Wave   By Rich Tennant

"I ADVISE TO COMPANIES WHERE THE USE OF HURTFUL LANGUAGE APPEARS EPIDEMIC. THAT'S RIGHT, YOUR HONOR— I'M AN INSULTANT CONSULTANT."

In this part . . .

Are you ready to become a consultant? Before you can answer that question, you have much to consider. In this part, we talk about some of the most important things to keep in mind, such as why people become consultants, what consultants do, how to determine whether consulting is for you, and how to make the transition from full-time employment to independent consulting as painless as possible.

Chapter 1

Why Consult? (And When to Make the Leap)

• •

In This Chapter

▶ Exploring what a consultant is and why people become consultants

▶ Taking the consulting challenge quiz

▶ Deciding when to become a consultant

• •

People become consultants for many reasons. And there are all kinds of consultants. A consultant can be a partner in a large management consulting firm or a freelance writer. A consultant can be a self-employed computer programmer or a part-time cosmetics salesperson. A consultant can be an architect who works out of his or her home, an expert witness hired to testify at the latest Trial of the Century, or a virtual stock trader who does business with clients around the globe over the Internet.

In this book, we use the term *consultant* quite loosely. We define a consultant as someone who provides his or her unique expertise to someone else. This expertise can be anything from showing someone how to properly lay out a flower garden, to donating time to an organization such as a church or community, to analyzing and recommending changes to a complex manufacturing operation.

So why would anyone want to become a consultant?

If we have to sum up the reasons for becoming a consultant in one word, the word is *freedom*. You have the freedom to chase your dreams, to live life on *your* terms, and to really enjoy the work that you do for others. Most consultants do what they want to do, when and where they want to do it. If you want to work on a client's proposal while you're sipping a steaming grande café latté at your local Starbucks, that's just fine. If you want a commute that consists of walking the 39 steps from your bedroom to your home office — in your bathrobe — it's yours for the choosing. If you're tired of punching a time clock and you've always wanted to be your own boss, relief is within your reach.

Although many people think of consultants only in terms of the narrow field of professional management consulting — firms like Price Waterhouse, KPMG, Bain & Co., and others that specialize in fixing "broken" organizations — the world of consulting is much bigger than that. Anytime someone pays you for your unique expertise or advice — whether it's creating a snazzy Web page for a friend's business or measuring the stress that a Category 4 hurricane might exert on a new home or suggesting where to dig a new water well on a ranch in Wyoming — you are acting as a consultant. And don't forget: Some companies hire *internal* consultants — employees whose job it is to address a wide variety of problems within their organizations. Working as an internal consultant can be a good compromise if you're not quite ready to strike out on your own but want to use your skills and expertise in a new way.

In this chapter, we consider the many reasons why energized and talented people like you are becoming independent consultants. You then have the opportunity to test your consulting aptitude to see whether consulting is right for you. Finally, we briefly discuss some of the factors that enter into the decision to become a consultant.

The Reasons for Consulting

Men and women from all walks of life with all manner of experience and expectations have reasons for becoming independent consultants. Some are leveraging their knowledge to help their clients, and others are simply tired of working for someone else. Still others are looking for a way to make some extra money. You may have noticed that more and more of your friends, family members, and coworkers are becoming either part-time or full-time consultants. A new model has replaced the old model of having a career for life. This new model is flexible — both for organizations and for the workers who get things done. The new model calls for skilled workers who can be brought into an organization on short notice, fix a problem, and then move on to another organization in need.

And although some think that *money* is the main reason people choose to become consultants, that's not really what it's all about. Sure, a lot of people make good money as consultants — make no mistake about it. But to many people, the benefits of being a consultant go far beyond the size of their bank accounts. This section talks about some of the most compelling nonmonetary reasons people enter the consulting field.

Leveraging your talent

Everyone is especially knowledgeable about at least one thing. You may, for example, have worked for 20 years as a construction loan specialist for a large bank. When it comes to construction loans, saying that you are an expert is probably an understatement. And because of the huge network of contacts that you have developed over the years, many other organizations could benefit from your unique experience.

Or you may enjoy exploring the Internet in your spare time. You've built many Web pages for yourself and your friends, and you always keep up with the latest in authoring tools and other developments. Although you work at a grocery store as a cashier ten hours a day, five days a week, you always manage to find time to pursue your favorite hobby. Would it surprise you to find out that many businesses would hire you and pay you good money to build and maintain Web pages for them? Imagine getting paid to do your hobby — *wow!*

Being tired of working for someone else

Most people have dreams of what they want to do with their lives. Some dream of buying their own home. Others dream of establishing a career or family. Still others dream of winning the lottery and moving to Bora Bora. However, in our experience, one of the greatest dreams — the one that *everyone* who works in an organization dreams at least once or twice a day — is the dream of being your own boss.

It's not that all bosses are bad. Both of us authors have had many *great* bosses over the years, and we hope that we have been good bosses to those who have worked for us. Most people, however, are born with a strong desire to be independent and to make their own decisions rather than have others make their decisions for them. And when, as time goes on, you begin to know more about what you do than your supervisors or managers, working for someone else *really* becomes difficult.

Getting laid off or are about to be laid off

The days of having a job for life are long gone. Today's economy is one of rapid change and movement. As companies continue to search for ways to cut costs, they increasingly turn to hiring temporary workers or contracting work out to consultants. Having a job today is no guarantee of having one tomorrow. When you work for a company — no matter how large — you can be laid off at any time, for almost any reason, with little or no notice. If you're lucky, you'll get a severance package of some sort — maybe a few weeks' or a few months' pay. If you're not so lucky, your last day will be just that, and you'll be on your own.

Becoming a consultant is a good way to ensure your financial future in the face of economic uncertainty. Why? One, because *you* control the number of jobs you take on and how much or how little extra work you want to keep in reserve. Two, because you can often make more money consulting for a firm than you can as an employee of that same firm. Many companies are more than willing to pay a premium to hire an expert consultant to do the same job that an employee could do for much less money.

Having a flexible second source of income

If you want a flexible second source of income, then consulting is just what the doctor ordered. When you are a consultant, you set your own schedule. If you want to work only on weekends, you can decide to work only on weekends. If you want to do your work late at night, that's fine, too. And because *you* decide exactly how much work you take on, you can work for one client at a time or many clients at once. Decisions about your schedule and your workload are all up to you.

And another thing: If you conduct your business from your home, this second source of income can mean a sizable write-off on your income taxes. The government allows owners of home-based businesses to take a variety of tax deductions that are not available to most other individuals. Even if you don't work out of your home, you can write off the majority of your business-related expenses. Check out Chapter 17 for some basic information about the tax benefits of becoming an independent consultant. For *detailed* information about taxes and your business, we highly recommend *Taxes For Dummies* (published by IDG Books Worldwide, Inc.) by Eric Tyson and David Silverman.

Finding a higher calling

Many organizations benefit greatly from the services of good consultants because they generally bring an independent and objective perspective. Unfortunately, many small businesses and noncommercial organizations cannot afford to pay for a consultant's expertise like most larger, well-established businesses can. Schools, churches, charities, and other community-based organizations rely on members of the community to provide expertise and assistance. Many consultants make a regular practice of providing their expertise to community organizations at no charge. If you are one of these people, you may already be consulting without even realizing it!

Why would anyone want to do that?

- ✔ If you really believe in something — whether it's the goals of a particular political candidate or your kid's elementary school — then the psychological benefits are much greater than any financial benefits.

- ✔ The work you do for your favorite charity or community group may get you noticed, resulting in paying work. Most community organizations are supported by a variety of people from all walks of life. The network that you establish with these individuals can be invaluable to you in your working life as well as your social life. Although establishing a network of contacts may not be the main reason that you decide to offer your services to the group of your choice, it's not the worst thing that could happen to you, is it?

Peter Economy consults!

Since 1990, Peter Economy (bizzwriter @alumni.stanford.org)—coauthor with Bob Nelson of both *Consulting For Dummies* and *Managing For Dummies,* published by IDG Books Worldwide, Inc. — worked toward his goal to leave his 9-to-5 career as an administrative manager and build a successful full-time consulting practice. In 1996, this dream came true when he finally cut loose the anchor that he called his job and began consulting full-time. In addition to cowriting books, Peter provides editorial advice to other authors, writes magazine articles on a variety of business topics, and corresponds with *...For Dummies* readers worldwide via e-mail. Bob interviewed Peter to get an idea of why someone would leave a "secure" 15-year career to work as a consultant.

Consulting For Dummies: Good morning, Peter. Long time no see.

Peter Economy: Yeah right, Bob.

CFD: Okay, here's the million-dollar question: Why did you decide to become a consultant?

Economy: Geez — you're getting right to the point, aren't you? I guess there are three main reasons why I wanted to become a consultant. Number one, I always wanted to be my own boss. I've been a manager for years, but during the entire time that I was working in the world of business, I always had to respond to someone *else's* needs and priorities — not my own. It seemed that I was so busy fighting other people's fires that I didn't have enough time left to prevent my own.

CFD: Even when you were a vice president for that computer operations company?

Economy: Probably more so than when I was lower in the hierarchy. The higher up I got in an organization, the more I was subject to the personal whims and foibles of those in upper management. If they sneezed, I jumped! Anyway, now *I* decide my priorities. *I* decide the projects I want to work on, how much I'm going to charge my clients, and when and where I will do the work. I don't have to show up early at the office or stay late just to impress my boss. The color of my tie or the size of my pinstripes is no longer an issue. My work speaks for itself.

CFD: So your clients are more concerned with the final product, not what you were wearing when you created it or whether you called in sick on Friday or whether you attended the mandatory off-site management meeting?

Economy: Right. They don't care *how* I create products; they care only about the *quality* of the products I create and that I deliver them when I promise to.

CFD: So what is your second reason for becoming a consultant?

Economy: The second reason is for economic security. Back when I started getting serious about building a consulting practice, I could see that the government business that the companies I worked for depended on to remain prosperous was quickly drying up. Many of my friends and coworkers were laid off by

(continued)

(continued)

their employers, and I was afraid that I might very well be next. This suspicion was borne out when I was laid off from my last career job twice due to lack of funding.

CFD: Yeah, there's nothing like getting laid off to light a fire under you!

Economy: That's for sure. The first time I was laid off, I wasn't yet ready to make the transition to a full-time consulting practice. The second time, I was ready, willing, and able! Now the amount of money I make is directly proportional to the amount of effort I put into my work. If I work, I get paid. If I don't work, I don't get paid. However, I know that if I work hard and do the best possible job for my clients, I will have plenty of business to do, and I will be much more successful than I could ever be working for someone else.

CFD: But how were you able to build a consulting business while you were working in a full-time job?

Economy: Well, that leads to the third reason for my wanting to be a consultant: flexibility. By nature, consulting is a very flexible way to make a living. Because of this fact, I was able to squeeze occasional jobs into my schedule — usually at night and on the weekends. I might review a book for a publisher or ghostwrite a few chapters for a textbook or help fix another writer's manuscript — all in my spare time. Eventually, I was able to increase the level of consulting I did so that I could replace my full-time career job with a variety of different consulting jobs.

CFD: Wasn't leaving a steady paycheck and benefits scary? When you work for an organization, you can rely on a steady paycheck —

regardless of your level of productivity. When you work for yourself, you never know where your next paycheck is coming from.

Economy: That's all true, but to me that's part of the price of freedom. Freedom is a two-edged sword. Not only do you have the freedom to succeed beyond your wildest dreams, but you also have the freedom to fail beyond your wildest nightmares. However, I honestly believe that each one of us has a skill or talent that, if developed, can be the basis of a successful consulting business. The hard part is taking the first step and putting your dreams into action. It's not easy, but if you are willing to put your heart and soul into it, the rewards — both psychological and financial — soon outweigh the costs. And besides, then you too can sing, "I did it *my* way...."

CFD: How did you overcome the financial and emotional adjustments that you obviously had to make?

Economy: To address the financial issues, my wife Jan and I sat down together and drew up a budget for our family — the first we've ever done in our eight years of marriage. Once you work through the numbers and see that everything is going to be all right, a lot of the fear goes away. The emotional adjustments can't be made quite so easily. It takes a little time to get used to the idea of being dependent on yourself rather than on your employer. But it helped that, when I left my full-time job, I was emotionally *ready* to make the move. I wanted to be my own boss.

CFD: One last question. Is Peter Economy really your real name?

Economy: Put it in your ear, Nelson!

The Consulting Challenge Quiz

Maybe you're thinking that this consulting thing may not be such a bad idea. Now the big question is: Do you have what it takes to become a consultant? Do you want to find out? Then simply take the Consulting Challenge Quiz. It's quick, it's easy, and it's guaranteed to help you sort fantasy from reality. Don't forget to total your score at the end of the test to see where you fit.

Answering the questions

Here are the questions. Read each one and circle the answer that comes closest to your personal feelings. If you're not sure how to answer a question on your first attempt, move on to the next question and come back to the tricky one later.

1. Do you like to solve problems?

  A. Yes, solving problems is my sole reason for being.

  B. Yes, I like solving certain kinds of problems.

  C. Can I trade one of my problems for one of yours?

  D. Is there someone else who can solve them?

  E. No. Yuck. Never.

2. Can you set your own goals and then follow them to completion?

  A. I don't know what I would do if I didn't always have goals to pursue.

  B. Yes, I set my own goals, but I don't always follow up on them.

  C. I haven't tried before, but if you show me how I will.

  D. I don't set my own goals; they set themselves.

  E. Sorry, I don't have any goals.

3. Are you an independent self-starter?

  A. I don't need *anyone* to tell me what to do — let's get going!

  B. I'm independent, but I sometimes have a hard time getting motivated to do things on my own.

  C. No one has ever let me make my own decisions before. I kind of like the idea of doing things on my own, though.

  D. Hum a few bars, and maybe I can sing it.

  E. Do I have to be?

4. Are you confident about your ability to get the job done?

    A. Without a doubt.

    B. I'm fairly certain.

    C. I'm not sure.

    D. Can we discuss this some other time?

    E. Absolutely, unequivocally not.

5. Do you enjoy pursuing tasks to completion, despite the obstacles in your path?

    A. I am *very* persistent.

    B. Usually, although I sometimes avoid tackling problems directly.

    C. As long as we understand up front that no one is perfect.

    D. Is any task ever *truly* complete?

    E. Some things were just never meant to be done.

6. Can you adapt to rapid changes?

    A. My middle name is change.

    B. It's easier for me to adapt to good changes than to adapt to bad changes.

    C. If you've seen one change, you've seen them all.

    D. As long as it's *you* who changes and not me.

    E. I don't even like to change my socks!

7. Are you creative?

    A. Just give me a pencil and a piece of paper, and you'll have your solution in five minutes.

    B. Usually, but it depends on what mood I'm in.

    C. Let me think about that for a while.

    D. Why spend a lot of effort creating something that someone else has probably already figured out the answer to?

    E. I once taught my dog how to fetch the morning paper.

8. Do you like to work with people?

A. Working with people is what makes work fun.

B. Definitely — some people more than others, however.

C. Yes — it definitely beats working with trained seals.

D. I really prefer my computer.

E. I want to be alone!

9. Are you trustworthy, loyal, honest, and brave?

A. All of the above and more!

B. Well, three out of four isn't bad, is it?

C. How about two out of four?

D. I'd like to believe that there are other, more important human qualities.

E. Next question, please.

10. Are you interested in making a decent living?

A. My opportunities are unlimited.

B. Sure, as long as I don't have to work *too* hard at it.

C. I don't know; I'm pretty comfortable the way things are now.

D. Just how do you define *decent?*

E. I'm going to win that lottery one of these days!

Analyzing your score

Get out a calculator right now and add up your results. Give yourself 5 points for every A answer, 3 points for every B, 0 points for every C, –3 points for every D, and –5 for every E. Don't worry. We'll wait right here until you're done. Finished? Okay.

We have divided the possible scores into six separate categories. By comparing your total points to the points contained in each category, you can find out whether consulting is in your future.

> **25 to 50 points:** You are a born consultant. If you're not already working for yourself as a consultant, we strongly suggest that you quit your job right now and start passing out your business card to all your friends, acquaintances, and prospective clients. Well, you *may* want to line up one or two clients first! Read this book for tips on how to sharpen your already well-developed skills.

1 to 24 points: You definitely have potential to be a great consultant. Consider starting your own consulting practice in the very near future, but make sure that you keep your day job until your consulting practice is well under way. Read this book to understand the basics of consulting and find out how to grow your new business.

0 points: You could go either way. Why don't you try taking this test again in another month or two? Read this book to ensure that you pass next time.

–1 to –24 points: We're sorry to tell you, but consulting is not currently your cup of tea. We strongly recommend that you read this book and that you take this test again. If you don't do better after all that, then maybe working for someone else isn't the worst thing that could happen to you.

–25 to –50 points: Forget it. You were clearly born to work for someone else. Sell this book to one of your coworkers right now. Maybe he or she will score higher on this test than you did.

More than 50 or less than –50 points: Take your calculator to the nearest repair shop and get it fixed! Or if your calculator isn't broken, go straight to your nearest bookstore and buy a copy of *Everyday Math For Dummies* (published by IDG Books Worldwide, Inc.) by Charles Seiter. It's never too late to learn some new tricks!

The Best Time to Take the Plunge

Congratulations! Either you have decided to join the growing ranks of men and women who are taking control of their lives *and* their financial futures by becoming consultants, or you're seriously thinking about making the move. Consider some of the factors that determine exactly when the timing is best for you. Don't be surprised if your answers differ from those of your family, friends, or coworkers — everyone has a unique schedule.

In this section, we examine some of the key issues that help determine exactly when you should make your move into consulting. This list is by no means exhaustive — feel free to add any considerations that affect you directly.

Professional considerations

Before you can become a successful independent consultant, you have to attain a certain level of professional expertise. For example, if you expect someone to hire you to set up a new manufacturing quality system, you should have a strong base of experience in the area of manufacturing quality systems. If you spent your 20 years of experience behind the cash register at Burger King developing a callus on your forefinger, you may have a tough time selling yourself as an expert in manufacturing (although you may have a great future in fast-food franchise consulting).

If you're thinking about making a living as an independent consultant, be sure to keep the following professional considerations in mind:

- **Subject matter expertise:** Most people hire a consultant because they want the benefit of a consultant's extensive expertise. They know that a good consultant isn't cheap, but they also know that the overall price is less than specifically hiring or training an employee to do the same task. Before you become a full-time consultant, become an expert (or pretty darn close) in your field. When you ease into consulting by working on a part-time basis, you gain the benefit of learning while being supported by your full-time job.

- **Certifications and licenses:** In some cases, you may need to obtain special credentials before you can pursue your chosen vocation. For example, if you plan to become an independent tax adviser, you should have your Certified Public Accountant (CPA) certification before you jump into the fray. Many other professions require extensive certifications or licensing before you can practice them. If you work for an organization that pays for your required training and testing, by all means take advantage of these resources. Getting a regular paycheck while earning your certification is better than trying to earn a living on your own while you pursue the necessary paperwork.

- **References:** The ability to point to a long list of satisfied clients is a critical selling point for any consultant. Try to do as many jobs as you can with as many customers as possible before you go out on your own. Not only can you take your current clients with you when you make the move to independent consulting, but you also create a valuable network of associates that you can tap to locate new clients.

- **Organizational ability:** Making a business work takes more than printing up a set of business cards. You have to be organized, you have to have a plan, and you have to know (or learn) how to run a business. Running a consulting business is no different than any other business in that you have deadlines to meet, bills to pay, and associates and clients to coordinate with. Before you launch your new consulting business, take the time necessary to plan ahead and get organized. The time you invest *before* you get started pays for itself many times over after you are under way.

Financial considerations

Certainly, financial considerations weigh heavily in deciding when to become a consultant. Becoming complacent is easy when you're earning a decent wage and you're getting an attractive benefits package. However, what's here today can easily be gone tomorrow — you just don't know for sure *what's* going to happen. We have far too many acquaintances who have been pushed out of organizations that are desperate to cut costs in any way possible. Businesses often don't care how many years you've worked there or how talented you are. When the budget ax falls, the results can be devastating if you're not ready with your *own* plan. So when you hear "Breaking Up Is Hard to Do" on the music system, get ready to boogie.

Before you go out on your own, however, you must be able to support yourself and any significant others who depend on you. Consider the following financial issues before you launch a consulting practice:

✔ **Weigh your income versus your expenses:** It's a simple rule of business and of life in general. To survive, your income has to be more than your expenses. If it's not, you go into debt. And if you go far enough into debt, eventually you'll be forced out of business when you file for bankruptcy. As you plan your consulting business, review all your projected sources of income and expenses. If your income exceeds your expenses, no problem — you can go forward confidently. However, if your expenses exceed your projected income as a consultant, figure out how to put yourself in a more favorable position before launching into full-time consulting. How? Try the following ways, and then turn to Chapter 15 for detailed information on how to project and optimize the amount of money you can make as an independent consultant:

- Increase the amount of work that you do.

- Increase the rates that you charge your clients.

- Decrease your expenses.

- Change the type of clients you pursue as partners.

✔ **Assess how much you have in savings:** It's been said that most people are only a few paychecks away from bankruptcy. That's why having money squirreled away in a savings account or other highly liquid asset, such as a money market account, is important. You should have some money saved whether you are working for an established organization or working for yourself. Do you have enough money saved to get you through times when your business is down and your clients aren't paying their bills as quickly as you might like? You need at least three months' worth of living expenses, preferably more. Assess your savings account and, if you find it lacking, direct as much money to it as you possibly can before you go out on your own. Believe us — when you need the funds to get through a particularly rough spot, you'll be glad you did.

✔ **Plan for the inevitable surprises:** Life is full of surprises, which can be both good and bad. A good surprise in business is an early payment from a client or a large, unexpected contract from a client you had just about written off. A bad surprise is finding out that a client has decided to go bankrupt before paying your bill — or receiving a notice that the Internal Revenue Service wants a much larger piece of your income than you planned to contribute this year. *(What?!? My Jacuzzi isn't a deductible expense?)* Again, you have to be financially prepared for surprises — especially bad ones. Make sure that your income is sufficient and that you have adequate savings to get you safely past bad surprises.

Personal considerations

You certainly have other considerations besides professional and financial when you decide to become an independent consultant. Think about these personal considerations:

✔ **Friends and family:** What will your friends and family think about your choice to become a consultant? In some cases, everyone may be incredibly supportive of your move. In other cases — especially when you already have a good-paying career — your friends and family may question your sanity in deciding to become an independent consultant. *Have you lost your mind? Why would you want to do that?* You may have to counsel your family about your reasons for consulting and about your new role so that you don't become the "soccer spouse" if you have kids. You may also want to be clear with your friends that becoming a consultant was *your* choice — and not a reaction to the latest organizational purge. Before you make the move to consulting, make sure that *you* are clear about why you want to make the change. Explaining your decision to others is easier when you can first explain it to yourself!

✔ **Lifestyle:** Becoming a consultant can mean quite a change in your lifestyle. For example, when you work for an organization, you're almost always directed to complete a long list of tasks and assignments. However, when you're an independent consultant, suddenly you have to direct and motivate yourself to get things done. Self-motivation can be a liberating but frightening prospect for someone who has been told what to do and when to do it for years. Consulting requires *lots* of self-discipline. You still have to get up each morning and go to work, even when your office is only a few steps down the hall — or at a coffee-house down the street — rather than 20 miles on the other side of town.

✔ **Personal goals:** How does consulting fit into your personal goals? Do you have personal goals? Becoming an independent consultant isn't something that you should do on the spur of the moment. It requires serious advance planning and preparation. For example, consulting is one step in Peter's long-range plan to eventually become a university business professor. (If any of our esteemed readers are affiliated with the University of Hawaii, Hilo, please watch your mailbox for an offer you simply *won't* be able to refuse!) Whatever your personal goals, be they financial, professional, or whatever, make sure that consulting fits into them.

Only you can decide when the time is right to leave your day job and step into a new world of unlimited opportunity — a world where *you* control the reins of your destiny. If the prospect of consulting seems too overwhelming right now, don't forget that you can make the transition from your current job to a career in consulting at your own pace — one small step at a time or one great leap forward. The choice is yours.

Chapter 2

What Consultants Do

*W*hen you ask most businesspeople what they think of when you mention the term *consultant,* the likely response is the traditional management consultant. Organizations hire management consultants to research and diagnose the causes of significant problems in organizations — anything from poor product quality to employees' excessive sick leave usage to explosive growth of corporate overhead.

However, an incredibly diverse array of consulting occupations exists outside the archetypal model of management consultant. We can probably safely say that for every possible thing an individual or organization needs to do, a consultant is available to advise how to do it cheaper, quicker, and better.

In this chapter, we identify some of the many different kinds of consultants and explain what they do and who they do it with. We also look at the specific roles of consultants in the consultant-client relationship and the things that consultants should never, ever do.

A Consultant for Every Occasion

Consultants are nothing more than experts in a particular field who sell their expertise for a fee. So what do you imagine when you hear the word *consultant?* Someone brought in by upper management to try to straighten out a big problem at work? An expert of some sort?

Many people tend to think of consultants in terms of their own experience. However, consultants work in almost every possible endeavor. They may not always be as visible as the individuals or organizations that they consult for, but they are definitely out there.

If you pick up a copy of the Yellow Pages, you can find accountants, interior decorators, promotional products and services, and more, but you probably won't find a category called *consultants*. This is because consultants specialize in such a wide variety of areas, most of which are totally unrelated to one another. Although our Yellow Pages directory doesn't list *consultants* as a category, we *can* find audiovisual consultants, child care consulting and information services, educational consultants, and others scattered about. Bob even used to be a job-hunting consultant!

To get a better sense of exactly what consultants do, we set our AltaVista Web search engine to overdrive and asked it to find the number of documents containing the word *consulting* in the title. The result? Two million documents. Talk about going from famine to feast! Unfortunately, this response is a bit overwhelming. Turning to the Yahoo! Internet search tool, we pared the list down to a manageable number. Here are just some of the categories of consultants that Yahoo! lists under the heading "Business and Economy: Companies: Consulting":

- Advertising
- Aerospace
- Anthropology and Archaeology
- Collectibles
- Computer
- Construction
- Entertainment
- Financial Services
- Food
- Furniture
- Health
- Hobbies
- Information
- Law
- Media
- Political
- Resumes
- Set Construction and Design
- Small Business
- Telecommunications

  ✔ Web Page Designers

  ✔ Woodworking

 While writing this book, we interviewed several successful consultants to see what kinds of things worked — and didn't work — for them as they established and grew their businesses. Here is a sampling of some of the consultants we interviewed and what *they* do for a living:

  ✔ Jamie Zebrowski, president of The Lawyers Network, Inc., located in San Diego, California, provides attorneys for hire on a temporary basis by matching her clients with the lawyer who has the best mix of experience for the job.

  ✔ Richard Vaaler, owner of Springfield, Virginia-based Vaaler Associates, advises his clients on how to most effectively work within the complex and ever-changing world of the federal government's vast acquisition and procurement bureaucracy.

  ✔ Jim Harris, founder of The Jim Harris Group of Indian Rocks Beach, Florida, has acquired a large in-house database and has done extensive online research. He uses this information to develop unique best-practices programs that show his clients' executives and management how to build and maintain a world-class work environment.

  ✔ W. Lee Hill, an independent legal consultant in Boulder, Colorado, works closely with Native American tribes to help them communicate effectively in order to traverse the vast cultural chasm that separates them from government agencies, regulators, and businesses.

  ✔ Cindy Kazan, president of Communi-K, Inc., in Milwaukee, Wisconsin, assists her clients in making the best use of their marketing, promotion, and publicity budgets. She helps her clients write industry-specific articles and then places the articles in trade magazines and journals that have the greatest impact on a targeted audience.

This is really just a small sampling of what consultants do. Other Web sources include listings for antiques consultants, aromatherapy consultants, color consultants, funeral consultants, fashion consultants, recycling consultants, wine consultants, and just about anything else your heart might desire. Undoubtedly, a consultant somewhere advises or provides services to clients in *every* kind of vocation or interest.

That consultant could be you!

What Consultants Do

It's easy to think of consultants as modern-day witch doctors who wear blue pinstripe suits, dance around, and wave a magic wand to make things better for the organizations or individuals that hire them. Of course, being a consultant requires a bit more effort than simply waving a magic wand. Quite a bit more effort. Whether you are a computer network consultant, a management consultant, or a beauty pageant consultant (yes, they do exist!), almost *all* consultants do a few key things to get their jobs done.

Listen

Listening is really the number-one job of any consultant. Clients hire consultants to solve a problem or to provide advice or services. To do so effectively, consultants must first understand *exactly* what their clients want. And not only do they need to be good listeners to learn what their clients want, but they also have to ask the right questions and then *listen* to the answers. Listening is one way to get a sense of the symptoms of what's wrong with an organization. This means that consultants periodically need to stop talking and listen to what their clients tell them — instead of focusing their attention on what they're going to say when their clients stop talking!

Investigate

One fun thing about being a consultant who solves problems for clients is investigating *why* something has gone wrong in the first place. Investigation leads consultants to the people, information, and data that they need to properly analyze a problem. As outsiders to organizations in trouble, consultants bring with them a fresh perspective that isn't tainted by the politics and hierarchy of their clients' organizations. They can ask the tough questions, talk to people, and gather information throughout organizations with little regard to the often-petty fiefdoms that constrain employees. If consultants run into resistance, a brief discussion with someone in top management usually makes the roadblocks disappear.

Analyze

After consultants have the information they need about a particular problem, they study it closely to see whether they can discern the causes of the symptoms of an organization's problems. For example, by listening to a company's chief financial officer, a consultant may learn that the organization is in poor financial health because revenues have dropped sharply over the past several months. After investigating to find the information that gives the consultant a better idea about the *sources* of the problem, the consultant must analyze all the data available to figure out why revenues dropped. This data might include company financial reports, sales reports, and interviews with product managers.

Consultant resources on the Internet

With the widespread popularity of the Internet, many consultants — both those working independently and those working for established firms — have created a presence in cyberspace. In addition, many organizations representing consultants or answering frequently asked questions about consulting have sprung up online. Check out some of these Web sites to get a taste for the resources available to you as a consultant:

✔ **Association of Professional Consultants:** This nonprofit organization, whose Web site is located at http://www.consultapc.org, provides a variety of services, such as networking opportunities, professional development, and publicity and promotion, to its member consultants.

✔ **Inc.:** *Inc.* magazine runs an excellent online service of interest to consultants and consultants-to-be through the Net at http://www.inc.com. In its "Virtual Consultant" area, you're treated to access to lots of free stuff, including interactive worksheets, software libraries, and a reference desk.

✔ **Expert Marketplace:** You can find the Expert Marketplace, which claims to contain listings of more than 214,000 individual consultants and consulting firms who specialize in the manufacturing sector of business (sorry, we lost count after 53,216!), at http://www.expert-market.com/em. Besides these incredibly vast consultant listings, the Expert Marketplace

also contains a searchable database, performance benchmarking, consultant performance reviews, and much more.

✔ **Fast Company:** Billed as the "handbook of the revolution," *Fast Company* magazine presents the latest thinking on cutting-edge business management and leadership issues and techniques, such as teams, participative management, the impact of information technology, and more. Of special note is Fast Company's consultant debunking unit, which presents — and skewers — popular consulting myths. You can find it on the Web at http://www.fastcompany.com.

✔ **Consultant's Corner:** Consultant's Corner (http://www.pwgroup.com/ccorner) is a great source for listings of consultants, consultant resources and training materials, sales and marketing resources, and small-business survival guides.

✔ **SBA:** The Small Business Administration (SBA) offers a variety of online resources to small businesses of all kinds, including independent consultants. You can find anything from advice on starting and financing your business to promoting and expanding it. Find the SBA online at http://www.sba.gov.

This is just a small sample of some of the resources available to consultants on the Net. Check these out for starters and then use your browser's search tool to find more. You'll be amazed at the amount of information available to you.

Recommend

After consultants analyze the data that they gather, their next task is to synthesize their findings into conclusions and recommendations to their clients. A consultant's experience base plays a huge role in the quality of the recommendations that result. This is, ultimately, what clients pay consultants the big bucks for: to make recommendations that improve the organization, the process, the operation, or whatever they have been asked to work on. Consultants make their recommendations via face-to-face meetings, written reports, presentations, and other methods of communication.

Catalyze change

In many situations, consultants may find themselves in the role of advocate. Whether they're urging the implementation of a set of recommendations or pushing for the adoption of a product or service, consultants advocate new ways of doing business all the time. Sometimes a long-established organization needs a gentle (or not so gentle) push from an outsider to jump outside its well-worn ruts. In this way, consultants act as *catalysts* to make things happen in the organization. Insiders are often at a distinct disadvantage when trying to gain management's ear. The recommendations of an outside expert often spark the kinds of momentous changes that managers would not accept from their own employees.

Implement

Many clients want and expect their consultants to help them implement recommendations. Being external to the organization helps consultants remain separate from and above the internal crises, politics, and distractions of the typical organization. In this position, consultants have a clear advantage in implementing recommendations over staff and managers who are *within* the organization. Just don't forget (and don't let clients forget) that if clients want a set of recommendations to *really* make a difference with their employees, managers must support the implementation of the plan every step of the way. If they don't, then the consultant is wasting his or her time, the clients' time, and the clients' employees' time (but invoice them anyway). Being involved in the implementation of recommendations is good because the consultants get to see the fruits of their labor and extend the consulting engagement at the same time.

What Consultants Should Never Do

After considering the things that consultants do, you need to know the things that consultants should never, ever do. (Don't even think about it!) Continued attempts to do any of the following will likely do nothing more than ensure that the organization where you transgress won't find a reason to hire you in the future.

Be arrogant

When you are truly skilled in a particular area of expertise, your ego can easily get the best of you. As business guru Peter Drucker puts it, "A little humility goes a long way."

Although there's nothing wrong with being self-confident, arrogance has no place in a consulting relationship. One time, Peter (Economy, that is) participated in a consultant-led, long-term planning session with the rest of the organization's management team, including the executive director. On the second day of what was to be a year-long relationship, the consultant, who was quite full of himself, made the mistake of publicly humiliating the executive director for speaking out of turn. That was the *last* day that particular consultant was heard from in the organization. And the long-term planning effort went with him.

Pull punches

As a consultant, you have to be ready, willing, and able to be completely forthright. You must tell your clients exactly what they need to know to make intelligent decisions politely and tactfully — even if you have to tell them bad news to do it and even if the bad news is about the person who hired you! Sure, no one likes to be the bearer of bad news, but you're being paid to assess the situation honestly and completely. When you sugarcoat your observations and recommendations, you're being dishonest with your clients, and you're doing both your clients and yourself a great disservice.

Create problems where none exist

In an effort to show their clients that they are earning their fees, some consultants (not any *we* know, of course) create problems where none exist. For example, an interior designer may tell clients that stripes are out this year (although stripes are just fine) in hopes of generating more business. Or a strategic planning consultant may tell prospective clients that their old plans are worthless (when they are just fine) and promises to put together new plans for a small fortune. Whether they are self-employed and dependent on every job that they get or partners in a large consulting firm who are expected to bring in a certain amount of revenue each year, consultants are often under a great deal of pressure to build a strong base of long-term clients. Unfortunately, this pressure often translates into creating problems where none exist.

Here's a tip: Consultants who address the issues they are paid to address and move on generally receive outstanding referrals from satisfied clients.

Bite off more than you can chew

Fooling Mother Nature is not nice, and fooling your clients isn't nice, either. Although consultants may have scads of experience in a particular area, they may have little or no experience in another related field. Similarly, a consultant who can take on the problems of a small business in his or her sleep may be like a fish out of water when thrown into the exponentially bigger pond of a large, multinational business. Would you want to hire a birdhouse builder to build your next home?

You have two ways to avoid this problem: Either turn down the job or collaborate with other consultants to help fill the gaps.

Overcommit and underdeliver

Similar to representing skills you don't have is representing *time* you don't have — no matter how much you'd like to. Although turning away a profitable business opportunity is hard, accepting a job that you can't do well because you are already overcommitted is not fair to your clients or yourself. When you take on more jobs than you can adequately support, the work you are doing for your current clients, as well as the additional work you accept, suffers.

Before you turn down work, see whether you can farm some of it out to a subcontractor or associate, or see whether the client can slip the delivery schedule. If neither option is possible, turn down any additional work until you catch up on your current work. Clients respect this professionalism.

Neglect current customers while pursuing new customers

Yes, lining up future clients in advance is important; otherwise, when you finish your current jobs, you're out of work until you can get your next job. However, too many consultants neglect their *current* clients as they run around chasing their *next* clients. The unfortunate byproduct of this situation is a number of dissatisfied clients. Not only do your current clients pay your bills right now, but by referring you to their network of contacts, they are your best source of future clients. Although keeping an eye to the future is important, ignoring the present in the process doesn't pay.

TRUE STORIES

Jamie Zebrowski's Lawyers Network, Inc.

Jamie Zebrowski is the president of The Lawyers Network, Inc. (phone 619-490-9164), a firm based in San Diego, California, that provides attorneys for hire on a temporary basis. Her three main clients are corporate counsel, corporations without their own lawyers, and law firms. Jamie founded her firm four years ago as an alternative to reentering the ultra-competitive, ultra-stressful environment of the large corporate law firm that she left behind when she had her second child. We met at her office to discuss why she left her law firm to start her own consulting business, and to explore some of the pluses and minuses of consulting versus working for a large, established firm.

Consulting For Dummies: What exactly do you do as president of The Lawyers Network, Inc.?

Jamie Zebrowski: My job is to evaluate the needs of my clients and then to match them up with a lawyer who has the best mix of experience for the job. My clients call me up, and they give me specifications as to experience and different areas of expertise — the things that they need in an attorney to help them with an assignment. The assignments can vary from four hours to several months. I've got one attorney who was on a job for seven months.

CFD: Why do your clients go to you instead of directly to a law firm? There are certainly plenty of law firms and lawyers listed in the Yellow Pages.

Zebrowski: It all comes down to cost. I charge a fraction of the price of most law firms in southern California. Most law firms charge $175 to $300 an hour for the services of a lawyer. Because our overhead — mine and the

lawyers' — is so much lower than the typical law firm, we can provide the same quality of lawyer for $75 to $100 an hour.

CFD: Wow — I'll bet that makes you *very* popular!

Zebrowski: It definitely keeps me busy! I really knew I was successful when some of the attorneys who I placed as temps years ago began to call *me* to provide attorneys to help *them* out.

CFD: I understand that you left the largest law firm in town to start your business. Why?

Zebrowski: I left the firm to raise my children. I always told my husband, Mark, that, when we decided to have kids, I planned to quit working. And then when I had the kids, I loved my job so much that I couldn't quit. But the problem was, I had *no* life. When I first took the position, I went from working 40 hours a week to working 60 hours a week. It was okay — for three years it was fine. No kids, my husband worked 60, 70 hours a week — what did I care? But when I had my first child, there was a problem. After my second, it was impossible.

CFD: Why impossible?

Zebrowski: My daughter was in preschool, my son had a nanny. We were running around from place to place, paying everyone extra for staying later. We all suffered — especially the children. So I left to concentrate on my kids.

CFD: So what led you to start your own consulting firm?

Zebrowski: When I left my job at the law firm, I kept in touch with my friends and my colleagues. And it was really interesting because we both looked at each other with envious eyes: They looked at me thinking "you're so

(continued)

(continued)

lucky," and I looked at them thinking "you're so lucky." My goal was originally to find jobs for new attorneys fresh out of school and for attorneys who were out of work. This original goal evolved into the full-service firm that I have today.

CFD: What are the advantages of having your own firm as opposed to working for a traditional law firm?

Zebrowski: Control. Control over time, that's the biggest advantage. That, and never having to put nylons on.

CFD: And high heels?

Zebrowski: And high heels. And another thing: There are two ways you can go when you work for yourself. You can either become very inefficient with your time, or you can become very efficient. When I worked for a law firm, part of my job was appearance. I needed to be there from 7:30 a.m. to 5:45 p.m. The more time I spent in the office, the better.

CFD: Face time.

Zebrowski: Right. Now, working for myself, anytime I'm in my office, I perceive I'm away from my kids. Therefore, the less time I spend in my office, the more time I can spend with my kids. So when I'm in my office, I'm *very* efficient and effective. I may not look as presentable as when I worked in the law firm, but I am not making money on my looks. I'm doing what needs to be done and achieving that quickly and getting done with it.

CFD: So having your own business allows you to spend more time with your kids *and* have more personal time for yourself.

Zebrowski: Yes.

CFD: What are some of the disadvantages of having your own firm?

Zebrowski: There are definitely disadvantages. In the case of *my* firm, *I* am it. I do everything within this business, from paying the bills to typing out my letters — no support whatsoever on a professional or an emotional basis. However, what I really miss is bouncing ideas off another professional: getting another opinion.

CFD: Independent consultants can definitely tend to get isolated.

Zebrowski: Right. I think a business can lose because of that. I think that you can sometimes take the path of least resistance when you're on your own.

CFD: What kind of advice can you give to someone who is thinking of leaving an established business to start his or her own thing?

Zebrowski: I think one of the key things about working on your own and by yourself is that you really have to know yourself and be self-motivated. There's just no Big Brother watching over you. It's a mixed blessing. Another thing: You need to identify *why* it is that you want to do what you want to do. I think the worst reason to go into your own business — the *worst* reason — is to make a lot of money, because you *will* fail. There's absolutely, positively, no free lunch. The other thing for me that has been key to the success of this business is to have it separate from my home.

CFD: Why's that?

Zebrowski: Because, for me, one of two things would have happened had I had my business physically in my house. I either would always be working or never be working. Both create an unsuccessful situation. Having it detached separates the entities. It separates the home from the business. And it allows your friends and family to separate the two. That's *very* important, especially for children. This setup works just great for everyone.

Chapter 3

Reading Your Compass: Picking a Route That Is Right for You

For some reason, most people draw a very distinct line separating *work* from the things that they *really* like to do. Work is work. Fun is fun. And rarely do work and fun meet. So you may work all day long as an office supplies salesperson, a lawyer, or a grocery store clerk, all the while dreaming of what you plan to do when you get off work and can enjoy doing the things *you* want to do. Maybe you'll head to the lake to do a little fishing, putter around in the garden, or fix a gourmet meal to share with your significant other. The reality is that few people go to work to have fun; they assume that work is work and that fun has to wait until later.

A friend of Peter's worked for years as a software programmer for a high-tech research and development firm. You may know that programming can be a very solitary profession — programmers tend to spend much one-on-one time with their computers. However, Peter's friend John is very social, and although he enjoyed programming — and the good money that it brought in — he really would have preferred to make a living doing something that allowed him to interact with people more often than with his computer. Instead of spending his life dreaming about it, John took action. He sold his stock in the company and used the proceeds to start a successful cantina in a busy college town in Arizona. Now, instead of working his days away in a sterile, climate-controlled cubicle, John surrounds himself with people and music. John's work is his love, and he is making more money than he did as a programmer. If you drop in at Palapa in Tempe, Arizona, on New Year's Eve, you'll find John and his band playing to a full house of happy college students. (Just be sure to tell him that Bob and Peter sent you!) By the way, John *never* plays "I Can't Get No Satisfaction."

Can we let you in on a little secret? Your work *can* be your love. You don't have to spend the rest of your life working in a job that brings you little or no joy or satisfaction. Becoming an independent consultant can be the key that unlocks the door to the rest of your future if you just take a small step forward and give it a try. And you don't have to do it all at once. You can keep your current day job while you try out consulting in your spare time. Becoming a consultant is as simple as deciding exactly what you want to do, making a plan for your transition to consulting, and then executing that plan.

In this chapter, we help you determine what you *really* want to do with your life and what skills you have that can get you where you want to go. We also help you determine whether what you want to do is marketable enough to allow you to make a living at it. (Making a living at whatever you decide to do is always a plus!) Finally, we tell you how to do some simple test-marketing of your business ideas to see which ones will fly and which ones may be better suited to papering your parakeet's cage.

Assessing Your Preferences

Undoubtedly, you like to do certain things at your job more than others. And when you are away from the office, you probably enjoy a wide range of hobbies and activities even more. Take a moment right now to think about the things you most like to do at work. Perhaps you love to create massive computer spreadsheets. Maybe you really like to read and analyze legal contracts. Or is your number-one favorite duty making travel reservations for your organization's salespeople?

One problem with a career in most organizations is that you may very well be promoted right out of the things that you enjoy doing the most, into new duties that you may find much less enjoyable. If you are talented in a particular area of technical expertise — whether it's chemical engineering, writing complex machine code, or building houses — you'll inevitably be recognized for your skill and promoted into a supervisory or management position. When this happens, suddenly your job changes from one of, say, creating advertising campaigns to one of coaching a team of *employees* to create advertising campaigns. And although you may still do *some* creative work, suddenly your day is chock-full of management activities, such as budgeting department resources, controlling expenditures, counseling employees, building teamwork, attending endless meetings, and filling out forms for anything and everything you can imagine. Before you know it, you're doing tasks that have nothing to do with what you really enjoy doing — creating advertising campaigns, building houses, or playing rock and roll guitar.

In this section, your job is to decide exactly what you enjoy doing the most — at work and otherwise. Your goal is to identify new work opportunities that allow you to do what you enjoy doing. Think in terms of a new career where *you* — not someone else — decide which things you do. Don't worry now about whether you can make money at it. We look into that later in this chapter.

What do you really like to do?

Start this exercise by considering which things you really like to do. Our logic is that if you like to do it — *really* like to do it — you can do it well. And doing it well generates success. For the moment, forget about the things you just sort of like to do or the things you feel wishy-washy about. We want strong, positive feelings here! Use the space below each question to write in your ideas. Or photocopy the pages so that you can go through the exercise again in a few months or a few years.

What would your ideal day look like ten years hence? Divide it into 30-minute increments and describe what you'd be doing during each part of your day.

What would your perfect job be? Visualize it. Smell it. Taste it. (Okay — don't taste it.) What would you do every day? How would you spend your time? With whom would you work?

List your most positive and enjoyable work experiences. What about these experiences made them so enjoyable? Exactly what skills were you applying?

What are your five favorite things to do at work? Why do you like each of these five things?

1.

2.

3.

4.

5.

What are your five favorite things to do away from work? Why do you like each of these five things?

1.

2.

3.

4.

5.

What strengths would you bring to your dream job? What gaps in knowledge or experience would you need to fill to start work in your dream job today?

What do you really dislike doing?

Just as you have things that you really like to do — both on the job and off the job — you invariably have things that you really can't stand to do. For example, Bob dislikes not being able to make the final decision as often as he'd like. Peter dislikes getting stuck in meetings that have no purpose and, seemingly, no end. (Unfortunately, attending meetings is a required duty when you become a manager.)

The next step in this exercise is to zero in on the things that you really don't like to do. Be honest with yourself — now's the time to get it all out on the table. (Don't worry; we're not going to show this to your boss.)

What would your worst job be? What would you be doing every day? With whom would you be working? How would you be spending your time?

List your most negative and unenjoyable work experiences. What about these experiences made them so unenjoyable? Exactly what skills were you applying?

What are your five least favorite things to do at work? Why are these your least favorite things?

1.

2.

3.

4.

5.

What are your five least favorite things to do away from work? Why are these your least favorite things?

1.

2.

3.

4.

5.

A visualization exercise

As you work on getting in touch with the things that you like and the things that you dislike, you can amplify the effectiveness of this process by participating in a visualization exercise. First, find a nice, cozy chair where you can relax — away from the phones or the hustle-bustle of your home or office. Turn down the lights and let your mind wander. Visualize your ideal life. What is a typical day like in your ideal life? Start at the very beginning of your day when you wake up and work through it until you go to bed at night. Ask yourself the following questions:

Where are you living?

How do you wake up?

With whom do you wake up? (That is, do you have a spouse? Children? A dog?)

What time do you wake up?

What clothes do you put on?

What do you eat for breakfast?

With whom do you eat breakfast?

Where do you go to work?

How do you get there?

Whom do you see at work?

What does your work environment look like?

What does it smell like?

What do you do at work?

Whom do you talk to?

What do you talk about?

Continue to work through your typical day in your ideal life — the rest of the morning, lunch, afternoon, the commute home in the evening, dinner, after dinner, and bedtime. Ask detailed questions about what you are doing, where you are doing it, when, and with whom. Use the results of this exercise to help guide you in your answers to what you really want to do with your life.

Assessing Your Skills

It's one thing to want to do something — to be in tune with your likes and dislikes — but it's another thing altogether to have the skills and expertise needed to carry out your selected endeavor successfully. To get a sense of whether a particular brand of consulting is really in your future (or in your *present*, for that matter), you've got to first take the time to assess the skills that you bring to the task. In the sections that follow, we help you do just that.

What are you really good at?

In your years of experience in the business world, you undoubtedly excel in certain tasks. Perhaps you are the world's greatest budget forecaster, or maybe you have an incredible eye for displaying products in department store windows to increase sales. Whichever skills you excel in, now's the time to get in touch with them.

What are your most outstanding job skills (for example, accounting or negotiating), and what makes you so skilled in those particular areas?

What things have other people told you that you do well?

What personal qualities (for example, analytical ability or persistence) do you possess that support your most outstanding job skills?

What are the top five essential duties of your current job?

1.

2.

3.

4.

5.

What special training or classes have you taken to improve your job skills?

What special certificates, licenses, or registrations do you possess for your current job (for example, CPA or general contractor's license)?

What aren't you so good at?

Figuring out what you're *not* good at is just as important as figuring out what you *are* good at. However, deciding what you're not good at is often easier said than done. Why? Because many people have an idealized vision of what they *think* they ought to be good at, whether they are or not. For example, you don't admit that you are lousy with figures and discard that option from your list of possibilities. Instead, you say, "One of these days I'm going to concentrate on getting better at working with numbers," leaving open the possibility. The implicit assumption is that you should hang on to every possible avenue to the future, regardless of the probability that you will ever travel upon it. Although the motive behind doing this type of thinking is noble, it only diffuses your focus and concentration on the things that you do best.

> *What job skills (for example, accounting, negotiating, and so on) are you least comfortable with, and why are you uncomfortable with them?*

> *What personality traits (for example, decisiveness or persistence) would you work on to enhance your job skills and why?*

> *What tasks do you avoid and why?*

Putting It All Together

After you assess your likes and dislikes, your skills, and the areas that you are less skilled in, you should put together all this information to create a coherent picture of who you are and what kind of consultant you should be. You may be surprised to find that the perfect job for you bears little resemblance to your current job. On the other hand, you may be surprised to find out that you're not cut out to be a consultant. Whatever the result, you need to know one way or the other.

To begin this exercise, review all the comments that you wrote under the section titled "What do you really like to do?" The point of this section is to allow you to unleash your imagination and consider what kind of work you really want to do. For a moment, forget that you have been a bank teller in Toronto your entire working life or a waitress in a truck stop in Little America, Wyoming, for the last ten years. As you read through your responses, take time to step back, close your eyes, and visualize your answer to each question.

Think about what kinds of consulting businesses you could start that would allow you to apply your life's preferences. Don't be shy — now's the time to let your imagination go wild. If you need a little help, review the listings of different kinds of consultants in Chapter 2. Try to list *at least* five or more possible consulting businesses. Jot them down here:

Next, review your responses under the section titled "What are you really good at?" Your responses to the questions in this section don't necessarily indicate that you want to *do* something, only that you're good at it. And if you need some additional training to get the credentials you need, weigh the amount of time and money that you need to get them. Step back and visualize the kinds of consulting businesses that you could start based on your answers. Again, think of five or more business possibilities and list them here:

Now compare your lists. Do you have any possibilities in common? Yes? Great! Circle them right now with a big red marker. You don't have *any* in common? Go through the exercise again and *really* let go of yourself. When you start your new consulting business, pick something that lets you do what you want to do with your life, but also choose something that you're good at or that you could get good at in a reasonable amount of time.

Finally, review your responses to "What do you really dislike doing?" and "What aren't you so good at?" Would any of your responses to the questions in these sections cause you to delete any of the consulting possibilities that you circled with that big red marker? Yes? Then take that big red marker and put a big *X* through it. No? Good. Enter the surviving items of this exercise in the space below:

Now complete the following sentences:

I am in the _____ consulting business.

I help my clients _____.

Congratulations! You have identified the consulting businesses that best match your desires *and* your talents. Because of this synergy, you have the best chance for success if you pursue one or more of these opportunities. Of course, success takes more than a great idea. You have to have clients who are willing to pay you for your services, and your idea has to be profitable. The next section addresses these issues and more.

Is Your Idea Marketable?

Should you or shouldn't you? When deciding whether to become an independent consultant, only you can make that decision.

Unfortunately, trying to predict whether your consulting business will be successful or go down in flames is a difficult task. Many new businesses succeed each year, but many fail. How will yours fare? Only time will tell. Many factors add up to potential success or disaster in running your own business: your drive to succeed, the availability of clients who are willing to pay for your services, and your ability to make a profit.

In this section, we address some of the most important issues surrounding your decision whether to take the plunge. Before you quit your day job, give serious consideration to these issues.

Who are your clients and what are their needs?

You may have a great idea, but unless you also have clients who need your services and are willing to pay for them, all you have is an idea. Ideas don't pay your bills; *clients* do. Identifying your clients and their needs is an important step in determining whether you have a viable idea.

So who are your clients, and what do they need? You need to be able to list real names and phone numbers, not just stuff like "anyone who needs an online presence for their business" or "a vast quantity of investors who aren't being served adequately by big brokers." You should be able to easily complete the following sentence: My target clients are _____
_____ .

As you consider exactly who your clients are and what they need, ask yourself the following questions:

- ✔ **Who are your most likely clients?** Make a list. Name names and list phone numbers and addresses. You can find clients by looking in the Yellow Pages or in industry trade magazines, by networking, or by researching possible firms of interest on the Internet. Vague, ambiguous, pie-in-the-sky entries do not cut it on this list!

- ✔ **Exactly what do your clients need?** As you develop your list of likely clients, also note what each client needs. For example, your targeted clients may need someone to perform limited maintenance on their office server. The best way to find out what your clients need is by talking to them one-to-one. Will you provide *exactly* what they need, or are you going to try to sell them on something they don't need?

- ✔ **What advantages do you offer over your competitors?** Although you may have a great idea, other consultants can probably offer much the same services to your potential clients. Determine why your clients would pick you over your competitors, and then concentrate on those advantages. If you're not sure what advantages your competitors offer over your consulting business, ask your clients. They'll probably be happy to point out the pluses and minuses of you *and* your competition.

Can your business become profitable?

Doing what you want to do with your life instead of working as just another cog in the wheels of some humongous bureaucratic maze of an organization is a great goal. Consulting is, above all, about freedom — the freedom to decide what *you* want to do and then to pursue it. However, don't forget one minor detail. Unless you recently won the lottery, found the largest undiscovered diamond mine on the continent in your backyard, or inherited the Heinz ketchup fortune, you have to make a profit if your consulting business is to live long and prosper.

To determine whether your business can be profitable, do your math and take the following items into account:

✔ **What are your anticipated revenues?** Consider potential clients and decide the level of revenues that you can reasonably anticipate bringing in for several different periods — a month, a quarter, and a year. Be conservative; this is not the time to go manic. Do some outside research to discover what your competitors charge and the amount of business that *they* bring in each year.

✔ **What are your anticipated expenses?** List all your potential expenses for several different periods — a month, a quarter, a year. Think hard. You don't want to forget anything. Do a reality check by examining your canceled checks and credit card statements.

Here's a tip: It's always best to underestimate revenues and overestimate expenses.

✔ **Do your anticipated revenues exceed expenses or vice versa?** This is the $64,000 question. When your revenues exceed your expenses, the leftovers are called *profit*. Profit is good. When your expenses exceed your revenues, this is called a "going-out-of-business plan." This kind of plan is *not* good. Although you should expect that your consulting business will need several months to a year or more to become profitable, the sooner you can make more money than you spend, the better! Remember — Fido needs to be fed!

Is the timing right?

In business, as in life, timing can be everything. Although hard work and persistence can overcome almost any obstacle, having the right product for the right client at the right time is also important. For example, if you had started an Internet consulting firm in 1990, you would have starved — and quick. However, if you had started the same business yesterday, you'd have more than enough to do for a long time to come.

Consider the following when you try to determine whether your timing is right:

✔ **Does what you want to do provide a needed service?** You may have the greatest idea since sliced bread, but you may find that no one wants or needs your product. This is why all the big companies spend tons of money on marketing studies, focus groups, and product opinion surveys. You don't want to spend a great deal of time and money chasing a market that just isn't there. Before you start your consulting practice, survey the market you want to enter and determine that real clients will spend real money for what you have to sell. You can find out if people need your service by making phone calls to potential clients, conducting focus groups, or using a variety of other market research methods.

✔ **Are you too far ahead of your time?** You may have an idea that is so great, and so far ahead of its time, that your clients aren't even aware that they need it. When you're *too* far ahead of your clients, convincing them that they need your services can take a great deal of time and effort. If you're on the cutting edge of the kinds of services you offer, don't get so far out on the edge that your clients can't catch up to you!

✔ **Are you too far behind the times?** On the other hand, jumping into a hot field only to find that your potential clients' attention has already moved on to the next big thing is even easier. For example, total quality management (TQM) was a pretty hot field for several years and attracted loads of attention from a wide array of clients and consultants. Now, however, firms that once embraced TQM have forgotten about it. If you were to start a firm specializing in TQM today, you'd be hard-pressed to line up enough business to keep your lights on, much less make a profit. As you decide on a consulting specialty, look toward the future — where your customers are heading — instead of to the past, where they have already been.

Do You Have What It Takes?

This question goes way beyond the nuts and bolts of starting and running a successful business. It goes to your personality, your motivation, your personal support systems, and more. If you prefer the security of working for a large corporation and the thought of being out on your own makes you break into a sweat, maybe *full-time* consulting isn't for you. Take it slow and work your way into it.

Don't forget that you can consult on a part-time basis while you continue to hold down a conventional full-time job. You *always* have the option of increasing the amount of time you devote to your consulting business and decreasing the amount of time you devote to your other job. If you become a victim of a downsizing, rightsizing, or reengineering, you'll be ready for it.

Consider these things when you're trying to decide whether you are cut out to be a consultant:

✔ **Do you dream of being your own boss?** Perhaps that's not quite the right question. Maybe it should be, "*How often* do you dream of being your own boss?" Being in control of one's life can be a very strong motivator for a consultant — a motivator strong enough to bring your enterprise great success through the sheer force of your desire to succeed.

✔ **Are you independent and a self-starter?** When you're an independent consultant, you don't have anyone to hold your hand. No one is there to make sure that you get out of bed in the morning, to tell you that you're not working hard enough, or to praise you for doing a great job. It's all up to you. Are you up to the challenge? If you need to be jump-started on Mondays, then maybe consulting just isn't for you.

✔ **Can you support yourself as you establish your practice?** Although supporting yourself financially is important, supporting yourself emotionally is just as important. Are you mentally ready to make the move to consulting? Do you have the support of your friends, relatives, and significant others? Are you ready to answer the inevitable question: "Why would you leave that great job you have?" When you are comfortable with your answer to that question, you are truly ready to become an independent consultant.

Chapter 4

Getting There: Making the Transition to Consulting

*M*aking the move to independent consulting is a big step for most people — *especially* those who have cut their teeth in business while working for traditional, established organizations. For many, letting go of a traditional 9-to-5 job can be a time for deep soul-searching, introspection, and worry. *Am I disciplined enough to be my own boss? Will people be willing to pay for my knowledge and services, and how much will they pay? What will my family think if I decide to leave my regular job to start my own business? Am I ready to quit my job? Can I survive without getting a paycheck every other week? How will I obtain benefits like health insurance and a dental plan?* Ultimately, you must answer these questions and many others like them. Listen carefully — your answers will determine whether you are ready to make the transition to independent consulting and whether you will succeed in your new endeavor.

Our society values entrepreneurship, and the maverick entrepreneur who creates a successful business against great odds is a hero to many. However, most people inevitably end up as employees for someone else's organization, whether it's a small business, a large business, the government, or a nonprofit or educational institution. And instead of *owning* a piece of the rock, people often find themselves breaking the same rocks over and over again for their employers — chained to their jobs by the golden handcuffs of steady paychecks, health insurance, and pensions.

If you're like most people, however, you find that you can't squelch the dream and desire to be your own boss and control your own destiny. Instead, these wishes intensify each time you read a magazine story or see a television report about an employee with a promising future in an organization who has started a successful consulting firm, or when you hear about someone who left behind an established career to do what he or she *really* wants to do.

So how do you make the transition to starting your own consulting business? And, perhaps more important, how do you know whether you're *ready* to make the transition? Is there a way to find out the answer to this question *before* you put your career (and potentially the welfare of both you and your significant others) on the line? Can you make the transition a little at a time, or does it have to happen all at once? Funny you should ask. Those just happen to be the very questions that we address in this chapter.

Making the Move

Every great journey starts with a single step. To become an independent consultant, you have to make the first step — however small — on your journey. For some, the journey from a career in an organization to a career as an independent consultant may be very short. A reorganization and resulting layoff may be enough to show some workers the light and path. For others, the journey may take years of planning and gradual transition. One path is not right for everyone. The path that's right for you may be completely wrong for someone else.

That's why considering exactly *why* you want to become an independent consultant is particularly important. Are your reasons a part of a long-term plan for your life, or are they instead a reaction to some short-term issue that you have at work or in your personal life? Quitting your job and becoming a consultant won't instantly solve all your problems; indeed, taking such steps may create a whole *new* set of problems for you. Ideally, you are *drawn* to consulting because of your desire to control your own destiny and perform outside the constraints of your current organization — not *repelled* from your current organization because everything isn't going your way at the moment.

If you *do* decide to proceed along the path to becoming an independent consultant, the potential rewards to you are colossal. However, you must watch for many potential obstacles. If you aren't prepared to deal with them quickly and completely, these obstacles can dramatically slow your transition or stop it completely. The obstacles that you should be concerned about include the following:

✔ **Financial considerations:** You need to eat, keep a warm and dry shelter over your head, and take care of some of the other necessities in your life, such as cable television, Nintendo 64, and your Internet service provider. When you make the transition to consulting, unless you significantly decrease your personal cost of living, you need to ensure that your income as an independent consultant at least equals the income you were making in your traditional job. Don't forget to include employer-paid invisible income, such as health, dental, and life insurance, a pension, and paid vacation time that your employer contributed to your overall compensation package. And be sure to consider additional expenses, for example, self-employment taxes and other taxes (such as social security), that your employer used to contribute on your behalf.

✔ **Lifestyle considerations:** Maybe you're accustomed to using your corporate American Express card to pay for expensive business lunches and dinners with your customers. Or maybe you're used to receiving a car allowance or flying first class while on business travel. Although you don't necessarily *have* to change your spending habits when you become an independent consultant, don't forget who is paying the bills now: you! The money that you *don't* spend on maintaining a lavish lifestyle becomes money in the bank — *your* bank. When spending is put into those terms, many independent consultants have found that flying coach isn't necessarily such a bad way to go. Besides, if you fly often, you may earn enough frequent-flier mileage to upgrade your seat — a well-deserved reward for your hard work.

✔ **Long-term professional considerations:** Depending on the nature of your current job, stepping off the ladder at this point in your career may mean stepping off forever. Is this the right time in your life and in your career to make the transition to your own consulting business? If not, when is the right time? Three months from now? A year? Five years? Make sure that you have a long-term plan for your work life — not just a short-term one. And after you have a long-term plan, review it annually and keep it up-to-date.

✔ **Self-image considerations:** Many people were raised with the idea that they would eventually have a lifelong career — working for a large company, getting a steady paycheck, and retiring after 30 years of dedicated service. Parents, schools, friends, and associates all helped to reinforce this picture. You may find it *very* difficult — especially if you have been working in a traditional career for some time — to imagine yourself stripped of the protective identity of your organization, separated from your coworkers, and removed from the customers with whom you have worked over the years. Are your self-image and motivation strong enough for you to take wing all by yourself? The only way you can *ever* find out is to give yourself a chance: Leave the security of the nest and fly.

✔ **Significant-other considerations:** We all have significant others — husbands, wives, life partners, kids, pets, and so on — who depend on us for their financial, psychological, and physical well-being. How will the move from employee in an organization to independent consultant affect them? Will you have to sell off an extra car or tighten up your spending to make your dreams come true? Or will you suddenly be so busy traveling to client sites that your family will see far less of you than they did before you became your own boss? Although *you* may be ready to tighten your belt or make other sacrifices to become a consultant, consider what kinds of sacrifices your significant others will have to make. Don't forget, the decisions you make in your life also affect the lives of those closest to you. Make *them* a part of your long-term plan, too!

Finally, after you consider all the potential obstacles, look at the big picture: Does the upside of going out on your own outweigh the downside? If it does, then the time is probably right for you to make the move. If not, then you probably should wait until the upside does outweigh the downside.

Stops Along the Way

Becoming an independent consultant isn't something that just happens to you one day. It's something that deserves and requires significant planning to make it a successful reality in your life. Yes, some people do walk into their offices one day and quit to start their own businesses *before* they have developed an adequate client base, and others are fired or laid off before they have the chance to prepare. Most independent consultants, however, build successful businesses by making a stop or two along the way.

Big organization to consulting firm to self-employment

Many consultants have found a very natural transition from a full-time regular job to independent consulting by making a stop along the way as an employee for a consulting firm. For example, Peter has a friend who worked for a company for 15 years — all the while gaining valuable experience and company-paid training. He was lured away by a large international consulting firm and was put to work doing consulting jobs for firms in the industry that he had left. Eventually, after he sharpened his consulting skills and established a huge network of industry contacts, he started his own successful independent consulting business.

Moving from a big organization to an established consulting firm to your own independent consulting business offers numerous advantages:

- ✔ If you stay with your big-organization position long enough, you can collect retirement or a pension after you leave.

- ✔ While working for an established consulting firm, you develop and hone strong consulting and client skills while you learn the ins and outs of the consulting industry. Plus, working for a recognized consulting firm represents a seal of approval of your expertise.

- ✔ You have the opportunity to develop a valuable network of contacts that may become the client base of your *own* consulting business.

- ✔ Former employers frequently retain you as a consultant. Because you already know the company, its customers, and its competitors, you can contribute immediately with no additional training or orientation.

Part-time work

Easing into your consulting business on a part-time basis is one of the safest *and* least painful ways to make the transition. If you so desire, you can keep your regular job as long as you like while you maintain your consulting business on a part-time basis. Doing both jobs can create occasional scheduling headaches, though. For example, imagine what you would do if an emergency at your regular job required you to fly to Boston on the same day that you were supposed to present your final recommendations to an important consulting client.

Both jobs can peacefully coexist, however, with careful planning and extra work on your part. For example, you can keep one master calendar to ensure that you don't have surprise scheduling conflicts. And, if you need to take a leave from your regular job to do some work for a consulting client, you can request permission for the leave far enough in advance to minimize the negative impact of your absence on your current organization. You also should set up regular "office hours" — time when you're not at your regular job — so your consulting clients can contact you. Who knows — you may build up such a successful business that you have no choice but to quit your regular job and go into independent consulting on a full-time basis.

Here are some of the pluses of doing your consulting on a part-time basis:

- ✔ You can try various consulting alternatives and build a strong client base while maintaining the security of your regular full-time job.

- ✔ You retain your health insurance and other important job benefits (a steady paycheck, for one!) as long as you remain in your regular job.

- ✔ If your foray into the wonderful world of consulting doesn't work out, you can easily return to your regular job and try consulting again some other time.

Full-time work

Pursuing a regular full-time job while running a full-time consulting business can be very demanding on your schedule *and* on your sense of reality *(Where am I? Who am I working for today?),* and it may be one of the least preferred options. Yet holding two full-time jobs *is* an option for many people as they make the transition from their regular jobs to careers as independent consultants. On the plus side, not only can you fully immerse yourself in the wonderful world of consulting, but you can start developing a solid client base and generating significant consulting revenues — greatly accelerating your transition — all within the safety and security of your regular job. On the minus side, you could possibly quite literally work yourself to death. (This is probably not what you had in mind when you decided to become an independent consultant.)

We can't with a clear conscience recommend taking on full-time consulting business on top of a full-time job. However, if you decide to go that way, moving from a regular job to independent consulting by pursuing your new business on a full-time basis can work to your benefit in the following ways:

- ✔ You get the best of both worlds — a steady salary and benefits from your current job *and* full immersion in your new consulting endeavor.

- ✔ By building a base of consulting clients and income more quickly than you can by consulting on a part-time basis, you can greatly accelerate your transition to full-time independent consultant.

- ✔ You can get some excellent tax write-offs as a consultant that you can apply against your regular job.

- ✔ You'll sleep great at night because you're so tired from working two full-time jobs.

Landing a big contract

For some people, starting an independent consulting business is an all-or-nothing kind of thing. Bob has a business acquaintance who submitted proposals to a variety of potential clients while working in a full-time position as an employee of an organization. When Bob's acquaintance was selected as the successful bidder on a million-dollar contract, she had all the motivation and reason she needed to quit her job and dive into independent consulting on a full-time basis. If you consider this route, have an adequate base of consulting contracts lined up before you make the move to full-time consulting, and don't, we repeat, *don't,* submit your resignation before you have a signed contract in your hands! We discuss the ins and outs of writing winning proposals in Chapter 5.

Starting up your independent consulting practice by landing a big contract offers these advantages and more:

- ✔ You don't have to leave the security of your full-time job until you win a big contract.

- ✔ Producing and submitting contract proposals to potential clients in your after-work hours is easy. You must limit such work to after-hours to prevent conflicts of interest and future legal hassles with your current employer.

- ✔ If you don't land a big contract, all you have lost is some of your time and the cost of copying your proposals and mailing them out.

Total immersion

Finally, you have another way of shifting to independent consulting: total immersion. You may go to work one day and, because of a reengineering, be notified that you have been selected to be laid off: *Here's your check, please clean out your desk, thank you very much for all your fine work, don't call us, we'll call you.* Or you may reach the end of a long career of service to your organization and decide to retire. Or maybe you just can't stand the idea of spending one more day in your office doing the job you do, and you quit.

There's nothing quite like being out of a job to motivate you to get something going — and quick. Although some individuals immediately seek a new job with an established organization, others use a termination, retirement, or resignation as an opportunity to launch their own consulting businesses. For many successful independent consultants, termination — whether voluntary or involuntary — was the push that they needed to start their own businesses.

Although total immersion isn't always the *best* way to start an independent consulting business — you may not be able to keep your personal financial boat afloat very long without a steady paycheck, for example — it *does* offer the following benefits:

- ✔ You can focus *all* your work energy on establishing a successful consulting business.

- ✔ Being out of work has a special way of focusing your attention on the real necessities in life: paying your rent or mortgage, buying food, and making your car payments. Who was it — Louis Something-or-other — who during the French Revolution stated, "Standing on the gallows really focuses the mind"?

- ✔ If your former employer established a pension or retirement plan for you, you may be able to tap into those funds to help get your business off the ground and buy yourself time as you establish a client base.

Richard Vaaler's Vaaler Associates

As the founder and owner of Springfield, Virginia-based Vaaler Associates (phone 703-451-6380), Richard Vaaler acts as an adviser to companies that are dealing with the government's — particularly the *federal* government's — contracting bureaucracy. Richard's bread and butter is helping government contractors interpret complex and ever-changing acquisition and procurement laws and regulations, advising them on how to work within the system efficiently and effectively, and identifying the key people for them to deal with. Although Vaaler Associates has clients of all sizes, Richard has focused his marketing on providing resources to small businesses that may not be able to afford those resources in-house. We spoke with Richard by telephone to find out why he started his independent consulting business and the kinds of obstacles that he faced in doing so.

Consulting For Dummies: What did you do before you started Vaaler Associates?

Richard Vaaler: I was a government contracting officer for 33 years, primarily in the research and development (R&D) business, although I bought just about everything except for major weapons systems and construction. I was responsible for lots of subcomponents and quick reaction kinds of things.

CFD: You mean quick manufacture and production turnaround?

Vaaler: That, plus quick turnaround contracts. Many were high-priority, rush kinds of jobs.

CFD: What made you decide to start your own independent consulting business?

Vaaler: I knew when I retired that I was going to have to do *something*. Although I was a licensed real estate broker, I just thought I would rather stay in a business that I knew better than anything and see if I could make my own way. The business has been going well for ten years now.

CFD: What kinds of obstacles did you encounter in setting up your own consulting firm?

Vaaler: I didn't have any personal obstacles — family or financial — in my way. The obstacles that I faced were generated by the people within the government who I dealt with who looked at me differently when I retired. Now, I was a "contractor."

CFD: You mean you were sort of like the enemy all of a sudden — an outsider instead of an insider?

Vaaler: Right. I became an enemy — they didn't know me, and that kind of thing. I have dealt with that all along, even today. There's a certain amount of hesitation to do business with you.

CFD: What do you do to overcome that hesitation on the part of your clients?

Vaaler: The problem isn't with my clients — *they* are very open to the things that I tell them and to doing business with me. The problem is with my clients' *customers* — the government agencies that my clients do work for. I find, therefore, that I wind up doing a lot more work with my clients directly and not with *their* customers. That's proven to be the right thing to do. My clients have their own relationships with their customers. My job is to tell them what I think their government customers are looking for, how they're working it, and what their concerns and issues are. We go from there.

CFD: How did you start your business? Did you rent some office space, install a phone, and hang up an "Open" sign in your window, or what?

Vaaler: I figured I would start out of my home and see how things went. I incorporated as a Subchapter S corporation in the state of Virginia and set up a separate set of books for the business. That's worked out real well because most of the work that I have done has been outside of my home — either in somebody else's office or with my clients' customers.

CFD: What does incorporating under Subchapter S do for you?

Vaaler: It treats your income like it's corporate income, only it's all treated as personal income. That way, it's only taxed once, which is a benefit. Also, since it's a corporation, my personal legal liability for the business is limited.

CFD: Are there any personal traits that you see in yourself that were important in making your consulting business a success?

Vaaler: Staying with it. Perseverance has kept me going. One more thing: I learned a long time ago that you can't please everybody all the time, so you just roll with the punches as they come along and always try to rise above the fray. I really believe the old baseball analogy: The more times you get up to bat, the better chance you've got of getting a hit.

CFD: What kind of advice would you give to someone who is thinking of starting his or her own consulting business?

Vaaler: I wasn't as focused as I would have liked to have been at the beginning, and I didn't really have a marketing area precisely defined. I kind of took a shotgun approach to marketing my services. But that's part of my nature — I wasn't apprehensive about being out on my own, and so I thought I would start my business and see what happened. Of course, I had a pension to fall back on, so it wasn't a financial issue. It was more an issue of: What could I do, and did I have something to market? Looking back, I would definitely hire a marketing consultant to help focus my marketing efforts.

CFD: So what happened to your marketing efforts?

Vaaler: I made the assumption that a lot of small-business people out there needed my help, but I found out that, even though they need help, they don't necessarily want to pay for it.

CFD: Minor issue, right?

Vaaler: Not exactly. I've found that many businesses would almost rather muddle along on their own — this goes for large companies, too — than pay somebody to help them. I once ran across a situation like that where the guy had been muddling along for two years before he finally decided to call me in. I was able to help solve his problem promptly and for less money than he was throwing at it before he hired me.

CFD: So, in essence, you *make* your clients time *and* money.

Vaaler: That's exactly right. It's a small investment on their part for a large payoff in results.

How to Tell If You're Ready

Many people talk about making the move to independent consulting, and many dream about becoming their own bosses. Making the transition from organization employee to self-employment, however, is a *big* change in anyone's life. Are you *really* ready to make the move, or should you put your dream on the back burner for a while longer? Circle your answer to each of these questions, and you'll know for sure!

1. **How strong is your drive to succeed in your own independent consulting business?**

   A. I can be a success, and I will be a success. Period.

   B. I'm fairly confident that if I put my mind to it, I will succeed.

   C. I'm not sure. Let me think about it for a while.

   D. Do I have to start my own business? Can't someone do it for me?

   E. Did I say that I wanted to become a consultant? You must have been talking to someone else!

2. **Are you ready to work as hard or harder than you have ever worked before?**

   A. You bet — whatever it takes to succeed!

   B. Sure, I don't mind working hard as long as I can see the benefits.

   C. Okay, as long as I still get weekends and evenings off.

   D. Not *too* hard, I hope.

   E. What? You mean I'll still have to work after I start my own business?

3. **Do you like the idea of controlling your own destiny rather than having someone else control it for you?**

   A. I don't want *anyone* controlling my destiny but me!   & God.

   B. That's certainly my first choice.

   C. It sounds like an interesting idea — can I?

   D. I tried it once, and it didn't work.

   E. Do I *have* to control my own destiny? Can't someone do it for me?

4. **Have you developed a strong network of potential clients?**

   A. Yes, here are their names, needs, and phone numbers.

   B. Yes, I have some pretty strong leads.

   C. Not yet, but I've started kicking around some ideas with potential clients.

   D. I'm sure that as soon as I let people know that I'm starting a consulting business, clients will come in droves.

   E. I don't have time to worry about that right now.

5. Do you have a plan for moving to consulting?

A. Here it is — would you like the executive summary or the *full* plan?

B. Yes, I've spent a lot of time considering my options and making plans.

C. I'm just getting started.

D. Is any plan ever *truly* complete?

E. Never needed one, never will.

6. Do you have enough money saved to tide you over while you get your business off the ground?

A. Will the year's salary that I have saved be enough?

B. I have six months' expenses hidden away for a rainy day.

C. Three months' worth.

D. I'm still trying to pay off my college student loans.

E. Do you have change for a five?

7. How strong is your self-image?

A. Like a rock! I am self-esteem incarnate!

B. I strongly believe in my own self-worth and in my ability to create my own opportunities.

C. I feel fairly secure with myself; just don't push *too* hard.

D. I don't like that question — it makes me nervous.

E. Next question, please!

8. Do you have the support of your significant others?

A. They are all on board, are an integral part of my plan, and have been assigned responsibilities.

B. They're in favor of whatever makes me happy.

C. Well, I'm pretty sure they'll support me.

D. I don't really know at this point.

E. I thought it would be better to tell them about it later.

9. If it's a necessary part of your plan, will you be able to start up your consulting business while you remain at your current job?

A. Sure — in fact, my boss wants in!

B. If I make a few schedule adjustments, there's no reason why I can't.

C. Would you please repeat the question?

D. That's going to be a tough one.

E. Maybe I'll be able to work on it for a couple of hours a month.

10. What will you tell your friends when they ask why you quit that great job?

A. I'm free at last!

B. That the benefits clearly outweigh the potential costs.

C. I don't know; maybe they won't ask.

D. I'll plead temporary insanity and ask for a loan.

E. I know — I'll pretend that I'm still working for my old organization.

So how did you do? Take a few minutes to tally up the numbers. Give yourself 5 points for every A answer, 3 points for every B, 0 points for every C, –3 points for every D, –5 points for every E.

We have divided the possible scores into six separate categories. By comparing your total points to the points contained in each category, you can find out whether you're ready to jump into independent consulting.

25 to 50 points: You are *ready!* What are you waiting for? There's no time like the present to take the first step on your journey to success with your own independent consulting business. Whether you decide to drop your day job or work into consulting gradually, you should have no doubt that you're ready to give it your all.

1 to 24 points: You're definitely warming up to the idea of starting your own independent consulting business. Consider beginning your transition to starting your own consulting practice in the very near future, but make sure that you keep your day job until you have your practice well under way.

0 points: You could go either way on this one. Why don't you try taking this test again in another month or two?

–1 to –24 points: Unfortunately, you don't appear to be quite ready to make the move to consulting. We *strongly* recommend that you read this book from cover to cover and take this test again in a few months. Maybe working for someone else isn't the worst thing that could happen to you.

–25 to –50: Forget it. You were clearly born to work for someone else. Take this book right now and sell it to one of your coworkers. Now get back to work!

Testing the Waters

Assume for the moment that you have decided that you're ready to take the consulting plunge. Whether you decide just to stick your toe in first or to give it all you've got, testing the water before you jump in is always a good idea. Testing the water is simple when you're at home in your bathtub, but when you're starting a new business — *your* new business — you have to do more than just check the temperature to make sure that you don't get burned!

Here are a few tips that can help you determine once and for all that consulting is the right thing for you and get your consulting business started.

Talk to people who do what you want to do

You don't need to reinvent the wheel. Many people before you made the transition to independent consulting — including some, no doubt, who are doing exactly what *you* want to do. Some have succeeded beyond their wildest dreams, and others haven't. You can learn more from someone who is already doing what you want to do than you can from going to any school or sticking a book under your pillow at night.

Before you start your new business, seek out people who do what you want to do and talk to them — as often and for as long as you can. Schedule an appointment to meet them at work, or invite them to an informal get-together after work. Find out what things worked for them and what things didn't. Ask them about the good times and the bad times, and what you can do to bring about more of the former. You may find the flames of your desire to start your own independent consulting firm fanned to new heights by your acquaintances' enthusiasm. Or the embers may die when you learn that what you *thought* you wanted to do really *isn't* what you want to do. Either way, you learn important lessons that can make you and your business much stronger. Besides, you are building an informed network of consultants who can help you expand your business.

Start small

Given a choice, you are better off to start small and work your way up to larger projects as you hone your consulting skills. Why? One reason is that you can devote more of your time and attention to a small project than you can to a large one. If you are still working full-time in a traditional job, you'll have to fit the project into your schedule whenever you can — most likely at nights or on the weekends. We can guarantee from our personal experience that finding extra time to work on a small project is easier than finding time to work on a large project. Not only that, but you can learn the ropes of your chosen field at a pace that is comfortable to you, *and* you have a lot more time available to refine and polish your work.

Evaluate the results

How do you know whether your tentative first steps at consulting are taking you in the right direction? The way to find out is to evaluate your results:

- ✔ **Is consulting what you expected?** Many people have a glorified view of how wonderful consulting must be. Consulting *is* wonderful, but for many, the reality of consulting doesn't quite match up with the fantasy. Is consulting what you expected, or is it something less or more? If it's something less, then reconsider the kind of consulting that you have decided to take on or your approach to doing it. Don't worry — you may need several tries before you get it right!

- ✔ **Do you like what you're doing?** Don't forget: You're supposed to be having fun doing what you're doing. If you enjoy the consulting work that you're doing, great! If not, why not? Is your view likely to change as you get more involved in consulting and devote more of your life to doing it? Don't forget that the first few months (perhaps even the first few years) of transitioning to your own consulting business may be an emotional roller coaster for you and your loved ones. These highs and lows are a natural part of making a major life change. If you hang in there and keep trying, things probably will soon get better. If, however, you have been trying for some time and things *aren't* getting better, then maybe independent consulting isn't your cup of tea.

- ✔ **Do your *clients* like what you're doing?** Liking what you do is a great feeling. But knowing that your *clients* like what you do is equally important (at least if you want to pay the bills). If you plan to consult on a part-time basis only to supplement your current income, you don't need a lot of clients to keep your enterprise afloat. However, if you plan to pursue consulting on a full-time basis, you'll need lots of *very* satisfied clients to keep you fully employed. How do you find out whether they're satisfied? Ask them. You can do so in the form of a direct interview, a casual conversation, a feedback form, or a question-naire. If you do good work at a fair price and are dependable, don't worry — they will come.

So are you ready to become a consultant? Look closely at your answers to the preceding questions and weigh them against what you are doing now. If your current job still has the advantage, don't feel that you need to make your move right away. However, if consulting has the edge, now may be the time to make the switch. If you do, we wish you the very best and offer this advice: Don't look back.

Part II
The Consulting Process

In this part . . .

All consultants — whether they are experts in planting organic gardens or in managing organizational change — apply a uniform process for determining what their clients' problems are and what needs to be done to fix them. In this part, we take a look at the consulting process: defining the problem, collecting data, problem-solving, presenting recommendations, and implementing recommendations.

Chapter 5

Defining the Problem and Writing Your Proposal

- -

In This Chapter

▶ Meeting your client prospects for the first time

▶ Putting your best foot forward

▶ Asking questions

▶ Creating partnerships with clients

▶ Writing great proposals

- -

*E*very business process has a beginning, a middle, and an end. The consulting process is no different. It begins with defining the problem, moves through collecting data, analyzing that data, and making your recommendations, and then ends with implementation. Because the first step — defining the problem — sets the stage for all the other steps that follow, it is particularly critical. Not only do you have to quickly determine whether your potential clients have a problem and, if so, what exactly that problem is, but you also have to build a relationship with them and determine how to approach the problem and whether you are the best one to solve it. It's a tall order, but we're sure that, with a little help from this chapter, you'll perform magnificently!

For most consultants, this first step — defining the problem — takes place in a one-on-one meeting with the client-to-be. Although this meeting is usually in person, it can take place over the phone or even in writing, through letters or electronic mail. The process can take more than a single meeting — especially for complex problems that require complex solutions. For most purposes, a face-to-face meeting is best because it allows you to develop a much stronger relationship with your client and a much deeper understanding of your client's problems than you can get from other methods of communication. However, regardless of which method you ultimately choose, your meeting has three key purposes:

- ✔ To identify your client's problem
- ✔ To determine whether you can be of help to your client
- ✔ To develop rapport with your client

Note that this simple list of purposes for your first meeting with your client is appropriate for *any* kind of consultant. Whether you teach homeowners how to recycle their trash (and sell them the sorting systems to do it) or conduct management audits for a huge, multinational consulting firm, the purposes underlying your initial client meeting remain the same. At your meeting, you must determine your client's problem, decide whether you can help solve it, and develop rapport with your client.

In this chapter, we identify specific goals for your initial client meetings, as well as some things you should do and questions you should ask. We discuss building a partnership with your client and, finally, how to put together a winning proposal that summarizes the understandings that you reach as a result of your client meeting.

Goals of Your Initial Client Meetings

At first blush, you may think that you have only one goal when you meet with potential clients about a new project: to sell them on hiring you to do the work. This may very well be your overall objective. However, you need to know much more about your clients and the problems they face before you can be sure that the work fits well within your base of experience and that you can develop the kind of partnership with your clients that is so important for ensuring a successful project.

The initial meetings with your client are ones of discovery: meeting someone new and developing a basis for a strong business relationship, learning about your client's organization, learning about the organization's successes and problems, and deciding whether there is a fit between you and your prospective client. To help yourself through this discovery process, you need to take a series of steps in order to answer these questions. These steps represent the goals of your initial meeting:

- ✔ **Develop rapport and build a partnership.** Consulting is very much a business built on relationships. If you have a talent for developing rapport with potential clients quickly, you are well on your way to building strong relationships and, ultimately, partnerships with your clients. If you have problems developing rapport with your prospects, you're going to be an awfully lonely consultant. Work hard at breaking through the first-meeting jitters and establishing the kind of rapport that helps develop the foundation for long-term, fruitful relationships.

✔ **Assess your client's personality type and adjust your style accordingly.** If your client has an assertive, take-charge style, you want to get to the business at hand sooner than if the client is more social and personable. With the latter style, the client may need to be comfortable with you personally before he or she can devote full attention to your abilities.

✔ **Help identify the problem and get a feel for your client's desire to change.** Clients agree to discuss consulting projects with you because they believe that you may be able to resolve significant problems in their organizations. Most likely, your clients already have some idea of the problems, and they may very well have decided what needs to be done to solve them. Your goal is to identify the *real* nature of your client's problems and then determine whether you can be of value in helping fix the problem.

For example, your client may be convinced that the organization's high rate of employee turnover is related to the low wages paid to employees. You may suspect, however, that the turnover problem is actually a result of poor management skills. Although your client may be willing to address the *perceived* problem by giving employees a pay increase, the client may not be willing to address the *real* problem of poor management. We have known many consultants who feel that clients initially almost never report the real problem but only a symptom of their true problem. You'll get the opportunity to test your client's perception of the problem versus the real problem after you collect data, the second part of the consulting process.

✔ **Define project objectives and deliverables.** After you determine that your clients indeed have problems that need to be solved and you have a good idea what they are, you need to work with your clients to define the objectives of the project and the products that you will deliver at its conclusion. Your clients typically know the results that they want; they just don't know how best to reach them. When you meet with your clients, ask them what results they want, and then help them translate those results into objectives that are concrete and measurable and that can be achieved realistically. A good exercise is to ask clients to define "what it looks like" when the problem(s) is solved. After you define your objectives, decide which "deliverables" you will include in your proposal — perhaps a final report containing recommendations for top management, a customer perception survey, training for the client's employees, or an advertising campaign.

✔ **Decide who does what.** To ensure that possible confusion due to overlapping (or *dropped!*) responsibilities doesn't come back to haunt you during the project, take time during your initial meetings to sort out exactly who is going to do what. Will you distribute surveys to your client's employees, or will your client take care of that? Will you be responsible for scheduling and setting up employee training sessions, or will your client take care of those details? Who is going to be responsible for implementing your recommendations — you or the client? Now is the time to resolve these issues — not after the ball gets dropped.

✔ **Determine the information and client support that you'll need.** During the course of your initial meetings, try to determine the information and support that you're going to need from your client and get the client's buy-in to providing it. For example, suppose that you propose to redesign a client's ventilation system to incorporate improved air circulation as well as better filtration and absorption of mold spores and other particulates. Then you certainly need your client to provide a set of blueprints that shows you the exact location and measurements for the existing system. Work with your client to mutually determine the information and support that you'll need during the course of your project and from whom specifically you can get such assistance.

✔ **Define the project schedule.** A lot of things depend on your clients' desired project schedule and your ability to meet it. When your clients decide that they have a problem that is serious enough to require them to hire an outside consultant, they are usually in a rush to get the work done. For example, if you are an engineering consultant brought in to recommend actions to repair a leaking dam, your client isn't going to be very receptive to a completion date that is a year away. A week may not be quick enough in a situation like this, in which people's lives are at stake. Work with your clients to define a project schedule that meets their needs but that, in your best judgment, allows you sufficient time to do the project right.

✔ **Decide whether to proceed.** Despite the impression that some consultants (and clients, for that matter) may have about who decides whether a project goes forward, it is *not* the sole province of your clients to make that decision. In reality, the decision whether to proceed with a project is very much mutual. Just as your clients can decide that you're not the best consultant for the job or that your personality doesn't mesh well with theirs, *you* can decide not to work for your clients for a variety of reasons, including your belief that they are not prepared to make the necessary changes or that there's something you just don't like about your clients' personalities. It takes two to tango, and this is just as true with the consulting process as it is on the dance floor. If you decide to proceed, your next step is to develop and submit a project proposal to your clients.

As you can see, your initial client meeting is much more involved than simply trying to sell the merits of hiring your business to do some work. If you conduct this meeting in the manner we describe, you set the stage for submitting a winning proposal and for completing your project smoothly and successfully.

Tips for Your Initial Client Meetings

With so much riding on the first meeting with your client, it's easy to become nervous or apprehensive about it. Our advice is to take a deep breath and relax. Even if you're relatively new to consulting, you undoubtedly have a lot to offer your clients, and they will be glad to hear what you have to say.

Here are a few tips to help boost your confidence in your client meetings and leave your client with a positive impression of you and your abilities:

✔ **Relax!** Sure, those first meetings with your client are always critical. If they go well, you may be up to your ears in work for months, or even years. If they don't, well, you at least learn something. If you want to build rapport quickly with your clients, you must put them at ease right away. This means that you need to be confident and at ease yourself. Relax! As long as you are prepared for the meeting and you're confident in your ability to do what you do best, you shouldn't be nervous or apprehensive. In fact, if you've done your homework, you should be positively overflowing with the excitement of having the opportunity to help your clients solve their problems. Channel your anxiety; it can inspire your best thinking.

✔ **Know who will be there and why.** Before you meet with your client, find out who will be attending from your prospective client's organization and what their roles are in the proceedings. After you know who will be in the meeting with you, you can prepare yourself to address any topics that might be of particular interest to individual attendees. For example, if you learn that the company's chief information officer (CIO) is planning to attend, you can mention that you have extensive experience working with computerized management information systems — a topic that is sure to cause the CIO to pay attention to what you have to say.

✔ **Make your best impression.** You only have one chance to make a first impression, and this is the time and place that you want to make a *great* first impression. The way you greet your client, the way you dress, the way you speak, and the way you carry yourself should all lend weight to the fact that you are a professional. If you do financial consulting for banks, you had better look like a banker. If your expertise is squeezing an extra knot or two of boat speed out of a 12-meter racing yacht, then shorts, a polo shirt, Sperry Top-Siders, and a windbreaker are the uniform of choice. Without boasting or resorting to name-dropping, tell your client about some of the successful projects you have worked on in the past and about some of the better-known clients you have done work for. If you provide a formal reference with contact information, make sure that you get permission from your previous clients first. Be energetic, attentive, and sincerely interested in helping your clients solve their problems, and you leave your clients little choice but to be impressed with you.

✔ **Be prepared.** In an effort to test your knowledge and see exactly how you will respond to questions as they arise, your client may ask you highly technical questions or questions that require good judgment to answer well. The best way to handle these kinds of situations is by being fully prepared for your meeting *before* you show up. If your client is new to you, you should find out everything you can about the organization: its markets, its technology, its people, and its successes and failures. Not only will you impress your client with your knowledge of the organization, but your client will be impressed that you took the time to learn about the organization. This gives you an opportunity to wow them.

✔ **Listen.** To understand exactly your client's problem and get some idea of how best to address them, you have to *listen* to your client. Some consultants mistakenly believe that they have to do all the talking in order to show their expertise. This is simply not the case. In fact, in *any* meetings with your client — except, perhaps, ones where you are making a presentation of some sort — you should do more listening than talking. This is the *only* way that you can hear what your client is really saying and understand what is really needed.

✔ **Take notes.** After you and your client decide to proceed with a project, you need to draft a proposal for the work and submit it for your client's review and approval. During the course of your first meeting and in any subsequent meetings or phone calls, you will discuss a multitude of ideas, concerns, concepts, approaches, and understandings with your client. Taking notes of these critical discussions is invaluable to you both when you develop your project proposal *and* during the course of project performance. Not only that, but your client will be favorably impressed by the importance that you accord what he has to say. Right after the meeting, you should make additional notes of your impressions while they are still fresh in your mind.

That wasn't so bad after all, was it? After you go through more than a few client meetings, your confidence increases, and you have less and less reason to be concerned about them. Before you know it, these meetings become second nature to you, and you handle them like a pro. Until then, keep working at these skills and keep meeting with your clients.

Ask Your Clients Lots of Questions

If you want to create great proposals — ones that have your clients reaching for their checkbooks minutes after they receive them — you need to know the answers to a *lot* of questions. And after your client selects you to do the work, the answers you receive in this preliminary stage of the consulting process help to guide you through the rest of the consulting process.

Your job, therefore, is to ask the questions that get you the answers you need. Here are several different questions for you to try. Feel free to add others that have provided you with good information:

- ✔ What is the problem that you would like me to address?

- ✔ Why do you think that the problem is occurring?

- ✔ How long has your organization had this problem?

- ✔ Have you tried to solve the problem? How? What happened?

- ✔ What suggestions do you have about how I should approach this problem?

- ✔ What are your objectives for this project?

- ✔ Are there any organizational obstacles in the way of a finding a solution?

- ✔ Are there any organizational obstacles in the way of implementing my recommendations?

- ✔ Is your management team committed to making the organizational changes needed to make this project a success?

- ✔ What measurable outcomes do you want to see at the end of the project?

- ✔ When would you like this project completed?

- ✔ How do you see your role during the course of the project? After project completion?

- ✔ What kinds of information and other support can your organization provide?

- ✔ Will I be responsible for helping to implement the project recommendations?

- ✔ Do you have a budget in mind for this project?

- ✔ Do you have any personal concerns about this project?

- ✔ How soon would you like me to start?

The questions you ask now can save you lots of time and anguish down the road. Make asking questions a central part of your first client meeting.

TRUE STORIES

Jim Harris is getting employees to fall in love with their companies

Jim Harris, founder of The Jim Harris Group (phone 813-596-5749, e-mail to 74442.2232 @compuserve.com), is a consultant with more than 20 years of combined experience in university teaching and administration, operations management, and executive corporate work with a Fortune 250 retailer. He also has five years of experience on his own as a speaker, writer, and consultant on people-best practices. The Jim Harris Group specializes in studying how some of the most profitable and best-run companies around the world build world-class work cultures. Jim's book, *Getting Employees to Fall in Love with Your Company*, presents over 130 of the best practices that companies are employing to build better work environments for the future. We spoke to Jim to get his perspective on defining his clients' problems and how to build a successful consulting business.

Consulting For Dummies: How important are the initial meetings that you have with your clients, and what do you personally do to get the most out of them?

Jim Harris: The first meetings are critically important, and even before you get into defining the problem, you've got to make sure that you're building a positive relationship with that client. As a consultant, one of the key things that you're doing is building a relationship and not just making a sale. You have to build that trust from the very beginning. So the first couple of meetings that I have with my clients are focused on building that relationship, making sure that my personality and style will match their personality and style and that my expertise will meet their needs. That happens in the

first couple of meetings — sometimes before we even start talking about the problem.

CFD: So you spend a lot of time building a foundation for your consulting relationship up front.

Harris: And very often, as you know, sometimes that takes months before they say, "Okay, can you come back and help us? We have an issue here we think that you can help us with."

CFD: Some of the best long-term consulting relationships are built over a long period of time, not just a quick here-today, gone-tomorrow kind of thing.

Harris: That's right. In fact, I just got off the phone with a prospect I've been calling on for two years who I'm now finally about to present a specific proposal. Some consulting relationships take a long time to develop.

CFD: How do you actually determine what your clients' problems are? And how do you separate that from what they might *think* their problems are?

Harris: I specifically look to do three things as I define or help my clients uncover what their problems or perceived problems are. Number one, I believe one of the most important things we must do as consultants is help our clients define reality. What I mean by that is that, as an outsider and giving an outside perspective, we must help our clients define what is real and what is just perceived. When I was writing the book *Getting Employees to Fall in Love with Your Company* and studying some great companies like The Home Depot and Southwest Airlines, one of my most enlightening experiences dealing with these companies was that they said to themselves, "We're not that good. All we see is the bureaucracy, the in-fighting, and the budget battles." Sometimes it takes an outside perspective to not only tell people how good they are but to also define the negative reality. So I believe that a really important thing for consultants to do up front is make sure that they are going to define reality whether the client wants to hear that or not. I know that in one particular case, a retailer I was working with believed that its front-line employees needed a videotape on how to smile.

CFD: You're joking, right?

Harris: It's true. They believed that that's what they needed. But the reality of the situation was that their management quite frankly was disempowering. The managers of this particular retailer had a checklist for all the checklists that they had to complete for management. So I had to define reality for them. It's not what they wanted to hear, but my job as a consultant was to do that.

CFD: It doesn't sound like the employees had much to smile about in the first place!

Harris: Well, not in that particular case, but I was able to help them solve that problem. On the other side of the continuum, very often your clients can be pleasantly surprised. A current client of mine is a medical services company, specifically in cancer treatment services. They believed that they had a front-line morale problem because of the new CEO and the new direction this gentleman was taking the company. Well, we just conducted a quick, confidential employee survey, and to their surprise, reality was that the front-line employees really liked the new CEO a lot, and they liked the new direction. What we uncovered was that branch management is not listening to the front line. So the first thing that I do is help our clients define reality, whether or not

they want to hear it. Sometimes it's a positive surprise.

CFD: What are the other two things that you do to help your clients through the process of identifying their problems?

Harris: What I have found very important as an outside consultant is, number two, to define the problem through the customer's eyes. What I specifically recommend is that we must consider our customer's customer. In other words, we're looking at the problem down the line. Not just the managers or front-line staff, or even the executives that we are dealing with, although technically they are our first-line customers. We have to define the problem through *their* customer's eyes and maybe even the *next* customer's eyes. So we have to be willing to go two or three levels deep. When I was leading the executive and management training services internally for a $4 billion retailer, I once made the fatal mistake of only listening to our middle managers in developing a program for the front line. We developed it, and it flopped because I was not going to the customer's customer. Here's another example. One of my clients is a courier service. We found during a customer roundtable that I helped facilitate that one of their key reasons for using this company was simply that the couriers wore uniforms. Internally, my client thought of it as a problem, an expense, but actually the customers loved it because it distinguished them from the competition. It was a value-added factor in terms of their professionalism.

CFD: So you really have to look outside the organization, too — not just internally — to see what their customer's environment is.

Harris: Yes, and what I have found is that I not only define reality and define the problem in the customer's eyes. I have also found that those two things fall very much in a line with each other. Those are not really distinctive

(continued)

(continued)

steps at all. They really all combine into one bigger step.

CFD: So what's the third thing that you do to help your clients better define their problems?

Harris: The third point — and it's so important — is to be flexible. Now, that might not make a lot of sense on first sight, but what I have found is this: As you're defining the problem — defining reality and defining the problem through the customer's eyes — really what you're beginning to formulate is the pathway to the solution. Very often as consultants, we get our egos involved, and we believe that we can solve all problems. We can't. What we are is a resource. Remember, we're building relationships — preferably long-term relationships. Often, I get in with a client and say, "I'm not the best person for your solution. What I can do is bring in someone else who *is* because I want you to have the *best* resources to solve the problem." In fact, it happened with the courier service. They wanted to improve their initial employee selection methods. Now, I'm pretty good at that, but that's not my expertise. However, I have a friend and fellow consultant who is an expert in employee selection. I referred my client to the other consultant, and they worked up a wonderfully good deal. What has happened in the courier service is that my value is heightened. So one of the things that I do when helping my clients define the problem is not to assume that I am the best person to deliver the solution — I have to be flexible. Maybe someone else needs to get involved, or maybe I need to pass on the entire situation to someone else who has that particular expertise for that client.

CFD: So you may not be the expert on that particular issue, but you're an expert in putting together the resources necessary to tackle the project. Your clients can rely on you to take care of their problems, however you go about doing it.

Harris: That's exactly right. You know and I know that, very much — particularly with those of us who run smaller consulting firms — we go into virtual relationships depending on the particular client issues. That's becoming a very popular approach — bringing in the expertise you need for a particular project and then dismantling it when the project is complete.

CFD: What's great about that is that your clients can rely on you to pull all those resources together as they need them.

Harris: Right. And sometimes I'm a project manager, and other times I'm in the project with other consultants. What goes around comes around. So we have to be flexible when we're defining the problem.

CFD: How important is it to involve your clients during the process of defining their problems and working through solutions?

Harris: They have to be involved in 100 percent of all of the steps because you're an extra resource within their own environment, and they have to be involved from the very beginning through to the very end. And involvement has to start as high in the organization as we can possibly go. In fact, when I'm defining the problem or building that relationship, I try to get the people at least two levels above the person I'm dealing with involved in a big organization. I try to move up the ladder, as well as keep in mind the front line of the ultimate customer. In smaller companies — if it's a mid-sized company, say, $100 million in sales or so — we're probably already dealing with the president or senior operations manager. But I go at least one step, and preferably two steps, above, and I get their buy-in to help define the problem because really, in my step one, defining reality, the reality may not be what they want to hear. I want them to be involved from the beginning so that they understand what we're really talking about in that situation.

CFD: What would you advise prospective clients to look for when they are shopping for a consultant?

Harris: I believe I would look for a consultant just like I would look for a top-notch employee — a top-notch executive manager or front-line person — and to me the critical component is a positive values match. I say that because I believe the most important thing that can occur with a positive client relationship is that you believe in the same type of basic approach to business that your clients do. If you don't have values that match, regardless of your expertise, regardless of who you bring in, it's probably not going to be a good fit. So the first thing that I would do if I were hiring a consultant is ask, "What do you stand for in your business? What are your values? What is your mission, and how do you make that come to life?" And then, secondly, I would get some references and ask follow-up questions on how they represent themselves. Do they really have integrity? Do they follow through? Do they meet their time constraints? Do they pad their bills? Do they have surprises at the end?

CFD: What advice would you offer to a consultant who is just starting up a consulting business?

Harris: Be patient. Build your reputation slowly. Don't bite off more than you can chew. When I stepped away from a corporate management position with that $4 billion retailer and opened up my own shop, one of the things that helped me so much financially was not asking myself, "How am I going to attain the same cash flow the first year?" I asked the question from the other perspective: "How little do I need to survive the first year?" and that was my goal. So ask, "Okay, how much is my mortgage? How much minimally can I afford in terms of office?" and then it may only be $25,000 or $30,000. And that's your goal for your first year: to bill $30,000. And if you do that and you're successful, you've got the momentum going.

CFD: And then you can grow your business as your reputation grows.

Harris: And if you're getting that values-based matching and you're building that long-term relationship, your clients will come back to you with new situations where they want your advice or where they want you to put a consulting team together and be a project manager for them. About 80 percent of my business now comes from word of mouth or from referrals, and it's probably going to be more than that as we go down through the years. Quite frankly, I don't have an extensive marketing plan except in terms of referral business.

Building Partnerships with Your Clients

You have a choice: You can either work *with* your clients or work *against* them. We're going to let you in on a little secret: The wonderful world of consulting isn't always a bowl of cherries. In fact, if you have to deal with hostile clients or with uncooperative, troublesome employees, you may wish that you had followed a different career path — taxidermy, perhaps. The problem with working against your clients is that *nobody* wins and *everybody* loses. You lose because you wasted your time on a project that no one appreciated or even wanted, and your clients lose because the original problem remains unresolved.

If something doesn't feel right or you are getting bad vibes, you may want to terminate the relationship and find clients with whom you are more compatible. If the client-consultant chemistry isn't right at the beginning, it's not likely to get better farther down the road.

Clearly, building strong partnerships with one another instead of working against one another is in the best interest of both you and your clients. Your clients win and you win, too. Here are some dependable ways to build partnerships with your clients:

- ✔ **Collaborate, collaborate, collaborate.** Collaboration between consultant and client is an absolutely essential element in any successful consulting project. If the so-called "expert" consultant sits up in an ivory tower — remaining aloof from the organization and the people who work within it — the client may decide that the consultant is out of touch with the organization and quickly discard the consultant's reports and recommendations. Conversely, if the client decides to treat the consultant as just another employee — directing everything the consultant does and approving (or disapproving) every move the consultant makes — then the results and recommendations will be far less credible than those that a consultant would produce. The solution is for consultant and client to work together — *collaboratively* — and build a partnership to ensure that the project is successful.

- ✔ **Make all communication two-way communication.** Good communication is not a one-way street. You can't do all the talking and expect to understand your clients' problems or what outcomes they want to achieve. The strongest partnerships are built on a firm foundation of trust and mutual respect, where each party can speak openly and the other party listens. In a real partnership, the opinion of one partner is just as important as the opinion of the other, and all communication is open, honest, and moves freely in *both* directions.

- ✔ **Discuss and negotiate the tough issues.** In any meaningful partnership — including ones between consultants and their clients — tough issues have to be addressed and dealt with head-on. Dancing around issues or avoiding them to keep a relationship "pleasant" doesn't allow you to resolve the issues that need to be resolved, nor does it result in a better set of conclusions and recommendations. In fact, your conclusions and recommendations will be incomplete and, quite possibly, inaccurate because you failed to address crucial issues. Discuss and negotiate the tough issues with your clients *directly*. Though you can and should be diplomatic and respect your clients, you should attack tough issues without hesitation. The result is a real partnership — not a fantasyland version that is handicapped from the start by its artificiality.

✔ **Make mutual decisions.** Whenever possible, include your clients in making the big decisions that have the greatest effect on your project. Making them feel part of the team can prevent Monday morning quarterbacking. In the same vein, encourage your clients to include you in the decision-making process for issues pertaining to your project. Doing so helps you to build and strengthen your partnerships with your clients and leads to better project results and recommendations.

✔ **Deal with the people problems, too.** In some organizations, the consultant may be pressured to ignore people problems — weak or overbearing managers and supervisors, employees who consistently show up late for work, executives who have a habit of taking long lunches — and focus only on technical issues. This is a mistake. If you are to reach your goal of successfully solving your clients' problems, you can't leave people out of the equation. Although faulty policies, systems, and procedures can wreak havoc in an organization, so too can faulty employees. For the consultant-client partnership to be successful, artificial boundaries and fears have to be left behind, and the consultant must have free and unfettered access to the entire organization. Be sure to discuss this issue with your clients at the beginning of your projects — not after you have already gotten them underway.

Although establishing partnerships with your clients doesn't solve *all* your problems, it sure makes your relationships much easier to live with, your work more productive, and your results more meaningful.

Creating Winning Proposals

After you wrap up your initial contacts with your client, you next need to write and present an out-of-this-world, bang-up proposal. The length, depth, and breadth of your proposal greatly depend on the nature of your business, as well as your client's expectations.

For example, suppose that you are a computer consultant and you are simply going to install a new 3.5 gigabyte hard drive in someone's computer. You certainly don't need to present your client with a 35-page proposal describing all the benefits of the hardware upgrade and the reasons for selecting you over the competition — heck, your client will probably give you the go-ahead after briefly discussing your experience, your price to do the job, and how soon you can do it. However, for a complex, multiyear proposal to do some serious management consulting, 35 pages may not be enough!

Regardless of how long your proposals are or how much they weigh, they should always be easy to understand, attractive, and concise. Here are a few more tips for your next proposal:

- **Respond directly to your clients' needs, questions, and concerns.** Listen to your clients and determine exactly what their needs, questions, and concerns are. After you figure them out, respond to each one with a solution.

- **Place your clients' perceptions above your own.** When it comes to proposals, your *clients'* perceptions count, not your own. If your clients absolutely love color photographs in their proposals but you hate to use photos because you think they detract from your image, you better use *lots* of color photographs in your proposals, regardless of your own opinions.

- **Don't wait until the last minute to start working on your proposals.** Get to work on your client proposals as soon as you decide to do them; avoid the temptation to put them off to the last minute. Not only are you more relaxed when you write them — resulting in a better, more thoughtful product with fewer errors — but you improve your ability to get them in on time (or even early!).

- **Take time to review your proposals before submitting them to your clients.** Always set aside time after you write your proposals to review them before you submit them to your clients. If you submit sloppy proposals, your clients-to-be will probably assume that your work will be of similar quality.

- **Don't ignore your competition. Your proposals should be at *least* as good, or better.** Keep an eye on your competitors, and don't get too complacent or settled in your ways. Plenty of competition is out there, and in most cases, your competition isn't standing still. Always strive to make each proposal better than the one that preceded it, and stay up-to-date with your competitors' innovations.

- **Create a database of proposals.** Our experience is that after a while, 50 percent of any proposal becomes boilerplate; that is, content that is used time and again.

Proposals can be of any length, but for most situations, you submit either a short, letter-type proposal or a longer, narrative-type proposal. In the following sections, we check out each approach.

The letter proposal

In many consulting situations, all you need is a brief, one- or two-page proposal that concisely and simply presents the most important information that your prospective clients need to know. Letter proposals are particularly useful for projects that are simple, are short in duration, or don't cost your clients very much money.

At minimum, your letter proposals should contain the following information:

- **The point!** After a word of thanks for meeting with you or requesting your work, get directly to what you have to offer, focusing on results and on the advantages of working with you and your firm.

- **Proposed project:** What are you planning to do for your client? Make sure that you include a brief description of your project in your letter proposal.

- **Anticipated outcomes:** Summarize your anticipated project outcomes. If you are going to make recommendations that will save your client $1 million, tell him so here. If you are going to train your client to program a VCR, this is the place to present that particular bit of information.

- **Action plan:** Briefly outline the steps you will take to reach your anticipated outcomes, along with any assumptions that you are making and any other details that your client should know.

- **Price:** The bottom line.

- **Payment terms:** It's wise to break up your payments so that you are paid during the course of project performance instead of at the very end. Not only is this payment schedule better for the health of your bank account, but it also helps to ensure that you don't complete and deliver a project to a client only to have the client refuse to pay for it. Although you may have provisions in your contracts to protect you legally from this eventuality, collecting may take you months or even years if you have to take your client to court.

- **Next steps:** Put the ball in your prospective client's court — explain what the client needs to do to initiate the project and get you working. The simplest way is to ask your potential client to accept your proposal by signing it at the bottom and returning the original, signed proposal to you, along with the first project payment. As soon as the client signs and returns the proposal to you, you have a contract binding on both parties.

To give you an idea of what the heck we are talking about, Figure 5-1 (see the next page) shows a sample proposal for a consultant who does freelance software development and troubleshooting for a living. Of course, the names have been changed to protect the guilty!

September 28, 19xx

Ms. Stella Bella
The Nova Corporation
33 Rue d'Orleans
Shreveport, LA 71103

Dear Ms. Bella:

Thanks for taking the time with me today to discuss your forthcoming software program. As I mentioned at our meeting, I honestly believe that millions of computer users around the world are ready, willing, and able to pay their hard-earned cash for a Windows version of the popular children's game "Hula-Hoops." As I looked over what you have done to date, however, I noted many areas where I can help improve the program's functionality. Beyond the simple issues of color and graphics, I will be able to help you bring your entire presentation into sharper focus and tighten up its response to user input. I also have questions to ask you regarding your overall vision for the program, your intended audience, and the graphic look that will best meet the needs of the audience.

As a result of my initial review of your beta program, I propose the following:

- Conduct an initial telephone interview with you to discuss your overall vision of the program. This interview will be conducted within one week of execution of an agreement and payment of the first installment.

- Based on the telephone interview and a further review of the beta program, provide creative input to you in the form of a written report. This task will be completed within one week after the telephone interview with you.

- Completely troubleshoot your beta program for functionality and aesthetics and incorporate any changes that you may approve from the previous step. I will provide the revised program to you via e-mail within two weeks of receipt of your go-ahead.

- Provide online support and answers to your questions (limited to the scope of this project) via telephone and e-mail.

The price for this project is $3,500. Payment will be as follows: $1,000 upon execution of an agreement and $2,500 upon completion of the final program. If you are interested in proceeding, please sign both originals of this letter and return one of them to me by U.S. Mail with a check for $1,000.

I'm looking forward to working with you on this project. I know that you will be happy with the final product. Please don't hesitate to call me if you have any questions.

Sincerely,   Accepted:

J. Edgar Gerber   Stella Bella

The narrative proposal

When you make a proposal for a job that is complex, that you anticipate to run for a long time, or that requires a substantial investment on the part of your client, you'll most likely be required to submit a narrative proposal. In a narrative proposal — which can run anywhere from ten pages to hundreds of pages — you generally address the same kinds of information that you do in a letter proposal, but in much greater detail. For example, while the anticipated outcomes take up all of a sentence or two in the preceding example letter proposal, the section of your proposal describing anticipated outcomes could take five pages or more in a narrative proposal.

Because we don't have enough pages available in this book to provide you with a complete sample narrative proposal (sorry, but our editor says *no way*!), we instead summarize a typical approach to putting one together:

- ✔ **Cover letter:** The cover letter contains a brief overview of the proposed project, along with your name, phone and fax numbers, and e-mail address. For some projects, you can also put expected benefits in the cover letter.

- ✔ **Title page:** As you might expect, the title page contains the title of your proposal, along with the date, the name of your business, and the name of your client's organization.

- ✔ **Table of contents:** We told you that this proposal would be big. Your clients need a table of contents keyed to page numbers just to find their way around this monster!

- ✔ **Executive summary:** For the client who is too busy to read the 75 pages that you labored over for three weeks or more, this paragraph summarizes the entire proposal in a quick, 30-second reading.

- ✔ **Anticipated outcomes:** As in a letter proposal, you present the anticipated outcomes here — albeit in a much more complete fashion.

- ✔ **Detailed scope of work:** A scope of work is a presentation of every task that you will perform as a part of the project. For some narrative proposals — especially those for the government — a proposal's scope of work can easily run for 25 pages or more of highly detailed tasks and subtasks. We hope you have lots of toner left in your laser printer cartridge to print this one out!

- ✔ **Schedule:** In a narrative proposal, your schedule is likely to be much more complex than a simple, "The project will be completed six months after go-ahead by the client." In complex, long-term projects, you may assign each task presented in the statement of work a start date, a duration, and an end date. If your scope of work contains lots of tasks and subtasks, you should present your schedule in the form of a chart or graph that shows the information visually for greater understanding and impact.

- ✔ **Fee:** The price to your customer for the work you plan to do. You should first propose your fee in the way *you* prefer it to be, for example, a monthly flat rate or an hourly fee. You can modify it later if your client wants you to price your work in some other fashion. In some cases, your client may want you to break down your price by task, by outcome, or by deliverable (for example, your interim or final report). If so, your pricing is going to get awfully complex very quickly.

- ✔ **Qualifications and experience:** Here's where you can go to town about all the great experience you have and all the years of training you underwent to get where you are today, as well as that great high school or college you attended. If it's okay with your present and former clients, you can even mention their names if you want to augment your credibility.

- ✔ **Resumes:** If you feel that it will help support your proposal, include a copy of your resume along with the resumes of other key project personnel. One caution: Make sure to tailor your resume to the kind of work you are proposing!

- ✔ **Letters of reference:** If any of your clients were so overwhelmed by the work you did for them that they were moved to write you letters of thanks or reference, include those letters here if your prospective client asks for them.

After you submit your proposal, follow up with your clients to be sure that they received the proposal and that they have what they need to make a decision. And don't forget to ask when you can expect a reply. Don't pressure your clients *too* much, or you may not like the answer you receive — *no!*

After your proposal is accepted, you can proceed with the next part of the consulting process — data collection — which just happens to be the subject of the next chapter of this book.

Chapter 6

Data Here, Data There, Data, Data, Everywhere

• •

• •

*A*fter you meet with your clients to help determine whether they have a problem and, if so, what that problem is (see Chapter 5 for more information about this step), your opinion of what your clients' problems are and why they're happening are preliminary. It's sort of like being a doctor examining a patient complaining of chest pain: The patient (the client) may be convinced that a heart problem is causing the pain, and you, the doctor (the consultant), may *suspect* that that is the case, but until you run some tests and gather further data, you don't really know for sure what your patient's problem is. The heart problem could turn out to be a simple case of indigestion! You use the data you gather to test your assessment of what is wrong or determine the best approach to achieving your clients' goals. The data could prove you right or prove you wrong, but whatever the results, you need complete, accurate, and timely data to know one way or the other.

In any data-collection exercise, you face a dilemma. Every organization generates an incredible amount of information — internally in the form of memos, reports, plans, graphs, and more and externally in the form of investor relations materials, newspaper and magazine articles, and other documents. When deciding what information you need, you can easily get bogged down in a flood of information, much of it irrelevant to the problem. On the other hand, if you are too selective in your approach, you may miss an important source of information. The challenge is to obtain just the information you need — no more, no less. This is often much easier said than done, but you should always make it your goal.

Another problem with collecting data is that you often have to dig deep into the organization — and into its hierarchy — to get to the *real* answers. As you speak to people in an organization, their awareness of a problem moves from an external focus to an internal one. When you first question your client, for example, she may perceive that the "payroll system is all messed up." If you press her a little bit, she may move down one level and focus on *external* causes for the perceived problem: "If those darn payroll clerks would stop taking those long lunches, maybe we wouldn't have this problem!" If you continue to press your client, you may get to the heart of the issue: "Well, I guess I *did* forget to turn in my time sheet on time a few weeks ago — maybe that caused the problem with payroll." Questioning a variety of people throughout the organization — employees on all levels and with all types of work assignments — invariably leads you to the truth.

Collecting the kind of data from your clients that is useful in your efforts on their behalf is an art. In this chapter, we describe the most common and reliable sources of client data, and we tell you how you can involve your clients in helping you get that data. Finally, we consider some of the most dangerous data disasters and explain how you can take steps to avoid them.

Identifying Key Data Sources

Selecting the sources of data you need and then obtaining that data in an accurate and timely manner is a critical step in the consulting process. The secret to knowing what data to gather is simple: You must have an analytical model — a hypothesis — to explain the problem or demonstrate your preferred approach. Start by gathering data that can prove your idea or model true or false. The initial identification of the problem or approach gives you a starting point for which specific data to gather.

When you look at the universe of places from which you can gather data, your task can seem incredibly difficult. (Indeed, when you are pulling together a large quantity of complex data from a variety of sources, the job *can* be difficult.) However, if you work with your clients to determine the exact information that you need — and where to find it — you'll have a much easier time completing your task successfully.

Fortunately, the number of sources for gathering data is not unlimited. The following six categories pretty much sum them up:

✔ **Direct observation:** One of the best ways to gather data — especially when you want to know how people *really* carry out a job, task, or procedure (not how they *say* they carry it out) — is to actually watch people do their jobs. It's amazing how people's *perceptions* of how they do their jobs can differ from the *reality* of how they do it. The only way to get past the discrepancy is to directly observe them in the business environment.

✔ **Internal documents and records:** Every organization — no matter how large or how small — has internal documents and records that document the way it does business: accounting records, purchase orders, internal company memos, policies, procedures, product marketing plans, vision statements, and more. As a part of your data-collection efforts, you need to determine exactly which internal documents and records are most useful for your project and then work with your clients to obtain those items. For example, if you believe that your client's security problem is a result of security guards who aren't performing their duties in accordance with prescribed policies, then you can seek security logs and similar data that indicate the daily activities of the security guards.

✔ **External documents and records:** Every organization distributes numerous external documents and records outside the company, including such things as press releases, magazine and newspaper articles, radio and television interviews, licenses and permits, health inspections, and tax records. In your search for external data, you'll find libraries, government offices, and research services to be invaluable assets. And as you likely know if you have ever logged onto the Internet, a heck of a lot of information is out there in cyberspace just waiting to be grabbed. You may be surprised at what comes back when you do a global Yahoo! or AltaVista search on the name of your clients' organizations or the names of the people in charge.

✔ **Surveys and questionnaires:** Surveys and questionnaires — especially anonymous ones — offer a structured and confidential way for an organization's employees and for your client's customers, vendors, bankers, and other business associates to provide you with data. As with interviews, you get to decide exactly what information you need and what questions you need to ask to get the information you need. And because you control the way the questions are asked, you can direct the response — from a simple yes or no to an expansive, essay-type, multipage response. For example, if you are trying to find out how your client's customers rate your client's efforts at customer service, you can design a survey with questions that help you gauge the opinions of your client's customers. To conduct the survey, obtain a list of your client's customers, call them — using either the entire list or a sampling of the list — and ask them to answer your questions. Their responses can provide valuable data for your investigation.

✔ **Interviews and group meetings:** Any data-gathering exercise worth its salt includes interviews with people in the organization as a basic foundation. Interviews can take the form of one-on-one question-and-answer sessions ("What do you do after you weigh the package on the postal scale?") or small group meetings ("Do you have any idea why so many accidents are occurring on the night shift?"). Interviews should always include the people who are directly involved with the problem, as well as others who aren't directly involved but who may have a good perspective on it. One-on-one interviews are often better than group meetings because the participant can tell you what's on his or her mind without fear of retribution from management or coworkers. However, group meetings often offer their own insights — especially when they reveal rivalries between individuals or departments or expose raw nerves in the organization. One method of dealing with extensive data is to use these sessions as opportunities to get the participants' interpretation of the data. For more information about these and other potential land mines in the data-collection process, check out the "Watch Out! Data Disaster Ahead!" section at the end of this chapter.

✔ **Personal experience:** The longer you have worked in your field of expertise — whether as a consultant or as an employee — the more personal experience you have to draw on. For example, you may have 20 years of experience in integrated pest management with the Agricultural Research Service of the USDA and may have written scores of articles on the topic. Your own opinions and experiences can be important sources of data, supplementing the other data you gather directly from your clients. In some cases, you may have seen identical problems in other organizations. If you have extensive experience in a particular field, take advantage of it!

Of course, gathering data from all these different sources, depending on which ones you finally settle on, can involve an incredible amount of time and effort. Fortunately, there *is* a solution: You can have your client help gather the data for you! Not only do you save time and money, but you have the opportunity to better cement the relationship with your client. Why? Because you and your client will naturally work together more closely as you strive toward a common goal: obtaining the information that you seek. Thus, you strengthen your relationship with your client while you reduce your own effort. That combination is hard to beat.

Getting Help from Your Clients in Collecting Data

Collecting client data is an important part of the consulting process, but it's often an incredibly time-consuming part of the process as well — for both consultant and client. If you allow it, you can quickly get bogged down in your data-collection efforts — slowing or even halting your progress on a project. Not only is this outcome potentially expensive and frustrating for you, but it also can make your client question whether you are the right consultant for the job.

One way to avoid getting bogged down in the data-collection process, while improving the quality and timeliness of the data you collect, is to enlist your client's help. The old adage that many hands make light work applies in consulting, too. If you decide that getting your client involved is in your best interest — and in the best interests of your client (and it generally is because you get better access to the data you seek) — then ask your client to do the following to help you through the process. If you are concerned that your client may tamper with the data, then you may not want to ask your client to help you collect data.

- ✔ **Mutually decide what data is best.** After you have a general idea of the data that you need to get, meet with your client to decide the kinds of data and the sources that are the best for what you are trying to accomplish. For example, you and your client may determine that the organization's weekly sales reports are a better source of near-real-time data than the quarterly financial reports released to shareholders. After you determine *what* data is best, then you can turn your attention to finding it.

- ✔ **Identify where the data you need is located.** Who better to know where the data you seek is located than your client? You can play detective all you want and try to track it down yourself, but you can save yourself (and your client) a great deal of time and money if you ask your client to help direct you to the data you need. If, for some reason, the data is not what you expected or is incomplete, *then* you can dig in more deeply in your own search for it. However, getting your client to direct you to the right source to begin with is certainly worth a try.

- ✔ **Prioritize your effort with employees.** If you are an experienced consultant, you probably already know that many employees (that is, anyone in the organization besides the person or persons who hired you) look forward to dealing with consultants about as much as they look forward to trips to the dentist. As an outsider, you can be stone-walled, misled, obstructed, and otherwise thrown off track by employees who not only don't want to cooperate with you but also may be actively fighting your efforts. Your client can help to smooth out these little bumps in the data-collection road by explaining to employees that their cooperation is not only encouraged but also expected.

- ✔ **Help you physically obtain the data you need.** The data you need may be archived in an organization's warehouse, or it may be squirreled away at a variety of sites scattered around the country. After you know exactly what information you need, your client can pull it together for you. All it takes is a simple memo or a phone call to your client, and before you know it, you have everything you need, *when* you need it. Not only do you save the time and money that it would have taken you to physically gather the data yourself, but you avoid organizational red tape and employee resistance that may otherwise have caused you problems.

✔ **Grant the ongoing support of the keepers of the data.** Sometimes you need one or more of the keepers of an organization's data to, in essence, act as your guide and translator as you review the many different pieces and sources of data that you uncover during your project. This person can be an invaluable resource as you try to understand the context of the data that you are reviewing. *When was this policy last updated? Why was it updated? Was it intended to address some sort of organizational problem?* Find the individuals and departments responsible for generating the data and have them tell you two things: what it means and how it was used. If necessary, your client can grant you the help of one or more employees on a part-time or full-time basis.

As you'll find out, your clients may be very willing to help you out; alternatively, your clients may expect *you* to take care of the data-collection aspect of the project. The best way to solicit the assistance of your clients in the data-collection process is to include this discussion in your initial client meetings and sell your clients on the benefits of involving them in the search. You can encourage your clients' involvement by pointing out two benefits to them. First, the quality of the data-collection efforts is enhanced (thus enhancing the quality of the results of your efforts). Second, you can pass on the savings that result from the reduced number of hours that you devote to collecting data. You'll have much better luck getting your clients signed up if you make data collection a part of the original contract instead of springing the request for help on the client during the course of the project. Be sure to include in the contract a section listing the exact support that the client is to provide.

Watch Out! Data Disaster Ahead!

If you aren't careful, you may conduct an involved data-collection effort only to find that key data is missing, incomplete, or suspect because the source was biased. These data disasters not only can cause you additional work and heartache, but when they become a part of your project assumptions, they can also destroy the validity of your work as well as your credibility as a consultant. For these reasons, it's especially important to validate your sources and to examine them closely for problems that could lead to data disaster!

Here are some of the most common data problems and suggestions for ensuring that they don't cause *you* problems:

✔ **Overlooking key data sources:** It's easy to overlook a source of data — perhaps a disgruntled employee who has been moved to an offsite location or a disheveled box full of audiotapes recorded at executive team meetings. Such an oversight may occur because your clients direct you to information sources that are less embarrassing to them or simply because you inadvertently omitted some information. Unfortunately, the data you overlook may be a crucial link in the success of your project. Be exhaustive and relentless in your search for the data that you need to complete your project successfully.

✔ **Overlooking client biases:** Regardless of what they may say or think, every employee — from the mailroom clerk to the chairman of the board — comes with a unique set of biases. For example, a design engineer may tell you that the problem with product development is absolutely, positively the result of late input from the marketing department. But you may not be aware (and you won't be aware until you start digging into the problem more deeply) that he harbors a personal grudge against the head of marketing because she got a bigger bonus than he did last year. The secret to gathering accurate data from interviews with employees, group meetings, and questionnaires is to recognize that bias is a part of most data gathered directly from employees, to understand the source and nature of the bias, and to filter the bias out of the data that you have gathered.

✔ **Overlooking personal biases:** Believe it or not, you may harbor a bias or two yourself. Perhaps your client is from Tierra del Fuego, and you've never trusted anyone from Tierra del Fuego. Or maybe you don't think that your client knows what he's talking about, and you think that you have all the right answers. Take a close look at yourself and any biases that may color your data-gathering efforts, and work to overcome them and make your approach as balanced as you possibly can.

✔ **Accepting incomplete data:** Sometimes you know exactly what information you need from someone and ask for it, but what you get in return is incomplete or not what you asked for. You may be greatly tempted — especially when you are under a lot of pressure to complete your project or you have tons of data to analyze — to simply let it go and accept what you are given. This can be disastrous to the successful outcome of your project. When you get incomplete data — or no data at all — follow up with your source and insist on getting what you need. If you meet with continued resistance in obtaining necessary information, ask your client to help prioritize the effort with the difficult employee.

✔ **Failing to fully document data:** When you are in the middle of fast and furious data gathering, the sheer amount of data that comes your way can be overwhelming. Before you know it, you can find yourself focusing your efforts on data that is already documented for you — reports, policies, staffing plans, product schedules, and the like — at the expense of data that isn't documented, such as employee interviews and surveys. Often, the data that you gather from *your* sources turns out to be the most useful in getting to the heart of an organization's problems. Don't let these important sources of information slip through your fingers; document your conversations, interviews, and other interactions with client personnel as soon as you can after they occur.

The data that you collect in this phase of the consulting process forms the basis for the ensuing steps of the process. Be sure that the data you collect is accurate, complete, and timely, and check it thoroughly before you send it on to the next step of the consulting process: problem-solving and developing recommendations. In Chapter 7, we consider how to take the data you gather in this phase of your project and start making sense of it.

Chapter 7

Problem-Solving and Developing Recommendations

• •

In This Chapter

▶ Organizing client data

▶ Problem-solving and weighing alternatives

▶ Developing, prioritizing, and selecting your recommendations

• •

*W*hat are you going to do with all that great information you gathered? As you may recall (if you started at the back of the book and are working your way forward, we're talking about Chapter 5), the first step in the consulting process is defining the problem. The point of collecting data, which is the next step of the process, is to test your assumptions of what the real problem is. For example, if you and your client make a preliminary decision that the organization's problem is a lack of training for line supervisors, the data you collect should either support that conclusion or point you in a different direction altogether.

Before you can tell whether the data supports or refutes your conclusions, you need to organize it and make sense of it. This means sorting it into recognizable categories and then looking for commonalities and trends. Through this process of sorting data — discarding irrelevant data along the way — and then focusing on the data that is most compelling, a range of possible alternatives for problem-solving naturally opens up.

The point of this exercise is to arrive at the very best recommendations for your client. By considering your client's needs, the cost of your recommended courses of action versus the benefits to be derived from them, and the organization's culture, you can arrive at recommendations that not only solve your client's problem but also are right for your client's organization. In our experience, if your recommendations don't mesh with the organization — its culture *and* politics — then your report gets filed away and is soon forgotten.

In this chapter, we consider how to take a flood of data and organize it so that it makes sense to both you and your clients. We explain how to apply an effective model for problem-solving and discuss the best way to go about deciding which recommendations you present to your clients.

Making Sense of All That Information

After a week or two (or three) of collecting data, most consultants find themselves up to their ears in data of all kinds, sizes, and formats. Surveys, interviews, focus groups, archives, management reports, and much more are available to you. This is good because the more data you have to draw from, the higher the probability that you're going to get to the bottom of your client's problem. However, all this information can be overwhelming. If you don't have a good system for organizing it and separating what's important from what's not, you're going to find yourself bogged down in a flood of data. And if you can't pull yourself out of the flood, your project progress is going to slow to a crawl, and your client is going to begin to wonder whether hiring you was the wrong choice. This is not the best outcome for you *or* your client.

Fortunately, you can make sense of all that data and identify the trends and patterns that point you to solutions. Just follow the steps listed here, and before you know it, you'll have the right information at your fingertips.

Sort and consolidate the data

After you pull together all the data, you're likely to be faced with a stack (or perhaps a small mountain) of information from many places: project status reports, computer diskettes and printouts, receivables forecasts, promotion plans, internal memos, press releases, and the like. Your first task is to synthesize all this data by sorting it into collections of similar *kinds* of information. For example, you might organize a year's worth of data on an organization's financial performance into monthly categories. Within each month, you might further organize the data into the categories of sales, expenses, and so on. How you decide to organize your information is up to you; you should base your decision on the nature of your project and your personal preferences.

After you sort your data into collections of related items, you can consolidate it. You may have multiple copies of the same data or the same data from several sources; if so, toss the extras.

If you use surveys to collect data, first read the ones on which the respondent made numerous comments. Because those respondents cared enough to take the time to give you additional information, you undoubtedly get the most productive and thoughtful feedback from them.

Put steps and processes in time sequence

When people take on a task, they normally do so in a logical and stepwise fashion. Part of organizing and synthesizing your data is to figure out the sequence of the steps your clients take to carry out tasks and processes. What do employees *say* they do first, second, third, fourth, and so on? What do they *really* do first, second, third, fourth, and so on? What then are the differences between what employees say and do, and why is there a difference?

For example, a mailroom clerk may claim that he delivers all incoming overnight mail to employees first, processes and routes incoming regular mail second, and then prepares all outgoing mail third. However, upon personal observation, you may discover that incoming overnight mail is actually handled second, causing delays in the receipt of important correspondence.

A great way to work out time sequences is to draw the steps and processes on flowcharts or write the steps on stick-on notes and then stick them on a wall in sequence. This technique is commonly known as *process mapping*. Using computerized flowcharts or stick-on notes makes it easy to rearrange the steps as you enter the problem-solving and recommendation phases of the consulting process.

Look for patterns, trends, and themes

As you pore through all the data you pull together, you may soon begin to notice certain patterns and themes emerging. For example, if you're reviewing a company's sales performance, you may notice that sales are strong at the beginning of the month but then consistently dip at the end of the month. Or you may notice that more accidents occur on an assembly line during the night shift than during the day or swing shift. These emerging trends tell you where to delve deeper when it comes time to problem-solve.

Ignore and set aside extraneous data

As you begin to refine your data further — noting which information is starting to point to recurring themes and possible solutions — you notice that some of the data you collected is extraneous to your efforts. Set that data aside and remove it from further consideration. Doing so allows you to focus your efforts and attention on the most promising data while ignoring the information that has little or no bearing on your recommendations.

Focus

Concentrate your full focus on the most relevant data, and consolidate it to the lowest common denominator — that is, the information that keeps coming back to you as a possible solution. For example, suppose that you are investigating the reasons for the poor morale of an organization, and a large amount of the data that you collect through employee interviews and one-on-one meetings points to uncaring managers as the source of the problem. In that case, you focus your efforts on the information that tells you exactly which managers are at the root of the morale problem and what they are doing to cause it. Focused information forms the basis of your problem-solving efforts, which are at the heart of this process.

Whew! Organizing your data is a tough job, but somebody has to do it. Fortunately, now that you have the heavy lifting of collecting your data and sorting it into recognizable collections of information out of the way, you can begin having fun with this phase of the consulting process.

Bill Eastman on developing client partnerships

Bill Eastman is president of Applied Innovations Group, a business consulting firm located in Gloucester, Virginia (804-693-3696, e-mail epriseos@aol.com). Applied Innovations specializes in using the Internet to maximize its impact in markets that traditionally have been underserved in the consulting industry — service companies at $20 million in annual revenues with plans to make the leap to $100 million, and those companies in the manufacturing sector that are currently at $100 million in annual revenues with plans to make the leap to $500 million. We spoke to Bill about how to develop client partnerships and the secrets of running a successful consulting business.

Consulting For Dummies: What do you do to develop partnerships and long-term relationships with your clients?

Bill Eastman: We're convinced that for an organization to make change, most of the recommendations we provide cannot be created inside the organization. Why? Because either our clients are too busy, there's too much on their plate, or they are up against entrenched forces. To solve this problem, we create a temporary and joint organization from our operations plus key players from the client's organization. The joint project is run independently, and as a beta operation for the duration outside the boundaries of the client organization. What this allows is the testing of new ideas: bring the best inside the organization and integrate with current operations. Consulting is not about staying around; it is about transferring technology — the temporary organization should cease to exist as soon as its mission has been accomplished.

CFD: That's an innovative approach. Many projects conducted *within* organizations are subject to all kinds of employee resistance.

Eastman: Definitely. And if your client is not willing to do that, then you've really got to ask yourself whether or not partnering is appropriate. You may still want to work with them and sell them your expertise, or sell them the products and services that they need, but clearly understand that you're not dealing with a partner; you're much more into a customer-vendor relationship as opposed to a true partnership. And that's okay, because every client is different. What we try to do is to focus on those companies for whom we don't have to explain that concept to them twice — they get it. Their issue is not resistance to change as much as it is "My plate is full, I know I've got to do this, I can't because I don't have time, so we commission you to do it."

CFD: Most successful organizations have a plan. What's yours?

Eastman: We have a five-part business plan for running our business. And this isn't something for bankers or accountants — it's really the way we keep our eye on the ball every day of the week. By the way, we run an entire cash business. We have no loans because we don't have to — we run a virtual company. The first thing that we do is attempt to gain visibility and exposure — it's a word that I got from somebody about 20 years ago called *visiposure*. What we're looking for are visibility and exposure in our targeted industries. This includes membership in trade organizations, writing articles, being present in newsgroups and user groups on the Internet, and executing a number of other promotional

strategies. However, we focus on only a couple of industries that we want to own.

CFD: What industries do you own?

Eastman: The industries we are attempting to own are something that we call "infocom" — information and communications. We view our business in the same way that a stockbroker does in that we're managing a portfolio. We try to bundle a number of companies together within a portfolio that we call infocom. Our portfolio includes software manufacturers, organizations into interactive media and programming, organizations such as phone companies that do distribution, and companies that manufacture hardware — computers or switching equipment. Though we work in other areas, this is the one we want to stay in.

CFD: So what's the second part of your business plan?

Eastman: The second step is the gathering of mindshare. In other words, by creating an image in the marketplace, we're trying to get mindshare for integrated solutions. And we focus predominantly in the service arena. Although we know a lot about product quality, we don't work in that particular arena — the competition is brutal. Service quality is a lot more difficult for organizations and consultants to handle, and that's the arena that *we* want to play in. We look at companies — companies that live or die on the quality of their customer service — that are in very complex types of businesses and that have incredibly rapid rates of change — a perpetual state of white water.

CFD: What do you mean by "perpetual state of white water"?

Eastman: It used to be that being in business was much like riding the Mississippi — for the most part, the ride was slow and wide. In business today, it's much more like shooting a river

(continued)

(continued)

that's got an incredible drop, lots of rocks, currents, and eddies, and almost no flat water whatsoever to rest and catch your breath. It's all white water. So, although you can put together plans to run your business, those plans can only be put together strategically. Tactically, you need to, as you approach a rapid, have the people in your organization standing on the rocks *in the river* figuring out how to shoot it. It's an immediate decision made at the front line.

CFD: And as soon as you get through that first rapid, there's another right behind.

Eastman: Right. The best thing that management can do for people is to walk the rim of the canyon so that they can inform their team that there's another set of rapids coming.

CFD: How about the third step in your business plan?

Eastman: The third step is to create a temporary organization where the project that we're engaged in — where it's both strategy and implementation — is run as a beta. We briefly discussed this concept earlier in this interview. Not only do we feed the information that we learn back into the organization so that they can incorporate it as we go, but we train the people from the company who join us how to handle it.

CFD: And what's step number four?

Eastman: The fourth step is reintegration. This step allows our clients to reintegrate our findings from the third step back inside the organization. We can then shift our role to an expert

provider, and our role is to provide expertise to keep them upgraded and updated on what's happening. Once clients pick up our technology in the third step, for a small fee they get a download of the latest technology. So we're now selling information to our consulting groups who are internal to the companies that we sold contracts to.

CFD: Once a client, always a client?

Eastman: That's certainly our goal. In the fifth and final step of our business plan, we publish what we've learned — the successes *and* the failures. That information then goes back to step one and gives us added visiposure.

CFD: What's the key to the future for consultants?

Eastman: You've got to be able to find a way of providing new, identifiable, and significant value. For example, I used to subscribe to *Business Week* magazine. I still read *Business Week,* but I don't subscribe anymore. Instead, I check out their free Web site. But that's not where the *future* is. The future is having a Web site that people can customize to fit their own needs, one they can interact with. We have our portfolio that's made up of information and communications firms — infocom — and we provide and gain cutting-edge insights. We work hard to stay ahead of what's happening in our clients' industries in regard to how technology is going to alter them and then we help them integrate this information so they can run more efficient and effective business operations. The net result is that our clients *win.* And when our *clients* win, *we* win.

The Right Way to Problem-Solve

In consulting, problem-solving is really where the rubber meets the road. While problem-solving, you review the data that you sliced, diced, and otherwise processed to develop a set of solutions, one of which will ultimately become the recommendation that you present to your clients. Because of this, you want to open the net as wide as possible at the beginning of the problem-solving process — sucking in as many possibilities as you can. Then you need to throw some of your catch back into the sea (and keep the good ones for yourself) by weighing the alternatives until you are left with the best possible courses of action. At this point in the process, you aren't narrowing the field down to one possible course of action, but only down to the few *best* ones.

There's a right way and a wrong way to problem-solve. Fortunately for you, we present the right way here:

1. **Brainstorm possible solutions.**

   The first step in the problem-solving process is to take the data that you collected and consolidated and to brainstorm possible solutions to the problems that the data raises. Although you can brainstorm by yourself or only with other members of your firm — if there *are* other members of your firm — you get a much wider variety of options when you include your clients in your brainstorming sessions.

   The secret to conducting productive brainstorming sessions is to encourage *every* possible idea — no matter how far out it may seem. This means suspending judgment for the duration of the session and welcoming everyone's input. Record every idea on paper, flip charts, or a white board so that you don't lose track of any of them.

2. **Consider the implications of each possible solution.**

   Isolate each alternative that was generated during your brainstorming sessions and follow it to its logical conclusion. For example, if a client has a problem with the quality of the circuit boards leaving the factory floor, one possible cause is that workers are not using the correct soldering techniques. If you follow this possibility to its logical conclusion, a solution may be to provide more training to employees on soldering correctly or to provide better supervision and monitor employees' work more closely.

3. **Weigh alternatives and narrow your focus.**

   After you work through all possible alternatives, weigh them one against another to determine which are most likely to be relevant to the outcome and which ones are least likely to be relevant. As a part of getting to your final recommendations, you have to focus your efforts more sharply at this point and move ahead on a few fronts instead of many. Discard the alternatives that are *least* likely to become viable recommendations, and continue to narrow your focus to those that are the *most* likely.

4. Pick the best courses of action.

By this time, you should have your list of possible alternatives narrowed down to a manageable number. Continue to work through this list with your client until you whittle it down to no more than five or so of the best courses of action. If you look up for a moment, you should be able to see the light at the end of the tunnel. After you complete this step, you are ready to go on to developing your recommendations.

So you managed to wade through all your data, problem-solve, and arrive at a reasonable number of alternatives from which to draw your recommendations. This is the reason your clients hire you: to take advantage of your expertise by obtaining your advice and recommendations on ways to solve their problems. Don't worry — you're almost there!

Developing Your Recommendations

Your clients hire you to get your recommendations on how they can solve their problems. However, you have to test every set of recommendations to ensure that they are in the best interests of your clients and that your clients will readily accept and implement them. All the most wonderful recommendations in the world — bound in attractive report binders and accompanied by lush multimedia presentations — aren't worth a hill of beans unless they are heeded and implemented. (Has anyone ever figured out how much a hill of beans is worth? If you know, please e-mail the answer to us.)

The best client recommendations are effective and honest but take into account clients' budgets, needs, resources, and culture. Here are some guidelines to help you develop recommendations for *your* clients:

✔ **Evaluate the best courses of action.** At this point, you have approximately five possible best courses of action that resulted from the problem-solving phase of your effort. Take another look at them in light of the following criteria:

- **Cost versus benefit:** Before settling on your final recommendations, consider each recommendation in terms of its cost versus its ultimate benefit. If a recommendation is potentially very expensive for your client and the benefits are marginal at best, it may not deserve a position at the top of your list. However, if a recommendation costs your client relatively little and the payoff is great, it should make a speedy trip to the head of the class.

- **Client needs and resources:** Your best recommendations not only address the very real and concrete needs that your research and brainstorming uncover, but they also address the unique situation that your client's organization and employees are in right now. Each client has particular needs and can muster differing amounts and kinds of resources. Whereas some companies may be short on cash and long on employees, other companies may have plenty of cash to throw at their problems but have no excess personnel to assign to the needed repairs and solutions. Be sure to account for these kinds of differences as you finalize your recommendations.

- **Client's organizational culture:** Every organization has a unique culture, and your client's culture is an important consideration in molding your final recommendations. You may have the greatest recommendations in the world, but if they run counter to the organization's culture, at best they will be adopted only grudgingly. Much more likely, they will be discarded altogether. For example, if you recommend laying off half of a company's workforce but the founder is rightfully proud that throughout the company's history no employee has ever been laid off (and layoffs are not about to start now), your recommendation will be quickly discarded.

- **Client's people and politics:** Politics plays a major role in how things are done in every organization. Your recommendations have to take into account your client's political landscape and the way that people relate to one another to get things done. If they don't, your recommendations may *look* great but be unworkable in the organization. For example, you may determine that an organization needs to get its employees *much* more involved in the decision-making process. However, if the middle managers in charge of implementing this change are dead set against it and they have the political power to block it, the recommendation will die a quick death.

✔ **Draft recommendations.** After taking the preceding criteria into consideration, the next step is to draft the recommendations to present to your clients. Although you still have a *little* bit of time to rework them before you make your client presentation, they should be fairly definite, settled, and stable at this point in the process.

✔ **Rank your recommendations.** After reviewing all the potential recommendations and running them through the gauntlet of criteria such as cost versus benefit, client needs and resources, and organizational politics and culture, you're ready to take the last step: ranking your recommendations in order of practicability. After you do that, you're in business. Provide options for your client. Let the client choose among lower price, faster completion, and higher quality. It's best to use a min-max strategy: Build a first-class, top-note strategy, and then build a bare-minimum strategy. Doing so tells you when to walk away and helps your client build a solution between your two viable ends of successful solutions.

Well, you've made it through one of the most difficult, yet most rewarding, parts of the consulting process. After you compile your draft recommendations, you're ready for the next step: presenting them to your client. Good luck!

Chapter 8

Tell It Like It Is: Presenting Your Recommendations

. . . .

In This Chapter

▶ Giving feedback to your clients

▶ Designing your feedback meeting

▶ Building client ownership of your recommendations

. . . .

*A*t some point in your consulting project, you're going to develop a set of recommendations for your client. This, after all, is what your clients pay you the big bucks for. They pay their hard-earned money to have you look at their problems and, applying your unique brand of skill and expertise, develop a set of recommendations that lead them to the promised land of improved products, practices, or ways of doing business. Just as important as developing a set of recommendations is presenting those recommendations to your clients in a way that captures not only their interest, but also their hearts and minds. That's what this chapter is all about.

So how do you go about presenting your recommendations to your clients? Should you write them a letter, drop it off at the receptionist's desk, and then run? Although that's sometimes a very tempting option, you'll more likely communicate your recommendations in the form of both a written report and a presentation. As a rule, you should always give your clients a tangible product of some sort at the end of the project. In most cases, this product takes the form of a written report. And to ensure that your clients understand and ultimately act on the recommendations in your report, presenting your recommendations personally — whether directly to your client or to a group of managers or other members of your client's organization — is definitely a good idea.

Your primary goal in this phase of the consulting process is to get your clients to accept your recommendations. Bringing your clients around to the point where they are ready to embrace your recommendations is very much a selling process; running through a few charts is not enough. You should be passionate about your recommendations and feel strongly about your clients' need to adopt them.

In this chapter, we consider the importance of presenting your recommendations to your clients, plus we give you some tips for making the feedback meaningful and lasting. We also review the steps involved in presenting your recommendations in an effective and successful client feedback meeting and discuss ways to help your clients take ownership of your recommendations to build the momentum necessary to carry them out. Although this chapter explains how to submit reports of recommendations and how to make presentations to your clients, Chapter 13 covers in greater detail the content to include in your reports and detailed presentation techniques and tips.

Giving Client Feedback: Setting the Stage

As you prepare for a client feedback meeting, you can do several things to help yourself (and your client!) get the most out of your presentation. By following this advice, you help open up the channels of communication between you and your client and pave the way for client acceptance and implementation of your recommendations.

You can have great impact on whether your client ultimately accepts and implements your ideas. Keep these tips in mind as you prepare for your presentation; they'll pay you back many times over in the form of happier clients and a greater probability of implementation of your recommendations. And don't forget, a happy client is a client who will likely contract with you again — and refer you to *new* clients.

- **Don't forget your selling cap.** Sure, the point of communicating your recommendations to your client is to explain exactly what the organization should do to solve its problems, whatever they are. However, making your recommendations involves more than that. In most cases, presenting your recommendations to an organization is as much (or perhaps even more) a *selling* job as it is a *telling* job. No matter how much an organization wants to solve its problems, you always run across at least some resistance from some of the people within it. As you present your recommendations, keep this in mind and be consistent in highlighting the benefits to be gained by the organization and the people who are part of it. Your case must be compelling!

- **Keep your clients involved.** If you have been playing your cards right throughout the consulting process, your clients are very much a part of your presentation and the recommendations you make. They are involved because you keep them abreast of your findings as you encounter them and you ask for their feedback and input. Not only do you gain great insight from their feedback, but you give your clients the opportunity to begin to buy in to your recommendations before you formally make them. By keeping your clients involved — and, actually, an integral part of the process — your recommendations are better suited to the organization *and* more likely to be accepted and implemented than those that are created in a vacuum and announced to a resistant audience. You can anticipate objections and have that information incorporated into your solutions.

✔ **Unleash no surprises.** Clients don't like surprises. If your recommendations will shatter your clients or embarrass any of the principals of the firm, you haven't involved your clients enough in the consulting process. A good sign that your clients *have* been adequately involved is that not only are your clients not surprised by the recommendations, but they are already sold on them before you make your presentation. Make that happen by involving your clients closely in the problem-definition, data-collection, and problem-solving phases of your work.

That said, if, for some reason, you *do* have a surprise or two up your sleeve, first present it privately to your client or to a key member of the client's organization.

✔ **Be honest and frank.** Sometimes the truth hurts. Despite the fact that you probably would much rather give your clients good news than bad, you're getting paid to lay it all on the line. Be sure that your client gets the *complete* benefit of your expertise — not just the parts that are politically correct or easy for you to communicate.

✔ **Be nonjudgmental.** Avoid being judgmental about the decisions your client made that got the organization into its current mess. Opening your presentation by saying something along the lines of "In all my years of consulting, I have never seen such a mess as this!" is definitely not good form. Not only are you never going to work for *that* particular firm again, but your recommendations also will find their way into the wastebasket sooner than you can say, "Oops!" Maybe the management team has some problems, but you have a much better chance of helping if you present your findings in a way that your client will accept.

✔ **Support your client.** Change is tough for any organization, and the recommendations that you present may set the stage for tremendous change in your client's organization. Reorganization, downsizing, streamlining, and more are often inevitable results of consultant recommendations. Be prepared to support your client — both emotionally and organizationally — as the organization prepares to confront the need for change.

Now that you know some things that you should definitely do when you present your recommendations to your clients, the next step is to plan and conduct your client feedback meeting. In the section "Conducting a Feedback Meeting," we review each step of this very important meeting.

Janice Seto is learning the ABCs of management consulting

Janice Seto of Bowmanville, Canada, is currently studying for her master's degree in business administration at the University of Victoria, in Victoria, British Columbia. The MBA program at the University of Victoria is unique in its emphasis on management consulting and is noted for the cooperative relationships that it develops with the western Canadian business community. Janice came to the school after several years in business; she served on the board of directors of the Malaysia-Canada Business Council in Kuala Lumpur and is a member of the Ontario College of Teachers and the Greater Victoria Chamber of Commerce. Janice discussed her experience at the University of Victoria and her opinions on how to develop good client-consultant relationships.

Consulting For Dummies: Why did you select the University of Victoria MBA program? There are certainly plenty of MBA programs out there for you to choose from.

Janice Seto: I've worked overseas, and I didn't want to go into a program that was very traditional — one that took students from their undergraduate programs, but with no work experience, and then put them in a two-year program with lots of lectures and classes of 100 or 200 students. That's not for me. I went to a very good university — the University of Toronto — and I've already had that type of experience. That's why I wanted a small, innovative program. I'm not one of those New York, Wall Street types who goes around annihilating people. I wanted an MBA that was more team-based, more innovative, more creative, and with an international focus. I wanted a very practical type of program that backs up the theory with real-life experience.

CFD: So that's what the University of Victoria offers you?

Seto: Yes. They pride themselves in doing it. The School of Business is only about five years old, and they built it from the ground up. They looked at the new trends going on in business schools and they got together to design a program which has a co-op module, as well as the regular accounting, finance, and other MBA courses. But they have a lot of emphasis on practical skills. For example, they have a mentor program. They also have integrated management exercises (IMEs) where, twice a semester, the students are organized in groups of five to conduct weeklong consulting projects. One of the major companies here in Victoria approaches the school — they pay no fee — and the MBA class works on the project for them. In order to graduate from the University of Victoria with an MBA, you have to do a consulting project or a thesis.

CFD: Wow.

Seto: It's great. Our compulsory consulting and research methods course is very focused, and even though it's very, very short, they focus on the entire consulting process. We go all the way from needs, to problem identification, to requests for proposal, to actually doing the proposal, to contract negotiation, to data collection and analysis, and then to presenting our recommendations to our clients.

CFD: So you learn how to do it all.

Seto: Yes. Now, of course, when you have that approach, you can't get into too much depth. I suppose you could compare it to when I was in teacher's college. They teach you the *theory* of teaching, but you actually have to go out and *do* it. So this is what they set us up for. They give us the theory of consulting, and client relationships, and analysis, and research methods, and then they make us do it by assigning integrated management exercises and through the consulting project graduation requirement. We've just finished an IME project about the British Columbia forest industry. Yesterday we were in front of a panel of environmentalists and foresters, and boy did we have questions coming in. *Hostile* questions — coming in from everybody. We were in the bush for a couple of days looking at the coastal rain forest and listening to very angry loggers, and then we talked to some very angry environmentalists and then some very angry government people.

CFD: It sounds like you were right in the middle.

Seto: That's right, but it beats sitting in a classroom all day!

CFD: Tell us, how important is it to develop good relationships with your clients?

Seto: Well, compatibility is very important because you have to develop trust. Let me give you an example of what I am doing now with a local credit union. When we were first introduced to the credit union's management team, I think they were a little skeptical. They said, "You know, you have a lot of work cut out for you. If you don't know anything about credit unions and banking, then you're going to have to go through a very steep learning curve." To build some initial rapport and trust, I let them know that we had already done an IME consulting project with their organization, and I mentioned the name of their senior manager who worked with our faculty coordinator. Once I did that, the whole tone relaxed. They said, "Fine, we know that you folks are very competent." But, in order to be a good consultant, you have to do these things. I'm a member of the Chamber of Commerce downtown, and I know there are only two students who are members, and people ask me

afterwards, why? Well, why not? When I was overseas in Malaysia, I joined the Malaysia-Canada Business Council and I sat on their board. Why? Because it's very important when people see your resume or see your name across the e-mail, they have to know who they're talking to. And they also have to know your personality and perhaps a little about your track record. You can prove it right then and there, and your clients will have some idea of whether or not you'll be compatible with them.

CFD: What recommendations do you have for establishing strong relationships with your clients?

Seto: If you've got a specific project, it's good to have regular meetings. You have to be honest with your clients and let them know what problems you are encountering. If you're being stonewalled by a particular department, you need to diplomatically tell them that you need that information in order to do a good job. Each party keeps one another informed. Basically, make sure that you stick to your original terms of reference — the scope of your project. Clients want people who are inquisitive and who want to do a good job, and I think that that helps the relationship. If you know that the company wants a certain thing that goes against what you want to do or against your own ethics, then you can't live with that. When that's the case, then maybe you shouldn't even work for them.

CFD: Right. The decision to consult is a two-way one. Both the consultant *and* the client have to be in agreement to proceed with a project. How can you get beyond a simple relationship and convert it into a partnership where you're working together with your clients instead of against them?

Seto: That's a very interesting question. Let me tell you a story that our professor for consulting told us when we asked him about this.

(continued)

(continued)

In a recent consulting project, he put his clients together in a weekend pressure-cooker environment — he flew all the way from Victoria to Ottawa to do this — and he acted as a facilitator and had them do a lot of team-building exercises and brainstorming. What is the mission of the company? What are their goals? He had to go back to the strategic vision of the company, determine whether there was top-level support, and identify the targets — the people who want to shoot it down, the people who are for the project. This clearly helped get everything out in the open. He did an action plan that everyone agreed on, and he had them break into little groups. One group focused on what the company would do to foster lifelong learning. One group focused on research and development. Then he had them figure out a list of priorities — and they had a list of 40. Then they developed targets — what can you do in the next two weeks, what can you do in the next month? Everyone was involved.

CFD: Is there a good way to give your clients bad news? If so, how?

Seto: I believe that clients usually come to a consulting firm knowing that there is a problem. They're not exactly sure what the problem is, but they're already prepared for some sort of bad news. However, you have to back it up with quantitative and qualitative evidence — focus groups, interviews, number crunching, all that stuff — and I think it's always a good idea to give the good side to the bad news. See it as an opportunity for change. It's basically how you sell it. It's more the medium than the message.

CFD: What advice would you give to someone who is thinking about a career in consulting?

Seto: Whatever interests you, be the expert — know everything about it. Learn what the different methods are, the pros and cons of each one, and so on. Therefore, you'll be the authority, and that will be a good foundation for your career. Of course, there are a lot of good products out there, so you have to have very good presentation skills. I believe that anyone who wants to become a consultant and move up will have to develop their basic skills for knowing one field very well and to be able to present it well.

Conducting a Feedback Meeting

Hours and hours of work — defining your client's problem, collecting data, and problem-solving — bring you to this point: your client feedback meeting. In this meeting, you present your recommendations to your client, and you plant the seeds for the eventual acceptance or rejection of your results. If the meeting goes well, your client will likely move to implement your recommendations. If not, your recommendations will most likely end up on the proverbial dust heap of history.

Client feedback meetings are first and foremost *your* meetings — you set the agenda and control the pace and flow of your presentation. Sure, you can and should be responsive to your client's needs and allow for some flexibility in the agenda, but be sure to get back to the topics that you planned to discuss.

Here are the five steps for conducting a successful client feedback meeting:

1. **Present project background, goals, and methodology.**

   The first part of your presentation consists of a brief description of the project, including the problems you were hired to tackle, your project goals, and the methodology you applied to arrive at your recommendations. Be sure to highlight your client's role in the problem-solving process and in helping you arrive at the recommendations you are presenting. Everything here must have been agreed to beforehand.

2. **Present your recommendations.**

   Getting to this point has taken a while, but, finally, here you are. At this point in the presentation, you give your key recommendations along with the reasons why they are the most likely solutions to the problems your client faces. Be sure to have an array of alternative recommendations for your client to consider (including options such as lower price, faster completion, and higher quality), and explain why you didn't select them as your primary recommendations.

3. **Encourage client discussion.**

   Getting your client to talk about your recommendations is a critical part of this phase of the consulting process. You want the meeting attendees to ask questions, challenge your assumptions, consider the alternatives, request further information, or do whatever it takes to help decide on an appropriate course of action. If your audience is silent after your presentation, encourage a healthy exchange of ideas by asking the participants whether they understand your recommendations and whether they have questions about anything you presented.

4. **Help your client decide on a course of action.**

   Your recommendations are exactly that — *recommendations*. Your job is not to make your clients' decisions for them — they have to absorb the data you present and make up their own minds. However, you should press your client to make a decision of some sort — preferably while you are around to help facilitate the process. After conducting your project, you are likely to be the person who is most knowledgeable about the problem and the fixes that have the best chance of working. You can offer your clients a great deal of help as they decide which course of action to take.

5. **Determine your role in future activities.**

   In some cases, presenting your recommendations to your client may be the last step of the project. In other cases, your client may want you to stick around to help implement your recommendations. In any case, use the client feedback meeting to determine what, if any, role you will play in further activities related to your project.

After your client has your recommendations, all that's left to do is to implement them. Of course, the streets of business are strewn with recommendations that were never implemented. Part of getting your recommendations implemented is to help your client gain a sense of ownership of your recommendations. Like passing the baton in a relay race, you need to make your recommendations your *client's* recommendations.

Would it surprise you to hear that we address that very topic in the next section?

Building Client Ownership of Your Recommendations

At some point in the consulting process, your clients have to take ownership of your recommendations and make them their own. Otherwise, your recommendations are doomed to be relegated to the recycling bin. You can directly influence the chances of your recommendations being implemented by working with your clients to build ownership of your recommendations. Although you have been setting the stage for this transition since the beginning of the project by creating partnerships with your clients and involving them in the consulting process, now is the time to press your point home.

Your recommendations are only as good as their implementation by your clients. Even the best recommendations miss the mark if they remain unimplemented. Here are some ways that you can help your clients take ownership of them:

- **Push for consensus.** Don't allow issues to remain unaddressed or unresolved. For example, suppose that you recommend instituting a mandatory quality program for all the businesses that sell parts to your client's manufacturing operation. However, if one or more of the participants in your feedback meeting is opposed to your recommendation because such a program may lead to increases in vendor-supplied part prices, don't just drop the issue. Work with your client to mediate the differences between the two positions and come up with a consensus that can then be implemented. If you let the issue drop in your meeting, your recommendation may be ignored.

- **Push for decisions and commitments.** The client feedback meeting is the perfect time and place for you and your client to work out the details of an action plan for implementation. It's also the perfect time for you to push your client to make the commitments that ensure that the action plan is followed. After all, unless you have completely missed the boat, implementing your recommendations is the only step that helps your client.

✔ **Offer to continue your partnership through the implementation phase of the project.** Do you still have that selling cap we asked you to put on at the beginning of the chapter? That's okay; we'll give you a minute or two to dig it out of your closet. Got it? Good! Your client may or may not want your help in implementing your recommendations. If implementation wasn't a part of your original client contract (and you almost always should try to make it a part), you can suggest it now.

You have two good reasons for offering. First, you can help ensure that your recommendations are actually implemented and that the implementation is indeed what you recommended. Second, you can continue to reinforce and build the relationship that you have already developed with your client by continuing your work through the implementation phase. If the implementation goes well, your client will surely ask for your help when other problems arise in the future.

Congratulations! For some of you, this is the end of the consulting process. Your clients are now going to take your recommendations and implement them on their own. If this is the case, be sure to check in on your clients periodically to see how it's going and offer to help them in any way you can. You never know when your clients may want to take you up on your offer.

The rest of you — the consultants whose clients have engaged them to participate in the implementation phase of the consulting process — still have work to do. In Chapter 9, we discuss working with your clients to implement your recommendations.

Chapter 9

Implementation: Making Your Prescriptions Stick

*Y*our recommendations to your client represent the fruits of your labors. Much hard work — both on your part and on your client's part — goes into producing them. However, if your recommendations are filed away in a drawer or set aside on some manager's desk, then the fruits of your labor soon rot away to nothing. No consultant alive can honestly say that it doesn't hurt just a little when the outcome of all that hard work is a recommendation that a client never acts upon.

As a consultant, you're in a difficult position. You may know *exactly* what needs to be done to solve your client's problem, but you're not the one who decides whether to implement your recommendations — your client is. Indeed, your client may decide to pick apart your recommendations and use only the ones that are politically or culturally palatable at any given moment. That's the client's prerogative.

You can participate in the process of getting your clients to adopt and implement your recommendations. This is, after all, the ultimate goal of your hard work — to see your recommendations implemented and to watch your clients' problems disappear as a result.

In this chapter, we show you how to work with your clients to put together implementation plans, and we give you some tips on making the implementation go easier for everyone involved. Finally, we consider why and how to assess the results of the implementation of your recommendations.

You Have to Have a Plan

To ensure the ultimate success of the implementation of your recommendations, you and your client need a plan that details the exact steps that have to be undertaken, who is responsible for carrying them out, and when they have to be done. Depending on the size of your project and the extent and complexity of your recommendations, your plan may be only a few paragraphs long, or it might go on for many pages. The best plan you can have is one you have worked out with the close participation of your client. Participation builds commitment, and commitment greatly increases the chances that your recommendations will be implemented successfully and completely.

As you work with your clients to put together project implementation plans, plan to do the following things:

- **Define the implementation tasks.** Every good plan has to include tasks that spell out each step in its completion. A plan for implementing your recommendations should also contain the tasks that ensure that the implementation phase of the consulting process is completed successfully and with a minimum of confusion and client resistance. Because your client plays such a critical role in bringing your recommendations to fruition, be sure that he or she plays a big part in defining the specifics of implementation.

- **Define implementation task schedules.** For a plan to be effective, it must have schedules for completion. Otherwise, the people who are assigned implementation tasks don't have a sense for their priority, and they tend to let other priorities — ones with specific deadlines — take the front seat. For every task in your implementation plan, make sure to establish a start date and an end date.

- **Assign roles and responsibilities.** Every task in your plan needs someone who takes responsibility for its successful and timely completion. The best way to avoid confusion in the implementation process is to assign the responsibility for each task to one and only one person. When you assign responsibility for a task to more than one person (or, heaven forbid, to a committee), *no one* is truly responsible for the task. Given the way that human nature often works, this can lead to confusion, dropped tasks, and missed deadlines.

Note: For employees to carry out their assignments effectively, they must also have the authority to do so. Ensure that your client gives his or her employees the authority to do the tasks they are assigned.

- **Consider pilot projects.** If you're working on a fairly minor set of recommendations for a fairly small organization, you probably can implement your recommendations in a straightforward manner with little or no need to do extensive testing along the way. However, as the size of the implementation phase grows, along with the possible impact on your client's employees and customers, creating a pilot project to test the implementation of your recommendations *before* they are actually put into service often makes sense. For example, a Web design consultant may want to set up a test Web page for a client before actually posting the real Web page to the Internet. The test page lets you check all text and graphics so that they look the way you (and your client!) want them to look and gives you a chance to ensure that all hypertext and links function appropriately. Pilot projects are a virtual necessity if the changes you recommend impact particularly important client business systems, such as computer-based accounting systems and inventory systems.

✔ **Define how you will assess the success of the implementation.** The final part of your implementation plan is a description of the baselines, measures, and outcomes that you will use to decide whether your implementation was successful. These link back to the original baselines, measures, expectations, and goals that you worked out and agreed to with your client at the beginning of the project. What are your client's expectations for success? What are your expectations? Make sure that both points of view are incorporated in the overall plan. If your implementation isn't successful, you need the information from this assessment to determine why.

Although you can follow any variety of formats to present your implementation plan, the plan should at least address each one of the points discussed in this section. Figure 9-1, shown on the next page, is a sample implementation plan, based on the recommendations of an audiovisual consultant, for the installation of a new public address system in an auditorium. Note how the plan incorporates the activities that should be part of an implementation plan, as described in this section.

Regardless of how extensive the implementation is or how long it may take, a plan helps to ensure that no confusion arises over who is supposed to do what when. Of course, every implementation program can have its ups and downs. In the section "Just Do It! Implementation Tips," we give you some advice on avoiding the downs and maximizing the ups of *your* implementation.

Just Do It! Implementation Tips

Wouldn't it be nice if you could snap your fingers and have all your recommendations implemented, just like that? Unfortunately, the implementation phase of the consulting process can be difficult — for both you and your client. If you aren't careful to attend to the details, the whole thing can unravel very quickly, and your client's organization quickly moves back to where it is most comfortable: the status quo.

Kennesaw Auditorium Public Address System Upgrade Implementation Plan

After a thorough study of the acoustics of the Kennesaw Auditorium and a review of the adequacy of the current public address system, the project consultant — Superb Audio Associates — recommended that the current system be upgraded with the Friztek Model 1000 public address system. Implementation of this recommendation involves accomplishing the following tasks:

Task 1: Purchase new Friztek Model 1000 public address system. Superb Audio Associates will seek competition to obtain the lowest price on the Friztek equipment, purchase, and take possession of it not later than May 25.

Task 2: Remove the current public address system from the Kennesaw Auditorium. Employees of the Kennesaw Auditorium Trust will remove the current equipment and repair any resulting damage to the facility not later than June 1.

Task 3: Install new Friztek Model 1000. Superb Audio Associates will install, mount, and wire all components of the new public address system not later than June 5.

Task 4: Perform system testing. Superb Audio Associates will completely test the installed new public address system, ensuring that it meets all published specifications for power output, signal-to-noise ratio, and distortion, not later than June 7. Superb Audio Associates will be responsible for making any required adjustments to bring the equipment within specified performance limits.

Task 5: Train Kennesaw Auditorium employees in the operation of the new public address system. Superb Audio Associates will train all Kennesaw Auditorium employees in how to operate the Friztek Model 1000 public address system not later than June 10. Consultant will also be available for retraining of employees as required.

Success Measures:

Superb Audio Associates will be considered to have successfully completed the project when all of the following events occur:

- New Friztek Model 1000 public address system is installed, mounted, and wired not later than June 5.
- New Friztek Model 1000 is tested to meet all published specifications for power output, signal-to-noise ratio, and maximum distortion not later than June 7.
- All Kennesaw Auditorium employees are trained in the operation of the new Friztek Model 1000 public address system not later than June 10.

You can actively do several things to help ensure that your implementation comes off without a hitch (well, at least with only a *few* hitches here and there). To facilitate the implementation of your recommendations, you need to do the following as you work through the implementation process:

✔ **Deal with resistance.** If you thought that your client's employees were resistant during the data-collection phase of your project, you haven't seen anything yet. Now that your recommendations are soon to become reality within your client's organization, the people who have the most to lose with coming changes will be sure to rally their forces against you in a last-ditch effort to preserve the status quo. If you hope to make your recommendations last, you have to identify all the possible sources of organizational resistance and then neutralize them one by one.

✔ **Be realistic in your expectations.** Organizations don't change overnight. Even after a massive reorganization, line workers still do their jobs in pretty much the same way they always have. Lasting change takes time to bring about, and you must have patience as the organization slowly moves in the right direction. Be realistic in your expectations for the implementation of your recommendations. As you develop your implementation schedule, allow plenty of time for employees to soak up the changes and work them into their day-to-day work routines.

✔ **Watch out for dropped responsibilities.** The successful implementation of your recommendations requires close attention to the performance of tasks — ensuring that they are completed when they are supposed to be — and to the continued participation of all personnel assigned to carry them out. Employees resisting change commonly do so by conveniently "forgetting" to carry out their assigned duties or by simply allowing other tasks to take priority. The best way to prevent this type of behavior is to establish clear tasks, assign definite responsibilities to specific individuals, track task completion closely against the established schedule, and hold individuals accountable.

✔ **Nourish your client partnership.** You need the complete and committed participation of your client to make the implementation of your recommendations work and ensure that it lasts. The ongoing care and feeding of your client relationship is an important factor in getting your recommendations implemented. You can demonstrate this care by keeping in touch with your clients, inviting their input and suggestions, and maintaining a good working relationship. If you find yourself on the outs with your client, your recommendations probably will soon find themselves there, too.

✔ **Beware of the perpetual implementation syndrome.** Some implementations drag on. And on. And on. Before you know it, the whole project — recommendations and all — falls off the radar screen and everyone forgets that it ever happened. By allowing implementations to drag on without end, you risk letting all your work go to waste. Be sure to work closely with your clients to establish a firm implementation schedule that has a clear beginning and a clear end — one that is written in terms of weeks or at most months, not years. Exact timetables depend on the nature of the project — its complexity and the desired speed of implementation — along with the availability of required client resources and support.

By following this advice, you're doing just about everything you can to do your part in the implementation process. Don't forget that your clients must do their part, too. As the old saying goes, you can lead a horse to water, but you can't make him drink. You can't *force* your clients to implement your recommendations. All you can do is to point out the many benefits to their organizations by following your prescription for change. If they decide to ignore your advice, the decision is theirs to make, and you have to accept it and move on.

The final step in the implementation phase of the consulting process is to assess the results of the project. We just happen to cover this topic in the next section.

Evan Rose knows the value of implementation

Evan M. Rose of Columbia, Maryland, is a business consultant for Continuous Improvement Systems (phone 804-262-7839), which specializes in assisting its clients by improving the utilization of resources such as people, equipment, facilities, and cash. This is done through the implementation of productivity programs, quality programs, and strategic planning. Evan started in the consulting business with the Alexander Proudfoot Company, an international consulting group located in Chicago, Illinois. Continuous Improvement Systems has clients nationwide, and all of its business comes from client referrals. We spoke to Evan about implementing the recommendations that his firm makes.

Consulting For Dummies: How important is it that a consultant be part of the implementation of his or her recommendations?

Evan Rose: I think that it is absolutely critical. Quite honestly, if I had to put a negative on the consulting industry, it would be that an awful lot of consultants are out there making suggestions and are not around to follow through to make sure the recommendations work. Any time you make a change in the client's or an individual's behavior pattern, there is a high likelihood that resistance will occur somewhere in the client's organization. With this resistance, there will be some specific issues that will come up that need to be addressed. If you are not there helping the client work through those problems or issues, then you're not really doing the job your client hired you to do. As a matter of fact, when I am asked what I do for a living, I always explain that we are implementers, facilitators, and trainers. We install programs with our clients that generate a positive result.

CFD: How do you encourage your clients to buy into your recommendations?

Rose: There are a number of different tactics that we use to accomplish this goal. The simplest one is a management style that we call "control and focus." In order to use this style, you need to have a clear picture in your mind of what you want to accomplish. You then ask the client a series of questions that lead them to the goal. People do not like to be told what to do. They like to be part of the decision process. Instead of saying, "do this" or "you must do it this way," we usually ask a question along the lines of "Do you think it would be effective if we were able to do this?" The idea is to secure their agreement and to make them part of the process. Once you have been able to do this, the implementation becomes significantly easier because the client has already bought into the idea and has made a contribution. With this style, you must also listen to the client. There are many times when the client's ideas combined with ours produce an even greater result.

CFD: That technique is a common one for salespeople. They ask their prospects a series of questions along the lines of "Wouldn't you like to increase your productivity and decrease your costs?" It all leads to the solution that they happen to sell. Ownership is everything.

Rose: Right! If the client doesn't buy into your recommendations, you don't stand a chance of making a change. The client really must take ownership of the ideas and programs.

CFD: What do you do when a client refuses to take ownership? Do you keep trying? Do you walk away?

Rose: If the client refuses to take ownership, it is my belief that we haven't presented our case well enough. Either there is information missing, or there is something in our approach that is not correct. Maybe we haven't provided enough information to make the right decision. If the client does not take ownership, we certainly need to understand why. We need to be able to work together to solve this issue. However, we don't need to be able to make a wholesale change to be effective. Sometimes we can make the change in stages. If we can secure agreement on the first part of the program and we are able to demonstrate an improvement, I'll take that and then build on the improvement. It is important that you and the client have an open and trusting relationship in order to be successful, and you must always do what is in the client's best interest.

CFD: What else do you do to encourage ownership of your recommendations?

Rose: When we walk into an organization, we perform an analysis that takes a broad look at the company — everything from the financial picture, to observations of the workforce, to diagnostics on the organization, to reviewing the systems that direct the business activity. By the time we complete this part of the program, we have a good indication of the opportunities, the management styles of the key people, as well as the climate of the company's management and workforce. Most of our clients know they have some issues that need to be addressed and have identified a number of the problems themselves. Their frustration comes as a result of not being able to resolve them. The result is that by the time we present our analysis findings, the client is saying, "Yes, all these issues are really problems, and we do need to fix them." We start the process of encouraging their ownership right then and there.

CFD: Are internal politics in your clients' organizations ever an issue for you?

(continued)

(continued)

Rose: All the time! The toughest part of the job that we face in most companies is overcoming the frustration and lack of trust of middle management. The owners see the problems that need to be addressed, and they are probably concerned that the middle management can't seem to fix them. So here comes this consultant from the outside who is charging a healthy fee and has identified some of the same problems and programs that middle management has identified. Unfortunately, middle management hasn't been able to implement these programs or solve these issues because they haven't been trained or they don't have the resources. All of a sudden, we are on board, and we are perceived as a threat to their authority. We need to overcome this barrier and build a trusting relationship with this group in order to be effective. This is accomplished when we are able to reduce some of their frustrations and train them to solve some of the problems. It is important that middle management receives all the credit for the improvement that is achieved.

CFD: How do you neutralize resistance in an organization?

Rose: I like to hit it head-on. Just last week I had a middle manager who told me that he thought it was unfortunate that his company had to bring in outsiders to help fix their problems. I told him that I couldn't agree more, but every organization sometimes needs somebody from the outside who can provide an objective point of view, and isn't it a good thing that the owners have recognized the need for help because these issues have been in existence for a long time. Maybe I could help him facilitate the changes needed to improve his department.

I found myself selling him on the idea of help. I asked him how long these issues have been a problem. His response was that they have been a problem ever since he started working there. My point to him was, since the organization has had the same problems since he started, maybe it *is* time to bring in an outside resource to help. I tell my clients that if there is anything that I say or do that they don't agree with, I would expect them to confront me and tell me they don't agree. Let's work through the issues together, and I'll do the same in return. I would rather have them confront me and then work through the issues than have them say yes to my face and then go off and do the opposite behind my back.

CFD: Do you have any thoughts for someone just starting out in consulting?

Rose: This is the only business I have ever been associated with where the longer I'm in it, the more I learn. That is the main reason I like it as much as I do. You're dealing with clients from different cultural and socioeconomic backgrounds and everyone from the bottom of an organization to the very top. It's *very* rewarding. One of the things that gives me great satisfaction is when the client says, "Here are all the changes that *we* made," *not* the changes that the consultant made. That's really where you want them to be. I'm not in this for the credit or the glory. Our clients become our best spokespeople for our future business — we get 99.9 percent of our business from referrals, and that is our reward.

The downside of the consulting business, at least the kind of work that we do, is the constant travel. It can be tough on the family, especially if you have young children. There are long hours, a lot of hard work, and travel headaches. Running through an airport at 10:00 or 11:00 at night is not always a fun thing to do. Fortunately, my wife is a very understanding person — her support has helped immeasurably.

Assessing the Results of Implementation of Your Recommendations

So you've reached the end of your consulting project. It's been a long haul, but you managed to develop a great set of recommendations with your client. In addition, those recommendations were implemented just as you planned. How do you determine whether they had the effect you intended? You do so by assessing the results of your project implementation and then comparing the results to your original plan.

Fortunately, your task is fairly simple because you developed an implementation plan that you can now use to measure the results. (You *did* do an implementation plan, didn't you?) Here's how to assess the results of your project implementation:

1. **Gather data.**

   Just as you gathered information in the data-collection phase of the consulting process, you need to gather data that tells you whether your recommendations are working. Some results of your recommendations may be readily apparent; others may take months or even years to come about. If, for example, you are implementing changes that impact employee morale, surveys may tell you within a few weeks whether morale is improved. However, changes to large and complex manufacturing systems to improve product quality may require many months of gathering product quality data to show whether the recommendations are working. Whatever the case, you don't know which way your project went until you collect the data that tells you whether it was a success.

2. **Assess progress against plan.**

   Keep close tabs on the progress of all implementation tasks against the plan you created. Depending on the nature of the project — its complexity and speed of implementation — daily or weekly checks wouldn't be too often. Assess whether some tasks should be accelerated or whether the schedules for other tasks should be lengthened.

3. **Assess your client's satisfaction and view of your effectiveness.**

   One of the most important measures of success (some might say the only measure worth worrying about) is how satisfied your client is with the implementation of your recommendations and his or her view of your effectiveness as a consultant. Ask questions; send surveys; call your client. How you choose to solicit and measure your client's satisfaction is up to you. The important thing is that you ask.

4. Assess your own satisfaction and view of your effectiveness.

Project satisfaction is a two-way street. Consider whether *you* were satisfied with the project. Did you handle your client in the right way? Did you approach the project in the most effective way possible? Would you change anything about what you did and how you did it? Do you want to do future work with this client? Did you make any money on the project, or did your work turn out to be pro bono? Ask yourself these questions and others like them to gauge your own level of satisfaction.

5. Use feedback to adjust future projects.

As you obtain feedback on the way you conducted the project and implementation, note the information that you should keep in mind for future projects. Use this feedback to adjust the way you approach the different steps of the consulting process — defining the problem, collecting data, diagnosing, presenting your recommendations, and implementing them. No one knows everything there is to know about consulting, and you can always learn something new that helps you do an even better job the next time.

6. Write an impact study.

This is a definite discipline of top-quality consulting firms. Writing an impact study forces you to document lessons, both positive and negative, that ensure that your process improves consistently and that provide valuable marketing data for future clients.

As you can see, assessing your project — whether it is the most successful project you ever pulled off or the least — is the way that you and your client's organization learn. By obtaining feedback and using it to figure out what you did right and what you did wrong, you improve your services to clients and become a better consultant. You can always learn something new from a project you participate in, and doing so is always in your best interest.

Part III

Key Consulting Skills

The 5th Wave   By Rich Tennant

"GET READY, I THINK THEY'RE STARTING TO DRIFT."

In this part . . .

Though there are many kinds of consultants in the world, some are clearly better at what they do than others. In this part, we address the consulting skills that can make you stand out from the rest of the pack, including focusing on image, reputation, and ethics; getting organized; communicating effectively; and using technology to your advantage.

Chapter 10

Walking the Walk and Talking the Talk: Image, Reputation, and Ethics

A big part of being a consultant is convincing prospective clients that you are the best person for the job, all things considered. Certainly, price and technical skill are both key factors when clients weigh the pros and cons of hiring various consultants. No one (at least no one in his or her right mind) is going to hire a consultant who is technically incompetent just because that person happens to offer the lowest price. However, beyond price and technical expertise, something less tangible and significantly more subjective weighs very heavily into the decision whether to hire a particular consultant.

This additional factor is image.

Image is the overall impression that others have of you. Many different things go into the mix that, when blended together and baked in the oven for 20 minutes at 350 degrees (we'll have no half-baked product here!), becomes your image. Besides the most obvious ingredients, such as personal appearance, success at what you do, professional business cards, and the like, reputation and ethical standards are *very* important factors in the impression that you make on your clients.

A favorable image and reputation and a well-developed set of ethics are important to most clients, and clients are generally willing to pay more for consultants who possess these attributes. If you had the choice between hiring a consultant with good technical skills but a so-so reputation and image and hiring one with equally good technical skills but an excellent reputation and image, wouldn't you be willing to spend a few extra bucks an hour for the consultant with the much better reputation and image? Most clients probably would.

The good news is that image, reputation, and ethics are all things that you can work on and improve. This chapter is about creating a positive image with your clients and clients-to-be and building your professional reputation. We also consider the importance of ethics to the consultant and why it pays to have a strong personal code of ethics.

Creating a Professional Image

Though image isn't everything for a consultant, it sure is a big part of the selection process when clients go shopping. Many things add up to make your image. The way you dress, the way you speak, the way you carry yourself, the kind of office you work in, the brand and model of the car you drive — all these things influence the way others perceive you and the impression you make.

Fortunately, you can always change your image. Although the adage that you have only one chance to make a first impression is true, the impression that others have of you can change over time. Some things, like the style of your business cards and the look of your office, are easy to change. Other things, such as converting your negative personality traits into positive personality traits, may take a bit longer. (Some of us keep trying, but we still haven't gotten it right!)

Anyway, here are a few things you can do to enhance your professional image:

- **Get real.** The first rule of creating a professional image is to *be yourself*. Don't try to be Mr. Big Man on Campus or Ms. Name Dropper. And definitely don't try to be Mr. Eager Beaver Salesperson or Ms. Know It All. Take advantage of your *best* personal attributes — perhaps your ingenuity, or your persistence, or your ability to perform under pressure — and amplify them. If you have any negative characteristics (not that you do!), whatever they may be, work hard to minimize these charming little personality traits.

- **Look like a duck, *be* a duck.** If you *look* professional, your clients and clients-to-be will perceive you to *be* professional. Despite the old saying that you can't judge a book by its cover, clients do so all the time. If you're asking someone to entrust his or her multimillion-dollar company to your care — a company that your client spent a significant part of his or her life building up from nothing — then you're going to have a hard sell if you look like you just came in from your morning jog or you don't appear to be serious about your work and the way that you do it.

✔ **Build trust through action.** Actions speak louder than words. Although your proposal or your PR package may rhapsodize enthusiastically about your commitment to quality and the satisfaction of your customers, the words that are printed on those pieces of paper really don't matter. The actions you take to follow up on the promises that you have made to your clients are what matter. Believe us: If you follow up your words with action, your clients will love you forever, and you'll soon have more business than you know what to do with.

✔ **Create an environment that matches the work you do.** If you're an investment adviser, your environment should be one that exudes an atmosphere of quiet success, conservatism, and stability. However, if you're a graphic artist or an interior decorator, your environment should be energetic, creative, bright, and full of life. The point is that when your clients come to visit your office, you want your environment to send the kind of message that tells them exactly what they can expect when they hire you for a consulting job.

✔ **Make your media your message.** Your business cards, your letterhead, your report covers, and all the other things that you give out to your clients and clients-to-be speak volumes about your professionalism and your commitment to quality. High-quality paper and printing; professional-looking brochures, newsletters, and mailers; and a well-done Web site send a message that you are the kind of consultant that your clients will want to hire — and retain far into the future.

Creating and maintaining a professional image can play a very important role in your ability to achieve the kind of success you're aiming for. Be aware that you are constantly being judged and assessed by your clients and your clients-to-be. With a little work (or for some of you, a lot), you can make your good image even better. And doing so translates not only into more business but also into better, higher-paying business to boot. That combination just can't be beat!

Enhancing Your Reputation

Just as a good reputation can enhance your image in the eyes of your clients, a bad reputation can tarnish it. And just as many different factors add up to your professional image, many different factors make up your reputation. The quality of the work you do, the time you spend in the public eye, the work you do for charity, and much more play a part in determining your professional reputation.

One thing about reputation: Enhancing and maintaining a good reputation is much easier than trying to rehabilitate a bad one. Once you develop a bad reputation, many clients won't bother to consider you for *any* sort of work, no matter how great your proposal or how low your price. And after your reputation is tarnished, many clients will *never* believe that your business has turned things around and changed for the better — even if it has. Turning around a bad reputation can take years. Therefore, doing whatever you can to enhance your reputation is clearly in your best interest. Your current clients will be proud to tell their associates that they are affiliated with you, and future clients will be more likely to seek you out.

With that point in mind, here are a few tips for enhancing your reputation or for helping to repair your reputation if you have fallen on hard times:

- **Do incredibly great work.** Of course, one of the best ways to enhance your reputation is to do great work. And if you do *incredibly* great work, that's even better. Your clients want and deserve the best you have to offer. Give it to them. Consistently deliver more than you promise.

- **Be easy to work with.** How do you get a bad reputation quickly and easily? By being difficult to work with. You can be a brilliant consultant and your price can be right, but if you're an incredible pain in the neck, clients will avoid you like a swollen can of tuna. Be someone whom your clients look forward to talking to, not someone they have their secretaries tell that they're in a meeting — even when they're not.

- **Keep your clients informed of your successes.** A great way to enhance your reputation is to keep your clients well informed about your doings. If you land a big new contract with a high-profile client, let all your other clients know about it! If you successfully complete a highly visible project, get the word out! (But be sure to get a client's okay before you publicize your work for that client.) If your business has been featured in a newspaper or you have appeared on television, get copies to your clients. Newsletters, e-mail, voice mail, brochures, clippings of newspaper and magazine articles, videotapes of television appearances — use all these methods to spread the word and raise your standing in the eyes of your clients and your prospective clients.

- **Get in the public eye.** Give speeches to community groups or groups of your peers. Write articles for trade magazines or submit op-ed pieces to your local newspaper or national publications, such as *The Wall Street Journal* or *USA Today*. Become an expert resource for your local newspaper or radio and television stations. Develop a press kit and a regular newsletter and distribute them to a wide variety of national media.

- **Teach.** Teaching at a local college or university can be a very effective way for you to enhance your reputation, broaden your skills, and expand your professional network. You may learn a few new things from your students, too!

✔ **Write a book.** Many consultants find their professional reputations greatly enhanced after writing and publishing a book. Not only can you enhance your reputation by writing a book, but organizations may hire you to present the ideas from your book to their employees. Much of the time that Bob spends on the road nowadays — making speeches and presentations and meeting with clients — is in support of the books that he has written. You may eventually find yourself making more money from activities related to your book than you do from consulting.

✔ **Work for free.** Many worthy nonprofit organizations — boys' and girls' clubs, environmental groups, churches, and more — could really use your expertise and skill but can't afford to pay for it. By offering to work for free for a few organizations that you really believe in, you are not only doing something good for your community but also building your reputation and network at the same time.

✔ **Work ethically and honestly.** It should go without saying that engaging in unethical and dishonest behavior is a sure way to destroy your reputation and lose all you have worked for. Because of the sensitive and confidential nature of the jobs for which clients often hire consultants, any hint of dishonesty or lack of ethical fortitude can be the death knell of a consulting relationship. *Always* work honestly and ethically. This topic is so important that we devote the entire next section of this chapter to it.

Work hard at developing and enhancing your good reputation and, at all costs, avoid doing the kinds of things that could tarnish it and destroy the client relationships that you have worked so hard to establish and nurture.

Do the Right Thing! Ethics and You

What would you do if your best and most profitable client asked you to divulge some new product information from another client? What would you do if a client asked you to take your payments "under the table" and not report them to the Internal Revenue Service? What would you do if a potential client offered to pay you a large amount of money to do a project that you know you are not qualified to perform?

Consultants face these kinds of ethical dilemmas every day of the week. Like a double yellow line painted down the center of an interstate highway, when it comes to ethical behavior, a clear line separates good behavior from bad behavior. The decisions you make in response to all the dilemmas you face determine which side of the line you walk on — the right side or the wrong side. Unfortunately, just as a thick fog can roll in and obscure the lines painted on a highway, so too can the line separating right from wrong become fuzzy and hard to see.

In this section, we consider some of the key elements of ethical behavior and ways to develop and implement a personal code of ethics.

Ethical land mines

A consultant is sure to face an incredible amount and variety of ethical land mines every day — sometimes over and over and over again. Temptations to stray from the right side of the ethical line to the wrong side are all around you. So why not take advantage of these ethical dilemmas? As long as no one gets hurt, why not make your ethical behavior situational — that is, moving the ethical line between right and wrong depending on the particular situation — especially if a large financial reward is in it for you?

You have a choice: You can do business the ethical way or the unethical way. It's that simple.

Our advice is to do business the ethical way. Not only will you sleep better at night, but your reputation will be enhanced and your clients will be glad that they have one less thing to worry about.

Here are the kinds of ethical land mines for which you should be on the alert. You never know when they'll make their presence known or who will plant one in your path.

- ✔ **Conflicts of interest:** A conflict of interest occurs when your personal interests or the interests of your business conflict with those of your client. An example is a government consultant who recommends that a client buy an expensive new fire-suppression system from one particular company without seeking competitive bids; unbeknownst to the client, however, the consultant is getting a kickback from the fire-suppression system manufacturer for each unit that clients buy.

- ✔ **Personal relationships:** When professional relationships between consultants and clients cross the line into the realm of personal relationships — particularly intimate personal relationships — ethical quicksand can't be very far away.

- ✔ **Ability to do the job (or lack thereof):** Are you *really* qualified to do the work that your client is hiring you to do? Do you already have far too many jobs lined up to be able to adequately handle new ones? Are you going to have to subcontract the work to another consultant or firm because you are too busy to do the work yourself? Your clients hire you because they assume — either through your telling them so or through your silence — that you are able to do the work. If in reality you can't, you'll soon find yourself in a major ethical quandary. You and your clients should agree to any subcontracting of work *before* you commence work.

✔ **Insider information:** As a consultant, you learn a lot of interesting and confidential things about your clients' operations, business plans, and strategies. If you misuse this information — such as by using information gained from working with Company A and providing it to Company A's arch rival, Company B, as a part of the work that you do for Company B — this is a serious breach of ethics with your client, Company A.

✔ **Fees and timekeeping:** Are your fees reasonable? Do you keep meticulous track of the time that you work for your clients? Do you have controls to ensure that one client isn't charged for another client's work and that clients aren't billed for work that is never done (like while you were out of town meeting with other clients or working on another client's project when you should have been working on a project for the client you just billed)? Ethical land mines abound in this dangerous area of your practice. To make sure that *you* stay on the straight and narrow path, check out our discussion on timekeeping in Chapter 18.

Stephen Crow and the playing field of work

Stephen Crow (phone 504-280-6482, e-mail scrow@ibm.net) is a professor of management at the University of New Orleans in New Orleans, Louisiana. Stephen received his Ph.D. in personnel and industrial relations from the University of North Texas in 1989. He joined the University of New Orleans in the fall of 1989 and teaches management courses at the undergraduate, MBA, and EMBA levels. From 1968 to 1989, he was employed as a human resource manager and professional in a variety of positions and industries, with most of his experience as the top-ranking personnel officer in the organization. Stephen consults and conducts management seminars and lectures in organizations. He is also a labor arbitrator on the American Arbitration Association panel of arbitrators. He is an active researcher and has published over 100 articles in academic and practitioner journals. He and

his wife, Suzanne, divide their time between their home in New Orleans and their tree farm in Lonesome Duck, Mississippi. He has four daughters, four grandchildren, and three Airedales, and he enjoys building bluebird houses in his spare time. We spoke to Stephen about the very important topic of consulting ethics.

Consulting For Dummies: Are ethics something that most consultants should be concerned with? Why?

Stephen Crow: There are more ethical dilemmas in medicine and law than in consulting. I base that remark on the consequences of being wrong. If the doctor is wrong, the patient may die. If the lawyer is wrong, an innocent client may go to the gas chamber. What are the consequences of a consultant giving bad advice? It's not as consequential as the bad advice of a doctor or lawyer, but it's close.

(continued)

(continued)

We now know from the research that aside from the fact that downsizing has enhanced shareholder wealth, it has not lived up to its promise as a cure-all for organizational ineffectiveness. Over the past ten years, many organizations threw away legions of good people in the name of downsizing, rightsizing, reengineering, becoming lean and mean, and a host of other euphemisms for gutting employees. Sadly, the research indicates that most of this was for *no* good reason. To the extent that consultants participated in and encouraged this carnage, they were acting in a highly unethical fashion.

Are ethics something that most consultants should be concerned with? I am convinced that ethics *are* the central issues of consulting. The consequences of giving bad advice when you know better or should have known better can be devastating.

CFD: What kind of guidance do you give your students in regard to ethics in business?

Crow: More than they want. But I don't moralize like their parents. I try to present ethical behavior as a necessary part of survival in the workplace over the long haul. For example, I tell them that there are no secrets in organizations. If you engage in hanky-panky with your secretary — unethical these days and generally considered sexual harassment — assume everyone will know about it because they will. And once they know, there is no longer any doubt about your ethics. The mystery is what forms your unethical behavior will take. We know that you sexually harass your secretary. Do you steal, too? People generalize. If you're unethical in one situation, it's assumed you will be unethical in other situations. Once they pin "unethical" on you, it may be career-ending.

CFD: What advice would you give to a consultant who finds himself or herself in an ethical quandary? What are some good ways to tell a client that you're ethically opposed to taking on a particular task without burning a bridge with your client in the process?

Crow: Do the right thing. If you sense that something a client wants you to do may be unethical, it probably is. Don't rationalize it to yourself by saying every consultant acts unethically from time to time. Discuss it with your client. Most clients want to do the right thing, too. But they don't always know right from wrong. Don't tell the client that what he or she wants you to do is unethical. In a friendly manner, discuss your concern about the *outcomes* of what the client wants you to do and suggest an alternative. For example, "I understand that downsizing may be the answer, but I'm concerned about the research about downsizing. Particularly the research that finds that downsizing may have no impact on effectiveness but will certainly be devastating to those employees who are forced to leave and those employees who have to pick up the slack. Here's an alternative that I have been thinking about...."

CFD: But what if the client persists in pushing you down the slippery slope of compromising your ethics?

Crow: If the client said, "Damn the employees, full speed ahead," my bulldog tenacity would require me to take another shot at the client — "Why not give me an opportunity to do some more research and let's analyze this further?" However, if the client then said, "Hell no, let's cross the Rubicon and loose the dogs of war," then it's time to fish or cut bait. In a situation like this, if the consultant is convinced that what the client wants to do is unethical, then the right thing to do is to tell the client that what he wants is contrary to the ethics of his profession and he has no choice but to decline. A cool head and a pregnant pause are in order here. Since this is the first time ethics has entered the picture, the client, in good faith, may want to discuss the ethical considerations and then change *his* mind. Assuming he does not and becomes irate, *quit!*

CFD: Aren't you burning a bridge with your client by suggesting that he is unethical and then quitting?

Crow: Yes. But what's the alternative? Compromise your ethics? Line up the employees and put them in the Downsizing Chamber anyway? How about recommending another consultant who has no qualms about ethics? No thanks. The very act of burning your bridge may cause your client to reconsider.

CFD: Is there some sort of absolute code of ethical conduct, or do ethics change depending on the situation?

Crow: There are no absolutes. If there were, we would all have them memorized. The fact is that people will never agree on a uniform code of ethical conduct — there is simply too much diversity of values and beliefs in the world. The situation is an important imperative in the ethical realm. I get a lot of flak from colleagues when I say this. However, let me explain it the way I discuss this in class with my lecture — The Playing Field of Work.

The playing field is where most of the judgments about behavior are made. Imagine the playing field of work as a football field — 100 yards long. From the goal line to the 20-yard line on one side of the field represents behavior that is clearly ethical — working hard, supporting the company, being a team player, and so on. From the goal line to the 20-yard line on the other side represents behavior that is clearly unethical — lying, cheating, stealing, and generally having too much fun at the expense of others. The rest of the field — 60 yards — is where people make judgments about how they will behave at work.

Behavior close to the ethical side of the field is generally deemed appropriate — for example, an employee with a good work record

stretches her lunch hour by 15 minutes from time to time. On the other side of the field, behavior becomes progressively questionable as one's behavior nears the 20 yard line of unethical behavior. Behavior on this side involves improprieties, dirty pool, cheap shots, putting a whoopee cushion in the boss's chair, and other such transgressions.

It's against the rules for an offensive lineman to "hold" his opponent. Yet, all good offensive linemen hold their opponents about 60 percent of the time. It is clearly against the rules — unethical — to grab your opponent around the neck and wrestle him to the ground. You will get flagged if you do. It is clearly within the rules to keep your hands open and push the opponent to the ground. Now, from time to time, you can hold on to your opponent's shirt — briefly, but as much as 60 percent of the time you block him — and get away with it.

CFD: How does your football analogy relate to a business environment?

Crow: It is against the rules for an employee to steal the assets of the company. Yet practically all employees steal — time, paper, paper clips, pencils, etc. It is clearly against the rules — unethical — to spend all day on the phone — you are stealing the company's time for nonwork. However, you probably will not get into too much trouble if you call home — steal the company's time — occasionally to make sure the kids have not burned the house down.

What's going on here? The fact is that rules, laws, and ethics are painted in shades of gray — we have a lot of room to "play." The speed limit may be 55 mph, but we all know that we will not get into trouble unless we speed past 63 mph. Right or wrong, the fact is that many of us see rules, laws, and ethics as "guidelines" that give us some leeway on how to behave.

(continued)

(continued)

CFD: Who gets to decide what's right and what's wrong?

Crow: The prevailing culture of the employees and the dictates of the organization.

CFD: Should a consultant ever make exceptions to his or her ethical standards?

Crow: Yes — when the consultant's ethical standards are wrong. The fact is that we all think we are ethical. Some of us are foolish moralizers and need to get off our high horse. It is a competitive world, and while we may be applauded for our moral valor by turning the other cheek, it is much more satisfying and realistic to counter-punch sometimes.

CFD: What is your greatest concern about ethical behavior and consultants?

Crow: That a consultant will be too self-righteous and mistake his neurotic love for rules for ethics. I'm not worried about the bad guys. An unethical consultant cannot survive in the field for long. An unethical person is pathologically programmed for the dark side of life and self-destruction. Eventually, if we disrespect rules and are inclined toward non-conformity, we will be hoisted by our own petard. Reputation is everything in consulting, and there are no secrets. If a consultant is dishonest, word will get out and he will get no work — except for the scraps.

Any consultant who thinks of ethics in absolute terms is doomed. The world of work is competitive. People use consultants because they want an edge up on the competition so that they can *win*. The client already knows right from wrong. He knows that holding is against the rules and that 55 mph is the speed limit. The client wants to know how to hold without getting flagged and how fast he can drive without going to jail. It seems that consultants can be more effective and still maintain their integrity if they know the boundaries that define what is right and what is wrong and how to win in the playing field between those boundaries.

Developing your personal code of ethics

Ethics are important for anyone in business. They are *particularly* important to consultants because of the high level of trust that organizations grant them and because of the access that many consultants have to the confidential and proprietary inner workings of the firms that employ them. There is no uniform code of ethics for consultants. So many different kinds of consultants exist that a set of rules that is appropriate for one group — say, real estate brokers — would have little in common with a set of rules that would be appropriate for a group of consulting engineers. However, some very basic ethical beliefs can and should form the basis for your personal code of ethics.

Here are some items that can form the basis for *any* consultant's code of ethics. Review them and consider using them as the basis for your own code of ethics.

✔ **Account for your time accurately and honestly.** If you are working on an hourly or other time-based system of billing, keeping track of your hours and reporting them to your clients accurately and honestly is up to you. Your client expects and trusts you to be truthful in your billing practices. To do any less is not only unethical but also a violation of your client's trust. And if your client can't trust you, he or she won't hire you or refer you to other associates.

✔ **Don't make promises you can't keep.** Although you may *really* want to impress a potential client with your amazing abilities, avoid making promises you can't keep in hopes of landing your client's account. Not only is this unethical — your client may be better off hiring someone who has more capacity or better qualifications in a particular area — but you end up setting up yourself and your business for failure. Though there's nothing wrong with a little good old-fashioned optimism, don't blatantly make a promise that you know you cannot keep. If you're hoping that your client forgets you made the promise or that you can change the promised action to something you *can* achieve after you are selected to do the work, then you're not only fooling yourself but also doing your client a great disservice.

✔ **Follow through on your promises.** Part of becoming a successful consultant is doing what you say you are going to do. If you say that you will complete the project on March 31, then you should deliver the results on (or before, if you can) March 31 — not a day later. Suppose that you promise to come up with a complete landscaping design for $1,000. Unless your client does something that causes your incurred costs to skyrocket, such as adding more work to your project but not adding more money to your project budget, you should deliver your design for $1,000 and not a penny more. If, for some reason, you can't keep your promise no matter how hard you try, then inform your client as far in advance as possible and present a plan for curing the problem.

✔ **Don't recommend products or services that your clients don't need.** You may speak with clients who are absolutely, beyond-a-shadow-of-a-doubt certain that they know what is wrong with their organization. You need only propose to do what they say that you should do to land what could be a very lucrative contract. This is the consulting equivalent to shooting fish in a barrel. However, if *you* know that this is *not* the proper course of action, you should tell your client so and decline the offered work. In most cases, your client will appreciate your honesty, and your reputation will be elevated a few notches in your client's mind (and in the mind of anyone else your client tells this story to).

✔ **Be candid and give your honest opinion.** Your clients pay you good money for the benefit of your skills and many years of experience. When your clients ask for your opinion, be frank and honest, and don't try to sugarcoat the truth to make it more palatable.

✔ **Protect your clients' confidentiality.** When you are a consultant, you may often be placed in situations in which you learn information that is proprietary to your clients, the release of which could cause them serious financial or other damage. Your clients have placed you in a position of trust. Don't violate that trust. If, for some reason, you want to publicize the fact that you are doing work for a particular firm — perhaps in a press kit or a proposal to another organization — ask your client for permission first.

✔ **Disclose conflicts of interest.** If you are a popular consultant in your field, preventing conflicts of interest from occurring can often be difficult. As organizations vie for your expertise, you may find yourself working on the same problem for two different companies that compete with one another in the marketplace. However, as soon as you learn of a conflict — whether it is a potential conflict or an actual one — you should always disclose it to the affected client or clients and then take action to resolve it. This may mean assuring your clients that you won't transfer their confidential data from one company to the other, or it may mean signing information nondisclosure agreements. If the conflict can't be resolved through these means, then you may have to drop one of the two firms as a client.

✔ **Don't use inside information to your advantage.** While you are working for an organization, you may learn information that is closely held within the company and unknown to others outside the organization. For example, you may learn that the organization is about to patent a process that will certainly lead to a huge surge in the price of the company's stock. Not only is it unethical to use insider information to your advantage — in this case, to buy a large amount of the company's stock before the patent becomes public — but it is illegal as well.

✔ **Don't break the law.** At times, a client may ask you to do something that is not only against your personal sense of ethics but also obviously and blatantly illegal. Do not pass go and collect $200. Just go. And don't come back. Ever.

These guidelines look great on paper, but in the real world, you're going to face many situations that aren't quite so black and white. Everyone has a personal set of values and ethics, and what's right for one person may be wrong for another. The challenge is to find ways to keep to your values while also finding ways to work with a client whose values may not be exactly the same as yours. If your values are too far out of sync with your client's values, then don't hesitate to pull yourself off the job and find other clients whose values more closely match your own.

If you ever find yourself in an uncomfortable ethical situation, first talk to your client about it in an effort to determine an alternate course of action that is in accordance with your own values. Most clients will respect your perspective, even if they don't share it. If you can't find a way out of your ethical dilemma by working with the client on alternative actions, then walk away from the job, but in a way that doesn't offend your client. Whatever you do, don't burn bridges with your clients or poison the well for referrals to other clients.

Take some time to develop your own code of ethics. Type it up, hang it prominently in your office, and make sure that your clients get copies. Above all, *live* the code of ethics that you have developed. A good operational rule is, if you have any doubts, don't do it!

The ICCA Code of Ethics

This is the Code of Ethics of the Independent Computer Consultants Association (ICCA), a national not-for-profit organization based in St. Louis, Missouri, that provides professional development opportunities and business support programs for independent computer consultants. (Visit the ICCA's Web page at www.icca.org for further information.) The ICCA publishes the following Code of Ethics, copyrighted by ICCA, to serve as a model for its members and for the entire computer consulting industry.

✔ Consultants will be honest and not knowingly misrepresent facts.

✔ Consultants will install and use only properly licensed software on their systems as well as the clients' systems.

✔ Consultants will divulge any potential conflicts of interest prior to accepting the contract or as soon as possible after the conflict is discovered.

✔ Consultants will only represent opinions as independent if they are free from subordinated judgment and there is no undisclosed interest in the outcome of the client's decision.

✔ Consultants will ensure that to the best of their knowledge they can complete the project in a professional manner both in terms of skill and time.

✔ Consultants will keep the client informed of any matters relating to the contract even if the information is unfavorable, or may jeopardize the contract.

✔ Consultants will safeguard any confidential information or documents entrusted to them and not divulge any confidential information without the consent of the client.

✔ Consultants will not take advantage of proprietary information obtained from the client.

✔ Consultants will not engage in contracts that are in violation of the law or that might reasonably be used by the client to violate the law.

✔ ICCA member firms, their principals, and employees will uphold the principles of the ICCA and not commit acts discreditable to the ICCA.

Chapter 11

Manage Your Time and Get Organized!

• •

• •

*B*eing an independent consultant is quite different from working in a traditional 9-to-5 job. When you work for someone else — whether for a small business or a huge multinational corporation — your employer is *very* interested in the number of hours you work each week, the level of your productivity, and the progress you make toward meeting your goals. If your employer is paying you a full-time salary, you're expected to work a full-time schedule — perhaps more if your job requires it. If you're self-employed, however, you have the luxury of working half-time — either the first 12 hours or the second 12 hours of each day!

When you're a self-employed consultant, you must answer to *yourself*. No one is going to tell you what to do, or how to run your business, or what time to show up for work in the morning or go home at night. If you decide to sleep in until noon every day, it's your choice to do so. If you decide to work for an hour and then go hiking for the rest of the day, that's just fine — it's up to you. If you go on a three-month vacation, you don't have to seek approval from anyone — you can just do it. However, when you're not working, you're not making money. And when you're not making money. . . . Well, you know what happens next.

Although time is a precious commodity for *anyone* who works, this is especially the case for consultants who are in business for themselves. Time really *is* money, and you can't afford to waste it. That's why you must learn to manage your time and get organized. If you don't, you're going to waste an awful lot of time *and* money as you stumble around looking for an important report, read and reread that stack of junk mail for the third time, or miss a crucial client meeting because you forgot to note the date and time of the meeting.

Fortunately, we can help you solve this problem. How? Just keep reading, and we'll tell you!

It's Your Time — Manage It!

Here's a little secret that we have learned in our many years of business experience: If *you* don't manage your time, someone else will manage it *for* you. For those of you who aren't yet self-employed and still work for an organization, take a moment to reflect on how often people manage your time for you. How many times have you been drawn into a meeting where you had no idea what the heck was being discussed or why the heck you were there? Or given a "rush" assignment that caused you to be late in completing your top-priority work? Or drawn into a half-hour conversation with a coworker who is anxious to fill you in on what he did Friday night?

One of the most satisfying things about being an independent consultant is that *you* are in charge of your time, your schedule, and your life. In this section, we discuss some specific, proven strategies to help make you a better manager of your time.

Deciding what's really important

Priorities are a good thing. Not only do they tell you *what* to do, but they tell you *when* to do it. The only problem is that a multitude of people, actions, and activities are constantly vying for your attention and for a place on your priority list. Some of these things should be on your list, and others shouldn't be given the time of day. Unfortunately, it's easy to find yourself — especially if you are self-employed — spending a great deal of time doing jobs that aren't on your priority list or are at the very bottom. The result is that you often fail to do the things that are most important to achieving your goals while you are caught up doing the things that don't get you any closer to those goals at all.

And the information revolution hasn't made the situation any better. Now it seems that *everything* you do has to be done *right now*. An associate needs you to review and comment on a 25-page report in the next hour? All she has to do is fax or e-mail the report to you, and the ball is in your court. A client has a problem troubleshooting a software installation that you did for him last month? A quick call to your pager or cell phone, and he has your immediate attention. Do you have a voice-mail system to handle your calls? As you know, if you have lots of clients and other business associates, messages from the many individuals who are competing for your time can quickly fill up your voice mail. Just ask Bob. In a flash, his voice-mail box reaches its 60-message limit. But Bob needs *hours* to listen to all the messages and sort, prioritize, and determine what to do with each one.

The point is to remind you that you now have more competition for your attention than ever before. And the pressures distracting you from completing your top priorities are relentless. At the same time, you have to be able to meet the technical and financial challenges of your competition. So how do you sort through what's not so important and concentrate only on the things that are most important to meeting your goals? As you fight against the rising tide of paper that spills out of your in-box and fax machine, the FedEx and Priority Mail packages, the endless stream of voice mail and electronic mail messages, and the requests of clients to capture a piece of your limited schedule, consider the following:

✔ **What is the impact to the bottom line of you or your firm?** If the task you are to accomplish is a high-payoff one — that is, it significantly increases your ability to meet your chosen goals — then place it at the top of the list. If the task you are to accomplish is a low-payoff one — that is, it does not significantly increase your ability to meet your chosen goals — then place it at the bottom of the list. For example, if your key goal for the year is to double your sales, then you should give priority to any task, such as generating proposals or making sales calls, that will directly help you to achieve that goal. If a low-payoff task makes your list at all, it should be at the very bottom.

✔ **Is it a client emergency?** Client emergencies are a consultant's bread and butter, and you should welcome them with open arms. Build enough time into your schedule to allow yourself to be flexible when the inevitable client emergencies arise and to give emergencies the priority that they deserve.

✔ **Can you delegate the task to someone else?** Depending on the size of your business, you may or may not have other people available to help you. Your job is to determine whether someone else is better suited than you to take on a task. If so, then delegate the task. Don't waste your precious time doing tasks that someone else can do more efficiently or cost-effectively than you. Save your time to focus on the work that you are uniquely qualified to do.

Making and keeping your priorities — and then revising them as necessary — is a vital task for every consultant. Make a point of reviewing everything you do during your workday and establishing priorities to help guide *if* and *when* they should be done. And above all, respect your priorities; do your most important tasks first and save the rest until you complete your top priorities.

Setting your priorities the Franklin Quest way

Franklin Quest Day Planners have become a popular way for businesspeople of all walks to keep track of their busy schedules and to set and track their priorities. Underlying the pages, tabs, and tables of information that make up Franklin Quest's planners is a philosophy of deciding what things are most important in your life — both personal and business — and therefore deserve the most attention. Franklin Quest calls this philosophy the "Personal Productivity Pyramid." The Pyramid is made up of four parts:

1. **Governing values:** Governing values — the activities that have the most value to you — form the foundation of the Personal Productivity Pyramid. To determine your governing values, ask yourself what you really want or what you really most enjoy doing.

2. **Long-range goals:** The next level of the Pyramid — your long-range goals — is the concrete expression of your governing values. So if one of your governing values is the importance of a higher education, then one of your long-range goals may be to obtain an MBA.

3. **Intermediate steps:** Going up one more level in the Pyramid, intermediate steps

are the near-term activities that you undertake to achieve your long-range goals. If, for example, you have a long-range goal of getting your MBA, intermediate steps may be requesting course catalogs from the schools you are interested in attending and scheduling your GMAT.

4. **Daily tasks:** At the very top of the Personal Productivity Pyramid are your daily tasks — the activities that you carry out each day to accomplish the intermediate steps that you set forth in the preceding step. Key to the Franklin Quest philosophy is that your daily tasks should be in concert with your governing values, that is, your highest priorities in life.

As a part of the Franklin Quest system, daily tasks are assigned priority codes when you record them in the Franklin Quest Day Planner. "Vital" tasks are assigned an A code, "Important" tasks are assigned a B code, and "Optional" tasks get a C priority code. If more than one task is listed in a letter code category, then each task is numbered in order of importance, for example, A1, A2, A3, and so on. By following this system of prioritization, you'll always be assured that your daily tasks support your personal governing values.

Becoming a better time manager

Sometimes there just aren't enough hours in the day to do all the tasks that need to get done. The bad news is that you get only 24 hours each day. The good news is that you can get much more done each day if you take the time to become a better time manager. Although you'll never be able to make more hours in your day by applying a few common-sense rules and principles, you *can* use the hours you have more efficiently.

Here are eight of the best ways to become a more effective time manager:

✔ **Get organized!** Organization is clearly next to godliness. Although the relationship may not be immediately obvious, getting organized is one of the best ways you can manage your time. Why? Because when you're organized, you're at your most efficient — you know where everything is, and you know how to get your hands on the items you need quickly. When you're *dis*organized, you lose messages, you miss appointments, and your business life is generally a great big mess. Take time to make time by getting organized and staying that way. For a variety of specific tips on getting and staying organized, check out the next section of this chapter, "Get Organized!"

✔ **Set aside time at the beginning of the day to review your priorities.** Far too many people have learned to become crisis managers — jumping from one crisis to the next without planning ahead to fix the problems that *cause* these crises. If you want to take charge of your own schedule, you simply have to set aside time to plan ahead and to review your priorities and then realign them as necessary. Think about which actions are *really* the most important and which actions bring you closer to achieving your goals. One of the best times to do so is at the beginning of your workday, before you do anything else.

✔ **Set aside time at the end of each day to tie up loose ends and review your priorities for the next day.** Instead of rushing headlong from your office when you're done for the day, take time to tie up loose ends and prepare for your next workday. Review the items on your desk. Did you forget to sign and mail a few letters or return a couple of phone calls? Go through your list of priorities, crossing off items that you completed and adding any new ones that you accumulated during the day. Put your phone books back on the shelf, file away papers, and leave yourself an organized, uncluttered workspace to come back to the next day.

✔ **Do your first priority first and drop your last priority.** Putting off doing your highest-priority tasks is really easy because completing lower-priority tasks first is often easier or more fun. You may think that you're being effective when you take care of a bunch of low-priority tasks and get them out of the way or when you respond immediately to a bunch of urgent but unimportant messages, but you're only creating an illusion of effectiveness. What you're really doing by taking care of your lowest-priority tasks first is procrastinating and actually preventing yourself from completing your high-priority tasks. Although you should always allow for flexibility in your schedule, commit to working on your most *important* items — not necessarily the most *urgent* items — first. The most important items move you closest to meeting your goals and are most critical to your clients. The most urgent items are the ones with the most pressing deadlines, regardless of importance.

✔ **Junk your junk mail.** Not only is reading junk mail an incredible waste of your time, but it can lead to a seriously messed-up desk and office if you don't dispose of it quickly and thoroughly. If you're like most people, you probably receive on the order of 10 to 20 million pieces of junk mail every year (at least it *seems* like 10 to 20 million). And we bet that you wouldn't miss it if you never even received it. Therefore, the best strategy is to junk your junk mail. Don't waste your time opening it or reading it; just toss it in the recycling bin.

If you're hooked up to the Internet and your in-box is constantly overflowing with junk e-mail, the same rules apply. If you don't recognize the sender or the subject is obviously another opportunity to strike it rich on the Internet through an unbelievable breakthrough in network marketing, hit your Delete key and send the message to cyberpurgatory where it belongs!

✔ **Take advantage of dead time.** You spend a considerable part of consulting life in airplanes, in cabs, and waiting for meetings. View these as opportunities to catch up on background reading, note condensing, and correspondence. Always have 30 to 60 minutes of work with you to maximize this otherwise dead time.

✔ **Use technology to your advantage.** Although technology has created some incredible ways to *waste* your time (just try to keep from spending an hour or more surfing the Web — with stops at CNN, the Exploding Macintosh page, and Archie McPhee's online store in Seattle), it also has created some incredible ways to *save* time. Computers are getting faster and more portable every day. Fax machines can transmit your letters, reports, and documents anywhere in the world in minutes. With cell phones, pagers, and e-mail, you can keep in touch with your clients no matter where you are. Take advantage of such time-saving technology by keeping up with the latest innovations and then determining if and how they can help *you* become more effective and efficient.

✔ **Upgrade your computer.** How old is your computer? Are you still making do with a 486 or (heaven forbid!) a 386 personal computer? Or an old, generic Apple Macintosh? If so, you're wasting *hours* of your precious time every week waiting for your computer to catch up with you. Not only are the microprocessors in these old computers abysmally slow by today's standards, but they also don't adequately support the most current Microsoft Windows and Macintosh operating systems. This means that you're unable to run the most current — and fastest — versions of business software programs. The best solution is to sell your old computer or donate it to a worthy cause (and take a tax deduction) and buy a *new* computer. As your business grows, you may want to lease a computer to get the latest technology at the best prices.

As a rule, buy the best computer you can afford — you don't want your computer to become obsolete only a few months after you buy it. See Chapter 14 for more information about computers and peripherals.

Get Organized!

You have seen what happens when you allow your workplace to get disorganized. As your desk gets buried in an ever-increasing stack of notes, letters, brochures, and such, you may start losing your mind before long. Suddenly, the most important things get lost in the shuffle, and you start missing client deadlines or forgetting to put together an important teleconference at the appointed hour. And what's worse is that disorganization breeds even more disorganization. If you allow this disorganization to continue unabated, you may end up losing business.

What's the solution? Get organized before it's too late! Being organized is a great quality in business. When you're organized, you always know where to find everything you need to do your job, and you don't waste time searching for things when you need them. And whether you choose to track your jobs by using a low-tech, simple solution, such as a wall calendar, or a high-tech solution, such as a complex project management software program, an incredible number of tools are available to help you get organized and stay organized.

In this section, we consider some simple solutions for getting organized and staying that way. As you read through these recommendations, don't forget that the best solution for you doesn't have to cost a great deal of money or take much time to learn and use. The secret of success in getting organized and staying organized is to pick a system and then *use* it — religiously.

Getting organized starts with you

As you look around your office, the reason why you feel like you aren't really in control of your schedule or your work may be pretty obvious. Not only is your desk a mess — buried under stacks of books, last week's mail, a couple of half-used packets of paper, three empty cans of soda pop, a partly filled cup of coffee that is starting to sprout some sort of green hair, a computer, a printer, and a telephone — but it looks as though a tornado passed through your office only moments ago. Although this kind of scene may lend a homey, lived-in look to your office, this disorganized mess can keep you from attaining the high level of efficiency and effectiveness that lies within you, if you'll only give it a chance to get out.

Getting organized starts with you. You can't blame disorganization on your coworkers (*what* coworkers?), clients, kids, boyfriend, dog, or cat. *You* have the power to organize your life, and if you approach it a step at a time, you can create organization out of even the most disorganized situation.

Organizing techniques

If you want to get organized, you need a plan of action. Fortunately, we have put one together for you. Here are some simple suggestions for converting that mess you call your office into a model of organization and efficiency. No more vainly searching for lost files or stepping over, around, and through stacks of paper on your floor or forgetting that important appointment with a client. Soon you'll be so organized that you won't know what to do with yourself.

- ✔ **Clean up your office.** Whether you work in your garage, your dining room, or a rented office suite downtown, the first step you need to take when getting organized is to clean up your office. Here's a tip: Get a big snow shovel and shovel all the stuff on your floor into a big pile. Then work through each item one by one. If the item should be filed, then file it. If it's obviously unnecessary trash, then trash it. Give the stuff that remains this final test: *If I throw this thing away, will I miss it?* If the answer is no, then toss it before you have second thoughts!

- ✔ **Clean up your desk.** After you clean up your office, your desk is next. Don't just scrape everything off your desk and onto the floor — you just got your office organized, and you want to keep it that way! Tackle those stacks of papers, envelopes, faxes, invoices, books, and so on that are overflowing your desktop. What can you file away or put in its place in your office? What can you mail to a client or note on your calendar and toss? What needs to go directly to your trash can without further ado? Also make sure that items are stored within reach of their use.

As you work through the stuff on your desk, don't forget this basic rule of getting organized: Try to touch each item only once as it makes its way from disorganization to organization.

- ✔ **Revisit your office layout.** Putting your computer on your desk, your printer next to the window, your office supplies stuffed into a closet, and the birdcage on the corner of your credenza may have made quite a bit of sense once. But does that arrangement still make the most sense? For example, maybe if you hang Budgie's cage from a hook in the ceiling and move your computer (not the monitor, of course) from your desktop to a place *under* your desk, you can free up valuable workspace on your credenza and your desktop. Look at your entire office with an eye toward what will keep you most organized and efficient in doing your work. Try out different arrangements until you hit upon the one that works best for you.

- ✔ **Buy an appointment calendar, daily planner, or personal digital assistant.** Keeping your schedule organized is just as important to your success as keeping your workspace organized. And the best way by far to organize your schedule is to buy an appointment calendar, daily planner, or personal digital assistant — you can't remember all your business commitments without one. You don't need to spend much money to keep your schedule organized — almost any kind of calendar will work, so long as you use it. However, if you're so inclined, you can find a wide array of personal planners and automated personal assistants — all standing ready to help you get organized — at a store near you.

✔ **Perform regular maintenance.** After you get your workspace organized, your desk cleared off, and your schedule duly recorded into your calendar, your job is to keep things that way! Instead of jotting down appointments on scraps of paper and stuffing them into your pockets, grab your calendar and write the appointments in it right then and there. Not only do you save time by cutting out some steps in the process, but you avoid cluttering your office with scraps of paper. You also ensure that the scraps of paper listing your appointments won't get lost before you have a chance to record them. At the end of each workday, move your working papers into a file cabinet and put everything into its proper place. Organizing a disorganized mess takes a lot of work, but after you get organized, staying that way is much easier.

✔ **Use scanners.** If the majority of your correspondence is by e-mail or fax, a scanner enables you to store the information in your favorite word processing program. The rule is scan information (or store it electronically) if you intend to cut or paste it into documents.

✔ **Adopt a "Do it Now" (DIN) philosophy.** Refuse to put off until tomorrow what you can do right now! Instead of touching a piece of paper four or five times before you decide how you're going to deal with it, give it your full attention and determine its ultimate disposition when you first receive it. You'll increase the speed of your decision-making while reducing the amount of time that you waste shuffling paper around rather than taking action.

Keeping Track of Your Busy Schedule

Today, you have your choice of any number of ways to keep track of your schedule. Some — such as paper and cardboard pocket calendars — are low-tech. Others — such as laptop computers — are high-tech. Most — including daily planners and electronic organizers — are somewhere in between. And depending on your personal needs and preferences, you can spend anywhere from the change in your pocket to thousands of dollars on your favorite solution.

In the following sections, we review some of the key features, advantages, and disadvantages of each key way to keep track of your schedule.

How we keep track of our priorities and schedules

As you can imagine, we are pretty busy guys. But we took some time away from our crazy schedules to enjoy a cup of coffee together and chat about the ways that *we* keep track of our often frenzied work lives.

Bob Nelson: It all starts with a basic philosophy of getting organized and then staying that way. Most any system will work if you just stick with it.

Peter Economy: Yeah, I know what you mean. I've tried a lot of different ways to keep track of my priorities and things to do over the years. Some have worked better than others, but through it all, I have always made a point to at least have a system in place and then to use it.

Nelson: I have refined my system down to two key pieces. First, I have a short to-do list — it's usually about six items long. I update it as necessary, but since most of my goals are long-term in nature, daily updates are the exception rather than the norm. Second, I have a weekly phone log where I list all the people I need to contact that week, along with their phone numbers and the reasons for the calls. I prioritize the list in order of importance — the most important calls are at the top of the list.

Economy: When do you put together your weekly phone log?

Nelson: Usually on Sunday night or Monday morning — at the beginning of the week.

Economy: I also know that you also have a third way of keeping track of your priorities, Bob. You write your overarching life goals on pieces of cardboard and then post them on the side of a bookcase in your office. Family and health rank high on your list, as I recall.

Nelson: How right you are, Peter. Since they are on pieces of cardboard, I can easily rearrange them anytime I like.

Economy: And what system do you use to keep track of your to-do list and weekly phone log?

Nelson: I don't use a specific kind of daily planner or binder to stay organized. My priorities are primarily phone calls and projects when I'm traveling, so what works best for me are the plain 8½-inch x 11-inch Franklin Quest Monarch lined pages. What's great about Franklin Quest's lined pages is that the lines are more closely spaced than any other product that I can find. So instead of having only 30 or so lines to work with, I get 50 with the Franklin Quest product. I just buy their lined pages — not the rest of the system. What's *your* system for staying organized?

Economy: Well, I have been through more than a few. I tried the Franklin Quest system for a while — one of my former employers paid to have all of its managers attend a special training session in how to use it properly — but I got tired of lugging that big binder all over the place. Also, I didn't like the fact that I could see only one day at a time. I've probably tried every possible calendar from pocket calendars that looked really cool to large wall calendars that I could write on with white-board markers. None of those really did the trick for me.

Nelson: You're pretty computer savvy, right? Have you tried any of the personal information management software?

Economy: When we were writing *Managing For Dummies,* I tried out Microsoft Schedule+, which came bundled with my copy of Microsoft Office. It's a pretty good program — it certainly does everything that I would ever need it for and more — but I don't want to have to boot up my computer every time I need to look up a phone number or confirm an appointment. I used it for a while, and then I dropped it. A couple of years ago, I decided to find a system that would fit me just right and, after much searching, I found it: Quo Vadis.

Nelson: Quo Vadis? What's that?

Economy: Quo Vadis is a company that offers a variety of different planning calendars. They're a little hard to find, but well worth the search. I use their Trinote model. What I like about it is that it's a comfortable size — about the same footprint as *Consulting For Dummies,* but only half an inch thick — and I can see a whole week at a time, which is a definite must for me. The heart of the system is built around a typical appointment calendar, with slots for appointments starting at 7 a.m. and going until 9 p.m. There's also plenty of room to note priorities and list people to phone, send faxes to, and visit that week, and so forth, plus a separate address book at the back. I can take it anywhere, all my information is in one place, and it never needs batteries.

Nelson: So how do you *use* your system?

Economy: Pretty much the same way that you use yours. In addition to noting all my appointments in my Quo Vadis, I start each week by compiling all my top-priority things to do and phone calls to make. I then fill in the number-one thing to do for each day of the week at the top of the page, along with my other priorities at the bottom of the page. While I try to keep my lists manageable, I sometimes find myself with up to ten or more things to do on a given day. If I don't make a note of them, I'll invariably forget them. It's the old TNT — Today Not Tomorrow — approach.

Nelson: If it works for you, that's what counts. Find a system that works for you and then change it when it's not working.

The problem that many people have — and this is often true for consultants — is that they create to-do list after to-do list, but they never finish any of the things that they put on these lists. You should have only one list, and you should be disciplined and make a habit of addressing the things on your list — not other things that might seem more fun to do at the time. I strongly believe that you have to look at the way you are spending your time and make sure that it aligns closely with your objectives. Even if it means that your to-do list has only one item, make every minute of every day count.

Economy: I'm with you, Bob. How about another coffee?

Nelson: Sure — *I'll* buy this round!

The low-tech but highly reliable paper calendar

Good old-fashioned paper-based calendars are the easiest and most flexible way to keep track of your schedule. You can quickly, easily, and efficiently record client meeting dates and times, project due dates, appointments, and more on a calendar. And if you need to make a change, no sweat — simply grab an eraser and pencil in the new date and time. Although good old-fashioned calendars aren't very trendy or fashionable, they are easy to use and incredibly reliable.

If you want choices, calendars are definitely the way to go. You can get a calendar in just about any color, size, and shape that you could ever desire. Need something that you can carry around in your pocket? No problem. Would you like a briefcase-size calendar covered in paisley? No sweat. Or how about a great big wall calendar that you can write on with colored marking pens? Easy. Whatever your heart desires, you can probably find a calendar out there with your name on it.

Some key advantages of calendars are that

- You can write your entries in pencil and easily remove them with an eraser (all the better to pencil in your lunch appointments!).
- The batteries never run out.
- If you drop your calendar, it won't shatter into a thousand pieces of expensive circuit boards, smoking hard drives, and silicon wafers. Simply bend over, pick it up, and brush it off, and it's as good as new.

What's more, calendars have stood the test of time. You have no fancy commands to learn or expensive accessories to buy. With a good old-fashioned calendar at your side, you need never worry about your batteries dying or your hard drive crashing just as you are checking your appointments for the week. Despite the inroads that other scheduling tools have made, consultants likely will be relying on calendars for many years to come.

A step up: the daily planner

For those who find calendars to be too limiting or to lack the requisite number of tabs, gadgets, and gizmos, the daily planner offers something for everybody. But what exactly *is* a daily planner?

A daily planner is basically an appointment calendar, but at the same time, it is much, much more. Popular models by companies such as Franklin Quest and Day Runner, Inc., are appointment calendars at heart, but they offer an incredible array of options:

- **Binders:** Most daily planners start with a choice of vinyl, cloth, or leather loose-leaf binders to enable you to add and delete accessories easily. Sizes range from pocket- or purse-sized binders to larger, notebook-sized versions.

- ✔ **Priority lists:** A daily planner is a convenient place to keep your priority lists close by throughout your workday.

- ✔ **Appointment schedule:** Appointments, meeting times, important phone calls, and other significant events go here. If you prefer, you can write down insignificant events, too. However, if you have time to write down insignificant events, are you really managing your time?

- ✔ **Expense records:** On a business trip? Great! With this handy feature, you can keep track of cab fare, entertainment expenses, and other business expenses. If you plan to write off any of your expenses against your taxes, this feature is a godsend. Believe us, getting through tax time is *much* easier when you've recorded the *who, what, when,* and *where* of your expenses instead of trying to remember a year after the fact! IRS auditors love expense records and abhor recollections!

- ✔ **Address/telephone directory:** Names. Phone numbers. Addresses. Fax numbers. Zip codes. All alphabetized and awaiting your command. Wow.

- ✔ **Tabs, tabs, tabs:** You want information? You've got it! You can get tabs to record your blood type and lucky lottery numbers; reference charts for metric conversions, time zones, and area codes; weekly and monthly calendars; and more. Need even more information? How about check registers, contact logs, menu planner/shopping lists, client files, a built-in straightedge shaped like a golfer, or a solar-powered calculator? The possibilities are truly endless (so long as your bank account is, too).

Although daily planners offer many advantages to their users through the sheer variety of planning tools that they can incorporate within their gold-embossed binders, you *do* need to consider a few minuses. First, after you load up your binder with every conceivable option, it can become incredibly bulky and heavy. If you travel frequently, the hassle of lugging around 10 pounds of daily planner quickly wears on your patience. Second, a daily planner requires a large commitment of time and energy to keep it up-to-date. This is okay if you don't have much else to do, but for a busy consultant (you *are* a *busy* consultant, right?), this task can quickly become a burden. Not only do you have to keep your appointments up-to-date, but you have to keep up with your priorities, phone numbers, life goals, and whatever else you committed to when you signed on to the program.

And whatever you do, don't even *think* about losing your planner. For those who use their daily planners religiously, these big binders full of paper and ink quickly become essential tools — some might say *crutches* — containing their most vital information. What would you do if you lost *your* daily planner? We're guessing that, if you left your binder on the subway or dropped it in the street, you could probably kiss your business life goodbye — at least for a couple of days.

Computers: big and not so big

Just as computers have taken over more and more work functions, so too have they worked their way into keeping schedules. If you're intrigued by the latest in information technology or if your idea of fun is sending an e-mail through your laptop's PCMCIA modem and a cellular phone to your Internet service provider, you're going to like what's waiting for you. Just be sure that your bank account can support the investment (don't forget — it's tax deductible).

If you think that daily planners have a great deal to offer, you haven't seen anything yet. But before you run out and buy the first gadget that you see in a *Groovy Computing* magazine advertisement, ask yourself the following questions:

✔ **What do I really need?** Good question. Do you want an electronic appointment calendar and a telephone book? Piece of cake. Something to track your projects and to send and receive faxes? Okay. Do you want to receive and send e-mail over a cellular modem? Fine. You can find an electronic organizer or computer to do almost anything you would ever want to do. Before you run out and buy, decide what features are essential. Then research the heck out of your choices by reading product reviews in computer magazines and doing some hands-on comparison shopping.

✔ **What's my budget?** You can buy a compact and useful electronic organizer for $50 or less, or you can spend a couple hundred dollars more to get a personal digital assistant. Although a simple electronic organizer does little more than keep tabs of your phone numbers and appointments, a personal digital assistant adds the ability to send and receive e-mail through the Internet and the ability to send and receive faxes and take on other computing tasks. Add a couple thousand more dollars, and you can buy a portable laptop computer or desktop system that does everything for you but feed your cat when you're away from home. You'll have to wait for the next upgrade to be able to do that!

✔ **Big or small?** You can get your organizer in any size, from a Timex/Microsoft wristwatch that downloads and displays appointment and other information from your personal computer, to laptop or desktop computers running a variety of personal information management software packages. Don't forget that the smaller it is, the fewer features a manufacturer can jam into it, and the more it is likely to cost.

Now take a close look at each major category of microprocessor-based organizers to see which one best fits your needs.

Electronic organizers: more than just calculators!

Electronic organizers — such as Sharp's popular Wizard or Casio's B.O.S.S. — are microprocessor-based, palm-sized devices that incorporate many features beyond the basic calculator functions that they all share. For example, the Sharp Wizard incorporates a word processor (with a miniature QWERTY keyboard), telephone and address directories, an array of calendars and priority lists, a project management function that carries uncompleted tasks to the next day's schedule, a 9,600 bps fax modem, world time clocks with alarms, and much more. Not bad for a package that's smaller than a paperback book and runs on two AAA batteries!

The advantages of electronic organizers are their combination of compact size and extensive features for a relatively small price. For a fraction of the price of a laptop computer, many consultants are discovering the beauty of getting organized.

The disadvantages of electronic organizers are their tiny keyboards, which are painfully inadequate for doing anything serious in the typing department. Look for systems that allow you to do heavy data entry on your desktop computer and then download the data to your electronic organizer.

They're personal, they're digital, and they're assistants

Personal digital assistants, such as the Apple Newton and the Motorola Envoy, are essentially handheld computers designed with a definite bias toward communication. Although the Newton was ahead of its time when it was introduced several years ago, improvements in assistants' capability to interpret handwritten input correctly is finally helping them to gain some measure of popularity in the market.

With your trusty personal digital assistant (PDA), not only can you keep your daily calendar, but you can also manage your business contacts, send and receive wireless electronic messages, send messages to fax machines, and much more.

Here's a typical scenario: Suppose that you're scheduled to meet with a client over lunch to discuss the delivery of your recommendations to management. Before you hit the road that morning, you fire up your personal digital assistant, pull up your daily schedule, and note the time and place for the meeting. To make sure that you don't forget, you set an alarm to go off exactly one hour before your appointment. In a cab on the way to the meeting, you decide to handwrite a note on the touch-sensitive screen of your PDA and fax it off to an associate in Blackpool.

Over lunch, your client informs you that your report must address certain issues. You reach for your PDA and start taking notes on its surface. When the meeting is over, you create a message outlining your client's instructions and e-mail it to your assistant back at the home office via the cellular phone built into your PDA — all while you are sitting at your table after lunch. A few minutes later, you're on your way. Let's see your old-fashioned calendar do that! Of course, your client may want instructions in how you do this magic — but that's more billable hours for you!

Personal computers: organizing power in laptop or desktop flavors

If you're a consultant, you surely have a computer. You may have it to write reports and carry out other word-processing tasks, to build mammoth spreadsheets or databases of client information, or to communicate with others via electronic mail. Whatever your reason for buying a computer in the first place, you can also use your personal computer as a powerful organizing and scheduling tool — one that blows away your old paper calendars or daily planners.

Laptop computers have revolutionized business by breaking the chains that once tied businesspeople to their desks and to their desktop computers. With their built-in modems, remote networking capability, and the capacity to run sophisticated organizing software, such as Microsoft Schedule+ or Franklin Quest's ASCEND, laptop computers enable consultants to take their offices with them wherever they go — in a cab, at a client's office, or in a hotel room.

Most of the computer-based organizing software packages allow you to quickly produce and print out to-do lists, track appointments and tasks, manage your client contacts, create and update an address book, schedule meetings, and more. These features, coupled with the standard computing power of your word-processing, spreadsheet, database, and communications software, add up to a winning combination for many consultants.

Clearly, whichever kind of scheduling system you choose — whether it's a regular old calendar or a Pentium II desktop computer — you have absolutely *no* excuse for not getting organized. Right now! Deciding on a personal planning system is a personal choice. Take the time to research your options and try them out. If the one you select doesn't work for you, try something else. With all the options available, you're sure to find a system that fits both your personality *and* your pocketbook.

Chapter 12

Communicate, Communicate, Communicate

In This Chapter

▶ Speaking your way to success

▶ Asking effective questions

▶ Listening actively to your clients

▶ Putting it in writing

ommunication this, communication that — what's the big deal? The big deal is that almost everything you do as a consultant involves some amount of communication. Whether you are calling a potential client to make an appointment for a marketing presentation, interviewing warehouse personnel about how closely they adhere to established client policies, or reporting your findings and recommendations to your client's executive team, communication is the one element that flows throughout.

If you hope to be a successful consultant (and how could you wish for anything less?), you first have to be a successful communicator. Communication is the foundation upon which all consultant-client relationships are built, and it's the glue that holds your relationships together. If you communicate well with your clients, not only do they have more confidence in your abilities, but they also enjoy working with you more and are more likely to hire you for other jobs later.

Of course, some people are better communicators than others. Some people just have a knack for presenting their thoughts in speech or in writing. Fortunately, for those of you who still have a way to go before you'll be paid $50,000 to speak before a large group of people or to write your life story, there's good news. You *can* learn to become a better communicator. How? All you need to do is follow some very simple advice (which we coincidentally plant in this chapter) and then *practice, practice, practice*. And when you're done practicing, practice some more.

The more you communicate with others — whether in speech or in writing — the better communicator you'll become. And the better communicator you are, the more confident you feel communicating, the more you enjoy it, and the more effective you are with your clients. Before you know it, your mailbox will be overflowing with requests for your services. (Just remember: We get 10 percent of everything you make!)

One thing about communication and your clients: Make sure that the way you communicate with your clients is based on *their* preferences — not your own. If your client prefers a personal phone call over an e-mail message, then pick up the phone. If your client prefers to have one point of contact within your business instead of several, then provide that single point of contact. If your client prefers long meetings over lunch for project briefings, then do it that way — even if you hate lunch meetings. Be sensitive to your clients' communication needs, and you're sure to have happy clients. Of course, you still have to do a good job on your projects!

This chapter is about communicating with others and, in particular, the *way* in which you communicate. We address the importance of communicating orally with your clients and asking the right questions at the right time. We consider that most important part of the communication equation — listening — and how to become a better listener. Finally, you can find out how to sharpen those rusty writing skills. For detailed information on another important aspect of communicating with your clients — making presentations — see Chapter 13.

Harnessing the Power of the Spoken Word

Speaking occupies a large portion of every consultant's day. Whether you are trying to sell a prospective client on the infinite wisdom of hiring you to appraise her Renoir, or asking an accounts payable clerk about how he processes payments to vendors as part of your audit of his firm, or presenting your recommendations to a company's management team, your success depends heavily on your ability to speak and be understood.

If there's anything that most people think they do pretty well, it's probably speak effectively with others. However, even if you have a great deal of practice talking to clients, you can do several things to become an even better communicator:

✔ **Think before you leap.** Whether you are responding to your clients' questions or preparing to ask some questions of your own, you should stop for a moment to get your bearings before you leap into the breach. Reacting rather than reflecting can be tempting, but your *first* reaction may very well not be your *best* reaction.

✔ **Keep it simple and brief.** When presenting information to your clients, keep the information as simple as possible so that your clients understand it clearly and easily. Also be as brief as possible so that you hold your clients' attention as you speak. Complexity begets confusion, and confusion makes it more difficult for you to control the outcome of your discussion.

We know one consultant who always talks on the phone while standing. Why? It helps him come to his point more quickly with his clients.

✔ **Ask lots of questions — and listen to the answers.** Not only does asking lots of questions show that you are genuinely interested in what your clients have to say, but it also is a great way to obtain information about your clients' needs and expectations. Vary the number of questions you ask, depending on the exact purpose of your contact and the amount of time available.

✔ **Be enthusiastic.** If you're excited by the prospect of doing a project for a client or providing an update of your progress, make sure that your client knows it. The more enthusiastic you are about doing your client's project, the more enthusiastic your client will be about having you do it (and about paying your invoices when they come due!).

✔ **Be empathetic.** Your client will receive your message more favorably if you tailor it to the listener's individual needs. As the old saying goes, you should "walk a mile in their shoes." For example, if your client is too busy to spend more than a few minutes at a time with you, you need to present your message much differently than if your client seems to have all the time in the world and likes to philosophize for hours and hours.

✔ **Get personal.** A key component of consulting is building relationships with your clients. The best way to do so is to get personal with them. Although you should maintain a certain amount of professional decorum in your business relationships, you should get to know your clients as *people,* not just as customers. Get to know their likes and dislikes, whether they have kids, and what kinds of hobbies or other non-job interests they have that you may share (tennis, anyone?). However, before you dive in too deep, be sensitive to where you draw the line between your personal relationships and your business relationships with your clients. Although some clients may prefer to develop friendly, personal relationship with their consultants, others may prefer to keep some distance. Regardless, keep in mind that the rapport that you develop with your clients helps you cement long-term relationships with them. And that's good for you *and* for your clients.

As you can see, you can do many things right now to increase the power and impact of your speaking skills. Give them a try! We guarantee that you'll see a marked difference in your client relationships almost immediately.

Asking the Right Questions at the Right Time

If consultants do one thing, it's ask questions. Lots of questions. *How much can you afford to spend to redecorate your house? When do you need this marketing survey completed? Did you know that my business has located more high-producing wells than any other in the valley?* Not a day goes by that consultants don't ask clients — or clients-to-be — questions about something.

Because asking questions is such a big part of your job as a consultant, how do you make sure that you ask the right question at the right time? Before we answer *that* question, first consider exactly why consultants ask questions.

Why ask questions?

If you stop and think about it, consultants ask questions for many different reasons. Although you may at first think that the number one reason to ask questions, such as *why, what, when,* and *where,* is to find out simple answers, asking questions goes far beyond those simple kinds of responses.

When asked the right way and at the right time, questions can give you direct insight into the heart and soul of your clients and provide you with a road map of where you should take your discussion. Here are some of the many different reasons that consultants ask their clients questions:

- **To obtain information:** You can solicit information from your clients by asking them questions along the lines of "Exactly what results are you hoping to achieve?" or "How soon do you plan to select a consultant for this project?"

- **To provide information:** You can use questions to inform your client about the capabilities of your consulting business and any number of other things. Try asking questions like "Did you know that, in addition to providing graphic design services, our consultants also produce press kits and other publicity tools?" or "Would you believe it if I told you that our largest customer is Apple Computer?"

✔ **To check comprehension:** Although your clients may be nodding their heads up and down throughout your presentations, do they *really* understand what you're talking about? You can check by asking questions like "Are you following me so far?" or "Do I need to explain anything we've discussed?"

✔ **To measure interest:** Of course, you want to quickly get a sense of whether your clients are interested in what you have to say or what you have to sell. Do so by asking your clients questions such as "Are you interested in contracting to have this work done?" or "Are you ready to make a commitment to this project right now?"

✔ **To encourage client participation:** Engaging your clients in your discussion is in your interest. You can encourage client participation by asking questions like "What do you think about our approach?" or "What is the biggest problem that you're having with your current system of production scheduling?"

You have many more reasons to ask your clients questions than to simply find out when they plan to issue a contract or how much money they have to spend. Now that you know why consultants ask questions, read about the two kinds of questions they ask.

Asking questions: how to do it

Although you can ask your clients an infinite number of questions, you can break down all the questions into two key *kinds* of questions — open and closed. Just like you can open or close a door, you can either open up communication with your clients or close it down just by the kind of questions you ask.

There's a right time and place to ask open questions and a right time and place to ask closed questions. The type of question to ask all depends on the particular goals that you have set for your question-and-answer session. Following is a description of open and closed questions, including when you should use (and *not* use, as may be the case!) each kind.

✔ **Open:** Open questions require some amount of explanation to be answered. When you want to explore what your client thinks about a particular topic, you should use open questions. However, if you need a simple yes or no response, then open questions are definitely out. Open questions, such as "What suggestions do you have that can help make our proposal fit your needs?" or "How should we approach obtaining that particular information?" encourage your clients to go beyond simple yes or no answers and to open up and reveal their personal opinions and beliefs to you.

✔ **Closed:** Closed questions can be answered with a simple yes or no or another such specific response. Closed questions, such as "How many years have you been in business?" or "Do you like our proposal?" are great for getting specific responses and information, but they are lousy for getting your clients to open up and offer you any sort of insight into what they are really thinking. If you merely want to get specific answers to specific questions — and to avoid wasting time with a lot of needless discussion — then you should use closed questions.

In addition to these two main types of questions, you can trigger a response from your clients in other ways. Simple words and sounds can often get your clients to continue with a response or elaborate on it. For example, when your client tells you, "I just found an extra $100,000 in our consulting budget," your questioning response of "Oh?" can trigger this additional response: "Yes, and I have no idea how we're going to spend it by the end of the year." No doubt, you have some great ideas to help your client solve this problem.

Other response triggers, such as "Really?" and "No way!" and sounds and grunts such as "Huh?," "Hmmm . . .," and "Uh-huh," can facilitate further discussion. Even silence can trigger a response by your clients who get nervous when there is a gap in your conversation. Maybe that's why they say that silence is golden!

We've delved deep enough into the whys and wherefores of asking questions. It's time to stop all this beating around the bush and find out the right questions to ask your clients. Determine the goals of your question-and-answer session *before* you start it and then apply the following rules when you ask your questions. Know *where* you want to go — and map out your route — before you start your journey, and you'll probably get there!

✔ **Do your research ahead of time.** Before you launch into your question-and-answer sessions, spend some time learning about your clients and the kinds of issues they face and may need you to help them with. Don't waste your time or your clients' time going through a list of issues that you easily could have obtained the answers to in advance.

✔ **Ask straightforward questions.** Don't beat around the bush or (heaven forbid!) try to trick your clients. Ask your questions in a straightforward manner, and you are most likely to get straightforward responses.

✔ **Move from the big picture to the little picture.** Start with broad questions that give you a general sense of what your clients are thinking. As your clients answer your broad questions, use their responses to ask more precise questions that take you to the heart of the information you need to know.

✔ **Use answers as a foundation for more questions.** You frequently may have absolutely no idea where your questions will lead. Use the answer to each question as a bridge to your next question. Tailor your questions to the responses that you receive from your clients.

> ✔ **Try different angles.** If one approach doesn't work, don't be afraid to try another. You may have to ask your question many different ways before you find the one that gets the response you need.

Listening: It's a Two-Way Street

Just like any other equation, the communication equation has two sides. On one side, you have to speak, and your clients have to listen to what you say. On the other side of the equation, your clients speak, and you listen. In many ways, listening to your clients is *much* more important than talking to them.

Why? Because anytime you provide a service or a product, you need to concentrate your attention on your clients' needs and desires, not your own. Focusing on your clients is extremely difficult when you're doing all the talking and none of the listening. In fact, it's virtually impossible.

We're not talking about a half-hearted, polite kind of listening here. We're talking about 100 percent, industrial-strength listening. You see, when you fail to give your clients your *full* attention, you're shortchanging both them *and* yourself. Not only do you miss your clients' messages, but your inattention sends its own message: *I don't really care what you have to say.* When you are in business for yourself and you depend on your clients to help you pay the bills, you cannot afford to send this message. Not only that, but when you listen actively, you increase the likelihood that you understand what your clients are saying. Depending on what you're talking about, this understanding can be quite important to you and your client relationships.

Don't leave listening to chance. Take an active role in listening to your clients by doing the following things every time you talk with them:

> ✔ **Express your interest.** It's a simple concept, but one of the best listening techniques is to be interested in what your clients have to say. No, nodding your head as you think about what you're going to have for lunch does not indicate that you're interested. We mean that you should display an honest, sincere, and genuine interest in your clients and the information that they are communicating to you. Give your clients your full attention and ask questions if they say something that needs further clarification. For example, you might say something like "Wow! That's a great approach! How did you arrive at that solution?" The more interest you show your clients, the more interesting they become — and the more interested they are in talking further with you.

> ✔ **Maintain your focus.** Have you ever been in the middle of a conversation and all of a sudden noticed that you haven't heard a word that the other person said? The problem is that sometimes our minds are moving far faster than the other person can speak — often so fast that

we start thinking about all kinds of other things besides the topic at hand. It's a fact: Most people speak at the rate of approximately 150 words per minute, but most people *think* at approximately 500 words per minute. This physiological gap leaves a lot of room for your mind to wander and for you to lose track of what your clients are telling you. Keep your mind focused on listening to what your clients have to say. If you do find your thoughts wandering, bring your mind back on track right away!

✔ **Ask questions.** Asking the right kinds of questions at the right time is an important tool in your communications bag of tricks. Asking questions also fills a role in your program of active listening. When something your clients say is unclear or doesn't make sense to you, ask questions to clarify your understanding. Not only do you better understand what your clients tell you, but you also demonstrate that you are interested in what they have to say. One particularly effective way of ensuring accuracy in communication *and* demonstrating your interest is through a technique called *reflective listening*. This is summarizing what the speaker has said and then repeating it back to him or her. For example, you might say, "From what I understand so far, am I right in assuming that you are dissatisfied with the service you are receiving from our competitor?"

✔ **Seek the keys.** What are the key points that your client is expressing to you? You can easily lose yourself in all the detail of a conversation and miss the key points as a result. As your clients speak, divide what they say into two separate categories: information that is relevant to the discussion and information that isn't. You may need to ask clarifying questions to help you decide into which category to classify your information. A question like "Would you please explain to me how that issue affects our overall goal of completing your project by the first of the month?" helps you decide whether the information is relevant.

✔ **Avoid interruptions.** Although you can ask clarifying questions or employ reflective listening techniques, you should not constantly interrupt your clients when they have the floor. You should personally avoid interrupting your clients needlessly and create a private environment where you and your clients can work uninterrupted. Although you can't control outside interruptions if you're at your *client's* office, you *can* control outside interruptions if your client is at your office. Close the door to your office or ask your assistant to tell visitors that they'll have to wait. Consider investing in a "do not disturb" sign. And one more thing: If someone telephones you, don't answer — that's what voice mail is for, after all.

✔ **Listen with more than your ears.** Communicating with your clients involves more than the verbal part that we all know and love so much. After spending tons of money studying exactly how communication works, scientists discovered that up to *90 percent* of the communication between people is nonverbal! And what is this nonverbal stuff that is so important to how we communicate? Facial expressions, head nods or shakes, posture, squints, position of arms and legs, and much, much more. Therefore, use *all* your senses when you listen to your clients.

✔ **Take lots of notes.** Can you remember all the details of every conversation that you had last year? How about last month? Last week? Yesterday? The problem is, remembering anything within a few hours, days, or weeks after it takes place can be quite difficult. Therefore, take notes as you listen to your clients speak. The act of writing notes actually helps some people retain longer the information that they hear. And note-taking offers an extra bonus: Notes provide a convenient way to organize your thoughts later, when you have the time to review them.

How W. Lee Hill keeps in touch

Due to the nature of his consulting practice, which often requires him to leave his home base of Boulder, Colorado, to travel across the country to meet with clients, W. Lee Hill (wleehill@aol.com) has learned the value of communication and of keeping in touch. Lee currently specializes in legal consulting — particularly for Native American tribes — and he was recently involved in developing casino opportunities for a Midwestern American Indian tribe. His role was to assist the Indian tribe *and* to assist the investment groups interested in working with the tribe, to come together across a variety of tables to work out a deal that pleased everyone. In this role, Lee also worked as a liaison to the various governmental regulatory agencies concerned with Indian gaming.

In addition to his work with Native American tribes, Lee also consults with new businesses to develop strategic legal planning. The goal of this work is to develop a comprehensive legal strategy that will reduce the amount of legal work required once operations commence, thus saving his clients time and money. We met with Lee to discuss his perspective on the role that communication plays in his consulting practice and how he keeps in touch with his clients.

Consulting For Dummies: Why is communication so important to your consulting practice?

W. Lee Hill: There's a great language difference — not the spoken language as much as it is the understood language that differs between many different Native American communities and many conventional business communities. It all boils down to cultural differences in Native America and the subcultures represented by individual Native American nations. Business, governmental regulatory, and jurisprudential networks have *their* own subcultures, too. The cultural reference points engender a lot of mistrust and misunderstanding between the two. So I view my role — having one foot in *both*, in the case of Native America and governmental regulatory/jurisprudential subcultures — as an interpreter, facilitating the different groups' abilities to more accurately understand one another.

CFD: The law is certainly hard enough for *anyone* to understand, much less someone who isn't a part of the mainstream culture.

(continued)

(continued)

Hill: That's quite true.

CFD: So communication is obviously a very important part of your practice. How do you keep in touch with your clients — particularly when you're away from your home base in Boulder?

Hill: Communication is definitely the key to expanding your availability as a consultant *and* expanding your access. For example, I can't imagine *anyone* not having Internet access, because of the expedient communication opportunities that it provides, as well as the obvious research opportunities.

CFD: Right. We both use the Internet on a daily basis to send e-mail to our business associates and to access company Web pages and such.

Hill: I have a client who is an Internet service provider, so I have a general access account through his firm. I also subscribe to America Online because it's a convenient e-mail address and most people *are* on America Online — it simplifies things. When I take my laptop on the road with me, I can usually access my America Online account anywhere I am by way of a free local phone call.

CFD: What else?

Hill: In addition to my Internet connections, I have a toll-free voice-mail service that pages me anywhere in North America whenever a message is left.

CFD: So whenever you get a message in your voice-mail box, you're notified on a standard pager?

Hill: Yes. I get paged to call the toll-free number where I can access my messages. By the way, the price is very reasonable. The money that I save by not having to dial long-distance from a pay phone to check my messages more than pays for the monthly service charge.

CFD: Anything else?

Hill: I have a cellular phone, two business phones, and two backup voice-mail services for the business lines when they are engaged, as well as personal answering devices tied into my computer that also page me when I want them to.

CFD: Your answering machine pages you?

Hill: Yes. Since I have caller ID, I can literally go in and select a number, and when that number rings, the caller doesn't even have to leave a message — my computer will page me and leave a specific numeric indicator on my pager. The software can run on either my desktop computer or my laptop.

CFD: With all those different voice-mail boxes and pagers and answering machines, how do you decide which one to answer first?

Hill: The 800 number notifies me by pager wherever I am, so that's always the top priority. This number is indicated on my business cards as a 24-hour message line. So clients that I've worked with for a while quickly learn from me that the most immediate way to reach me is by leaving a message on my 800 number. There's a general inclination for my clients to do that anyway since it's a toll-free number. The other boxes are more often than not used for general administrative purposes.

CFD: It sounds like you're already pretty well equipped, but is there anything you're dreaming about getting?

Hill: I want your digital PCS phone!

CFD: Sorry, Lee, you're going to have to buy your own!

Hill: It was worth a try.

CFD: Is there some piece of advice that you would offer to someone who is starting out as a consultant?

Hill: It's essential that you know what you are doing. The ticket is for people to follow their muse, their inspiration — do what they really want to do — and reach a point where they are very comfortable and confident that they are doing it well. And then they can consider the almost unlimited range of applications in other, unrelated endeavors. The challenge becomes informing decision-makers in those other, unrelated endeavors of their availability.

CFD: How you would go about doing that?

Hill: In my case, I do it by directly contacting people I know or people who know someone that I know. I send letters, I make phone calls, and I make visits — telling them that there are important issues they need to consider and offering to make a presentation. That's what works for me.

Putting It in Writing

Technology offers us a glut of pagers, telephone answering machines and voice mail, e-mail, and 1,001 other new ways to communicate with your clients. As a result, you may think that good old-fashioned writing is obsolete and soon to be replaced with something better. (Maybe the Psychic Friends Network *is* onto something!) If that's what you think, you couldn't be farther away from the truth.

The simple fact is, writing is more important than ever. Whether you're writing a proposal for new business, sending a thank-you note to a client, or responding to an associate's e-mail message, good writing never goes out of fashion; it's also an essential element of your success as a consultant.

What to put in writing

Although writing is not quite obsolete (witness this 300+ page book and its many yellow-and-black-covered brothers and sisters, for example), it has turned into a bit of a lost art. And although voice mail, e-mail, and the like have generally supplanted the need for a large amount of business correspondence that traditionally used to flow between consultants and clients, writing still has a vital role to play in the world of business communication. In fact, because of its increasing scarcity, well-written business correspondence can set you apart from the rest of the pack.

So now that you may be thinking that writing is worth considering, what things should you write? Here are a few forms of communication that can help you foster good relationships with your clients:

- ✔ **Business letters:** Business letters are the traditional backbone of all business correspondence between consultants and their clients. Consultants write business letters to their clients for many reasons, including persuading, thanking, selling, apologizing, communicating good news, communicating bad news, asking questions, and seeking information. Sure, crafting a good one- to three-page business letter may take more work than a two-sentence e-mail message, but the effort is worth it.

- ✔ **Notes:** Writing and sending notes to your clients and clients-to-be should be a central part of your writing campaign. Send your prospects thank-you notes after you meet with them or after you complete a project for them. Send your clients notes attached to copies of your latest newsletter or attached to newspaper or trade journal articles that may interest them (preferably ones that you wrote or that contain interviews with you!). Send notes just to let people know that you're thinking about them. Yes, you *can* send your notes via e-mail if you like. But whenever possible, take the extra effort to write your notes by hand. Your clients will appreciate the thought, and you'll appreciate their business.

- ✔ **Proposals:** Very few clients will hire you without some form of written proposal of what you plan to do for them. Proposals require a very precise and organized style of writing that conveys not only the fact that you can do what you say you can do, but that you can do it well and cost-effectively. A well-written proposal can make the difference between being hired and being rejected. See Chapter 13 for detailed information on how to write winning proposals.

- ✔ **Reports:** For many consultants, reports — and the presentations that go along with them — are the only products that they deliver to their clients. Because of this, the contents of reports — and the way that reports are written — are critically important in the acceptance of consultants' recommendations by their clients. Chapter 13 also addresses the important issues involved in writing good reports.

Seven steps to better writing

Like anything else, the more you write, the better you'll get. So how can you write better? Dust off that old pen and paper or boot up your word processor and get to work! Here are seven steps to writing better that you can start using right now:

✔ **Know your point.** Before you write a single word, think about the point that you want to make. What's your point, and what kind of reaction do you want from those who read what you write? Keep your thoughts tightly focused and sharp.

✔ **Get organized.** Writing clearly is hard when your thoughts are a disorganized mess. The solution is to organize your thoughts before you start writing. One of the best approaches is to create an outline of what you want to say. An outline — or even a few notes — can help you pull your thoughts together into a coherent written product. As an additional aid to getting your thoughts organized, bounce your ideas off clients and business associates.

✔ **Write the same way that you speak.** The best writing is natural, like everyday speech. Write the way that you speak. Don't be artificially formal or too businesslike and sterile when that's not your style. Not only will your writing be less accessible, but you'll squelch your individuality and personality.

✔ **Be concise.** Don't write just to fill up a sheet of paper with your words — every word should have a purpose. Avoid fluff and filler at all costs. When you write, make your point, support it, and then move on to the next point.

✔ **Simplicity is a virtue.** In writing, as in life, simple is better. Why waste your time writing a 300-word memo or letter when a 50-word note is sufficient? Why use jargon and indecipherable acronyms when plain English works just as well or even better? Make it your life's purpose to simplify, simplify, simplify.

✔ **Write and then rewrite.** There's no writer, amateur or professional, on the face of this green earth who doesn't need to rework much of what he or she has written until it's just right. We both have lots of experience in this regard — just ask Pam Mourouzis, our project editor for this book. When you write, first create a draft of what you want to say and then edit it for content, flow, grammar, and readability. You may need to write a few drafts before your work really shines, but the effort will be worth it.

✔ **Convey a positive attitude.** People naturally prefer upbeat, positive writing over writing that is negative and a drag to read. Falling into the negativity trap is easy, but don't let yourself become a victim! Even when you have to communicate bad news, be active, committed, and positive in the words that you choose and the way that you write. Your readers will really appreciate your approach!

If you want to learn more about how to write better, you can find plenty of books and classes to help you. Check your local library or bookstore for a wide variety of titles on improving your business writing skills. Contact your local community college, university extension office, or private training companies, such as The Learning Annex. People who write for a living and are quite good at it teach many of the classes offered in these outlets.

Chapter 13

Schmooze Like a Pro: Reports and Presentations

• •

In This Chapter

▶ Producing great written reports

▶ Making presentations like a pro

• •

*B*eing an effective consultant means more than providing your expertise and advice to your clients or even finding the answers to their problems. One of the most important parts of consulting is effectively getting your message to your clients. You may have a great solution worked out for a client, but if you fail to present it in an effective way, the message may well be lost, and all your work can fall on deaf ears.

So how do you ensure that you get your message across to your clients? Through written reports and presentations. Although we discuss the importance of the many different kinds of communication in Chapter 12, in this chapter we focus our attention on the pluses and minuses of two very important forums for consultants to communicate with their clients.

Each of these methods of communicating requires a unique set of skills, and you approach each method quite differently. Which method you use to communicate your results depends on the nature of the work you are doing, the nature of the results of your work, the preferences of your clients, and your own preferences. The main thing is to get your message heard and understood by the right people in your client's organization without wasting your time or theirs.

The Secrets of Producing Effective Written Reports

Although some consulting work may require only a brief verbal discussion or oral presentation to convey the results of your work, most consulting assignments result in at *least* a brief written report. In fact, whether or not your client asks for one, we recommend that you deliver some sort of written report — even if it's only a one- or two-page letter — to show your clients that you *did* do something for your fee and also to ensure that your message is clear and cannot be easily confused or misconstrued.

Regardless of the purpose your report fulfills, what it looks like, or what information it conveys, don't forget that the *best* report is the one that your intended audience actually reads. If your client throws your report into a corner and forgets about it — because it's too complex, it's untimely, or the results don't match your client's expectations — you have just wasted your time, and your client has wasted money.

Two basic consulting reports

No matter what kind of consulting you are doing, in most cases you will use two different kinds of written reports to communicate with your clients: progress reports and final report. In some cases — particularly in complex projects of long duration — your consulting projects will use both types of reports. In others — particularly projects that are relatively simple and short in duration — you may need to submit only a final report. In any case, you should plan to allocate approximately 20 percent of your time to the task of preparing and communicating results.

Although you can choose to employ many different formats to get your information across to your client, perhaps the most important consideration of all is your client's expectation. If your client expects a short report, make sure that you deliver a short report. If your client expects a long, detailed report, make sure that you tailor your format to meet that need. And while you're at it, make sure that you price your consulting proposal appropriately!

Progress reports

Progress reports — also known as milestone reports or project status reports — do just what they say: They report your progress on the way to completing a project. A progress report can be anything from a short, one-page update to a full-length, multipage extravaganza. Regardless of the length of your progress reports, make sure that they are concise and to the point. *Never* pad your progress reports with useless text or graphics in an attempt to impress your clients. You'll only succeed in convincing your clients that either you don't really know what you're doing, or you're being overpaid. Neither of these outcomes is exactly optimal.

The exact length and format of your report are up to you and your client, but you should make sure that your progress reports contain at *least* the following information:

- ✔ **Executive summary:** Write a brief but complete summary of the progress of the project during the reporting period, highlighting accomplishments and recommendations. This summary gives your busy clients a chance to get a quick overview of your progress without having to read the entire report.

- ✔ **Key accomplishments:** Your clients will be particularly interested in any notable accomplishments that you have achieved on the project. If you had any key accomplishments during the reporting period (and make sure that you *do!*), make them known to your clients in the progress report.

- ✔ **Work completed during the reporting period:** Summarize the exact work that you completed during the reporting period and discuss how it relates to the overall project. Your progress report should be a snapshot of your activity during the period of time that you are covering in the report.

- ✔ **Percentage of completion:** This information is simply an estimate of the percentage of completion of your project during the period of the report. If, for example, you are approximately one-third of the way through the project, simply note your percentage of completion as 33 percent.

- ✔ **Work to be completed:** Briefly discuss the work to be completed during the next reporting period and how it relates to the rest of the project. If you anticipate any particularly notable accomplishments — or particularly problematic issues — highlight them to your clients in this section of the progress report.

- ✔ **Issues:** If you have encountered any problems or other issues that need to be brought to your clients' attention, list them here. Make sure that you follow up this written presentation of project issues with personal, face-to-face discussions with your clients. You absolutely do *not* want to surprise your clients with project issues or problems. Bring up challenging issues as soon as you encounter them and ensure that they are promptly acknowledged and addressed.

How often should you produce progress reports? The specific answer to that question depends upon the exact nature of the project, how long the project is scheduled to last, and the expectations of your clients. If the project is a short one — say, only a few weeks' duration — you may not need to do a progress report. However, if your project runs for a month or more, then progress reports are clearly in order. Although monthly progress reports are the norm for most consultants and their clients, there's no rule that says you can't do your progress reports on a weekly, quarterly, or any other basis that suits your needs and the needs of your clients.

Final reports

Your final report presents the results of your project and, as such, is the culmination and central focus of the efforts you have undertaken on behalf of your client. Depending on the exact nature of your work, your final report may be the showcase of the project, and it may form the basis for company-wide changes or restructuring.

In many cases, your final report will be the only product that your client will receive from you; its importance cannot be underestimated.

Final reports are different from progress reports in many ways. Here are the key ingredients that you always include in your final reports:

- **Executive summary:** Your clients are busy, busy people, and they don't have lots of time to wade through long reports. Briefly summarize the information you are presenting in your final report and highlight key project accomplishments and problems.

- **Project background and scope:** Some of the people who read your report may not know much about your project and why you were selected to do it. Make this part of the final report your opportunity to discuss the nature and scope of the project, how it came to be, and your role in it.

- **Methodology:** How did you approach the problem? Did you conduct a market survey? A statistical analysis? A review of the literature? Your readers want to know how you came up with the results and conclusions that form the basis of your report. The right answers to those questions add to your credibility and strongly support your recommendations. The wrong answers detract from your credibility and possibly create doubt about your recommendations.

- **Findings and conclusions:** This section of your report contains the results of your work and any conclusions you can draw from what you found out in your investigation. All your good news — and your bad news — goes into this section of your final report.

- **Recommendations:** Even more than your findings and conclusions, your recommendations are probably what your clients are most interested in reading. In this section of your report, you apply all your experience to develop and present your prescription to cure your clients' ills. Make sure that your recommendations are concise and easy to understand and that they can realistically be acted upon.

✔ **Implementation guidelines:** Although your clients may not have asked you for specific guidance on implementing your recommendations, use this option to show your clients how your expertise can be of particular benefit to them. Do them a big favor by spelling out a step-by-step approach for putting your recommendations into place and include scheduling milestones and budgetary information. While you're at it, take the opportunity to propose *your* role in the implementation, along with a price and timetable to do so. Don't be shy — many consultants win a *lot* of business this way!

✔ **Summary of benefits:** Although your findings, conclusions, and recommendations may make perfect sense, most organizations need some sort of incentive to make *any* change to the status quo. Summarize the benefits of your recommendations in a way that shows your clients why they should be compelled to implement them. Increasing sales, decreasing expenses, avoiding litigation, improving customer satisfaction, and decreasing employee turnover are just a few of the possible benefits of your recommendations.

You have only one chance to make a first impression

It bears repeating that your reports may be the only tangible product you deliver to your clients. Therefore, both the quality of the contents of the report *and* the quality of your firm will be judged by how your reports look. Perhaps you can't judge a book by its cover, but you can surely get *some* idea of what's inside by looking at the outside. An inviting, attractive report is much more likely to be read than one that is either uninspiring or just plain shoddy looking.

What do *your* reports look like? Are they poorly organized, cheap-looking sheaves of smudgy, inkjet-printed paper, hurriedly stapled in one corner with a half-intact staple hanging on for dear life? Or are they laser-printed works of art, full of color graphics and bound tastefully with a comb, wire, or tape binding? Come on, tell us the truth. If your reports are more the former than the latter, then you need to take some time in the *very* near future to upgrade the quality of your reports.

We just happen to have a few tips to help make your reports as professional-looking as they possibly can be.

✔ **Composition and printing:** The easiest way to making professional-looking reports is to use a fully capable computer word processing program (such as Microsoft Word or Corel WordPerfect) and then print your report out on a good quality laser printer, such as those produced by Hewlett-Packard, Panasonic, Brother, and others. Typewriters are definitely out, and inkjet printers are only marginally acceptable because the ink tends to smear and the print quality is not nearly as good as laser printer quality.

✔ **Layout:** Don't try to jam too much information onto one page. Use lots of white space, indentations, margins, headings, and other layout features to make your reports more inviting to the reader. If you're not sure how to come up with your own distinctive report layout, ask your clients for some examples of reports *they* like or check your word processing software for standardized report templates. For example, Microsoft Word contains several report templates — or predetermined guides — already set up with distinctive fonts, heading formats, line spacing, table formats, and other layout tools. For more advice on layout, see *Word 97 For Windows For Dummies* (by Dan Gookin) and *Desktop Publishing & Design For Dummies* (by Roger C. Parker), both published by IDG Books Worldwide, Inc.

✔ **Graphics:** Whenever possible, use *lots* of graphics to break up the text of your report. Not only do graphics convey information more effectively than words, but they give your reader a much needed break. Graphs, tables, charts, photographs, drawings, and other graphical features make your reports much more attractive and professional in appearance. If you want to really go *all* the way, use full-color versions of the graphics in your reports. Keep in mind, however, that you can use *too* many graphics in your reports. Try to keep a comfortable balance of text versus graphics. If you're not sure whether you have gone overboard, ask an associate to look it over and give you an honest opinion.

✔ **Paper and covers:** This is definitely *not* the place to scrimp. Use top-quality, heavyweight paper (24 pounds and up) for producing your reports. (See your stationer for details.) A transparent front cover that both protects and provides easy access to the cover page of your report and a heavy, color-coordinated back cover are pretty much the norm. Your local office supply store or stationer will be glad to give you a complete tour of the many different papers and cover stock selections available to you.

✔ **Binding:** For small- to medium-sized reports, use a comb, wire, tape, or special binding (such as Velobind) to hold your reports together. If you don't have your own binding system, you can take your reports to almost any printer or copy shop to get them done. Staples are definitely *not* the best way to make an impression with your clients. For larger reports, use good-quality three-ring binders.

✔ **Proofreading:** Don't, we repeat, don't let *any* report out of your hands until you take the time to check it closely for grammatical and typographical errors. Nothing can torpedo your credibility more quickly than to submit a report that is poorly written and riddled with mistakes and errors. Not only will the results of your work be judged suspect by your client, but so will you and your firm. *Guaranteed.*

You Can Make Great Presentations

Making successful presentations is a key skill for every consultant. Whether you are a management accountant recommending a new inventory-tracking system to a corporate operations team or a wedding consultant advising a happy couple on the optimal use of colors and flowers, a significant part of your job is the presentation of your advice and recommendations. And you'll do important presentations many, many times during the course of your career.

Although some people seem to be natural-born presenters, others grapple with making presentations before groups of *any* size or shape. If, like most of us, you think you fall in the second category, the good news is that you can dramatically improve your presentation skills with a little preparation and a little practice. And the better your skills, the more confident you'll be when you make your presentations. The net result of this cycle of improvement is that the presentations you make to your clients are much more convincing and successful.

Getting prepared to present

It's a very rare person who gets called up to a lectern with no warning and no preparation and gives a great presentation or speech no matter what the topic. For the rest of us, *preparation* is the key to giving a great presentation. In fact, for "knock 'em dead" presentations, you can figure on spending anywhere from one-half to one hour of preparation time for each minute of your presentation. In addition to the hints presented in the section that follows, be sure to check out *Successful Presentations For Dummies* (by Malcolm Kushner), published by IDG Books Worldwide, Inc., for a wealth of information on making great presentations.

The following tips can help you in preparing your presentation:

- ✔ **Describe what are you trying to accomplish.** What are the goals of your presentation and what are you going to have to do to achieve them? For example, the goals that you have in mind when you pitch a project to a prospective client (sell, sell, sell!) are substantially different from the goals you have in mind when you present an interim progress report on an ongoing project (to inform and to seek client buy-in). And because your goals are different, your presentations will be different, too. Be sure to tailor your presentation to achieve the goals you set and the outcomes you require.

- ✔ **Assess your audience.** You want your presentation to be as effective as it can be, so you need to think carefully about your audience and write the presentation exactly for those people. Although an audience of scientific researchers is likely to expect and appreciate a jargon-laden, highly technical presentation, the same presentation would quickly put a group of corporate administrative managers to sleep. Before you make your presentation, be sure to assess your audience. Just as a written report will end up in the circular file when it doesn't meet your client's expectations, a presentation that fails to "speak" correctly to your audience will miss the mark in communicating your message effectively.

✔ **Develop the heart of your presentation.** Start writing your presentation by outlining the major points that you wish to communicate to your clients. After you have developed your major points, note any subpoints and visual aids that you will use to support your presentation. Don't get overly ambitious; limit your major points to no more than three to five. If you have more information to communicate than you can "fit" into the actual presentation, convert the extra information into handouts that you give to your audience at the beginning of your presentation.

✔ **Write the introduction and conclusion.** The introduction of your presentation should do three things:

- Capture your audience's attention

- Provide a brief overview of the presentation

- Sell the members of your audience on the importance of the presentation

The conclusion of your presentation is just as important as the introduction. Your conclusion should do three things:

- Briefly revisit your key points

- Remind the members of your audience why your presentation is important to them

- Leave your audience feeling energized and inspired

✔ **Prepare your notes.** If you've given the same presentation many times before, you can probably get away without using notes. However, if you're making a new presentation or you're simply not 100 percent confident when you make presentations, preparing notes to assist you is not a bad idea. Having notes in your hand is a real help if you momentarily lose your place — a real confidence builder, by the way! — and they also ensure that you don't forget to cover any of your planned topics. Notes should be brief and specific; they aren't a word-for-word script of your performance, but merely a reminder of your key points.

✔ **Bring in reinforcements if necessary.** Depending on the nature of your project, its complexity, and the number of people you have working on it, you can consider bringing other project participants from your business into the presentation. This idea is particularly good when your project is highly technical. If you have experts on your staff who can add credibility to your recommendations and solutions, ask them to address specific aspects of the project as part of your presentation.

✔ **Practice makes perfect.** Depending on your personal comfort level or on the complexity of the information that you plan to present, you may find it advantageous to run through your presentation a few times before you present it. On one end of the spectrum, you may be comfortable simply running through your notes a few times the night before the big event. On the other end of the spectrum, you may prefer to rehearse your presentation in front of another person or even a video camera. If you're new to making presentations, don't worry. The more presentations you make, the better you'll get.

You can't be *too* prepared for a presentation. Make the most of the time that you have before your presentation because it pays off in a big way when the time comes to get up in front of your audience and start your performance. And believe us, every presentation you'll ever make is a performance, and, each time, you are the performer. Actors rehearse before every play — so should you.

The art of using visual aids

Did you know that scientists have proven that approximately 85 percent of all information received by the human brain is received *visually?* Think about that the next time you make a presentation. Though your spoken remarks may convey a lot of valuable information, the people in your audience are likely to understand and retain far more of the information when you present it to them visually.

Here's an example of what we mean. Peter actually saw someone make an hour-long presentation to the executive team of a high-tech computer software development company using viewgraphs full of tiny little words and numbers just like the ones in Figure 13-1. Needless to say, if you were sitting anywhere farther away than front-row center, the text and numbers became a blur of hieroglyphic-like gobbledygook. What really iced the cake was that the presenter read each and every figure directly from the transparencies. Ouch!

Not only was the presentation a needlessly painful experience for those of us who actually tried to focus our eyes on the screen and follow the presenter's train of thought (much to the delight of the aspirin industry), but the effective impact of the presentation was lost because the transparencies were impossible to read.

A much better alternative: Convert the mass of text and numbers into some simple graphs that convey the very same information. Figure 13-2 illustrates exactly what we are talking about. Use a viewgraph like this one instead of the viewgraph in Figure 13-1, and your audience has an instantaneous, visual understanding of the numbers. As the presenter, you can concentrate on explaining the meaning *behind* the numbers instead of wasting time just reading them to your audience.

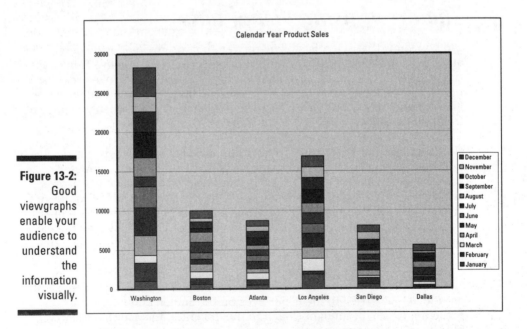

Calendar Year Product Sales						
	Washington	Boston	Atlanta	Los Angeles	San Diego	Dallas
January	1010	575	447	1819	554	150
February	2332	748	695	365	784	275
March	964	888	856	1635	254	365
April	2550	969	523	1450	699	184
May	3552	611	965	1788	955	432
June	2648	821	763	1193	419	231
July	1250	1352	712	1385	648	951
August	2451	1293	575	1230	499	785
September	3245	452	951	1721	744	626
October	2612	852	842	1521	654	441
November	1943	456	625	1352	951	239
December	3675	952	725	1420	842	855

Figure 13-1: A viewgraph that's painful on the eyes.

Figure 13-2: Good viewgraphs enable your audience to understand the information visually.

It took us many years of concentrated effort, but we eventually captured the essence of the visual element in presentations. Here for your consideration is the Nelson/Economy axiom of visual learning:

Information seen is remembered; information not seen is easily forgotten.

So how does this handy little axiom impact *your* presentations? It means that you should always consider your *visual* presentation as important as your *spoken* presentation. Whenever possible, think of ways to present your information *visually*. Maps, displays, product samples, prototypes, photographs, charts, and graphs are just a few of the many options available to you.

Visual aids serve a variety of purposes. First, visual aids are generally understood by your audience much more quickly than is spoken information. Second, your audience will retain the visual information that you present for a longer period of time than the information that you present verbally. Finally, visual aids help to make your presentation more interesting to your audience — especially when your topic is complex. Here are some of the most common kinds of visual aids used in presentations:

- **Handouts:** Providing your audience — no matter what size it is — with handouts of the information that you plan to cover — both text and graphics — can sometimes help your audience better follow your presentation. But heed this warning: Don't fall victim to the practice of providing handouts and then reading from them word for word; nothing is more boring to an audience than getting stuck in such a presentation. If you can break away from the text and speak directly from your heart and from your experience, not only will you be a more interesting and engaging speaker, but you'll dramatically improve your credibility with your audience, too.

- **White/chalk boards:** If you are working with a smaller group — say, up to about 30 people — using white boards and chalk boards is a very handy way of jotting down your main points as you proceed through your presentation. And if you make a mistake, you can simply erase it and write in the correct information.

- **Flip charts:** Like white boards and chalk boards, flip charts (those big pads of paper that mount on an easel) are good for making presentations to groups of up to about 30 people. However, the big advantage that flip charts offer over white boards and chalk boards is that you can prepare your entire presentation on the flip charts *before* the big event, in the privacy of your home or office. As an added bonus, you can scribble notes on the pages for emphasis as you speak. Want to get *really* wild? Use different colors of markers!

- **Transparencies:** When presenting a piece of information visually to a group of people — especially a *large* group of people (30 or more) — transparencies are hard to beat. With your computer, a printer (color would be nice), and a box of transparencies, you can turn anything on your computer into compelling visual aids quickly and easily. Need some help coming up with exciting graphics and formats? No problem. Simply load one of the popular presentation software packages onto your computer — Microsoft PowerPoint, WordPerfect Presentation, and Lotus Freelance Graphics all have their fans — and watch your presentations come to life. If you prefer, you can have your presentation graphics converted into 35mm photographic slides. As long as you don't mind carting around the special projector required to show them (few of your clients are likely to have one sitting around in the office), they are inexpensive, yet very professional in appearance.

✔ **Computer projection devices:** Wow! With the right equipment, you can put together a complete multimedia presentation on your laptop computer and then take your computer anywhere you like and project the whole presentation onto a full-size projection screen. For small groups, a color LCD computer projection panel hooked up to your laptop computer easily sits on top of any overhead (viewgraph) projector and adequately displays whatever is on your computer screen to your audience. For large groups, you can hook your computer up to one of the new, high-power multimedia projectors that can crank out a super-bright, 1,000+ lumen image onto a 30-foot-wide screen *and* integrate full-motion video, graphics, text, and sound capabilities all into one package. Taking your favorite technical guru along with you to these gigs may be a good idea, however!

Before you get too crazy with your visual aids, keep a couple of things in mind. First, don't try to squeeze too much information into any one aid. Use a large typeface (font), keep the number of words and numbers to a minimum (16 words or less, please!), and use color to improve the professionalism and readability of your visual aids. Second, have your presentation ready *before* you show up to make your presentation! You definitely won't impress your clients if you start your presentation by spending five minutes fumbling with your projector or paging through a disorganized stack of transparencies. Finally, don't forget that *you* are the heart and soul of your presentation — not your visual aids. Visual aids help to support your presentation, but they won't make up for a lack of preparation or for not being an informed presenter.

You're on stage: making your presentation

Okay, the time to prepare has come and gone, and you're ready to make your presentation. All your hours of hard work and preparation are about to pay off. Heed this advice as you start your presentation and you're sure to do a great job:

✔ **Relax!** Breathe deeply and visualize making a successful presentation before your audience. There's no need to be nervous. Don't forget: Your client is paying you because you are an expert in your chosen field. And you are, *right?*

✔ **Greet the members of your audience.** Besides making sure that everything is in order for your presentation, the opportunity to meet your audience is one of the main reasons for arriving early. Before you start your presentation, try to greet as many members of the audience as you can. Not only does this practice help you break the ice with your audience — reducing your nervousness in the process — but as a result, it helps generate more interest in you and what you have to say.

✔ **Wait for your audience's attention.** When you make a presentation, try to capture the full attention of your audience right at the start. You can ask for your audience's attention, or you can seek it by standing in front of your audience and saying nothing until everyone's attention is focused on you. If *that* doesn't do the trick, a couple of well-timed blasts from a portable air horn or megaphone are sure to get your audience's attention!

✔ **Make your presentation.** Jump in with both feet and don't look back. Start your presentation at the beginning and end it when you're done (and in even less time than you were allotted, if you can!). It's that simple. One more thing: When presenting, move about the stage a little and try to make eye contact with the critical decision-makers. Moving around helps make your presentation much more interesting to your audience. Making eye contact enables you to pick up on critical cues from your key clients. (For example, a finger rapidly drawn across your client's neck means that you have a *big* problem!)

As this chapter explains, there is a real art to getting your ideas across to your clients in an organized and effective fashion. Don't expect to be able to just wing it — it takes a great deal of work and preparation to prepare and execute killer reports and presentations. Fortunately, computers have done much to make preparation easier than ever before. In the next chapter, we consider how to make that technology work for *you!*

Chapter 14

Making Technology Work for You

*T*echnology plays a *big* part in your life as a consultant, regardless of what kind of consulting you do, where you do it, and who you do it for. Whether you need to make a phone call to a client across town, fax a contract to a subcontractor on the opposite coast, or type up a proposal on your computer and send it to an Australian colleague via electronic mail, technology makes all this and more happen — quickly and conveniently. And though the things that technology does for you are often truly awe-inspiring, much of the technology is as easy to use as simply picking up the phone and dialing, or clicking your mouse to send an e-mail message over the Internet.

You can easily devote a lot of effort to trying to stay up-to-date. But as soon as you think you've caught up with technology, it passes you again. You face a virtual smorgasbord of technology choices and decision points. Should you get a new PCS phone, or will a regular cellular phone suffice? How about a fax modem — should you buy one now or wait a few months until faster ones are available? Are a nationwide pager and 800 number best for your purposes, or is an answering machine attached to the phone in your office adequate? And what about a computer? Is a fast, slim laptop best, or would a powerhouse Pentium II multimedia desktop unit anchored to the desk in your office be even better?

The answers to these questions and others like them depend on the kind of consulting you do, where you do it, and your personal drive to be on the cutting edge of technological trends. If you're way out on the edge, you won't be happy unless you've got the newest, fastest, most exciting technology at your disposal. However, if you're like most people, you want someone else to work out the bugs and prove the worth of the latest technology before you buy into it.

In this chapter, we explore the most common technology and tools that consultants use to make their jobs easier, communicate more effectively and efficiently with their clients, and save time. Our intent is not to sell you on any one technology or provide an exhaustive look at *every* feature of *every* possible technology option or alternative at your disposal. The goal of this chapter is to present you with the latest information on the technologies that independent consultants commonly use to get their business done. Every consultant develops a unique set of tools. You may find that *your* needs differ considerably from the needs of your colleagues.

Keeping in Touch

Consulting is all about communication. Although old-fashioned face-to-face, one-on-one communication is still the best, sometimes you just can't be there with your clients, and you have to reach out and touch someone. You can use the latest technology to keep in touch with your clients in many different ways. In this section, we review some of the most important ways.

Let's talk: telephones and such

Ever since Alexander Graham Bell said, "Mr. Watson, come here; I want you," telephones have played a pivotal role in conducting business worldwide. Although the inherent physical qualities of these thin copper wires are being stretched to the outer limits through the use of fast modems, video transmissions, and the like, plain old telephones still work just fine, thank you.

Even if all you have is a plain-vanilla phone, you can subscribe to a variety of handy services through your local phone company. Call waiting, call forwarding, caller ID, conference calling, speed dialing, and many more calling features are available anytime for a small fee. All you have to do is order them.

Plain old telephones

Plain old telephones have served people well for the last hundred years, and they're probably going to serve us well for another hundred years. The simple fact is that most people have at least one or more copper phone lines going into their home or place of business, and standard analog phones are quite simple to use and very reliable. If you have only one tool to do business, it's most certainly going to be a telephone. Given the phone's versatility, its amazing range of access — you can call anyone in the world anytime you want — and its ubiquitousness, plain old telephones are also the hands-down winner in the contest of cost versus benefit.

When you set up your consulting business, consider these options:

- **Plain old telephones:** These are the no-frills, reliable, and rugged workhorses that you grew up with and learned to love. All you need to do is plug one of these babies into a telephone jack and it *works*. Period. If you prefer a few frills, you can get many basic features, such as redial, speakerphone, hold, caller ID, and other functions, built right in. And unless you want to buy a phone with extra-special features, such as 500-name personal phone directories, on-screen directory assistance, built-in digital answering machines, and more — which are admittedly quite fascinating (and often time-consuming and complicated to learn and use) — then you don't need batteries, outboard power supplies, or anything else.

- **Portable phones:** These are the wireless versions of plain old telephones. They are great for letting you run around your home or office while you look for something or for catching a few rays out on your deck while you follow up on your client calls. Forget the old-tech 49 MHz flavors and go with the newer 900 MHz varieties — preferably digital. Not only do these newer models work better and give you a longer range from handset to base, but they offer more security (you never know *who* is listening to your most intimate business or personal conversations!) than the older 49 MHz models.

- **Multiple phone lines:** While you're thinking about the basics of telephones, also consider the need for multiple phone lines. Most consultants quickly discover that one phone line is simply not enough to conduct business efficiently. If you're talking to a client on your single phone line while another client is trying to fax you a set of urgent questions in response to your proposal, someone is going to lose. (Guess *who?*) Two phones lines are considered a minimum for most single-person offices nowadays — one for voice and another for fax and Internet. And if you spend a *lot* of time online or you get a lot of faxes, you may need three lines to keep all your information moving along.

- **ISDN:** ISDN — which stands for *Integrated Services Digital Network* — is a special kind of digital signal transmission that enables you to put two separate phone numbers on one standard phone line. Or, if you choose, ISDN can enable your computer to send and receive data faster on a standard phone line —144 Kbps, or enough to transmit approximately 22 pages of single-spaced text every second — than the current conventional standard of 56.6 Kbps. However, ISDN is expensive and quirky, and you need to buy a special ISDN modem for your computer to handle the additional bits and bytes. And when and where ISDN is available (it still isn't in many areas), most local phone companies charge high fees for installation as well as for monthly access and usage. Our advice? Forget about ISDN. Enjoy your 56.6 Kbps modem and wait to replace it until you can get a cable modem through your cable television provider. At around 20 times the speed of ISDN, *that* will be cool.

Cellular telephones

Cell phones sparked a revolution in business. With the widespread introduction of cellular phones over the past decade, businesspeople were suddenly freed from their desks and their offices and were able to conduct business anywhere, anytime. Whether you're in your car, outside a client's office, at the airport, or anywhere else you can possibly imagine, you're now only a phone call away.

However, although cell phones are undeniably useful business tools — and will undoubtedly remain so for some time into the future — they are already starting to show their age. As any user of cell phones will tell you, dropped calls and ragged transmissions when crossing cells (as when you are driving across town in your car) are not uncommon, and you'll probably need a spare battery pack or two to get you through a typical workday. Not only that, but unscrupulous people can eavesdrop on most cellular phone conversations (they operate in the upper 800 MHz and lower 900 MHz radio bands) and easily clone your phone and sell it to people with even *fewer* scruples. So the next time you get a cellular phone bill with $3,500 worth of phone calls to Outer Mongolia, you'll know why.

Buying a cell phone and a calling plan is sort of like leasing a car — *lots* of options are available, and you have *lots* of fine print in the contract to worry about. Here are some of the things to consider when buying a cellular phone and signing up for a calling plan:

- ✔ **The phone:** You have at least a million different choices when picking out a new phone. Your first choice is whether to get a portable phone that you can carry anywhere or one that is hard-wired into your car — or both. Although portable phones offer the ultimate in convenience, they are not as safe to operate while you're driving your car. Plus, the batteries can get eaten up quickly when you're away from a source of power. Most phones share a number of convenience features, such as programmable one-touch speed dialing, alphanumeric displays, and the like. In a portable phone, key features to consider are size (most people like smaller phones), battery life (longer is better), and ease of use. Having lots of nifty programmable features doesn't do you much good if you can't figure out how to use them!

- ✔ **Phone purchase price and subscriptions:** Although you can spend several hundred dollars for your cell phone, a wide variety of high-quality phones are *free*. The catch is that you need to activate your cellular phone account with a particular carrier and subscribe for a year or more of service. Don't be surprised if you find, when you read the fine print, an activation fee of $25 to $50 *and* substantial penalties (up to $300 or $400) for early withdrawal. Whenever you buy a cell phone — whether it's free or not — make sure that you read the fine print of the agreement to see exactly what you're signing up to pay.

- ✔ **Monthly fees:** Most subscriptions require a minimum monthly fee of anywhere from $20 a month up to $50 or more. You pay this fee whether or not you make any calls in a given month. To make the monthly fees a bit more palatable, cell phone companies often offer a limited amount of "free" minutes of calling time each month, "free" weekend calling, or other incentives.

- ✔ **Airtime:** This is the charge that you pay for every minute that you use your cellular phone. If you are new to cell phones, you'll soon learn that — surprise, surprise — not only are you charged for the calls you make, but you're also charged for the calls that people make to *you*. No matter who initiates the call, you're charged a set rate per minute for airtime. And with most calling plans, the calls that you make during so-called *peak* times (conveniently scheduled during normal business hours) cost you more than the calls you make during *off-peak* times (on weekends and when you are normally asleep at night). If you call long-distance, that, of course, costs you even more, but fortunately, you don't have to pay more if someone calls *you* long-distance.

- ✔ **Bells and whistles:** Many cellular phone services offer lots of bells and whistles, such as call forwarding, three-way conferencing, paging, voice mail, and more. Sometimes, many of these options are offered for "free" with a subscription. Otherwise, you need to order each feature that you want and pay for it separately. Call forwarding and voice mail are both particularly useful additions to your cellular phone service.

Personal Communication Services (PCS)

When it comes to telephones that you can take anywhere, Personal Communication Services (PCS) phones are the next big thing, and they're here *today*. Although they look, feel, and work much the same as regular cellular phones, digital PCS phones are light years ahead. Sprint PCS — one of a number of firms that have been recently awarded PCS licenses by the government — launched its new service in San Diego, and Peter just *had* to jump on board. Not only did he buy one within a week of its introduction, but now he's one of PCS's biggest fans. Although PCS availability and service areas are still limited, expect to see it in your town soon if it isn't already there. Here are some of the features that separate PCS phones from the soon-to-be-ancient world of analog cellular:

- ✔ **100 percent digital:** Digital signals are much quieter than the old-fashioned analog signals that drive most cellular and portable phones, and calls are far less likely to be dropped or disconnected. And because digital signals already speak the same language as computers, you'll eventually be able to use your PCS phone to connect to your personal computer, reroute e-mail, download faxes, and more.

✔ **Encoded for security:** PCS phones use a special digital encoding process that assigns a unique code to each phone call. This process makes eavesdropping and cloning — a practice that's not uncommon with cellular phones — virtually nonexistent. To eavesdrop on your conversation, a potential listener would have to sort some 4 *trillion* individual codes. Good luck!

✔ **Batteries that go on and on and on:** You can keep your phone on standby — ready to receive calls — for up to 48 hours, and you get an honest four hours of talk time on *one* battery pack. That's more than twice as long as on conventional cellular phones.

✔ **Great pricing plans:** Peter is particularly proud of the pricing plan that he locked in for his new Sprint PCS phone. Not only did Sprint PCS guarantee no monthly access fees for the life of his account, but the cost of local calls will never exceed 35 cents a minute, and the first incoming minute is always free. Furthermore, Peter did not have to sign a contract or pay an activation fee, nor will he have to pay a penalty if he decides to terminate the service. As PCS phone services roll out in more and more places, expect the competition between PCS and cellular providers to get white-hot. This is good news because phone companies are beginning to offer some truly incredible pricing plans.

✔ **Lots of bells and whistles — for free!** Not only does Peter's PCS phone include all of the above features, but it also includes free voice mail and notification, free caller ID, free call waiting, free call forwarding, free three-way calling, and more. All for *no* monthly fee. Overall, the package is hard to beat.

Because PCS phones are so new, coverage areas will often be incomplete until the PCS companies finish building local infrastructures of transmission equipment, antennas, and other electronic stuff. Not only that, but a PCS phone from Seattle is currently useless when you try to use it in, say, Boston. To get around this problem, you can buy a phone that combines PCS *and* analog cellular capability into the same device. The phone automatically switches to one mode or the other, depending on whether it can tap into a PCS system. For those of you who travel a lot, this is really the best of both worlds.

Answering machines, voice mail, and pagers

What would phones be without their close relatives: answering machines, voice mail, and pagers? Unfortunately (or perhaps fortunately), you can't be available to answer your phone every minute of every day. That's where these little guys come in. Although they are essential tools for any consultant, they really can't fully replace a real, live person who answers the phone and is available to assist your clients in real time. Check out some of the basics of each tool, including pluses and minuses:

✔ **Answering machines:** Since distant, long-forgotten times, the way that most people answered calls after hours was to use an answering service where a real, (hopefully) living person actually picked up the phone and took a message. Unfortunately for the answering service industry, but fortunately for you, answering machines now make it possible for you to automate the process inexpensively and efficiently. When you look for an answering machine, forget the ones that use those old-tech cassette tapes and go for a digital machine. If your budget permits, consider one that shares the electronic innards with your telephone or fax machine.

✔ **Voice mail:** Voice mail is like an answering machine, but much better. Not only can you usually set up multiple mailboxes, but you also can speed up and slow down calls as you listen to them, archive them for future reference, and, if you're on the same system as your associates, forward messages to *their* mailboxes. Many voice-mail systems offer receipt of message notification by a light on the phone, a pager, or other method. As you know from calling almost any large organization within the past few years, voice-mail systems are now the receptionists of choice for telephone callers. *If you know your party's extension, please enter it now.* Independent consultants can obtain their own voice-mail systems in many ways. Many multimedia personal computers, as well as stand-alone modems, now come with built-in voice-mail systems — some of which can page you when you receive a message. And if you like, you can easily add voice mail to your home and business phone lines, as well as most paging and cellular phone services.

Two pieces of advice: Keep your greeting message up-to-date (Bob records a new message each week, informing callers of his general whereabouts and availability), and *religiously* check for new messages.

✔ **Pagers:** The biggest advances on the paging front have been the introduction of pagers that both receive *and* send messages, and the shrinking of pagers into packages as small as a wristwatch. Although pagers are inexpensive and reliable, they are gradually being supplanted in the market by portable telephones that incorporate paging features. If you're in the market for a pager, first check to see whether you can get the same service through your cellular or PCS phone and whether it makes sense from a cost perspective.

Internet phone

It didn't take long for some very smart people to develop a special kind of software that allows you to use your computer like a telephone over the Internet. "So what?" you say. The "so what" is that you can call someone in Ankara, Turkey, if you like, and talk as long as you want for no cost beyond the charge that you're already paying your Internet service provider for unlimited Internet access — for most people, about $20 a month. Hmmm . . . *very* interesting.

Before you get *too* excited, you need to know that some bugs in this software are still being worked out. The voice quality that most Internet telephone software provides really stinks, and to date, none of the Internet telephone software packages are compatible with any other Internet telephone software packages. For example, if you decide to buy Brand X's version of Internet telephone software, anyone you call *also* has to be using Brand X's software for you to communicate with one another.

Although it may be some time before Internet telephony comes into its own, keep your eye on these products. Because software technology changes so rapidly, the current problems with Internet telephony software may soon become a thing of the past, and the Internet telephone may become the bargain of the year.

Fax machines: essential business tools

Fax machines have made sending documents anywhere — from across town to around the world — simple, fast, dependable, and affordable. For no more than the price of a phone call, you can send reports, letters, memos, and other documents to your clients instantly. With the advent of the fax machine, along with its widespread acceptance and popularity (what business *doesn't* have a fax machine by now?), the speed of business has increased dramatically.

Along with a phone, a fax machine is truly an essential piece of business equipment for any consultant. The question then is not *should* you get a fax machine; the question is *what kind* of fax machine should you get. Consider a couple of the options:

- **Stand-alone fax machine:** The stand-alone fax machine is still the standard for most offices. As time goes on, it is getting faster and offering more features for less money. If you plan to fax original paper documents, such as signed contracts, newspaper articles, and photographs or other graphic images, a stand-alone fax machine is essential. Steer clear of the old-style faxes that use long rolls of thermal paper to image documents. Insist instead on a plain-paper fax machine — one that uses inkjet or laser printing technology to image regular $8^{1}/_{2}$-x-11-inch copier paper — that has at least a 14.4 Kbps modem. A multifunctional fax machine (fax, copier, scanner) can take care of your light scanning and copying needs. If funds permit, really splurge and buy your fax machine its own dedicated phone line. Your clients will really appreciate it!

- **Computer fax:** Most new computers already come with installed fax modems that allow you to send and receive faxes of document files. Computer fax software is *very* handy when you want to send documents that don't require signatures or you want to broadcast a fax to a large directory of clients. Just click your mouse a couple of times, and your computer does the rest. If you want to send signed original documents, photos, and such from your computer, you need to scan the documents first to create a file. This is a big pain in the neck, so it's better to save that task for regular stand-alone fax machines. One other thing: If you rely on your computer to *receive* faxes, you have to remember to keep your computer turned on 24 hours a day, 7 days a week — a practice that may reduce the life of your computer. Your best bet is to use your computer only to send faxes, and a standalone fax machine to receive them.

Electronic mail: It's free (well, sort of)

Although the jury is still out on whether the Internet has lived up to the tall expectations that many businesspeople and computer prognosticators and pundits had for it, e-mail is one of its shining successes. Now anyone can send electronic mail messages *and* attached computer files through the Internet to anyone who is online anywhere in the world. And if you're signed up for unlimited Internet access with an online service, such as America Online, or with an Internet service provider, such as AT&T WorldNet Service, you get to send and receive as much e-mail as you want at no additional charge. Not a bad deal considering the alternatives of snail mail (regular postal service) or expensive overnight mail services, such as FedEx.

We wrote 100 percent of *Consulting For Dummies* on our computers in San Diego, California. As we completed our chapters, we e-mailed them to Pam Mourouzis, the project editor in Indianapolis, Indiana, via America Online. After Pam edited the files, she e-mailed them back to us for our final review, modification, and approval. Whereas overnighting the chapters to Indianapolis would have cost us hundreds of dollars, it cost us just pennies to send them via e-mail. And they arrived at their final destination in *seconds* rather than hours or days.

Computers, Computers, and More Computers

If you're a consultant, you simply *must* have two things. The first thing is a phone. The second thing is a computer. Everything else — the office, the copier, the receptionist, the fax machine, the desk, the chair (okay, keep the desk and chair), and so forth — comes *after* you have your phone and your computer. If you're already knowledgeable about computers, you probably already have a setup that you like. However, if you're not, then all the advertisements and lingo can be bewildering, to say the least.

When you're deciding what kind of computer to buy, first determine how much you can afford to spend for your computer. Next, find a computer that meets your needs and is within your budget. Your goal is to get the most computer you can get for the amount of money that you have. Because few people can keep up on all the new products, read product reviews in magazines such as *PC World, Macworld,* and *PC* or check out computer technology-oriented Web sites such as c|net (http://www.cnet.com). Finally, buy it!

Regardless of what kind of computer you get, consider these basic components as the minimums you should consider. Otherwise, you may end up with a computer that's obsolete about ten minutes after you bring it home. Insist on a Pentium processor of at least 166 MHz, or the equivalent Apple PowerPC microprocessor. Get at least 16MB of RAM, a 2GB hard drive, an 8x CD-ROM drive, and at *least* a 33.6/14.4 Kbps data/fax modem.

Little computers

Laptop computers are great for consultants who are often away from the office visiting clients or who use their computers as personal scheduling and planning tools. There's nothing like the feeling of going to a local coffeehouse, ordering a cup of java and a toasted onion bagel with cream cheese, picking out a table in a cozy corner of the room, and opening up your computer and getting to work.

When Peter was writing his parts of *Managing For Dummies* (published by IDG Books Worldwide, Inc.), heading to a coffeehouse was almost an everyday occurrence for him. Bob often carries a laptop with him when he's on the road making speaking engagements. Instead of sitting in his hotel room late at night watching David Letterman reruns, Bob is often hard at work on a variety of projects. With a laptop computer, your office is wherever you want it to be, anytime you want it to be.

✔ **The good news:** Not only are laptops great for taking your office with you wherever you go — on an airplane, to a client's office, or to your cabin at the lake — but they are also *almost* as capable as the larger desktop computers. Pentium processors, multigigabyte hard drives, color monitors, tons of RAM, and CD-ROM drives are all the norm — in a battery-operated package that can easily fit in your briefcase. And for many portables, you can purchase a docking station — a product that enables you to plug your computer into a module that drives a full-sized monitor and keyboard. This can make your eyes and fingers *very* happy indeed.

✔ **The bad news:** On the downside, laptop keyboards are a bit cramped (okay, *very* cramped), and a typical battery holds only enough electricity to power your laptop for a few hours of use at most. Though you may be able to access a wall outlet for power in some locations (hotel, home, or office, for example), you may not in others (such as an airplane, train, or coffee shop). You may have to depend fully on the capability of your laptop's batteries to hold their charge. You also pay more for a laptop than for a comparable desktop computer with similar features. However, if your work often takes you out of the office, consider putting a small computer in your future.

If you prefer a computer that's *really* small — perhaps an electronic organizer or other hand-held computer — check out our discussion about them in Chapter 11.

Big computers

Desktop computers are the standard by which all other personal computers are measured. They offer the most technically advanced features for the money, and they are the first to receive the latest computing bells and whistles. If you spend a *lot* of time working on your computer — for example, if you do investment consulting and spend most of your workday watching the markets and performing complex financial analyses — *and* you have little or no reason to take your computer on the road or out of your office — then a desktop computer is just the ticket for you.

✔ **The good news:** Desktop computers offer numerous features that make them preferable to their portable counterparts. Keyboards are comfortable and spacious, and you can even get ergonomically correct versions, such as Microsoft's excellent Natural Keyboard. Large, easy-on-the-eyes 17-inch monitors are now pretty much the standard for desktop computers, and you get a faster Pentium processor, a larger hard drive, and better features overall in the desktop package than you get in a comparably priced laptop. And large amounts of extra space in the case allow you to easily install new hard drives, CD-ROM drives, Zip drives, and more. Not only that, but there are no batteries to run down every couple of hours!

✔ **The bad news:** On the downside, you can forget taking your computer anywhere, except to the repair shop when it breaks. Oh, and you don't look nearly as cool as you would pulling that sleek new laptop computer out of your briefcase at your local coffeehouse.

Things that plug into your computer

Once you have a computer, you'll soon discover that *many* things are available to plug into it. Consider the pluses and minuses of these options before you run out and make a purchase that you may later regret:

- ✔ **Multimedia:** Though the addition of multimedia capabilities — sound cards, stereo speakers, 3-D video cards, and such — doesn't have much of a direct work purpose for most consultants, they certainly can make your computer a *lot* more fun to work with. However, unless you work as a computer multimedia consultant or Internet consultant, your money is probably better spent on a faster microprocessor, a larger hard drive, or more RAM. Stick with the most basic multimedia accessories — a sound card and simple speakers — and put your money into the things that make you a more efficient, effective consultant.

- ✔ **Printers:** Printers are a very important consideration for consultants. When you are a consultant, the impression you make with your clients is critical to your ability to land their business. The printer you use to produce letters, reports, and other documents makes a *big* difference in the impression you make with your clients. The standard printer for business purposes is the laser printer, and you shouldn't consider anything less for *your* business. Not only do your documents look professional, but they don't smear like the documents that inkjet printers produce can and often do. Get the fastest printer you can afford (Peter's laser printer produces 12 pages per minute), and stick with tried-and-true brands, such as Hewlett Packard's top-notch series of LaserJet printers.

- ✔ **Backup systems:** You may think that it will never happen to you, but someday your hard drive could crash and all your client data could be lost along with its last dying breath. Do you have protection? Little old 1.44MB floppy disks just don't make it when it comes to backing up a 3GB hard drive. The best solution is to get a tape drive or Zip drive and do regular backups, which are a lifesaver in the event of a catastrophic failure of your hard drive. You can easily set your computer's operating system to do regular backups when your computer is inactive. Don't wait. Do it now before it's too late!

Doing That Internet Thing

You can't pick up a magazine or newspaper or watch TV for more than 15 minutes without being reminded — *constantly* reminded — that the Internet is the end-all, be-all technological and business innovation of all time. In many ways, it is. However, although the Internet — specifically Internet e-mail and the World Wide Web — *is* bringing about dramatic changes in the ways in which people communicate and do business, you have to be careful about separating the flood of Internet hype from reality.

In this section, we focus on the *reality* of the Internet, presenting the basics of using an Internet service provider and the advantages and disadvantages of large online services, such as America Online and The Microsoft Network. We end our discussion of the Internet with a quick peek at the World Wide Web.

Internet service providers: a dime a dozen?

Everyone seems to be getting into the business of providing Internet access. Not only are the local mom-and-pop firms that have been providing access for years, as well as the well-known online services such as America Online and CompuServe, still in the game, but now local and regional phone companies have joined in the fray, along with huge multinational phone companies, such as AT&T. Cable television providers, such as Time-Warner, are hitting the market with super-fast connections through their new fiberoptic cable networks. As a result of all this competition, prices for Internet access continue to decline.

No matter where you live, you can probably find a wide variety of Internet access providers that would just *love* for you to sign up with them. But be careful. Some providers are better than others. Here are some things to consider when you start your search for an Internet service provider (ISP):

- **Price:** No matter *who* you get your service from, flat-rate monthly pricing is now the standard. For a predetermined price, normally about $20 a month, you get unlimited access to the Internet. Local ISPs often offer even lower rates, especially if you're willing to commit to paying for a year of service in advance. Carefully weigh the benefit of a lower monthly fee versus committing yourself to one ISP for a long period of time.

- **Accessibility:** Your ISP should provide you with a local access phone number that you can call for free. If you're far from a big city, some providers can provide you with a toll-free 800 or 888 number for access. The rule is to use a national provider if your business takes you on the road a lot, and a local provider if you don't travel much. But having a local access number is just part of the equation. When you call it, can you get connected? As more and more people jump online every day, these phone numbers are getting bombarded with calls from hungry Net surfers. Getting busy signals during times of peak usage is not uncommon. (Coincidentally, these times no doubt coincide with the very times that *you* want to get online.) If the ISP you're thinking about signing up with offers a free trial period, use this time to determine how accessible the system is before you make your final selection. Note how often you get a busy signal or are denied access to the system. If these problems are happening too often, shop around for another ISP with better capacity. There are plenty to choose from.

✔ **Speed:** Just as some ISPs are easier to connect with than others, some ISPs offer faster connections — or more *bandwidth* — than others. Bandwidth refers to the amount of information that can flow through a channel at once. More bandwidth means faster connections for you, the customer. Make sure that your visits to the World Wide Web don't become an exile to the World Wide *Wait!* Don't forget that you often get what you pay for. A super-cheap monthly rate may translate to super-slow service.

✔ **Reliability:** Dropped calls and service cutoffs are no fun — especially when you're 25 minutes into a 35-minute file download. If you find that your calls are getting dropped too often — as far as we're concerned, more than once or twice a month is *too* often — take yourself and your business on a shopping trip for a new ISP.

✔ **Other services:** In addition to being able to access all the wonders of the Internet in their full glory (the preceding message has been paid for by the Friends of the Internet Committee), including the World Wide Web, e-mail, newsgroups, chat, and more, most ISPs also offer a wide variety of other services to their clients. Many ISPs provide free space on their servers for their customers' Web pages, as well as fee-based services for designing and maintaining Web pages. If you just don't have the time or interest to do this yourself, make sure that the ISP you select *does*.

Online services: the dinosaurs of the Internet?

Although established online services, such as America Online and CompuServe, have taken some pretty big hits from Internet service providers recently, they aren't dead yet. Not long ago, these content-based information providers focused on offering such things as chat rooms, access to online magazines such as *Business Week* and *Inc.* and newspapers such as the *Chicago Tribune* and *The New York Times,* bulletin boards for a wide variety of affinity groups — from lovers of alternative music to organic gardeners to political junkies — and professions, online encyclopedias, and much, much more. Access to the Internet was merely an afterthought. However, the explosive growth of the ISPs has given the major online services a big wake-up call, and they are reorganizing themselves to become more Net-centric.

Should you choose a major online service over an ISP? If you are new to accessing the Internet, the answer is yes. Services such as America Online and The Microsoft Network are *very* user-friendly for the Net newbie. (See Doug Lowe's *The Microsoft Network For Dummies* or John Kaufeld's *America*

Online For Dummies, 3rd Edition, both published by IDG Books Worldwide, Inc., for more information.) An online service is a great place to learn *netiquette* — personal etiquette on the Internet — and how to get around. However, if you are already experienced with the Internet and you don't need the additional bells and whistles that the major online services offer (you can find most of them on the Internet, anyway), go with an ISP. Your connections to the Internet will be more direct and faster as a result.

The wonderful World Wide Web

The World Wide Web is the Internet version of the Holy Grail for most business people. With all the media hype about the billions and billions of dollars of yearly commerce that's waiting just around the corner (we're still looking to find the corner!), it's no wonder that many people feel compelled to establish a presence on the Web. Should you?

Although you may read a handful of stories about glittering successes that began through a company or person marketing its wares on the Web, many companies have sunk a *lot* of money in marketing on the Web with little or no return. In consulting, word-of-mouth referrals from satisfied clients will probably create a *lot* more business than establishing a Web presence will. If you do decide to use the Web to market your services, see Chapter 23 for more information about the how-tos and wherefores. Until you're sure that your efforts are going to pay off, keep your investment to a minimum.

Bill Eastman uses the Internet to his advantage — and his clients'

Bill Eastman is president of the Applied Innovations Group, a business consulting firm located in Gloucester, Virginia [(804) 693-3696, e-mail to epriseos@aol.com]. Applied Innovations specializes in using the Internet to maximize its impact in markets that have traditionally been underserved in the consulting industry — service companies at $20 million in annual revenues with plans to make the leap to $100 million, and those companies in the manufacturing sector that are currently at $100 million in annual revenues with plans to make the leap to $500 million. We spoke to Bill about the impact of the Internet on consultants.

Consulting For Dummies: Does your firm specialize in any particular area of business consulting?

Bill Eastman: About four years ago, we made the transition to consulting strictly on service quality, whether it's service quality to external or internal customers. We look at service quality throughout the entire delivery chain. As one of the coauthors with Ken Blanchard of

(continued)

(continued)

the *Raving Fans* training program, we took our consulting expertise, brought it together, and put it into *Raving Fans*. That has led us more into the areas of strategy formulation, strategic marketing, and so forth.

CFD: How do you use the Internet to your advantage, and to the advantage of your clients?

Eastman: Applied Innovations provides the same quality and type of consulting that the large companies such as McKinsey & Company and Andersen Consulting provide, but at a price our customers can afford by using the Internet as a delivery methodology — charge a fee that they can afford. But we can also maximize our labor because it's the face-to-face time that you're billing as a consultant and you can only be in one place at one time. Not even Star Trek can help you with the transporter! With the Internet, you can service many clients at the same time so the end result is that your per-day fees will actually be higher, but what you deliver to the client will be at a lower price.

CFD: So you're in essence parallel processing your clients.

Eastman: Absolutely. To do that in the old model, you needed a consulting firm with lots of people resources. The Internet allows fewer people who can multitask to provide the same quality as a huge operation.

CFD: Do you use the Internet to collect data on service quality when you work with your clients?

Eastman: Yes, we use the Internet extensively for research in two ways: searching the net and learning from our present clients. We can't use it for everything yet, because not everything is on the Net yet, but it's getting close. We engage in the usual visitations with newsgroups and user groups and track down anything that a particular company has done, or what's going on in a particular industry with the goal of performing background research before we make our first contact. I'm finding that if I don't understand a potential client's business as well as they do, then I don't have much chance at getting the job. You've got to wow them at your first meeting. You've got to leave them thinking, "Gee, I didn't think of that," or "I had never looked at it that way," or "I've never heard that." If you can get one or two of those in the first meeting, unless you've priced yourself out of the market, you've got the business. I'm looking for people to be blown away at least a couple of times in this half-hour to 90-minute meeting. The other and potentially greater competitive advantage is using artificial intelligence and fuzzy logic to mine with our existing clients. This one is really exciting because client intelligence will be our greatest asset.

CFD: There's been lots of talk about the future of business on the Internet and, for the most part, it seems that the results haven't matched the hype. Should consultants have a presence on the Net and, if so, why?

Eastman: I see the Internet as really the next domain for consultants. Right now consulting is a very large and unfragmented industry. If you look just at the United States, the top ten companies have less than 10 percent of the total market share. That means that there are a lot of small, "mom-and-pop" operations — university based or small boutiques. What I think the Internet is going to do is to provide smaller companies and organizations with the opportunities to get the same advice as the large companies get; and it is an excellent way for smaller firms to become a larger presence. That's why we focus on the smaller, growth industries. Companies that are thinking of growing at 10 percent annually are *not* on our list. Companies that are building strategies to grow at 10–20 percent quarterly *are*.

CFD: We're hearing lots about the future of virtual businesses. It seems that developing a talented and responsive network of other consultants to draw from is a definite must for any successful consulting firm today. Do you agree?

Eastman: Absolutely. You'll never be able to get big in the consulting business if you don't have access to resources. What the virtual mindset provides you is a way to do that without incurring costs, because — as in *any* consultant business — you want to avoid fixed costs like the plague. Everything must be variable cost, because then your cash flow demands are a lot less. The consulting business has tremendous yields, but it takes large sums to support client acquisition, delivery, and maintenance operations.

CFD: Sure, and since your overhead is low, you have the option of passing that on to your clients in the form of lower fees.

Eastman: That's right. Other than paying for my part of the building and paying the normal utilities and phones, I have almost no fixed cost. So everything can be billed to the client. Of course, that then gets into how you set up your accounting systems. We're using activity-based costing as our approach so we know what every activity costs. When we put together a contract with a client, we're pretty confident that we know where the margins are. So when we're negotiating on price, and the client thinks we're coming down or off the price — which we are — I know exactly what that means in terms of margins.

CFD: How do you use the Internet to create value?

Eastman: Number one is we're doing away with the need to be on site with the client except when it makes sense. Number two, we don't have to steal a lot of our clients' payroll hours by bringing vast numbers of people together in meetings. What we can do using the Internet, either through some sort of collaborative computing, chat rooms, or by e-mail, is that we can get a lot more project work done. As a result, we've reduced the amount of face-to-face meetings by two-thirds.

CFD: Wow — that's phenomenal! Have you done any videoconferencing yet?

Eastman: We've played with it some, but the technology is still a bit cranky. But I would say that by the end of 1997, videoconferencing will be a fact of life. Consider this: The average airfare is about $600 a plane ticket. By using videoconferencing instead of traveling, we can reduce our variable costs to the clients by 50% or more.

CFD: What do you think about *Megatrends* author John Naisbitt's assertion that as we get more high-tech, we have to become more high-touch?

Eastman: I agree — a *lot* of personal contact is going to be required to offset these great advances in technology.

CFD: How does that affect the consulting work that you do over the Internet?

Eastman: That's where I believe that we're going to see this convergence of technology and companies such as CU-SeeMe, which is probably the premiere operation in videoconferencing as we speak. Pretty soon, not only will you be able to videoconference, but also you'll be able to combine several technologies: whiteboards, videoconferencing, training networks, and so on where everyone will share the information and it will almost be like being there. What the Internet is going to provide is a medium where you're going to feel like you're all together, even though you're looking at a screen — a screen that more than likely will be a digital 35- or 40-inch television/computer screen.

(continued)

(continued)

CFD: What kind of computer, Internet, and telecommunications setup do you have?

Eastman: We're using a network of three computers. One is a Pentium 100 single processor that we use as our Internet node — our communications computer. It's networked with a dual-processor Pentium 200 MMX. The dual-processor computer is the workstation — the workhorse. To be on the Net, you have to be careful because of security concerns, so the node machine is a firewall that prevents viruses, obtrusion, or people somehow trying to sabotage your system. And I also use a laptop computer for roadwork and remote access to the office network. We are investigating satellite hookup for our Internet uploads and downloads, while currently we're using both an Internet Service Provider (ISP) and America Online (AOL). America Online is the backbone of our system. The rationale behind that is that, for the price, you can't touch it.

CFD: Some Internet pundits have said, perhaps prematurely, that online services such as America Online are on the way out and ISPs are on the way in. What's your point of view about that?

Eastman: Part of that depends upon your level of expertise and the depth of your pockets. If you are really a Net weenie, and technologically you're able to ride the wave, you can work with a local ISP and probably do a reasonably good job. The thing that AOL gives you is it's a no-brainer. You load the software, you click your mouse, and it works. AOL will build Web sites for you, their chat rooms are first-class — AOL is a Microsoft in the making. They have had some bad times, but, I'll be honest with you, part of AOL's problem has less to do with them and is more indicative of the entire telecommunications network.

CFD: But isn't the problem at least partly of their making? Their user base recently doubled from approximately 4 million to 8 million users virtually overnight.

Eastman: What AOL is suffering from is a bigger problem than that. The twisted-wire phone technology, in almost universal use today, is at its limits. Because AOL is so large, they're taking the beating for this technology limitation, but they're taking the beating for USWest, Bell South, GTE, and the other local phone companies. It's an infrastructure problem, and AOL, being the largest online service on the block, is also the largest target for the press, who just happens to love to beat on big companies. My recommendation to anybody in the consulting business (especially start-ups) would be to start with AOL and use their incredible expertise because they're the best in the business. And they will continue to be the best in the industry because Steve Case and the rest of the crew there run a great company.

CFD: So what does the Internet mean for most businesses?

Eastman: What the Internet is really about for businesses using it as a competitive tool is a shifting of power from the producers to the consumer, customer, and client. Now, because you can interact with the customer, the customer custom designs their product before they receive it. The revolution is, instead of the traditional view of markets where if the market doesn't have $500 million out there, you don't produce anything, you now can break the market into little niches — and the customer does it for you. If you're a one-person operation, a $15,000 to $25,000 niche has a decent margin; a $100,000 niche has incredible margins.

Part IV
Setting Up
Your Business

The 5th Wave — By Rich Tennant

"FIRST HARRY CONSULTED FOR BOWLING ALLEYS, SO WE TOOK UP BOWLING. THEN HE CONSULTED FOR GOLF COURSES, SO WE TOOK UP GOLF. NOW HE'S CONSULTING FOR SURGICAL INSTRUMENT MANUFACTURERS AND FRANKLY, I HAVEN'T HAD A FULL NIGHT'S SLEEP SINCE."

In this part . . .

Despite rumors to the contrary, becoming a consultant is not quite as easy as simply printing up a set of business cards and waiting for clients to come walking through the front door. Consulting is a business, and there are right ways and wrong ways to set up a consulting practice. In this part, we talk about the *right* ways to set your fees, negotiate contracts, establish an office, track your time and your money, and use support services.

Chapter 15

What Are You Worth? Setting Your Fees

• •

In This Chapter

▶ Establishing your value

▶ Structuring your fees

▶ Creating client value

▶ Changing your fees

• •

The topic of setting fees probably makes an independent consultant more uncomfortable than any other topic. Consultants are comfortable when they are recommending the placement of columns for proper support of a massive steel I-beam, the implementation of a new performance review system, or the installation of new software to run a company's Web server. After all, they are experts in those fields. But setting fees is another matter. Just ask consultants their price and watch the reaction. Many suddenly get all flustered, soft, and tentative. And if a client balks at a consultant's quoted price, explaining that other consultants do double the work for half the price, some consultants quickly discount their prices in a desperate effort to gain or retain the client's business, doing whatever it takes.

Why does fee setting make so many consultants so uncomfortable?

When you're a consultant, pricing your services is a constant balancing act. Set your fees too low, and you may not only be flooded with more business than you can handle, but you won't make enough money on the business to recover your expenses and make a profit. Set your fees too high, and you may get a few high-fee jobs but not enough to keep your business afloat. The end result is that consultants are in a constant state of uncertainty when pricing their services.

You don't have to operate this way. Although setting fees with clients and (heaven forbid!) increasing them from time to time can occasionally be a painful experience, it's essential to your ability to make a living as an independent consultant. If you're going to thrive as a consultant, therefore, you need to do three things soon after you set up shop:

✔ Develop a fee structure that allows you to achieve your goals for financial and personal independence.

✔ Become a master at selling the value that you offer your clients and at getting your client to focus on results, not rates, activity, or time. Your clients respond to your confidence!

✔ Quickly overcome any hang-ups that you have about putting a price on your time and selling your skills and services to others.

As your business becomes better established, you must constantly refine those three things.

This chapter discusses putting a value on the expertise that you bring to your clients, determining how much you need to make for your business to thrive, structuring your fees, and deciding when to modify your fees and when to stand firm on them.

How Much Are You Worth to Your Clients?

How much do *you* think you're worth? $1? $10,000? $1 million? More? If we really pressed you for an answer, we probably could get you to come up with a number. However, regardless of the number you select, it's meaningless unless it is based on what your *clients* think you are worth.

One of the first lessons to learn about pricing your services is that you should always focus on the value that you bring to your clients and not only on your *own* opinion of worth. In some cases, your clients' perception of your value may far exceed your own perception of your value. In other cases, your clients' perception of your value may be disappointingly less than your own perception of your value. The fact is that you really can't know how much you're worth to your clients until you talk to them and get a sense of the problems they face and the cost to them of alternate solutions.

In this section, we consider some factors that determine your value as a consultant to your clients.

Why hire a consultant?

When exploring the philosophical question of how much you are worth to your clients, you may find it useful to explore why organizations hire consultants in the first place.

When faced with a problem, your clients have many alternatives for resolving it. The primary options include assigning a current employee to the task or hiring a new employee to take on the assignment. However, these approaches can often bring their own problems, and they may not be the most cost-effective ways to arrive at the best solution. In addition, when faced with hiring their own employees, your clients may not be able to find *any* candidates with a consultant's unique credentials and high level of expertise.

So why do organizations hire consultants? The following reasons are some of the most compelling:

- ✔ **Because consultants are experts:** This is one of the main reasons that organizations hire consultants. Many people in an organization may be able to take on a necessary assignment, but none can do the job as quickly and efficiently as an expert who every day lives and breathes the issue to be addressed. The end result of hiring an expert consultant is an overall savings in time and money — often with better results than if the assignment were performed in-house by the organization's employees.

- ✔ **Because consultants are independent:** When an organization hires a consultant, it is hiring an independent contractor, not an employee. This simple fact has all sorts of implications. Consultants work closely with their clients, but consultants do not require the kind of direct supervision that employees performing comparable tasks do. And the client controls payment — an especially popular point for the people who hire consultants. If a consultant doesn't perform in accordance with the terms of the consulting contract, a client can by all rights withhold payment — or stop using that consultant.

- ✔ **Because consultants are objective, outside third parties:** Consultants often bring a fresh point of view to an organization that may have lost its perspective. In many organizations — especially those where employees are afraid to speak against the status quo for fear of losing their jobs — only an outsider can do the job. Sometimes only an outside consultant can clearly see the broken organizational systems and dysfunctional management behaviors that disable the firm. Outsiders also can make recommendations that break through to the decision-makers who most need to hear them.

- ✔ **Because consultants have dedicated time:** Time may be a precious element among an organization's existing staff. A person or group may be assigned to a project and then later taken off the project because of conflicting priorities. An outside consultant, on the other hand, can focus on the task or project until the work is completed.

- ✔ **Because consultants are a flexible resource:** Most consultants make themselves available to their clients — especially their *best* clients — on a moment's notice. If an organization had to hire someone new to take on an assignment, it could spend *months* to place ads, perform interviews and reference checks, make a final selection, and bring a new employee on board. On the other hand, if the organization wants to hire a consultant, all someone needs to do is pick up the phone and make a call. Before that person can say, "Where should I go for lunch today?" a consultant is at the organization's disposal.

- ✔ **Because there's no long-term commitment:** When an employee completes a special project, an organization may find itself scrambling to place the employee in another position within the organization. When a consultant completes a special project, he or she simply goes away. There is no two-week notice, no termination, no layoff, no severance pay, no nothing. Consultants *do* develop long-term relationships with organizations, but only when *organizations* desire long-term relationships with particular consultants or consulting firms.

- ✔ **Because the price is right:** When you tally up the costs of hiring an employee to take on a task versus bringing in a consultant to perform the same task, going with a consultant may be more cost advantageous. An organization does not have to pay for health insurance, vacation time, 401(k) plans, or other benefits when it hires a consultant. Using a consultant is a cost-effective alternative for organizations that need to solve a problem quickly and efficiently. We explore *why* this is true in the next section.

Can you do it better, for the same price or for less?

Although all the considerations named in the section "Why hire a consultant?" are important for determining your value to your clients, the ultimate question is: *Can you do the work better than anyone else, and can you do the work for the same amount or for less?* If the answers to both parts of that question are *yes*, then you provide value to your clients that justifies a hiring decision in your favor — regardless of the amount of money you charge.

The point is — and we're going to keep repeating this until you believe it — that you should focus on the value you provide to your client, *not* on the hourly rate or on the number of hours that you need to complete a job. Keep this distinction uppermost in your client's mind, too. On the surface, asking for a fee of $100 an hour may appear to be *very* optimistic at best and insulting to your client at worst. However, suppose that a client has to invest almost $100,000 a year to hire a full-time employee to have the same effect that you can have in 40 hours each month — for $48,000 a year. In that case, you provide incredible value to your client, especially if you also provide a better product than any employee can.

Here's an example of what we mean: Say that your client wants to create a media presence for her large mail-order clothing business. She has a choice: She can hire a part-time or a full-time employee, or she can hire you, the public relations expert to beat *all* public relations experts — for a fee that, at least on the surface, appears to be pretty steep. The first thing to consider is the cost of each alternative to your client. In Case A, your client decides to hire a full-time employee for $25 an hour. In Case B, your client hires *you* for $100 an hour. On the surface, hiring an employee seems to make the most sense. Right off the bat, your client is going to save $75 an hour — right?

Take a look.

Case A: Hire a new employee to take on public relations chores.

Hourly pay rate	$25.00
Fringe benefits rate @ 35%	+ 8.75
Overhead rate @ 50%	+ 12.50
Total effective pay rate	$46.25
Hours per year	× 2,080
Total annual labor cost	$96,200

In Case A, the new employee is paid a wage of $25 an hour. However, this wage is not the true cost to the organization. The cost of benefits for the employee (health insurance, life insurance, 401(k) plan, and so on) weighs in at 35 percent of the hourly wage, or $8.75. Overhead — electricity, facilities, computers, and so forth — costs the organization another 50 percent of the employee's wage, or $12.50 for each hour worked and paid. This brings the new employee's total hourly cost to the organization to $46.25 an hour — almost double the wage paid to the employee for each hour worked. When you multiply the hourly rate by the standard number of hours in a work year, the grand total for the new employee comes to a whopping $96,200.

So what happens if the organization hires a consultant to do the same job?

Case B: Hire a consultant (you!) to take on public relations chores.

Hourly pay rate	<u>$100.00</u>
Total effective pay rate	$100.00
Hours per year	× <u>480</u>
Total annual cost	$48,000

Surprise, surprise. Your client actually *saves* almost $50,000 by contracting with you rather than hiring a full-time employee. Although your hourly rate is *more* than the new employee's rate in Case A, your client saves the cost of the benefits and overhead that would have to be applied to a new employee's wage. Not only that, but because you are presumably more experienced, more efficient, and better connected than the employee, you'll need to devote far less time to the project to get the same results — only 480 hours a year versus 2,080 for the employee.

When your client contracts with your business, *you* bear the cost of fringe benefits and overhead. Your client has to pay only the hourly fee that you agree to. In addition, if things don't work out, your client can terminate the relationship quickly and easily; the client doesn't have to worry about messy employee firings or unemployment benefits.

Which deal do *you* think is the better one?

Are you selling a commodity or a customized solution?

Part of the final determination of your value to potential clients depends on whether the service you provide has been reduced to a commodity in the marketplace. By *commodity,* we mean that the services offered by various providers are equivalent in clients' eyes and that price is the primary factor that determines who is going to get the job.

For example, suppose that an organization is going to hire a consultant to prepare a business plan. If the organization has several business consultants to choose from — all with very good references — it will probably hire the business consultant who gives the best price. In this case, the service that this consultant offers has been reduced to a commodity in the organization's eyes.

Now, say that a unique organization is looking for a consultant who shares its vision and is compatible with the way the organization works. The organization interviews a variety of business consultants, but only one consultant shares the organization's vision and meshes well with its personality. This same consultant also proposes to deliver a customized solution that is unique and better suited to this particular business than the other proposals. In this case, the business consultant is delivering a customized solution, and price is not the determining factor in the client's mind.

These scenarios reflect the way the consulting business works. If your product is the same as everyone else's, then your clients consistently look for the least expensive solution to their problems. The eventual result of this kind of pressure is that *all* the consultants offering these kinds of services are forced to cut their prices until hardly anyone is making any money at all. You're stuck in the commodity trap, and you can't get out! This is *not* a good situation.

If you find yourself stuck in the commodity trap, your first priority should be to find a way to get out — and fast! Here are some tips for making the services you offer stand out in a crowd and for moving your offerings out of the dark and rainy realm of commodity and into the sunny land of customized solutions:

- **Add value.** Do more for your clients than they expect you to do, and you add value to your work — the kind of value that sets you apart from your competitors. You don't need to do anything dramatic; all you need to do is consistently give more — even a *little* more — than you promise, and your clients will know the difference. For example, if you promise to complete your project in 30 days, try to delight your client (and add value to your work) by delivering early — perhaps in 25 days. The little things *do* make a difference in the eyes of your clients.

- **Be different from your competition.** When you're caught in the commodity trap, do whatever you can to make the services that you offer *different* from those your competitors offer — especially in ways that your clients value. This means getting to know your competition, the services they offer, and how they deliver them to their clients. What can you do to make your clients realize that you're offering a unique solution instead of a run-of-the-mill solution? Offer free pickup and delivery? Use higher-quality materials than your competitors? Be available 24 hours a day for emergency service? Customize part or all of the products and services you deliver to each client? Decide how to make your services different from your competition and then do it!

- **Focus on customer service.** If you are in a business in which most consultants deliver pretty much the same products or services, one of the best ways to stand out from the crowd is by providing unparalleled customer service. Unparalleled customer service starts with something that doesn't cost any money at all: a positive, can-do attitude. Your attitude says that you are making your customer your number-one priority and that you are doing whatever it takes to make your customer's consulting experience the best one possible.

✔ **Do great work.** Despite being paid small mountains of money, some consultants simply don't do a very good job. Not only that, but some consultants deliver their products late, if at all. If you do great work and deliver on schedule at the agreed price, your clients will seek you out and will be happy to pay a premium for your work. We know from personal experience that finding consultants who are both talented and capable of following through on promises of quality and delivery can sometimes be a challenge. However, consultants who do high-quality work and deliver it on or before the deadline are well worth the extra money.

✔ **Build long-term relationships.** Nothing sets you apart from the rest of the pack more than developing long-term relationships with your clients. The more work you do for your clients and the deeper your work *and* social relationships with your clients, the less likely your clients are to shop around for other consultants to take your place. And the more work you do for the same clients, the better you understand their operations and their unique needs. This understanding can help you to continue to improve the work you do for them.

Establishing high value-added fees at The Poretz Group

Doug Poretz is the founder and principal of The Poretz Group (phone 703-506-1778, e-mail info@poretz.com), an investor relations consulting firm formed in 1991 and located in McLean, Virginia. Typical clients are the chairpersons, CEOs, and CFOs of publicly owned companies. The role of The Poretz Group is to help clients develop a strategy and implement a program to communicate with the investment community, including stockbrokers, mutual fund portfolio managers, money managers, analysts, and others. In this first part of our interview with Doug (the second part is in Chapter 17), we discuss his approach to obtaining high value-added fees from his clients.

Consulting For Dummies: Exactly how did you go about establishing high value-added fees with your clients?

Doug Poretz: Before I address that question, I need to tell you a little about how I came to start a business. The first question I had to face was "Why am I going into business?" I brought to the entire process the premise that you go into business either for wages — high salary — or for equity buildup, that is, to build an institution that will have value and therefore create wealth, or your goal can be a blend of the two.

CFD: Which way did you decide to go?

Poretz: At the time I started my business, I felt that a combination of factors — the economy at the time, my experience, my name recognition, my immediate market, and so on — didn't make feasible the goal of building a business for equity. So I would work for wages. As a consequence, if you want to work for wages, it's quite simple: You want as big a top line as possible and as small an expense line as possible.

CFD: The rest you get to keep.

Poretz: Right. So I decided that a small expense line would, of course, require low overhead — primarily in terms of people.

CFD: Sure, people are usually the largest expense for *any* business.

Poretz: Exactly. The second largest expense would be real estate. I *had* my own real estate. I had been vice president of a very large, publicly owned home-building company prior to forming my own company. I took that time to build a custom home with the space for an office built in. So to keep expenses low, I wouldn't have people. But if I were going to try to avoid employing people but still have as my clients the chairmen, CEOs, and CFOs of publicly owned companies, I had to provide a high-quality service in terms of accessibility. I thought that an investment in technology for voice mail, e-mail, and so on would cost less than a person and would be *much* easier to control for a one-person business.

CFD: Definitely.

Poretz: And I would be available 24 times 7 — that is, 24 hours a day, 7 days a week. I need to be accessible, so my "receptionist" needs to be accessible. I didn't look at the installation of that technology as an expense that was costly. I looked at it as an expense that, one, had to provide a high level of service and, two, was much less costly than a person — especially a good person. So I was willing to pay a premium for the technology that would replace the people. The other thing that I needed to do was provide high value-added services to get the high fees that I wanted. To provide that, I needed two things: first, my own experience, knowledge, contacts, and so on — which required a high-quality database to manage my experience — and second, the resources that would allow me to maximize my experience. That meant bringing in information services such as a Bloomberg box so that, when my clients called me, I could tell them about their stocks in real time.

CFD: What's a Bloomberg box?

Poretz: Bloomberg Financial Business News is a system that you'll find in stock brokerage firms. It is probably the most robust information system I discovered that's available.

CFD: So it's beyond just stock quotes?

Poretz: It's massively beyond stock quotes. It has news, analytical reports, fundamental data, historical data, and more, for every publicly traded financial instrument worldwide — and it's all in real time. I approached my office not in terms of any expenses per se. Instead I considered two things: whether those expenses helped me earn value-added fees for offering value-added service and whether those expenses helped maximize my service to my clients.

CFD: So you're really leveraging yourself through these tools.

Poretz: Yes. And it was based on the premise that, as a one-person business, I wanted to command value-added fees that were as high as possible while at the same time keeping expenses as low as possible. I did not go into business with the goal of creating a one-person home-based business. I went into business with the goal of creating a business that can solve problems for prospective clients who would pay me a high fee.

(continued)

(continued)

CFD: Why is that?

Poretz: If you're going to get paid a high value-added fee, then you don't need *every* prospective client to fall in love with you and hire you. You only need that if you're going to get a *low* fee — a commodity fee — in which case you need high volume. So if you're going to get a high value-added fee and you don't need every prospective client to fall in love with you, then you want clients to fall in love with you despite your quirks and peculiarities — or maybe even *because* of them. You want your clients to fall in love with you because you are who you are — the same as a spouse. If you try to pretend you're something that you're not, it's not going to work in a business relationship or in a marriage.

CFD: And obviously your clients respected that and sought you out *because* you were who you were.

Poretz: Yes, in large part. But then I also discovered that there was a chunk of businesses out there that wanted what I did, but with some arms and legs. So that was one of the things that I brought to the thinking process when my premise changed — that there was a whole other segment. See, I wouldn't have changed the orientation of my business from high value-added fees to commodity fees. I wanted to keep the high value-added fees but simply add more clients.

CFD: Right — just growing the number of clients, not lessening the impact of their fees.

Poretz: Right. So now we have an administrator who takes care of all the administrative things in the office and four principals — myself and three other people. We're searching for the next principal now. And everyone is the same as I was — people with a great deal of experience. As a firm, we rely on technology and information, and we want to provide high value-added services so that we can get high value-added fees. By relying on technology, we can keep our expenses lower, and we can also avoid the necessity of hiring "junior associates." That means that our clients never talk with anyone who doesn't have a wealth of experience at senior corporate levels.

CFD: You can maintain a low overhead by using technology to your advantage.

Poretz: Yes. So the technology that I learned as a one-person business — and the fact that I could be so efficient with it — is moving over to the new business and making *it* more efficient.

Setting Your Fees in Different Ways

When you go about the process of setting your fees, the first question to ask yourself is how much money you want or need to make. Unfortunately, we can't answer this question for you — you have to look at your own situation and go from there. We can, however, provide you with some general guidelines that have worked for many consultants.

If you are leaving a job to start your own consulting business, a common guideline says that you should take your hourly wage rate and multiply it by three to arrive at the hourly fee you should charge as a consultant. So if you are currently making $25 an hour, as a consultant you should charge your clients $75 an hour. Why so much more than your current job? Because not only are you paying yourself a wage, but you are also paying for the benefits — health insurance, life insurance, and so on — that you want to maintain as a consultant. And although you may be a full-time paid employee now, you may *not* be a full-time paid consultant when you make the move. Many consultants experience downtime between projects, perhaps going for days or weeks without paid work. The higher rate of $75 an hour helps to cushion that kind of financial shortfall.

Of the many different ways to set your rates and charge for your services, those described in the following sections are the most common.

Hourly rate

The hourly rate is probably the most common way that consultants price their services. Whether you are proofreading manuscripts, providing legal advice, or keeping track of a client's bookkeeping, you can charge hourly rates. Hourly rates are easy to understand and compare with one another, and clients can buy as many or as few hours as they like. That's the good news. On the other side of the ledger, clients and consultants tend to focus on different issues. Clients generally want to reduce the number of hours that consultants work. Consultants, however, often focus on increasing the number of hours that they work for a client instead of focusing on providing the best overall result in the shortest amount of time.

If you decide to price your services on an hourly basis, you need to have a basis for developing and supporting your rates. Here are some of the ways in which you can do just that:

- **Consider the market for your services.** The easiest way to set a rate for your services is to find out how much *other* consultants charge to do the same kind of work and then price your services within the same range. For example, if other consultants in your field charge between $25 and $45 an hour, then you can comfortably set your price anywhere you like within that range. If you step below the range, you may be swamped with low-margin business that doesn't really pay the bills. Step above the range, and you have to convince your clients that you're worth the extra fee.

- **Build your rate from the bottom up.** If you've been working in a regular job for a number of years, your goal may be to simply maintain your previous pay rate. If you were being paid $25 an hour at your job, that's where you would start. If you add the burden of paying for your own health and dental insurance and other benefits that your previous employer paid — say, $10 an hour — and an additional $10 to cover your overhead and profit, then you end up with a rate of $45 an hour.

✔ **Build your rate from the top down.** You may decide that you want to gross $75,000 a year from your consulting efforts. If that's the case, you first estimate how many hours you can work and bill to clients in a year. For example, if you estimate that you will work 1,500 hours, then you divide the total amount of money that you want for the year — $75,000 — by the total hours you've estimated that you will work. In this case, you have to charge at least $50 an hour to achieve your goal of $75,000 a year.

When setting your initial fee, remember that you have convinced your client that you are the best person for the task (and we're assuming you have — if you *haven't*, then go back to the drawing board and try again!). The client, therefore, will be relatively fee-insensitive as long as your fees are approximately 20 to 30 percent higher than those of your competitors. Most clients figure that getting the best consultant is worth a 20 to 30 percent premium.

Depending on the type of project, you may want to establish a minimum number of billable hours, such as four hours. This protects you from the client who "just wants to get together briefly for a 30-minute meeting." However, by the time you drive to the client's office, meet, and return to your office, you blow half a day — not a half hour. Remember, as a consultant, you are selling time and knowledge. For a consultant, time really *is* money.

And don't forget to bill your client for any expenses beyond those normally incurred in doing your everyday business. For example, a consulting job may require that you fly to a number of client sites nationwide and spend several weeks on the road — incurring charges for airfare, hotels, rental cars, and dining. Remember to add these expenses to your client's invoices in addition to the hours that you are billing for a particular period. Be sure that you fully explain to your clients what expenses you will charge to their accounts and any limitations placed upon them. For example, you may decide to charge a fixed per diem of $125 a day for hotel and dining expenses, or you may want to include an agreement to charge your clients only for the price of economy-class airfare, even if you fly business class.

Per-item or per-project basis

Many consultants price their services on a per-item or per-project basis. For example, if you do image consulting, you might price consultations at $50 each. Or if you are hired to audit a small electronics assembler, you might price the project at a flat rate of $7,500. The beauty of pricing your services this way is that you redirect the focus from the number of *hours* you work to the *results* that you achieve.

For example, if you agree to conduct a full review of the purchasing and receiving function of an organization, you might price this project at a total of $15,000. In return for the $15,000, you promise to present a report with recommendations to improve the operation. At the end of the four-week study, you deliver your report and submit your invoice for payment. Now, your client could care less how many hours you spent on the project. Your client cares only about the recommendations in your proposal. If the recommendations are good, then your client will be happy and won't ask whether you spent enough hours on the job. If the recommendations *aren't* good, you'll know soon enough.

Although you'll do much of your work — especially early in your consulting career — on an hourly or daily basis, pushing your business to a per-item or per-project basis is definitely in your interest. If you price it right, you'll have plenty of money left over after the job is complete, and you can focus all your efforts on creating the best product possible.

Retainer basis

Sometimes your clients want to ensure your availability to work for them, but they aren't able to define in advance exactly how much of your time they will need or exactly when they will need it. This kind of situation is tailor-made for setting up a retainer arrangement. A *retainer* is nothing more than a guarantee that your client will pay you a fixed sum of money each month. In return for this guarantee, you promise to be available to work for that client whenever the need arises.

Here's how it works: Say that you are hired under an annual retainer of $60,000, giving you a monthly income of $5,000. In January, your client uses exactly $5,000 worth of services. However, in February, your client uses only $2,500 worth of services. Despite this shortfall in usage, your client pays you the fixed sum of $5,000 for February. The shortfall of usage in February is carried forward to March, giving your client a total of $7,500 to work with that month. If, on the other hand, the client *exceeds* the monthly amount specified in the retainer agreement, then you can bill the client for the extra work. At the end of the year, you wipe the slate clean. If the client hasn't used all his or her money by this time, then the client forfeits the unused portion to the consultant.

Retainers are generally win-win situations for both parties. The client has a skilled expert ready to work at a moment's notice. In exchange for this privilege, the consultant gets a steady stream of income each month. And if you are a consultant, you know that happiness is a positive cash flow.

Keeping Client Value in Mind

As you consider the different options listed earlier, don't forget that you should base the price you charge for your services on the value that you provide to your clients, not on anyone's preconceived notion as to what a "proper" fee is. When you start out in consulting, you probably will charge your services to your clients by the hour or day, and your clients will pay you only for the number of hours that you devote to their projects. Your clients also will probably be hesitant to pay you any more than the other consultants who offer services similar to those that you offer.

That arrangement may be well and good, but as you gain experience in consulting, keep the big picture in clear sight and don't get bogged down trying to justify a particular number of hours or a particular rate. The goal is to move the bulk of your business into a project-based or retainer pricing arrangement. Reaching this goal may be easier said than done — especially if your clients are accustomed to dealing with you on an hourly or daily basis. But believe us; achieving your goal will be well worth the effort.

Making Changes to Your Fees

If you are a consultant, we can absolutely guarantee that you'll eventually decide that you need to either increase or decrease the fees that you charge to your clients. Although you should never make changes to your fees without a good reason, increasing or decreasing your fees definitely makes sense at certain times.

Although a client is unlikely to complain when you *lower* your fees — or to tell you if your fees are too low — this may not be the case when you *increase* your fees. In either case, prepare your rationale *before* you make the changes and be ready to explain the changes to your clients. The following sections describe the most common reasons for making changes to your fees.

Increases

Most businesspeople would love to pay the same amount for the same service forever and ever. Wouldn't that be nice? But real life just doesn't work that way. As everyone knows, the costs of doing business continue to increase, and as costs escalate, your fees are sure to follow. Although you may know exactly *why* your rates need to increase, you may not be so sure *when* to make the change or whether the change should apply to your current customers or only to new customers.

The general rule is to pass price increases on to new customers *immediately*. For your current customers, the answer is a bit more complex. If you are contracted to provide your services at a set rate for a defined period of time — say, six months or a year — then you need to wait until you fulfill your commitment before you raise your prices. If you're not bound to an agreement fixing your prices for a period of time, then give your current clients at least 30 days' notice — or more if you can anticipate far enough ahead — of the impending rate increase before you actually implement it.

Consultants raise their fees for many reasons besides the rising costs of doing business. Here are a few reasons that may compel you to raise yours:

- **Your expenses have increased.** If your expenses increase and you want to maintain the same level of profitability as you have in the past, then you have to pass on the price increase to your clients.

- **You've underpriced your services.** You may find that you have priced your services too low — especially if you are new to consulting. If this is the case, you must act quickly to raise your prices for future clients so that you don't lose money on the work that you do for them.

- **You want to test the marketplace.** Setting your fees is a balancing act. Periodically test the market with higher-priced offerings and then note how your clients respond. If all your prospective clients go away as a result, it's probably not a good time to increase your rates. However, if your clients don't seem to be very concerned about the increase, then you know that you can make the change stick.

- **You need to pay for a client's "hidden" expenses.** After you work for a client for a while, you may find hidden expenses that you didn't anticipate and that dramatically increase the amount of work that you must do to complete your assignments on time. For example, you may be expected to attend meetings that your client didn't tell you about in advance. Or you may find that obtaining access to the information that you need is more difficult than you first anticipated. If you must take on unexpected work, you may have to increase the fee that you charge your clients to cover the extra time required to complete the project.

- **You don't really want to do the work.** Sometimes you just don't want to do the work. Yes, at times you would rather turn down a particular client or job than suffer through it. When a client offers you work that you don't want to do, price your proposal significantly higher than you normally would. If the client turns down your proposal, fine; you didn't want the work anyway. However, if the client accepts the proposal, then you'll be paid enough to make up for the pain and agony of doing the job or for working with that particular client.

Regardless of the reason for increasing your rates, take the time to carefully consider *how* you're going to implement your increase. Your goal is to keep your very best customers (the ones who pay you the most and the ones with whom you most enjoy working) while continuing to attract new business. As you attract and do business with clients who are willing to pay you higher fees, letting go of your marginal clients — the ones who aren't willing to accept fee increases — is definitely in your interest. As a rule, after you have your business firmly established, you should always strive to lose the bottom 10 percent of your business to make room for a new 10 percent of business to move in at the top of your client roster.

Decreases

Yes, Virginia, there really are times when you may want to *decrease* the amount that clients pay for your services. However, because price decreases can potentially threaten to reduce your revenues and profit, you must carefully consider any price decrease before you implement it. You also have to be careful that you don't set a precedent for continued price decreases (unless you *want* to) that your clients may expect in the future.

Here are several reasons to decrease your fees:

- ✔ **Because you've overpriced your services:** You should always be suspicious that you have overpriced your services when, despite advertising, networking, and making plenty of personal contacts, your only customer is your mother. If you're not getting the level of business that you expected when you started your business, look closely at your rates. If they're too high, you need to bring them down to a level that is more consistent with your perceived value. Either that or improve the value that you offer to your clients so that the value matches the fees you charge.

- ✔ **To reward your long-term clients:** Everyone appreciates getting an occasional bargain, and this is certainly true for your clients. The most common ways of decreasing your pricing for long-term clients are either by giving them special premiums from time to time — such as reduced rates for a month — or by holding your fee constant. (You can still increase your fees for short-term and new clients.)

- ✔ **To get your foot in the door:** Although you run the danger of setting a precedent that will be difficult to change for future work, you may find that lowering your fees when you are trying to break into a new industry or line of business is advantageous. The simple fact is, if you can't get anyone to hire you at the rates that you have set — no matter how fair they may be or how much value you deliver — you're not going to make any money. And if you don't make any money, then you're out of business. When you're trying to break into a new market, dropping your fees to give your prospective clients an incentive to give you a try can often pay off in the long run. Just be sure to let your client know that you are making this exception on a one-time basis only and that you will bill any future work at your normal rates.

✔ **As a professional courtesy:** Doctors, lawyers, and other professionals often lower their fees as a courtesy to others in their profession. As a consultant, you may decide to extend a similar favor. Why? Because it can help you to develop better relationships with other consultants — consultants who may refer work your way someday or who may want to partner with you on a particular project.

One technique to address the fee issue for a new client is to quote rates as follows:

✔ Normal professional fee: $75 per hour

✔ New-client discount to demonstrate performance and build goodwill: $15 per hour

✔ Net fee for this project only: $60 per hour

This approach establishes your normal fee in the client's mind for future projects while positioning you as a vendor who really wants an opportunity to show your stuff.

Making a Stand

All consultants can tell you countless stories about clients who wanted them to reduce their rates — on either a short-term or a long-term basis. Don't forget that this is *your* business, and *you* are ultimately responsible for deciding how you are going to run it. If you decide to reduce your rates or make other concessions to your clients in exchange for their goodwill (and business!), that's fine. Just be sure that you have a good reason and definite goals in mind for doing so.

If you decide to stick with your guns, however, then by all means do so. Not only do you earn the respect of prospective clients (this reason alone often earns you their business), but marginal clients who are more worried about fees than results stay away. And that's really not so bad, is it?

As you prepare to (politely!) tell your clients what they can do with their demands to drop your fees, keep these tips in mind:

✔ **Just say no!** When you're in business, you hate to tell your clients no, but sometimes you just have to. When you have to say no to your clients' requests to lower your fees or make other concessions, do so promptly and be firm. If you drag your feet, your clients may be angered that you weren't forthright to begin with. And if you aren't firm in your response, then your clients may believe that they have room to negotiate with you — even when they don't.

✔ **Have good reasons.** When you tell your clients no, you should also be prepared to explain exactly *why* the proposed change is not acceptable. Explain to your clients, "Those rates don't allow me to cover the expenses of doing business," or "I can't deliver the kind of high-quality results that I demand and that you expect, if we compress the schedule as much as you have proposed." Clients don't enjoy being told no, but if you have a good reason for it, then at least they may understand *why*.

✔ **Be prepared with a counterproposal.** Although you may not be able to accept a client's proposed terms, you may be able to propose alternatives that you both find acceptable and that result in a win-win situation. For example, say something like "I absolutely can't reduce the price I proposed to complete your project, but I *can* get you your results faster if you like." The more alternatives you can muster for your clients to consider, the better.

✔ **Don't forget: "It's not personal, it's only business."** Avoid at all costs the temptation to get caught up in arguments about your fees and prices or about why you have to decline your client's requests to decrease them. These decisions are, first and foremost, *business* decisions, and you should never allow them to devolve into personality clashes or conflicts. If your discussions with a client take a turn for the worse, politely cut the conversation short, tell the client again exactly where you stand, and ask the client to call you if he or she has a change of heart.

Although setting your fees can sometimes seem like a random act, there really *is* a rhyme and reason behind the rates that you establish and the decision to change them from time to time. Regardless of your feelings about how you set your own fees, don't forget that you're running a business: You have to *make* money, not *lose* it. Set your fees so that you meet the financial goals of your business and can afford to take a vacation every now and then.

Chapter 16

Contracting for Business: The Artful Dance

· ·

In This Chapter
▶ Defining contracts
▶ Reviewing the different kinds of contracts
▶ Negotiating contracts and agreements

· ·

Money makes the world go around in business, and contracts determine *how much* money you're paid, *when,* and for *what,* in addition to clarifying other expectations. Contracts are the basis for most business transactions, and *every* consultant should be *very* familiar with them.

This chapter is all about contracts — what they are, why you enter into them, and which kinds you will most likely encounter during your career as a consultant. We also address another very popular topic that is near and dear to consultants from all walks of life: negotiating.

What Is a Contract?

What exactly is a contract? A contract is nothing more than an agreement between two or more parties to do something (or *not* do something) in return for something of value — called *consideration* amongst those who make a habit of practicing contract law. Contracts can be oral or written and range in size from simple one-page agreements to incredibly complex documents as thick as the Manhattan Yellow Pages. The details and complexities of a contract depend on the nature of the agreement and the number of lawyers who are involved in drafting the contract. (Economy's third law of contract dynamics states that the size of a contract is directly proportional to the number of lawyers involved, multiplied by the number of days they are given to work on it, squared.)

In some cases, oral contracts may be just as valid as written contracts. However, written contracts offer a variety of advantages over oral contracts, and you should insist on them whenever possible. Although some consultants are willing to work on a handshake (and they are doing *very* well, thank you), most have learned that, in the long run, it pays to get agreements in writing and not rely on memories — or the continued goodwill of others — for something as important as the financial future and continued health and viability of a business.

In this section, we review the key elements of a contract and tell you about the many different kinds of problems that can make a contract unenforceable. And believe us, there are more than just one or two! That said, this chapter is written to give you a general overview of the principles of contracts and negotiation. Because every contracting situation is unique, our advice is to seek out competent legal counsel before entering into *any* contract.

The key elements of a contract

Good morning, and welcome to Business Law 101. Today, our topic concerns what constitutes the key elements of a contract. Every contract — written and oral — has three key elements. Each of these three key elements has to be in place for a contract to exist. If even one element is missing, then the contract is not valid. Without further ado, here are the key elements of a contract:

- **Offer:** An offer is simply a proposal — either oral or in writing — by one party to undertake an action on behalf of another party in exchange for adequate consideration. To be valid, an offer must be serious and must contain definite terms. What is *adequate consideration,* you ask? Keep reading and you'll find out.

- **Acceptance:** An acceptance is a party's agreement to the terms of an offer as evidenced by an oral or written promise to pay the agreed consideration. (Still don't know what consideration is? Keep reading.) Acceptance can be made only while an offer is still open. If the offer is withdrawn before acceptance or rejection, then the offer has expired.

- **Consideration:** Consideration is something of value given in exchange for performance, or a promise of performance. Examples of valid consideration include money, goods, services, the promise to do something that there is no legal obligation to do (for example, build a Web site for a client at some future time), or the promise *not* to do something that there is a legal right to do (for example, take a client to small claims court for nonpayment of a bill for services rendered). *Adequate* consideration is generally whatever the two parties agree to, unless there is evidence of fraud or duress.

When these three elements are in place, you have a contract. However, that's not quite the end of the story. After a contract is in place, several things can be used to make the contract unenforceable. We take a look at these different things in the next section.

Things that can "unmake" a contract

So you have the three essentials of a contract: an offer, an acceptance, and consideration. Everything's cool, right? Well, maybe. A number of circumstances can affect the validity of a contract. After a contract is formed, either party can raise certain issues to try to break it, including the following:

- **Capacity:** This means that the parties who enter into a contractual agreement must be of legal age, sane, and sober for the contract to be valid. If not, you've got a *big* problem.

- **Duress:** One party of a contract must not use undo pressure — either mental or physical — to force the other party to agree to the terms of a contract. If this situation exists, the contract could be in jeopardy.

- **Form:** Due to the Statute of Frauds, certain kinds of contracts — for example, home improvement contracts and sales of goods worth more than $500 — *must* be in writing to be enforceable. Depending on your locality, oral contracts for these kinds of transactions may be unenforceable.

- **Fraud:** If a party to a contract intentionally misrepresents an issue of substance in the contract, this is considered to be fraud, and the contract may be unenforceable.

- **Constructive fraud:** This occurs when one or more parties to an agreement knowingly omits an important piece of information by failing to fully disclose a key fact. Again, a contract made under these conditions may be unenforceable.

- **Legality:** The contract must be for a legal purpose. For example, a contract to smuggle diamonds into the country is not legally valid. Contracts for illegal purposes are automatically considered void and unenforceable.

- **Mutual mistake:** Although a mistake by one party to a contract may not make a contract unenforceable, if *both* parties make a mistake on an important issue — say, where both parties relied on a faulty sales catalog that priced an item at $4,500, when it was actually $45,000 — then the contract may be unenforceable.

Did *your* contract survive all the tests? Yes? Great! Now take a look at the different kinds of contracts, along with their good points and bad points.

Different Kinds of Contracts

Although in some situations, both oral and written contracts may be equally valid in the eyes of the law (with the exception of those jurisdictions that, in accordance with the Statute of Frauds, require written contracts for certain kinds of transactions), each has its own set of pluses and minuses. Oral contracts are unintimidating and friendly, but they can be easily forgotten and hard to prove. On the other hand, written contracts can be easily understood and enforced, but they can also be complex and bureaucratic.

Ultimately, the choice of what kind of contract you use is up to you — it's *your* business, after all. However, many organizations will want you to sign a contract — *their* contract. Our advice is to develop your own written contract form — meet with your legal advisor to hammer out the details — and then use it for all the work you do. If you *do* decide to accept your client's contract form, read it carefully before you sign it. If you have any questions about any of the provisions, ask your client to explain them. And don't forget: Have your lawyer look it over *before* you sign — not *after*.

Oral contracts

Most people are involved in an incredibly wide variety of transactions every day — both business and personal — that are conducted on the basis of oral, or verbal, agreements. A kid in your neighborhood agrees to shovel the snow off your driveway and sidewalk for $5. She completes the job, and you pay her the agreed amount. The counter person at the deli down the street says that he'll make you the best ham and cheese sandwich you've ever had if you'll pay him $3 for it. You agree. He makes the sandwich, you pay him the money, and you're on your way. Think about all the other agreements that you enter into on an oral basis each and every day of your life.

Here's how an oral contract might be formed between you and a client:

Consultants R Us (You): I've taken a good look at my schedule, and I can commit to develop a marketing plan for your new product line within two weeks.

Acme Widget (Client): Great! That should fit the roll-out schedule perfectly. How much will you charge me to develop the plan? Don't forget — we're your number-one client!

Consultants R Us: Right, how could I ever forget that? You know that I *always* give you my best rate. I can do the job for $4,500. We can go with our usual arrangement of one-third, or $1,500 up front, and the balance to be paid within 30 days after I deliver your marketing plan.

Acme Widget: That sounds fine. So to summarize, you'll complete the new product marketing plan in two weeks for a total price of $4,500 — right?

Consultants R Us: Yes.

Acme Widget: And I can pay you $1,500 to start, with the balance due within 30 days after you deliver the plan to me?

Consultants R Us: Correct.

Acme Widget: Super! Here's a check for $1,500 to get you started. I'll see you in two weeks!

Consultants R Us: Okay — see you then.

You and your client at Acme Widget have just entered into an oral contract.

In many cases, a court of law may consider an oral contract to be just as binding as a written contract. However, this doesn't mean that oral contracts are as good for your business as written contracts. Oral agreements often have a number of problems:

- ✔ **People forget things.** Although your oral agreement may be very clear and precise at the moment you agree to it, either or both parties may soon forget the exact terms.

  For example, Peter once hired a landscaper to cut back four trees on his property. As they walked around the yard, Peter pointed out exactly which trees he wanted cut, and then left for work. When Peter returned, he was shocked to find out that his landscaper had cut down one of his favorite trees — three were right and one was wrong. A written agreement along with a detailed map of the yard might have saved this particular tree's life.

- ✔ **People go away.** Sometimes people get sick or die, and the terms of any oral agreements that they were party to go away with them. You've seen how hard it can be to sort out a business disagreement when there are written contracts and agreements to guide the parties. Well, imagine how difficult it is trying to figure out who owes what to whom when one of the parties isn't there to give his or her side of the story. Unfortunately, enforcing an agreement can be *very* difficult when there is no proof or evidence that it exists.

- ✔ **Complexity begets confusion.** If an agreement goes very far beyond the simplest terms and conditions such as who, what, when, and for how much, the complexity of the contract grows quickly. As the complexity of your contract grows, so too does the potential for confusion and misunderstandings. Clearly, oral contracts are inadequate for dealing with complex terms and conditions.

- ✔ **You just might end up in court some day.** You never know. You can be going along for years doing jobs simply on the word of your clients when, suddenly — *bang!* — a client refuses to pay for a project that you toiled many long hours over. Now, if it's a $50 job, no big deal. But if it's a

$5,000 job, or a $50,000 job, then you have a problem. Though most people never plan to end up in court, many do. And if you do, an oral contract is much more difficult to prove to a judge than a written contract.

✔ **You may not be able to recover your legal fees.** In many jurisdictions, you won't be able to recover the legal expenses that you incur to pursue a legal action against a client unless this provision is clearly spelled out *in writing* as part of a written contract.

If you decide that oral contracts are the way that you want to conduct business, make sure that you use a letter of confirmation when you reach agreement with a client. The letter of confirmation briefly outlines *your* understanding of the key terms of the agreement and allows your clients to double-check *their* understanding of the agreement against yours. And if you ask your client to sign and return a copy of your letter acknowledging agreement to the terms, then you have that much more assurance (and written evidence) that both you and your client are working off of the same sheet of music.

Figure 16-1, shown on the next page, is an example of a letter of confirmation *with* acknowledgment for your viewing (and contracting) pleasure.

Written contracts

Like it or not, written contracts are here to stay. Despite the nostalgic longing that many people have for the days when deals were done with nothing more than a person's word and a handshake to back them up, it's safe to say that most consultant business today is conducted with some sort of written agreement. If you're not convinced of the need to enter into written contracts with your clients, all it may take to change your mind is a couple of days in court attempting to recover the thousands of dollars that a client owes you.

A written contract can be anywhere from a page or two in length to hundreds — even thousands — of pages.

Whew! Written contracts sure sound like a lot of work. Why bother? The main reason is that a written contract provides clear evidence of the *intent* of the parties to be bound to an agreement at the same time as the written document shows exactly *what* the parties agreed to be bound to. In other words, a good contract also clarifies expectations of all concerned.

One more reason exists: the Statute of Frauds. Under this provision of the Uniform Commercial Code (UCC), any contract for the sale of goods that exceeds a total of $500 must be in writing. Not only that, but the contract must clearly state the key terms of agreement and must be signed by the customer. Many states and jurisdictions have their own versions of the Statute of Frauds.

June 14, 1999

Sara Grosvenor
Tertiary Technologies, Inc.
4242 Chairman Way
Land O' Orange, FL 33333

Dear Ms. Grosvenor:

This letter confirms today's agreement for the design of a genetic transporter and the delivery of a complete set of production drawings and blueprints. Here is a summary of the terms of our agreement:

Delivery date: Draft plans will be delivered on or before November 30, 1999; final plans will be delivered on or before January 31, 2000

Total price: $75,000
Payment schedule: One-third upon start of work; one-third upon delivery of draft plans; one-third upon delivery of final plans

Payment terms: Net/30 days

As always, it's a real pleasure working with you, Sara. I am confident that we will surmount the challenges of this unique project and provide you with the promised plans on time and within budget. If you have any questions, please do not hesitate to call me anytime.

Please acknowledge your agreement to the above terms and conditions by signing and dating the space below and returning a copy of this letter to me as soon as possible.

Sincerely,

Felix Wang
Chief Innovator

_____
Acknowledged by   Date

Although contracts *can* be very complex and lengthy, they don't *have* to be — especially for the kind of work that most consultants do. You certainly don't want to scare off potentially lucrative clients by pulling 50-page contracts out of your briefcase and requiring your clients to sign them in triplicate before you'll do work for them. The whole point of a written contract is to ensure that each party to an agreement understands what is required of each party. In most cases, doing so takes only a page or two.

Written contracts come in many different forms. Here are a few of the most common.

Purchase orders

If you consult for businesses or the government, purchase orders are a regular part of your diet of written contracts. A purchase order is a written offer to purchase your services for a specified amount of money. In some cases, your clients will issue purchase order *numbers* in lieu of a written document.

A purchase order is considered a *unilateral* (one-sided) contract when you accept the offer through your performance of the requested service. For example, if your client issues a purchase order for you to produce an environmental impact report, a unilateral contract is deemed to exist if you complete the requested work. A purchase order is considered a *bilateral* (two-sided) contract when both parties sign it before performance begins. Both types of purchase orders are equally valid.

Simple contracts

Simple contracts — normally one or two pages in length — are appropriate for the kind of work that most consultants do. Not only do they contain the most important parts of an agreement between consultant and client — such things as price, delivery or completion dates, payment terms, payment schedules, and so on — but, because of their simplicity, they are easy to interpret and unintimidating to most people.

For many consultants, simple contracts are just what the doctor ordered. Figure 16-2, shown on the next page, is an example of a simple contract that contains all the basic information needed for most consulting situations. Use it as a guide and feel free to modify it to suit your own individual needs. Whether you pick a version similar to Figure 16-2 or a variation of that format, be sure to have your attorney take a look at it before you start using it.

Sample only: Consult with competent legal counsel before entering into any contract.

AGREEMENT FOR CONSULTING SERVICES

Client's name and address: _____

Description of services to be provided to client: _____

_____

_____

_____

Start date: _____ *Completion date:* _____

Fees: $_____ per _____ (hour/day/other)

Total estimated hours/days/other: _____

Total estimated fee: $_____

Other costs: $_____ for _____

Payment terms: _____

Additional terms and conditions, if any: _____

_____

_____

For _____(consultant) For _____(client)

_____(signed) _____(signed)

_____(date) _____(date)

Complex contracts

In addition to the basic terms and conditions contained in simple contracts, complex contracts contain a slew of additional terms and conditions meant to address any and every problem or legal challenge that could possibly occur during the course of project performance and beyond. Instead of only the simple stuff such as price, delivery date, payment terms, and so on, all of a sudden you've got entire paragraphs or pages with titles like "Warranties," "Termination," "Governing Law," "Force Majeure," and much, much more.

It's funny how things work. As the amount of consideration that you contract for increases, so do your clients' desires to enter into complex agreements. For example, a client who is happy to issue you a purchase order number for a $500 order may demand that you sign a 20-page contract loaded with any manner of complex terms and conditions when the price of your work crosses the $10,000 threshold.

Unless you are highly experienced and conversant in the terms and conditions of complex contracts, our advice is to bring in competent legal counsel when you're confronted with a long, complex contract filled to the brim with such terms and conditions. And don't automatically assume that, after you establish a precedent with an organization, all future contracts will reflect this precedent. Most organizations work with lawyer-drafted, lawyer-approved "boilerplate" (standard) contracts that are modified to reflect the particular terms and conditions of each deal. Every time you enter into a new contract with an organization, you're really starting from scratch. Read all new contracts closely to make sure that they match your expectations.

If you need to draft a complex contract, or you need someone to review *any* contract or agreement that a client has given to you to review and sign, then grab your Yellow Pages, flip to the section titled "Attorneys," and find a good lawyer to help you out. The review may cost you a couple hundred bucks, but the investment can save you a lot of heartache (and sleepless nights) down the road.

The ABCs of Contract Negotiation

What would a chapter about contracts be without a discussion of how to negotiate them? It would simply be a chapter on contracts! Although it would be nice if all your clients would just accept everything that you propose (yeah, we know — that would truly be Fantasyland), there comes a time in every consultant's career where you are required to negotiate terms and conditions with your clients.

Without a doubt, each one of us negotiates every day for a wide variety of reasons and purposes. *I don't think I can make a 3:00 meeting — how about 4:30? $25 to do an oil change for my car seems too high — make it $15 and you've got a deal. There's no way that I can do everything that you want for only $25,000. Now, if you can raise the ante to $35,000, I think we may be in the ballpark. I said, you need to be in bed by 8:00 tonight — no ifs, ands, or buts! Okay — you can stay up until 9:00, but that's it!* In fact, it might not be exaggerating to say that life is one long series of negotiations.

As you may have noticed, there is no shortage of books available on the topic of negotiating. In this section, we distill the wisdom and tips gleaned from literally thousands of years of human negotiating experience into a concise package that fits neatly into your pocket. Well, it fits if you tear this section out and fold it a couple of times before you try to stick it in your pocket.

Carry on.

Anticipating the negotiation

No matter how simple a negotiation seems on the surface, or how trivial or small the amount of time or money involved, it always pays to think ahead and *anticipate* the negotiation on which you are about to embark with your client. Even if it's only to briefly outline your goals or do a little bit of research on your client's needs, the additional insight that you gain by anticipating your negotiation puts you in a position to better achieve your personal, business, and financial goals.

Although you can do many things to get ready to negotiate, you should always take these four essential steps before you open a negotiation:

1. **Prepare your goals.**

    If you don't have goals, then you never know where you're going. Goals are the ultimate targets that you are going to work hard to achieve in a negotiation. Take time *before* you negotiate to determine your goals and how important they are to you. Would you be willing to give up certain goals in exchange for others? Know exactly what *you* need to achieve in your negotiation, and be prepared to get it.

2. **Research pertinent background information.**

    What do you know about your clients? Are they in the news? Are there pressing issues for the company or the industry? What is the client's past experience with consultants? Is the company at the beginning of its fiscal year and anxious to start spending the money that it budgeted for consultants? Or is the company at the end of its fiscal year, thus trying to pinch every penny and make money stretch as far as possible?

A wide range of information about the organizations you plan to negotiate with is available. (Do a few different searches on the Internet, for starters.) Use this information to help plan your negotiation strategies for achieving your goals.

3. **Evaluate your client's positions.**

What do you expect your client's positions to be? Do you expect that the client may want to shorten or lengthen the period of performance? Or request that you cut your fee or increase or decrease the number of hours you have proposed to perform the project? Put yourself in your client's shoes for a moment and anticipate his or her positions. After you do that, determine how you will counter them if and when your client introduces them.

4. **Prepare your own positions.**

Before you enter into *any* negotiation, prepare the positions that *you* will present and defend. Positions are the wants that you communicate to the other party in a negotiation. They differ from goals in that they are interim stops along the way to achieving your goals. For example, your goal may be to make $50 an hour on a particular job, but your initial position may be to charge your client $60 an hour. It's likely that you will have already prepared your initial positions and submitted them to your clients in your proposal. However, before you negotiate, also prepare back-up positions in the event that your primary positions are not acceptable to your clients and you can't get them to see the infinite wisdom of going with your suggested plan.

Figure 16-3, shown on the next page, presents a quick and easy worksheet that you can use to prepare for *any* negotiation.

Basic rules of the negotiation road

In negotiation, a number of basic rules have evolved over millions of years of human existence. Master these rules, and you will be a real pro at negotiation. You'll always get *exactly* what you want and your life will be full of unlimited success and happiness. Well, maybe not. However, if you ignore these basic rules, or fail to practice them effectively, we can guarantee that you'll end up with a lot less from your bargains than you hope for.

Anyway, here are the seven — count 'em, seven — basic rules of negotiation:

✔ **Be prepared.** Being prepared gives you a definite advantage in *every* negotiating situation — so much so that the downside of not preparing for a negotiation far outweighs the small amount of time and effort that it takes to prepare. And what should you be prepared for? For starters, go back to the previous section titled "Anticipating the negotiation" and do the four things that we recommend there.

Prenegotiation Worksheet

- What are your top three goals for this particular negotiation?

    1.

    2.

    3.

- What do you expect your client's top three goals for this particular negotiation to be?

    1.

    2.

    3.

- What do you expect your client's initial positions to be?

    1.

    2.

    3.

- What do you expect your client's backup positions to be?

    1.

    2.

    3.

- What are your initial positions?

    1.

    2.

    3.

- What are your backup positions?

    1.

    2.

    3.

✔ **Leave plenty of room to maneuver.** Nobody likes to be boxed into a position with no room for compromise or for flexibility in meeting the *mutual* goals of both parties. When you develop your negotiation goals and positions, build in enough flexibility to allow you to modify them to better achieve both your clients' goals and your goals.

✔ **Have lots of alternatives in mind.** For every possible reason that your client gives for *not* agreeing to one of your positions, you should have one or more alternatives ready to go. For example, if your client says that four weeks is not an acceptable delivery schedule, then be ready with an alternative that gets your client the delivery in two weeks, for an increase in fee to compensate for the rush job.

✔ **Keep your word.** In business, as in life in general, your word should be your bond. Negotiation is built on a foundation of trust and mutual respect. If you aren't willing to keep your word, then you'll quickly lose both trust and respect. It's one thing to make an honest mistake — most anyone can understand and deal with that — but if you can't keep your word, then what do you have left?

✔ **Listen more than you talk.** One of the most important negotiating skills is the ability to listen — *really* listen — to the other party. If you ask the right questions and then let your counterpart talk about the answers, you usually find out exactly what it will take to successfully negotiate and close a deal. Don't forget: When you're talking, you're not listening!

✔ **Don't give up too much too soon.** In our experience, it pays to not give up too much too quickly when you're dealing with a tough negotiator. Not only do you appear weak and perhaps a bit desperate, but you also miss out on getting any significant concessions from your client. Take your time when you are negotiating with your clients. It's better for *them* to be in a big rush to close the deal than for *you* to be in a big rush to close the deal.

✔ **Learn to say no.** Telling a client no is a very difficult skill for many consultants to acquire. We all want to tell our clients yes to encourage positive client relations. However, when you're negotiating a deal, sometimes you have to say no if you want to achieve your own goals. For example, if your client wants you to cut your normal fee in half and you don't want to do so, then just say no, but offer an alternative, such as a slight reduction in fee in exchange for payment in 10 days instead of 30.

Closing a deal

Closing your deal successfully — that is, reaching final agreement on all terms and conditions and signing all the appropriate documents on all the appropriate dotted lines — is the ultimate goal of every negotiation. Countless business deals have lost their wheels and careened out of control and into the ditches of the backwaters of commerce when the parties couldn't reach final agreement and close their deals.

Closing is an art. The more you do it, the better you get. However, it's never too late to learn a few new tricks or brush up on old ones. Here are a few tips to help ensure that you close your deals efficiently and with a minimum of bumps along the way:

✔ **Give your clients lots of reasons to say yes.** The more reasons your clients have to say yes, the greater the chance that they *will* say yes. Find as many ways as you possibly can to make it easy for your clients to say yes. If you do, you'll *definitely* close a lot more deals.

✔ **Confirm your agreement.** To ensure that your understanding of the final agreement matches the other party's understanding, confirm your agreement — first verbally, and then in writing. If there's a problem, you'll undoubtedly hear about it very quickly!

✔ **Don't be surprised by last-minute surprises.** We have both been in many negotiations where we had reached (or at least *thought* we had reached) a final agreement with the other party only to have them toss in a new demand or condition at the last possible moment. Be prepared for clients who use this negotiation tactic to wring additional concessions from you. If this happens to you, it's a good idea to calmly tell your counterpart, "No, this is not what we agreed to," and demand that he or she stick to the original deal. If your counterpart refuses, you may want to find a more dependable negotiating partner.

✔ **Follow up with a thank-you note.** Not only is sending a thank-you note a nice way to express your personal thanks to your client for hiring you or your firm, but it is also a great way to build rapport. The best business, after all, is built on long-term relationships with your current clients and the future clients that they refer to you.

✔ **Move on if you can't close the deal.** Despite all your efforts to reach a mutually beneficial agreement, some deals are just not meant to be. If this is the case, and there's nothing you can do to bring negotiations to a successful close, then simply walk away. By breaking off negotiations, you show your clients that you're serious, and they may very well make the final concessions necessary to close the deal. If not, then you can get on with your life and direct your efforts to more fruitful pursuits — such as lining up your *next* clients.

Chapter 17

Setting Up a Home Office

· ·

· ·

*A*s you might imagine, becoming an independent consultant offers you many benefits besides the opportunity to become your own boss, take charge of your life, and get a handle on your own destiny. (Whew — isn't that enough?) Becoming an independent consultant also offers you the chance to trade your current work environment — with its twice-a-day rush-hour commutes, its dress-for-success-or-else dress codes, and its I'm-the-boss-and-you're-not hierarchies and political pecking orders — for a saner workplace much closer to home. In fact, becoming an independent consultant gives you the opportunity to trade your current workplace for a work-place right in your home.

Right now, millions of people are working at home through the modern miracle of *telecommuting* — using telephones, fax machines, and computer networks to do business away from the office. However, despite the promise of telecommuting and other innovative work practices, most organizations still prefer to have their employees close at hand more often than not.

But when you're an independent consultant, *you're* the boss. You get to decide when and where you do business. If you want to rent an office downtown or in a suburban strip mall, you can do so if you like. Many consultants (especially those who have employees) do rent office space, and they are very happy with that arrangement. However, you now have a chance to take a different path — one that offers an array of opportunities and benefits that you just don't get by working in a traditional office.

In this chapter, we focus on establishing a home office. We consider the good points *and* the bad points (yes, there *are* a few drawbacks) of having a home office, and we look into the space and furnishings you need to get started. We also review some of the financial incentives to establishing a home office and explain how you can take advantage of them. Finally, we talk about when you should move your home office out of your home and into a regular office.

Working at Home: Good or Bad Idea?

We absolutely love the prospect of working at home. Both of us have dedicated home offices loaded with computers, laser printers, fax machines, multiple phone lines, bulletin boards, bookshelves, storage cabinets, and much, much more. But we're going to be honest with you: Working at home has both good points *and* bad points. Although we are obviously big fans of home-based offices, we feel that you need to know both sides of the story.

In this section, we explore the good and the bad about working at home, and we invite you to consider whether working at home is right for *you*.

The good news

The first bit of good news about working at home is that the good news far outweighs the bad news. This *must* be the case because the number of people who are starting offices in their homes is growing by leaps and bounds every day — a fact that hasn't escaped the attention of the many big businesses that want to capture a great big chunk of this burgeoning market. A quick search of the Internet turns up all kinds of resources targeted to people who work at home. Whether it's Sprint's *Home Office Solutions Guide*, GTE's *Turnkey Solutions for Today's Telecommuters and Entrepreneurs*, or the Home Office area of BankAmerica's Web site, Fortune 500 companies have seen the future of business, and the future of business is the home office.

So why are more and more people moving into home offices? The simple fact is that home offices offer plenty of advantages to those who are willing to pursue them. What advantages? Take a look:

  ✔ **Home offices are convenient.** What could be more convenient than having your office in your home? If you've ever sat in bumper-to-bumper rush-hour traffic, you know that one good thing about establishing a home office is that you'll never have to commute to work again. (Not only is commuting a big waste of time — a couple of hours a day for some people — but it also can be a huge source of frustration, *and* it contributes to highway congestion and air pollution.) Home offices also enable you to work in comfort and security when you need to rush a fax to a client at 10:00 at night or stay up until 3:00 in the morning working on a client presentation.

- **Home offices are free (sort of).** If you're paying rent or making payments on a home mortgage, you are already paying for living space. If you designate your dining room table, a spare bedroom, or a corner of *your* bedroom as your home office, you don't have to pay a dime extra. Sure, you may cough up a bit more for your gas and electric bills, and you may have to install an extra phone line or two, but the cost of the workspace is already accounted for. Not a single commercial real estate broker anywhere can touch that deal!

- **You get neat tax advantages.** If you play your cards right, the government can help you pay for your home office by making all your business expenses — as well as the portion of your housing expenses that is attributable to your home office — tax deductible.

This tax deduction can be a real financial benefit to you and your business; however, the government is *very* particular about exactly who is eligible to take the home-office deduction and under what circumstances. Writing off a part of your home as a business raises a red flag for government tax auditors, so be sure that you know what you're doing. Consult with your tax adviser for more details on the home-office deduction, and while you're at it, pick up a copy of *Taxes For Dummies,* by Eric Tyson and David Silverman (published by IDG Books Worldwide, Inc.).

- **You take on minimal risk.** When you start a business in your home, the risks of start-up are minimal because you aren't laying out much extra money for your office — especially if you continue to hold down a regular job as you test the waters with your own business. Compare this to the consultant who decides to lease a suite of offices. The consultant who leases space is committed for a year or more to making monthly rent payments — whether or not the business makes any money. If your business works out, great! If not, what have you lost by setting up a home office? Not much compared to the alternative of committing to a long-term office lease.

- **It's your party.** If you have worked in the corporate world, you are no doubt used to the regimentation of business life. Many organizations have policies — both written and unwritten — to direct a wide range of employee behavior. Wear this, don't wear that. Be at work by 8 a.m., and don't leave for home before 5 p.m. You can post a calendar, but not personal photographs or posters, on the wall of your workstation. However, when you have your own business, *you* decide what rules to follow. If that means starting work at noon, then that's okay; you set the rules. If having your own business means working in your pajamas or taking a couple hours in the middle of your workday to work out at the gym, no one cares except you. *You* decide when you are at your best — and at your most effective and efficient — not your boss. It's *your* party, and *you* get to decide how to run it.

✔ **You can get closer to your significant others.** For many independent consultants, one of the biggest attractions of establishing a home office is the possibility of spending more time with family and friends. Most businesses today draw very sharp distinctions between their employees and their employees' families and friends. With roughly one-third of your life spent at work and another third spent asleep, you have just the remaining one-third of your life available to pursue your other interests — and that includes the time you spend with significant others. When you work at home, you can easily pop out of your office to spend time with your loved ones or schedule your work hours around their schedules.

The bad news

We'll be the first to admit that having an office in your home isn't *always* a bed of roses. In fact, sometimes it can be a downright pain in the neck. Despite all that, we still believe that the good news about home offices far outweighs the bad. After you read through the following disadvantages of setting up an office at home, you can decide for yourself.

✔ **Separating your work life from your home life can be difficult.** This can be one of the toughest things about setting up a business in your home. When you're away at a traditional office, a very clear separation exists between your work life and your home life. Your family and friends know that you are at work and that you can be interrupted only for brief periods of time, if at all. However, in a home office, you may find it *very* difficult to keep working when you hear your 4-year-old daughter crying outside your office door, when a neighbor drops by to chat, or when your favorite soap opera or a big playoff game is on the air.

✔ **Creating space can be a challenge.** If you live in a small apartment or house, finding adequate space to set aside for a home office can be difficult. And if you intend to write off your home office as a tax deduction, you must dedicate the space to your business activities. So if you use your dining room as your office for part of the day and as a place for your family to eat (what a novel concept!) for the rest of the day, you can't write off your home office. This distinction may make finding an appropriate space in your home doubly hard.

✔ **Discipline and motivation are sometimes hard to come by.** When you work at home and you're the boss, you have to be self-motivated. You can't ignore the alarm clock in the morning, allow your friends and family to interrupt your work during the day, or waste countless hours puttering around the house, cleaning, doing laundry, or watching television. The temptations to draw you away from your work are all around your home office, and they are relentless. If you can't establish a work routine — and stick with it — you're going to be in *big* trouble.

✔ **Appearances can be everything.** What will your clients think when they find out that you run your business out of your home or when they hear your kids screaming at the top of their lungs in the background? Will they consider you a shrewd businessperson who has decided to take charge of his or her life? Or will they look at you as a loser who is doing this consulting thing as a hobby and who may very well be teetering on the brink of bankruptcy? Appearances can be everything, and your home office creates an appearance for your clients. Ask yourself whether your clients will approve of your home office.

✔ **Zoning can be an issue.** Depending on where you live and exactly what kind of consulting business you intend to run out of your home, you may have a problem with local zoning regulations. In general terms, *zoning* is the restriction of certain kinds of land uses to certain established areas. The intent is to keep someone from opening up an auto body shop in the middle of your peaceful neighborhood. In practice, zoning means that your local rules may not allow you to establish a business in your residential neighborhood if the nature of your business requires clients to meet with you at your home office.

✔ **Getting close to your significant others isn't always a good thing.** If you were looking closely, you probably noticed that we also listed this reason under the good news about home offices. Your family members may have gotten used to having the house or apartment to themselves all these years. Then, all of a sudden, there you are — a part of the household. Your home office can seriously disrupt the equilibrium of your home, causing friction, discontent, and battles with your significant others. This disruption is *not* a desired outcome when starting a home office.

What's it going to be for you?

The sections "The good news" and "The bad news" describe some of the pros and cons about home offices. Creating a home office is very much a personal decision, and before you launch into it, you need to weigh the pluses and minuses of working at home. Talk to your family members and determine how having an office at home may affect them. Seek other work-at-homes and ask them what they did to make their home offices work for them. Take a good look in the mirror and determine whether you have the personal drive and motivation to get out of bed in the morning and keep working at home throughout the day.

If you decide to go ahead with your home office, the information presented in the rest of this chapter can help you get things off on the right foot. Making the decision to move forward is the biggest step; the rest is simply icing on the cake.

Doug Poretz built a better home office

Doug Poretz is the founder and CEO of The Poretz Group (e-mail info@poretz.com), an investor relations consulting firm formed in 1991. Typical clients are the chairpersons, CEOs, and CFOs of publicly owned companies. The role of The Poretz Group is to help clients develop a strategy and implement a program to communicate with the investment community, including stockbrokers, mutual fund portfolio managers, money managers, analysts, and others. In this second part of our interview with Doug (the first part is in Chapter 15), we address the topic of his custom-built home office and the pluses and minuses of establishing a home office.

Consulting For Dummies: You have quite a home office. How did you go about designing it?

Doug Poretz: I built it step by step by step. So if you think of all of the different components of a home office: the furniture, the technology, the telecommunications — the total environment — I addressed them all. In fact, I brought in so many computers and peripherals that my office needed a dedicated electrical system.

CFD: You had to bring a separate electrical service to your home office?

Poretz: Right. At the same time, I also had to put in my own heating, ventilation, and air-conditioning system in the office. I approached my environment as if it were a very professional office. I had it wallpapered. I brought in comfortable chairs to sit in. And I also designed my workstation itself. However, before I started my home office, I subleased a very small office from another business.

CFD: Outside of your home?

Poretz: Yes. I wanted to start my business in an office environment and to have my phones answered live. Once I got that started, then I just changed over to my home office — step by step. I put in phones at home and then every once in a while worked at home by call forwarding. I really didn't start out saying, "I'm going to build a home office." I needed phones, and I needed a work surface. I got one of those thin metal desks that you can buy for about a hundred bucks at any office furniture store. And since they were relatively cheap, I kept buying those desks and putting them in different configurations, finally deciding exactly how I wanted my office space to be. I was in the center of something that curved around me — not unlike a nautilus — with different slots and different places for different things and accessibility to computers and screens and fax and printers.

CFD: Right.

Poretz: So when it came time to have my desk and work center built, it was pretty easy to decide what I wanted because all I had to do was formalize what I had put together by contraption.

CFD: How many phone lines did you end up running into your office?

Poretz: I've lost count. I had ISDN and a dedicated line for the Bloomberg box [investor information device]. I had a line for a plain-paper fax and a line for a fax modem. I had three voice lines and a separate voice line that was off to the side that nobody really knew about. And I had different types of voice-mail boxes — some of which could page me. Plus I had a cell phone that I carried with me plus a phone in the car. I was always available.

CFD: Did your clients have any problem with all your electronic answering systems replacing a human receptionist or assistant?

Poretz: No, my business is basically dealing with publicly owned businesses, and I handle a number of them. I've built a career in it. I decided that what you do is that you take the hand that you're dealt and then you maximize it. If there are any negatives, you try to overcome them. If there are any assets that can be maximized, you try to maximize them. So I always thought that in a one-person, home-office business, there were certain assets that I would try to maximize. These would be things like access to your client, flexibility, quick response, and so on. Furthermore, since I was trying to get a high value-added fee and since a lot of my clients are technology-oriented, by using technology, I could reflect to my clients that I was on *their* wavelength. I *never* tried to pretend to be something that I wasn't — trying to be a "big business." I think that those ads that you see — "make your customers think that you're a big business...."

CFD: We've seen *lots* of those!

Poretz: I think that those ads are not only stupid but counterproductive. Why would you want to make your customer think that something that you're *not* is better than something that you *are*? I thought that what would be best would be to say, "This is what I am, and here are the benefits of it." Never try to hide it. This is a one-person business, and if you want to talk about it, I'm all for it. And if you don't like it, then don't hire me.

CFD: Were there any conflicts with family, friends, or pets by having an office in your home?

Poretz: I think that, first of all, there is a graph with the vertical axis representing the amount of intensive time you need for your business. At the bottom of the graph there is a red band, and at the top of the graph there is another red band. These are the danger zones. At the bottom of the graph, the danger zone is distraction of the home from the *business* — the refrigerator, the TV, the music, the other people, the dog, and so on. That's why, to avoid that distraction, I started my business in subleased space. At the top of the graph, the danger zone is the distraction of the office from your *home*. When your business gets *too* intense, that's what happens. And that was probably the biggest negative for me.

CFD: But in between the red bands, that's where there are tremendous opportunities to enjoy the benefits of a home office, right?

Poretz: Yes. For example, my wife, who is very active in charity affairs and the community, has an incredible schedule herself. She's in and out of the house all day long. And where most people get called on the phone by their spouse — hi, how are you doing — my wife could just drift down into my office. If I was busy, she'd wave and say, "See you later." But if I was between calls, she could sit down, and we could share a cup of coffee instead of a phone call. I found all that quite wonderful.

CFD: You've moved The Poretz Group out of your home office, right? Why?

Poretz: As I built my new firm, I thought through the idea of hiring the kinds of people who have joined me and letting them have home offices and just networking everybody. But if I'm going after high value-added fees, one of the things that I want to do is differentiate the business, and one of the ways I want to differentiate the business is by establishing a certain type of corporate culture. I came to the conclusion that I didn't think that I could grow a corporate culture deep enough, wide enough, and fast enough with a networked organization. Perhaps after we build the business and the reputation and the infrastructure and personalities become very, very strong — when the corporate culture becomes virtually an entity — I might be able to network new people into that.

(continued)

(continued)

CFD: It seems like it would be almost impossible to create a corporate culture when you start out as a networked organization. It's going to create *some* sort of culture, but perhaps not the one that you as a founder or owner want it to be.

Poretz: Definitely. I looked at it very, very seriously — let me tell you. It wasn't something that I gave just five minutes' thought to. I gave a great deal of thought to it. It *was* my first inclination. People I spoke to, things I read, and just my own conclusions made me think that the overwhelming aspect of the corporate culture of a "virtual" business or "networked" business is the fact that it is a virtual business or a networked business. That becomes the overriding characteristic of the corporate culture of that business, in my experience. I wanted the corporate culture of this business to be different. I wanted the corporate culture of this business to have as its most important characteristics things relating to service to the customer, collegiality of the principals involved, access to information, and so on. I just think that small businesses that evolve from home offices to networked business very often, when you speak to those people, what they talk about is how they're networked — not about how they're serving their customers.

CFD: And that's really the most important thing — the service that you give to your clients.

Poretz: Exactly.

Getting Set Up

Setting up your office is probably the most fun part of running a business from your home. Remember all the lousy offices that you were crammed into in your past jobs? Remember the too-small desks, the uncomfortable chairs, the barely adequate computers, the stuffy air, and the Muzak piped over the loudspeakers? This is your big chance to make up for all your previous employers' transgressions against your sensibilities and to design an office that meets *your* needs.

In this section, we explore the essentials of setting up your own home office — from the space to the equipment in it. Don't forget that you'll be spending a great deal of time in your office. Make it as nice a place to work as possible.

Your space

The total amount of space that you're going to need to set up a functioning home office depends on the nature of your consulting business. For most consultants, the ideal situation is to take over an existing bedroom or den and convert it into an office. Not only do you get plenty of space for all your furniture, equipment, and supplies, but a bedroom or den with a door also offers privacy — an important ingredient in *any* home office. In addition, a room that is 100 percent dedicated to your business is easier for you to use.

Here are some key ingredients to setting up an inviting and productive workspace in your home:

- **Find an out-of-the-way place.** You don't want your home office to be in the center of your family's traffic pattern during the morning get-the-kids-ready-for-school rush, nor do you want it to be in a garage that fills with smelly fumes every time someone starts up the car. Ideally, your office should be a private sanctuary where you can focus on your work, not on everything *but* your work. On the flip side, if you find yourself working late into the night, your activities shouldn't bother your significant others. That can be a little difficult if you select your bedroom as your home office.

- **Make the space inviting.** You're going to be spending a *lot* of time in your home office, so you want it to be comfortable and inviting. It should have adequate heat when you need it and plenty of cool air when needed. The walls should be freshly painted in a neutral color, and windows should have blinds that enable you to control the amount of outside light that enters your office. What goes on the walls is up to you. We hang a mix of photographs, framed newspaper articles, bulletin boards, and letters from satisfied clients on our walls.

- **Provide for easy access.** Make sure that your office is easy to access without disturbing the other members of your household. You don't, for example, want the only entrance to your office to be through the baby's nursery.

- **Have good lighting and plenty of it.** Good lighting is critical to your productivity. Ideally, your office will have both plenty of natural lighting from windows (most bedrooms are already well equipped in this department) and from artificial light sources, such as overhead lighting and desk lamps.

    Peter's home office — which is in a converted bedroom — has large windows on the west and north walls, as well as a desk lamp and track lighting installed in the ceiling. The track lighting allows Peter to direct three different light fixtures *exactly* where he wants their light to go.

- **Ventilate the space early and often.** Make sure that your home office has access to plenty of fresh air. This is especially necessary if you have computers, printers, copiers, and other office equipment that generate gobs of ozone, dust, and heat.

✔ **Get wired.** Your home office needs plenty of grounded (three-prong) electric receptacles to plug in all your office equipment. Not only do you need outlets for your computer, but you also need outlets for your printers, your fax machine, your adding machine, your battery charger for your cellular phone, your desk lamps, a radio, and anything else that you may need to plug in. In addition to electricity, you need at least one phone line — maybe more — as well as a coaxial television cable if you're hooked up to a cable modem for Internet access.

✔ **Security is the best policy.** What would happen if someone stole your computer, along with all your disks and backup media? For some consultants, this incident would be an unqualified, magnitude seven, please-shoot-me-now-to-put-me-out-of-my-misery disaster. If you don't have a home security system tied to an alarm and a monitoring service, consider getting one. While you're at it, buy a small fireproof safe to store your backup disks, tapes, or other media — and make sure that you use it!

Your furniture

Your home office can be nothing more than a desk and a chair, or it can be a fully equipped suite with everything found in any commercial office, including fax machines, computers, copiers, and more. When you decide to furnish your home office, get good-quality furnishings that are both comfortable and built to last. You're going to be spending a lot of time in your office, so you should make it a joy — not an ordeal — to work there.

If you're watching your budget (and who isn't?), consider buying your furniture *used* instead of new. With all the corporate downsizing that is sweeping the nation, a heck of a lot of high-quality used office furniture is available — at a fraction of the price of new furniture. You may also want to consider renting or leasing your office furniture, although doing so may not be a great idea in the long run. Check your Yellow Pages for a rental company near you.

With that advice in mind, here are some key things to consider when you go shopping for office furniture:

✔ **Your chair:** If you're looking for a place to invest a little extra money in your office setup, the chair is the place. Spend the extra money to get a high-quality, ergonomically correct task chair. If you have used an ergonomic chair at work, you already know the importance of being in the correct working position — especially when you spend most of your time at your desk. Using a quality chair reduces fatigue and helps to prevent back pain and other ills that can occur when your posture is out of whack for long periods of time.

If you expect clients to visit, make sure that you have comfortable chairs available for them, too.

✔ **Your desk:** When shopping for your desk, think *big!* No matter how large your desk, by the time you load it up with a computer, a printer, a phone, a calculator, and a personal planner or two, you have precious little space left over to do your work. Get a sturdy desk — you don't want it to be rocking to and fro as you type up proposals. Also be sure that your desk has more than enough room to accommodate whatever you intend to put on it whilst leaving you enough room to spread out your work. A large traditional desk or even a sturdy worktable will do just fine.

While you're shopping, make sure that you look for a desk that is at the proper height so that working on your computer is an ergonomic dream rather than an ergonomic nightmare.

✔ **Worktables:** A couple of worktables can give you the extra room you need to get your work done more efficiently and to stay organized. You don't need anything fancy here — a simple table with folding legs or a sturdy dining-room table works fine.

✔ **File cabinets:** You may be able to make do with a file drawer in your desk. If you deal with volumes of paperwork as a part of your consulting practice, however, you need additional filing space. An organized filing system is critical to your efficiency, so spend some serious time designing and implementing a filing system before you jump into your consulting business. Plenty of choices are available, and your ultimate decision depends on the amount of paperwork that you need to keep at hand. At a minimum, you should get a freestanding, four-drawer file cabinet. You can easily add more cabinets as the need arises. For long-term storage, pull the documents from your file cabinets and place them in the cardboard storage boxes commonly known as banker's boxes. You can then stick the storage boxes in a closet or in the garage. Reserve the space in your file cabinets for documents that you actively use and need to access regularly.

✔ **Bookshelves:** What would an office be without bookshelves? In addition to holding books, bookshelves are handy for a variety of other purposes. Peter's bookshelves — which are actually heavy-duty plastic storage shelves that he purchased at a large membership warehouse club — are filled with books, boxes of business-oriented computer software, his laptop computer and related accessories, stacks and stacks of magazines for research, laser printer paper, inkjet printer paper, mailing envelopes, FedEx supplies, and his cherished compact disc player and stereo. No matter how many bookshelves you get, we can guarantee that you'll fill them up.

✔ **Supply storage:** Make sure to set aside a drawer or shelf to hold your office supplies. Pens, pencils, paper clips, staples, markers, and all the other fruits of your office-supply shopping spree need a place safe from your dog, cat, or kids.

Your equipment

As with any office, your home office requires certain pieces of equipment and supplies for you to conduct business. For example, doing an in-depth automated spreadsheet analysis without a computer is pretty hard. And contacting your clients is hard as heck if you don't have a phone. And if you want to mail an invoice, some envelopes and stamps would be helpful.

This section discusses obtaining the basic equipment and supplies you need to get your business up and running. For a more in-depth discussion of the different kinds of technology at your disposal, see Chapter 14.

- **Telephones:** You definitely need at least one telephone — maybe more. If you have only one phone, get a basic, plain old telephone with a hold button and speakerphone. Consider getting two telephone lines: one for voice and one for fax and Internet. Allow at least 24 to 48 hours for your local phone provider to get your service hooked up — more if the provider has to run new wiring from the street into your home.

   If you also need a phone away from your home office, buy a cellular or PCS wireless unit. And don't forget to get an answering machine or voice-mail service so that your callers can leave a message if you're not around.

- **Computer:** Your computer is the nerve center of your home office. Get the best you can afford, and make sure that it has the kinds of software that you need to get your work done. If you'll do most of your work at your home office, get a standard desktop computer. If you will be on the road frequently or plan to spend much time with clients, consider getting a laptop computer. You computer should have at least a 166 MHz Pentium or equivalent Apple PowerPC microprocessor, with a minimum of 16MB of RAM, a 2GB hard drive, an 8x CD-ROM drive, and a 33.6/14.4 Kbps data/fax modem. For software, a complete office *suite,* such as Microsoft Office 97, is a smart way to go. Microsoft Office contains word processing, spreadsheet, presentation graphics, data-base, and personal organizing programs, all in one package.

- **Fax machine:** If your computer has a data/fax modem, you can use *it* as your fax machine. However, if you don't want to leave your computer turned on all day long, you should buy a dedicated fax machine. Be sure to get one that uses plain paper — not the old-tech rolls of thermal paper. New fax machines have an added bonus: You can use most of them as copiers, printers, and scanners. Wow!

- **Internet access:** If you're new to the Internet, sign up with an established online service, such as America Online or CompuServe. You get unlimited access to the Internet and World Wide Web for a very reasonable flat rate each month and can send and receive as much e-mail as you like. You also can learn about online life in a supportive, nonthreatening environment. If you're an Internet veteran, find a reliable Internet service provider and get the fastest access you can — through a 56.6 Kbps data modem, an ISDN telephone service, or a cable modem.

✔ **Typewriter:** Although computers have almost placed the last nail in the coffin of the typewriter industry, you can still do a *few* things with a typewriter that you can't do with a computer and printer — at least not as quickly and easily. You can address labels and envelopes, for example. If you decide that you need a typewriter for your home office, consider finding a nice used one instead of buying new.

✔ **Copier:** If you need to make only a few copies of documents on an irregular basis, you can use your fax machine as a copier or rely on a local copying service, such as Kinko's. However, if you make lots of copies on a regular basis, buy or lease a decent office copier. To save yourself grief and headaches down the road, get one that at a minimum has an automatic document feeder and can handle legal-size as well as letter-size paper. Also get a service contract that guarantees service within one business day after you make your service call.

Other business essentials

The big stuff is out of the way. Now it's time to get down to the little things that really make an office an office. Remember those lousy pens that corporate standardized on to save money? Or those tacky desk calendars? Or how about those cheap yellow legal pads that fell apart more often than they held together? You'll never have to use any of those again. Now *you* decide what kinds of pens, pencils, paper, calendars, and other office supplies that your office stocks.

When you set up your home office, stock up on plenty of office supplies. Visit your local office supply store or a large warehouse office supply store and shop until you drop. Most of the large warehouse stores offer their own charge cards that include discounts and other benefits for using them — get one! Here are a few essentials for any well-equipped home office:

✔ **Writing utensils:** Get plenty of your favorite pens and pencils — now's your big chance to really let go. When it comes to pencils, go for a high-quality brand, such as Ticonderoga or Eberhard Faber, or go for the mechanical pencil of your choice. While you're at it, get a nice eraser stick, such as the ones offered by Staedtler or Pentel (not that you'll ever have any mistakes to erase, right?). Buy an assortment of color markers in sizes ranging from fine to broad. If you have a whiteboard in your office, you need special markers for that. And don't forget to stock up on those handy yellow highlighters, too.

✔ **Paper:** If you use your computer printer frequently or have an office copier, consider buying your standard 20-pound paper by the case. Be sure to buy paper that is designed for the use that you intend; for example, laser printer or plain paper fax. Also get some fancy 24-pound paper for sending out letters to your favorite clients. Depending on your personal preferences, you may also want to buy some ruled pads of letter- or legal-sized paper, some note paper, and index cards.

✔ **Fastening devices:** If your office doesn't have a stapler, it is not truly an office. Pick up a stapler and some matching staples to go with it. Buy plenty of paper clips (we like the jumbo size best), binder clips (get an assortment of all the different sizes), and rubber bands. A roll of adhesive tape is a definite must, and a large of roll of packing tape can be a real lifesaver from time to time. Finally, cap off your collection of fastening devices with a Uhu glue stick, just in case you need to paste something to something else.

✔ **Envelopes:** Stock up on #10 envelopes — these are the standard business size. If you plan to run them through your printer, make sure that the box says that they are made for that purpose. Also get some 9-x-12-inch or 10-x-13-inch mailing envelopes so that you can mail documents without folding them.

✔ **Folders:** If you have a file cabinet, you need file folders to fill it up. You can choose from a wide variety of sizes, colors, and types — including hanging and nonhanging folders. Try out several different kinds of folders until you find the ones that work best for you.

Home Office Checklist

Here's a quick and easy checklist to use for setting up your home office that summarizes all the items listed in the section "Getting Set Up." Now you don't have an excuse for not setting up an office right away!

✔ **Space:** Pick out a space in your home that is out of the way, quiet, and inviting. Make sure that it has adequate lighting and that it is sufficiently wired for electricity, phones, and data communications. If you don't have a home alarm and a fireproof data safe, consider getting them.

✔ **Furniture:** Get a comfortable, ergonomic task chair, as well as some comfortable chairs for your clients if you'll be meeting with them in your home office. Invest in a desk that is sturdy and large enough to accommodate your computer, peripherals, *and* your work. Buy work-tables, file cabinets, and bookshelves, too.

✔ **Equipment:** Buy a telephone for your office and invest in one or more phone lines, depending on your needs. Get the best computer you can afford and buy a plain-paper fax machine. You'll definitely need Internet access for your e-mail, and you may need a typewriter and an office copier as well.

✔ **Office supplies:** Go to your nearest office supply warehouse, grab a shopping cart, and go wild! Pens, pencils, staplers, tape, and more are all awaiting the opportunity to serve you.

When to Kick Your Home Office Out of the House

For some independent consultants, a home office is all they ever need. For others, a home office is just the first step on the way to something bigger.

So how do you know when the time has come to kick your home office out of the house? When any or all of the following events occur, start thinking seriously about finding someplace new to run your business — someplace *outside* your home:

✔ **When your home life intrudes too far into your work life (or vice versa):** One of the great things about having an office at home is the chance to balance your home life with your work life. However, if you are constantly being interrupted by your significant others — boyfriend, wife, kids, dog — you may have to move your office out of your home. Conversely, if your business activities are causing turmoil with the other people who share your house, that may also be a reason for moving your office.

✔ **When you start getting out of touch:** Many consultants keep in touch with their clients regardless of *where* they maintain their offices. Some consultants, however, find that staying in touch with clients is easier when they locate their offices in the same part of town as their clients. If you find that you are losing contact with your clients, you're going to have to make a choice. Is your home office — located an hour and a half from the big city — allowing you to get your business done the way it needs to be done? Or is your home office, instead, interfering with the day-to-day personal contact with clients that you need to succeed? If your home office is getting in the way of doing business, you need to reassess your situation and consider moving out.

✔ **When your clients start wondering whether you're all you're cracked up to be:** Face it. Some clients are going to wonder if you're as talented as you say you are or worth the fees you are demanding when they find out that you work out of your home instead of a "real" office. For many consultants, this is not an issue because the clients that they work for don't care *where* the work is done as long as it's done *well*. However, in some cases you may have to maintain a conventional office to convey the appearance of success to your clients. This is why you'll probably never consult with a lawyer or a certified public accountant in his or her home office.

Chapter 18

Keeping Track of Your Time and Money

. . . .

In This Chapter

▶ Tracking your time

▶ Invoicing clients and collecting money

▶ Creating and monitoring budgets

. . . .

*W*hen it comes right down to it, keeping track of the financial aspects of your business is really quite simple. Only two kinds of money are involved in your business: the money that's coming in and the money that's going out.

This chapter is all about keeping track of your time — the hours of work for which you will bill your client — *and* your money. We start by talking about how to keep track of your time and how to track the work you do on specific projects for specific clients. Then we briefly consider the ins and outs of budgeting and the importance of staying on budget.

Tracking Your Time

Although some consultants bill their clients as they complete specific percentages of the project — say, every third or half — many other consultants charge their services on the basis of some increment of time (usually hourly). Although you always should track your use of your time (what better way to find out that you're spending more than half of each workday playing Doom or Solitaire on your computer?), you absolutely must do so when you're paid based on the number of hours you work on a particular project.

You can track the time that you spend working on client projects in two ways: the client activity log and the client time sheet. The following two sections examine exactly what each of these forms is all about.

The daily client activity log

If you're the kind of consultant who bills your time hourly or on another basis related to time, then the best way to track your time is to maintain an activity log. An activity log is a daily record of everything you do for your clients, broken down into your smallest billing increments — say, an hour, half an hour, or a quarter of an hour.

Figure 18-1, shown on the next page, represents a simple daily client activity log that is appropriate for almost any kind of consulting work that is billed on an hourly basis. Although it's up to you to decide the smallest increment of time that you use to bill your clients — most consultants use 15-minute blocks — for simplicity's sake (and to keep the log from taking up two whole pages of this book), we have selected 30-minute increments for our example. You can select any portion of an hour that you like (and to which your clients agree!).

The first thing you may notice is that the client activity log looks very similar to an appointment calendar — in fact, an appointment calendar makes a great activity log — with every half-hour noted, from 7:00 a.m. until 5:00 p.m. Of course, you can tailor your client activity log to fit your exact schedule. If, for example, you start work at noon and work until midnight, you can set up your log on that basis.

As you can see from the sample client activity log in Figure 18-1, the consultant worked on projects for four different clients on February 8. The consultant worked on the Ramsey project from 7:00 to 8:00 and worked on a draft report for Willis from 9:00 to 11:00. Just before lunch — from 12:30 to 1:00 — the consultant made phone calls for Martinelli, another client. After a satisfying break for lunch, the intrepid consultant jumped into an Internet search for Speedway Associates from 1:30 to 3:30, and then finished the workday with another phone call to Martinelli from 4:30 to 5:00.

What's the point of going through the trouble of keeping daily client activity logs? Before you decide that filling out an activity log every day is too much pain for you to endure, consider these advantages:

- ✔ **You're going to want to bill your clients someday.** Sure, working on all those fun consulting projects can be very satisfying in and of itself. However, you still have to pay your bills. And if you want to pay your bills, then your clients have to pay theirs! Keeping a client activity log makes it much easier to bill your clients when the time comes (and it never seems like that time is soon enough!).

- ✔ **One sheet of paper is a lot better than lots of little sheets of paper.** The temptation to scribble your hours on a scrap of paper or a stick-on note is often overwhelming, but you *must* resist this temptation at all costs! You can easily lose or forget about all those little scraps of paper; before you know it, you've done a heck of a lot of work for nothing because you can't bill your clients for it.

Jobs

Tuesday Morning - part time
Indeed 1-31   Carmel

Ask if Whole Foods is hiring

Daily Client Activity Log	
February 8, 19xx	
7:00	Internet search for Ramsey project
7:30	Internet search for Ramsey project
8:00	
8:30	
9:00	Worked on draft report of recommendations for Willis
9:30	Worked on draft report of recommendations for Willis
10:00	Worked on draft report of recommendations for Willis
10:30	Worked on draft report of recommendations for Willis
11:00	
11:30	
12:00	
12:30	Phone calls on behalf of Martinelli
1:00	
1:30	Internet search for Speedway Associates
2:00	Internet search for Speedway Associates
2:30	Internet search for Speedway Associates
3:00	Internet search for Speedway Associates
3:30	
4:00	
4:30	Phone call to Martinelli
5:00	

Figure 18-1:
Sample
client
activity log.

✔ **Your log has a better memory than you do.** You may think that you can rely on your memory to keep the ten different projects that you are working on for three different clients separate from one another and then to bill them properly at the end of the month. Though you may be blessed with a memory that would make *Jeopardy!* fans around the world green with envy, we guarantee you that the memory in your client activity log is longer and much more precise — especially when you're considering 260+ workdays in a year filled with a variety of projects for a variety of clients. Do yourself a favor and start using a client activity log to keep track of the time you spend on your consulting projects.

Now that we have convinced you that it's in your best interest to use daily client activity logs to record your time, what do you do with all the information that you have gathered? This is the best part. Now it's time to transfer all that information to your client time sheets. Coincidentally, that just happens to be the next section of this chapter.

Client time sheets

Eventually — perhaps once a month or maybe more, depending on your client billing arrangements — you need to send an invoice to each of your clients for the work you did for them during that billing period. Believe us, this task is *much* easier when you have been maintaining your client activity logs on a regular basis. (You *are* maintaining client activity logs, right?)

A client time sheet is simply a summary of the exact work that you do for a client, including how much time you spend on each task or project. Deciding what approach you want to use to present your information is up to you and your client.

Figure 18-2, shown on the next page, is a sample client time sheet that breaks down the consultant's work into specific tasks.

As you can see from the sample client time sheet, the consultant performed a total of 90 hours of work for Speedway Associates in February. This total was further broken down into specific tasks, including client consultation (20 hours), Internet searches (45 hours), draft product marketing plans (10 hours), and clerical support (15 hours).

Where did these numbers come from? They came directly from the client activity logs that the consultant completed and maintained for each and every workday. Because the consultant bills his clients on a monthly basis, he goes through the month's client activity logs and prepares client time sheets for each client at the end of each month. The client time sheet — which is merely a summary of the information contained in the daily client activity logs — can then be used as the basis for the consultant's monthly invoice.

Remember, you need only two things to track the time you spend on client projects: a daily client activity log and a client time sheet. With those two pieces of information, you can track your time and then bill your clients for your services appropriately and accurately.

Client Time Sheet	
Speedway Associates	
February 19xx	
Client consultation	20 hours
Internet searches	45 hours
Draft product marketing plans	10 hours
Clerical support	15 hours
Total hours	90 hours

Figure 18-2:
Sample
client
time sheet.

Billing Your Clients and Collecting Your Money

Although the entire topic of accounting is important when it comes to ensuring the financial health of your enterprise, the effectiveness of your billing and collections procedures probably has the greatest impact — whether positive or negative — on the health of your consulting practice. If you bill your clients quickly and accurately and then follow up to ensure that you collect your payments when they are due, you do a *lot* to ensure the financial viability of your business.

Please take a look at some different aspects of billing your clients and collecting your money when it is due.

Billing for your services

How you bill or invoice your clients for the work you do for them depends on your contract. If your contract is set up to pay you as you achieve specific milestones — say, completing one-quarter of the project or submitting a draft report of recommendations — then you invoice your clients for the amount due upon completion of each milestone. However, if you work on an ongoing basis and bill your clients for the number of hours that you work plus expenses (photocopying, travel, and so on), then you collect the charges and bill them to your client at the end of the agreed billing period, usually the end of each calendar month.

Figure 18-3, shown on the next page, shows a sample invoice based on the Speedway Associates example used earlier in this chapter. As you can see, Speedway simply totaled the number of hours for all the work done in February and multiplied that by its contracted billing rate of $50 an hour for a total payment due of $4,500.

Here are some tips on maximizing the effectiveness of your billing process:

- ✔ **Front-load your billing.** If you invoice on a milestone basis, try to load your fees into the front of the project rather than at the end of the project. For example, push for an advance payment to start the project, or simply make your first couple of payments higher than those that are due later in the project. Doing so gives your project a financial head start that is very beneficial to the financial health of your practice.

- ✔ **Bill your clients often.** The more often you get paid, the better the effect on the positive flow of cash through your practice. Although monthly payments are pretty much the standard for consultants who bill hours and expenses, you can agree with your client to bill them more often than that.

- ✔ **Invoice immediately.** Immediately after you complete a milestone or reach the end of your billing cycle, send an invoice to your client. The sooner you send an invoice, the sooner your clients pay their bills. And the sooner they pay their bills, the better off your practice is financially.

- ✔ **Offer a discount for prompt payment.** To help motivate your clients to pay early (or at least on time), offer a nominal discount — say, in the range of 0.5 to 1 percent) for paying their invoices within 10 or 20 days.

- ✔ **Monitor client payments closely.** Make sure that your clients pay their bills on time. If certain clients don't, call them personally to see what the problem is. If it looks like you're going to have a hard time getting them to pay the amounts they owe you, act quickly to initiate your collection procedures.

What? You don't have any collection procedures? Then it's a great time for you to read the next section of this chapter.

Collecting delinquent accounts

No matter how great your clients are or how wonderful they are about paying their bills, eventually you encounter a client who either pays you late

Invoice	
Speedway Associates	
February 19xx	
Client consultation	20 hours
Internet searches	45 hours
Draft product marketing plans	10 hours
Clerical support	15 hours
Total hours	90 hours
Billing rate	$50/hour
Total amount due	**$4,500**
All payments due 30 days after invoice date. A prompt payment discount of 1% will be granted for all payments made no later than 10 days after invoice date.	
Thank you!	

Figure 18-3: Sample invoice.

or doesn't pay you at all. What should you do? Do you ignore this behavior and just be glad that you have the work, or should you take action? Our advice is to take action — *immediately*.

The action you should take to collect the money owed to you depends on many things: the size of the job, the length of the relationship with your client, the total amount of money owed to your business, the number of days (or months) that the money is overdue, and more. When you decide to initiate your collection procedures, you need to weigh these factors in your decision. Whatever action you take, we recommend that you establish a clear order of precedence — starting with a simple phone call and then escalating your actions upward in intensity depending on your client's reaction — to guide you through the process.

If you decide that it's time to start the collections process, consider taking these steps as a part of your efforts:

1. **Call your client directly.**

   Ask your primary contact in the client's organization why you haven't been paid. Your client likely has much more leverage than you do from outside the organization and, therefore, probably will have more success getting your bills paid than you will if you call the payment department yourself. You often can solve the payment problem in only a few minutes with a call to your client.

2. Send a past-due letter immediately.

If the call to your client doesn't resolve the payment problem within a reasonable amount of time — say, a few days or a week — then send a past-due letter to your client along with another copy of your invoice. Send these letters regularly — weekly or monthly — until you receive your payment. Follow up your letters with phone calls to your client and to your client's billing department.

3. Stop work.

If you are not being paid, consider suspending your work until you are paid. Your work may be the only leverage — short of legal action — that you have to get your client to pay you.

4. Call in a collections agency.

If the client continues to ignore your requests for payment, you can turn your delinquent account over to a collections agency. The agency will pursue the collections process for you for a piece of the money that is ultimately collected, usually somewhere in the neighborhood of 20 to 40 percent.

5. Mediate.

In lieu of going to court, both parties can submit to mediation, in which an independent third party helps you resolve your differences, or to arbitration. If both parties submit to arbitration, an independent arbitrator listens to both sides of the story and then makes a decision in favor of one party or the other.

6. Take the client to court.

Taking your delinquent client to court is the last remedy that you have. You can sue your client in small claims court, which allows you to sue without a lawyer for a very small fee, as long as the amount is within the limits of your state or locality. For example, small claims actions are limited to $1,750 in Michigan, $5,000 in California, $6,000 in the Canadian province of Ontario, and £3,000 in England and Wales. If the amount owed exceeds the amount allowed by small claims procedures, then you need to hire a lawyer and file your lawsuit in a higher court.

Ideally, you'll never have to go to court to get your clients to pay you. By monitoring your payments closely and contacting your clients at the first hint of trouble, you minimize your risk of exposure due to late payments or payments that are never made.

Building Better Budgets

A *budget* is an estimate of the amount of money that you expect to bring *into* your organization or pay *out* of your organization for whatever business activities you undertake. For example, you may estimate (and budget) that you'll bring in $25,000 worth of client billings in October. Or you may estimate (and budget) that you'll spend $300 in telephone charges in January.

Why should you consider developing budgets for your consulting business? You should do so because budgets provide you with a baseline of *expected* performance against which you can measure the *actual* performance of your consulting enterprise. With this information, you can diagnose and assess the current financial health of your business.

Does your latest accounting report say that sales are way below the amount you budgeted? Then your job is to figure out why. Are expenses too high? Maybe you need to find less expensive ways to pay for outside services. Whatever the issues are, budgets allow you to see whether your business is doing what it's supposed to be doing, at least in a financial sense.

You can also use budgets to fulfill another important purpose: to provide a baseline against which you can measure your progress toward the successful completion of client projects. For example, if you are 50 percent of the way through a project but have spent 75 percent of the amount you budgeted, then you have an immediate indication that you may run out of money before you complete the project. This is not a good situation for any consultant. Either you have underbudgeted your expenses for the project, or you are overspending. Whenever budgeted performance and actual performance disagree, your job is to find out why.

Creating budgets also gives you the opportunity to put together all kinds of snazzy graphs and charts to impress your clients. Picture yourself in your client's auditorium: lights dimmed, the attention of every audience member riveted on your presentation. You alternately project full-color, multilevel spreadsheets with beautiful three-dimensional bar charts and graphs. You're in command as you click the buttons on your remote control. There's nothing like numbers presented in an interesting way to get the attention of your clients!

Different kinds of budgets

Depending on the size of your business, the budgeting process may be quite simple or, alternatively, very complex. Regardless of the size of your business, you can budget most anything in it. Here are some examples:

- ✔ **Project budget:** A project budget is an estimate of all the different potential expenses that you will incur during the course of a project compared to the amount of money that your client intends to pay you.

- ✔ **Labor budget:** Labor budgets are made up of the number and names of all the various positions in a company (if there are various positions in the company), along with the salary or wages budgeted for each position.

- ✔ **Sales budget:** The sales budget is an estimate of the total number of products or services that will be sold in a given period. You determine total revenues by multiplying the number of units by the price per unit.

- ✔ **Expense budget:** Expense budgets contain all the different expenses that you may incur during the normal course of operations. You can budget travel, training, office supplies, and other similar costs to your business within your expense budget.

- ✔ **Capital budget:** This budget is your plan to acquire fixed assets (those with a long useful life), such as furniture, computers, facilities, physical plant, and so forth, to support your business operations.

Creating a budget

There's a right way and a wrong way to create budgets. The *wrong* way is simply to take a copy of your last budget and stick a new title on it. The *right* way is to gather information from as many sources as possible, review and check the information for accuracy, and then use your good judgment to guess what the future may bring. A budget is only as good as the data that goes into it and the good judgment that you bring to the process.

Here are a few tips to consider when you put together your budgets:

- ✔ **Gather data.** Retrieve copies of your previous budgets from your filing cabinets and then compare the figures that you budgeted against your actual experience. Look at this historical data to determine whether you overestimated or underestimated figures in any of your previous budgets and to see what previous years or similar projects cost your firm. Take time to consider whether you will need to hire more people, lease new facilities, or buy equipment or supplies. Finally, consider what effect possible large increases or decreases in sales or expenses may have on your budget.

- ✔ **Meet with clients.** When you start the budgeting process, meet with your key clients to get a firm idea of the fees that you can expect your work for them to generate. You also want to get some idea of when the revenues will hit your system.

✔ **Apply your judgment.** Hard data and cold facts are an important source of information in the budgeting process, but they aren't *everything*. Budgeting is one part science and one part art. Your job is to take the data and facts and then apply your own judgment to them to determine the most likely outcomes.

✔ **Run the numbers.** Put your estimates of money coming into your business and money going out of your business into a budget spreadsheet and hit the calculate button on your computer. Review and modify this draft of your budget before you finalize it. Don't worry if the draft is rough or is missing information. You always have the opportunity to fine-tune it later on.

✔ **Check results and run the budget again as necessary.** Closely review your draft budget and see whether it still makes sense to you. Are you missing any anticipated sources of revenue or expenses? Are the numbers realistic? Do they make sense in a historical perspective? Are they too high or too low? When you are finally satisfied with the results, finalize your budget and print it. Congratulations! You did it!

Where your budget numbers come from

The accuracy of your budget hinges on two main factors: the quality of the data that you use to develop your budget and the quality of the judgment that you apply to the data you work with. Although judgment is something that comes with experience, the quality of the data you use depends on where you get it. You can use three basic approaches to develop the data for building a budget:

✔ **Build it from scratch.** In this process, widely known as *zero-based budgeting,* you build your budget from scratch — determining the people, facilities, travel, advertising, and other resources that are required to support it. You then assign a cost to each need, and the budget is complete. Perhaps not too surprisingly, the answer that comes out of building a budget from scratch is often quite different from one that results from using historical data. Not only that, but building a budget from scratch is very labor-intensive. Of course, if you're a first-time consultant, you have little choice but to build your budget from scratch.

✔ **Use historical figures.** One of the easiest ways to develop data for your budget is to use the actual results from the preceding budget period. Though the past is not always an indication of the future — especially if your practice is subject to significant fluctuations in revenues or expenses — using historical data can be very useful, especially as a starting point.

✔ **Use the combination approach.** Many consultants use a combination of both preceding methods for determining which data to include in their budgets. They gather historical data and then compare it to their best estimates of what they think performing a particular function will cost. They then adjust historical data up or down, depending on their view of reality developed from personal experience.

Staying on budget

After you start your consulting business and after you begin each client project, you need to closely monitor your various budgets to make sure that you don't exceed them. If your actual expenditures start to exceed the amounts that you budgeted, you need to take quick and decisive action before you dig a financial black hole that quickly sucks up all your financial resources.

Here are some things that you can do to get back on track if the money you send out of your business starts to significantly exceed the amount of money that you bring into it:

✔ **Freeze discretionary expenses.** Some expenses, such as computer repairs, telephones, and electricity, are essential to an operation or project and cannot be stopped without jeopardizing your ability to perform your contracted jobs. You can curtail discretionary expenses, such as purchasing new carpeting, upgrading computer monitors, or traveling first-class, without jeopardizing your ability to complete client projects. Freezing discretionary expenses is the quickest and least painful way to get your actual expenditures back in line with your budgeted expenditures.

✔ **Freeze hiring.** Of course, you can cease hiring new employees only if your business is large enough to hire employees in the first place. By delaying the hiring of new employees, you save not only on the cost of hourly pay or salaries but also on the costs of any fringe benefits that you provide, such as medical care, and overhead expenses like water, electricity, and janitorial services.

✔ **Increase your rates.** Part of the problem may be that you aren't charging a high enough rate for your services to cover your reasonable and necessary expenses. If this is the case, consider raising your rates for new business that you bring in.

When it comes to keeping track of your money, budgeting is really just the tip of the iceberg. Whether you like it or not, as the owner of your own business, you need to have a basic understanding of the process that your business goes through in order to account for the money it makes and the money it spends. Check out *Accounting For Dummies* by John A. Tracy (published by IDG Books Worldwide, Inc.) for all the information you need to know about the wonderful world of accounting.

Chapter 19

Multiplying Your Effectiveness: Using Support Services

· ·

In This Chapter

▶ Leveraging your experience and focusing your efforts

▶ Hiring support staff

▶ Creating a virtual office

· ·

*W*hether your business is small or large, there are certain things that only *you* can and should do — the things that bring you and your practice the greatest financial return. Similarly, you should always delegate certain things to others because doing them yourself takes you away from doing the things that bring you the greatest return. As an independent consultant, you may find yourself constantly balancing the temptation to do everything yourself against the very real need to free up as much of your time as possible so that you can focus on the things you do best.

Your job is to use your time and resources in the most cost-effective way while maximizing their return. Our humble belief — borne over years of experience in business and consulting — is that the best way to accomplish this goal is to make effective use of support services. *Support services* are the full range of business services available to you — from clerical support to photocopying to legal advice to a fully equipped rented office — that enable you to spend less time doing the things that have a low return to your business and spend more time doing the things that have a high return.

In this chapter, we address the importance of leveraging your experience and focusing your efforts in making your business a success, and we consider the variety of different staffing options available to you. We also take a look at the virtual office and explain how it can help make you a more efficient and effective consultant.

Keys to Your Success: Leverage and Focus

The larger the business, the more specialized your role in it seems to become. If you are a marketing manager, you probably don't have to worry about personally greeting clients at the front desk or soldering circuit boards on your company's assembly line. However, as the size of your organization *decreases,* your role in it *increases.* Ultimately, in a one-person consulting business, you find that you are responsible for *everything* — from answering the phone to performing analyses for your clients to taking out the trash.

If you do *everything* in your business, at some point you're going to reach a limit to what you can accomplish. And depending on how high or how low that limit is on the scale of your potential success, you may find that you're unable to meet the goals that you set for yourself and for your business.

So what can you do? We're glad you asked.

There are two keys to success in consulting: leveraging your experience and focusing your efforts on the things you are uniquely qualified to do. Each is critical to your ability to do the things you need to do to grow your business, and the best way to get as much as you can of each is by using support services judiciously. The bullets that follow describe exactly how leverage and focus can make you a more effective consultant:

- **Leveraging your experience:** *You* know what the opportunities are, *you* have the contacts, and *you* know the business. When you take advantage of support services by hiring an assistant, you can leverage your own experience and knowledge by teaching it to another person. That person can then go out and do many of the same things that you do now — dramatically increasing your own effectiveness and the financial return to your practice.

- **Focusing your efforts:** Do you *really* have time to make 2,000 two-sided, collated, and comb-bound copies of your presentation? Even if you *did* have the time, would standing at a copier at your local post office or grocery store really be the best way to use it? We think not. For your business to be successful, you have to focus on doing the things that you are uniquely qualified to do and that bring you and your practice the highest financial gain. Leave the copying to someone else while *you* prospect for new business or meet prospective clients.

Clearly, it's in your best interest to find high-quality support services and then use them to help you leverage your own efforts and focus on doing the things that you do best. In the sections that follow, we take a look at the wide range of support services available and consider exactly how you can benefit from using them. You can choose to use one service, or you can choose to use them all — it's up to you.

Your Staff

There's a lot of stuff to be done, and trying to do it *all* yourself just doesn't make sense. Maybe you *could* if you really wanted to, but is wading through the daily mountain of mail and e-mail, looking for a few nuggets among the flood of junk, really the best use of your time? Or picking up the phone yourself each and every time it rings, distracting you from taking care of important client business? Or driving to your local copy shop every time you need to photocopy a particularly lengthy document?

In our opinion, it isn't.

Although there are certain things that only *you* can do, other things are best left to someone else. For example, it may make a lot of sense to hire a part-time personal assistant to take care of your routine clerical needs. Or it may be much more cost-effective to hire a firm specializing in promotion to publicize your business rather than to do it yourself. This section addresses the many advantages of hiring other people to help you do your own job better.

A good assistant is everything

Hiring an assistant is one of quickest and most cost-effective ways to free up your time to focus on the things that *you* need to do and that bring your practice the greatest financial benefit. You don't have to make a major commitment to start out. Your assistant may be a spouse or significant other working on a part-time basis. Or perhaps a college student or a temporary employee who works for you a couple hours a day or a few days a week. As your workload increases, you can gradually extend your assistant's work schedule to meet your needs and the needs of your clients, or hire a full-time person or additional people as required. Using temporary employees is a great way to get the support you need and to get a sense of how many hours you need help with before you hire someone on a more permanent basis.

Carefully chosen, a good assistant can deliver benefits far beyond taking care of clerical duties. Here are some of the benefits of hiring an assistant:

- ✔ **You save time.** An assistant can take over your rote tasks — answering the phone, responding to client inquiries, sorting and prioritizing mail, voice-mail, and e-mail messages — freeing you to focus on client projects and securing new business.

- ✔ **You save money.** The financial value of your time probably far exceeds whatever you would pay an assistant. For example, you may make $100 an hour as a consultant, but your assistant may make a fraction of that — say, $8 to $10 an hour.

✔ **You make a more positive impression on your clients.** When clients are helped by an assistant, they are likely to be impressed and feel that they are receiving better service — and they probably are!

✔ **You create opportunities to get away from your office.** When you're a one-person business, it's easy to feel that you have to be in your office all the time to make sure that you don't miss important client calls. Hiring an assistant enables you to get out of your office to visit clients and network with prospective clients.

✔ **You get another point of view.** No one has a monopoly on the truth. An assistant often can give you a second point of view or a second opinion. For a one-person operation, this can be a refreshing breath of fresh air.

As soon as you can afford to hire an assistant (can you afford *not* to?), do it! You'll be amazed at what you can do with all the time that suddenly becomes available — and so will your clients.

Contracting for services

Every business passes through several stages during its existence. Most businesses begin with a startup phase, move through a period of youthful vigor and growth, and then move on to a phase of maturity and stability, followed by slow decline (unless the business is reinvigorated by an infusion of new products, new management, or other fundamental change). You probably wouldn't be surprised to learn that a wide variety of consultants and professionals are available to help you and your practice pass successfully through each of these stages and to its ultimate destination, wherever that may be.

Here are some of the consultants and other professionals that you may find of use during the course of your career as an independent consultant:

✔ **Business planning and startup:** These consultants can help you develop the right business plan for the kind of business that you intend to set up, as well as provide you with a wealth of advice and support as you start up your business. A good business plan can be a valuable road map as you begin your new business and can be an effective tool for helping you obtain business loans and equity investment.

✔ **Accounting and bookkeeping:** Even if you have only a few clients and your business is relatively small, engaging the services of a talented accountant to keep your books straight and do your taxes can be a very wise move. The tax laws continue to get more and more complicated (much to the delight of those who have chosen the accounting profession), and a good accountant can make sure that you take full advantage of all the deductions and tax credits that are available to you.

✔ **Promotion and marketing:** Although many consultants like to think that they know best how to market themselves, this may not really be the case. A promotions or marketing consultant can help you get your message to the right people at the right time, in the most attractive and effective format possible, for a fraction of the effort that you might put into a trial-and-error marketing push.

✔ **Legal advice:** Face it. At some point, everyone who is in business for himself or herself needs the services of an attorney. You may not need a lawyer very often, but whether it's to help collect a bad debt or to review a consulting agreement or to provide legal defense in a court of law, you'll want the very best attorney you can find when you *do* need legal advice.

When are employees not employees? When they're temps!

After you establish your consulting business, you may find that you have far more clients who need your services than you have the time to do work. Unfortunately, one person can do only so much. When your workload exceeds the amount of time that you can devote to completing it, you have one of three choices:

✔ You can tell the client to find someone else to do the work.

✔ You can subcontract the work out to another firm.

✔ You can hire new employees to help you complete your assignments.

Although you *should* turn away business that's not in your area of expertise or that's not profitable enough for you, few consultants have the luxury of turning away good, profitable work. If you repeatedly turn clients away, then after a while, they won't bother coming to you with their work.

The second choice — subcontracting the work out to another firm — can be a good idea, especially if the other firm occasionally sends work your way, too. However, no matter how cordial the relationship, you run the risk of having your clients decide that they would rather work with your subcontractor than with you. Not only that, but *you're* still on the hook with your clients to assure the quality of the work done by your subcontractors — regardless of how good or bad it is.

You're left with a third choice: to hire employees to help you complete your assignments. But what if the assignment is relatively small or short-term in nature? You don't want to hire an employee or two for a couple weeks and then have to lay them off. But through the modern miracle of *temporary workers,* you can expand and contract your staff as often as you like, without going through the trauma of hiring employees only to lay them off a short time afterward.

And "temps" — the common term for temporary workers — aren't limited to just secretaries and receptionists anymore. Computer programmers, technical writers, drafters, communications engineers, accountants, word processors, assemblers, customer service specialists, managers, and more are available through temporary employment firms. According to the people who keep track of such things, approximately 90 percent of all businesses use temporary workers from time to time. Why not you? To get an idea of what's available in *your* town, check out the Yellow Pages under "Employment — Temporary."

Here are some of the advantages of using temporary workers to help you get through the inevitable surges in your workload:

- ✔ **Temporary workers are as temporary as you want them to be.** You can use temporary workers for a day, a week, a month, or a year — it's up to you. And when you finish your assignment, you don't have to lay off your workers or give them two weeks' notice — the temporary employment agency merely reassigns your temps to another organization. No muss, no fuss.

- ✔ **There's no tedious hiring process.** You don't have to run an advertisement in the newspaper, read a mountain of resumes, and spend days interviewing job candidates. All you need to do is pick up the phone, call a temporary employment firm, and help is on the way — quickly and easily.

- ✔ **Temps are there when you need them.** You often can have a temporary worker at your office ready to work within a few hours of your call — certainly by the next business day. When you need someone *quickly* and you can't afford to mess around, calling a temp agency is one of the best and most reliable ways to meet your needs.

- ✔ **The temp agency pays all employee-related expenses.** You don't have to worry about trying to understand the tangled maze of payments that you have to make to the government whenever you hire an employee. In addition to an hourly wage, the temporary employment firm pays your worker's payroll taxes, social security, workers' compensation, and insurance, and, in some cases, provides health insurance, vacation pay, 401(k) plans, and other benefits.

- ✔ **Temporary employees can save you money.** You pay only for the time that your temporary worker works for you. You don't have to worry about paying for sick leave, vacations, or other downtime.

Your Virtual Office

The explosion of information and technology over the past several years has made it possible for small businesses — including one-person consulting businesses — to do things that once required significant expenditures in personnel or equipment. You don't *have* to have a live person answer your phone anymore; now your answering machine or voice-mail box can take care of those duties for you. You don't have to stay chained to your desk to stay in touch with your clients; you can take a cellular phone with you wherever you go or use your portable computer to send and receive e-mail anywhere in the world, any time of the day or night.

When you take advantage of this technology, you're creating a *virtual business* — one that has all the capabilities of a much larger business — all in a lean, mean, and incredibly flexible and adaptable package. In this section, we take a look at some of the ways in which independent consultants are creating virtual offices to leverage their time and effectiveness.

A new way to office?

All it takes is a short trip to your local Yellow Pages phone directory to find plenty of companies that will be more than happy to help you out with your business services needs. As your fingers do the walking, you'll quickly find that, whereas some companies specialize in copying or mailing services, others offer a much larger variety of services. If any company today has embraced and extended the concept of the virtual office, it's Kinko's, Inc.

Originally housed in a converted garage outside the campus of the University of California, Santa Barbara, and featuring film processing, an offset press, a smattering of office supplies, and one tiny copier (that had to be rolled out on the sidewalk so that customers could use it on a self-service basis), Kinko's has grown from that 100-square-foot space into an international chain of hundreds of business service stores. Open 24 hours a day, 7 days a week, Kinko's and other chains like it have made it possible for one-person and small businesses to leverage their time and focus on doing the things they are uniquely qualified to do.

Peter is fortunate to have a Kinko's only a few blocks from his home office in Pacific Beach, California. Although he doesn't need to use the store that often, it's a real lifesaver (and time and money saver) when he does. Here are some of the things that Peter's Kinko's does for its customers:

- ✔ Black-and-white and full-color copies
- ✔ Instant posters and banners
- ✔ Overhead transparencies
- ✔ Binding and finishing services
- ✔ Fax and mailing services
- ✔ FedEx drop-off and UPS services
- ✔ Macintosh and IBM PC self-service rentals

- ✔ Digital printing
- ✔ Digital camera rental
- ✔ Conference room rental
- ✔ Videoconferencing
- ✔ Free tape, paper clips, staples, glue, and more in self-service areas
- ✔ Retail office supplies and stationery
- ✔ Free local phone calls

Perhaps not surprisingly, the big office supply warehouse stores, such as Staples, Office Depot, and the rest, are jumping in with their own business service departments. Although they aren't nearly as comprehensive and available as chain stores like Kinko's, they are becoming more and more capable every day. Of course, if you prefer, many smaller, more personal places can take your copying jobs or drop off a FedEx package or assemble a stack of reports for your client. The keys are convenience, capability, cost, and quality. If the firm you select measures up in all four of these areas, then you have clearly found a winner.

Renting an executive suite

How would you like to have all the benefits of a fully staffed and equipped office without hiring any employees or buying any equipment? And not just any old office or one in the corner of your garage, nestled between the hedge trimmer and the geranium sprouts, but a *real* office with a desk, a door, and more. Don't get us wrong; we both have our own offices at home — and Bob has a traditional office as well — and we're very happy with them. Usually. But a home office (or a cold, empty, and lonely office in an office building downtown) may not be right for you.

Enter the *executive suite*. What's an executive suite, you ask?

An executive suite is a business that rents offices — by the hour, day, week, or month — to busy consultants and businesspeople like you. Everyone shares a common receptionist, conference rooms, kitchen, and more. Not only do you get access to an office in exchange for your money, but you also have a wide variety of business tools and services at your disposal — for a price, of course.

Why would anyone want to rent an executive suite? Many good reasons exist:

- ✔ **Flexibility:** You can rent an executive suite for an hour, a few hours a week, a couple weeks a month, or on a full-time basis for as long as you like. You can work out almost any arrangement.

✔ **Minimal capital outlay:** You have the choice of bringing your own furniture and office equipment or renting these items from your landlord. According to executive suite industry estimates, the cost of using an executive suite is approximately 40 to 50 percent of the cost of setting up and staffing a comparable conventional office.

✔ **Turnkey operation:** When you rent an executive suite, you don't have to waste your time designing an office, installing electric and phone lines, hiring staff, and taking care of all those other details. With an executive suite, you can make one call today and have a fully functional office tomorrow.

✔ **Convenience:** In most cities, a wide selection of executive suites is available. You can therefore decide to locate your office near your home or close to your clients. And because you aren't tied to the long-term leases (typically three to five years) that are common in the commercial real estate market, you can quickly and easily pull up your roots and move to another executive suite or office if things don't work out.

✔ **Camaraderie:** One of the biggest complaints of consultants who work at home is that they miss the stimulation and company of being in a traditional office setting with other associates. Executive suites solve this problem by placing you in the midst of a group of other motivated business people who share many of your goals and interests.

HQ Business Centers — with more than 150 locations worldwide — is typical of this burgeoning industry. In the executive suite business for more than 30 years, HQ is the largest single provider of shared office space in the world. And with clients ranging from individual consultants, salespeople, and entrepreneurs to huge companies such as Coca-Cola, Boeing, Microsoft, and US Sprint, HQ Business Centers clearly provides a much-needed service to businesses of all sizes and persuasions.

Here are some of the services that are available when you rent an executive suite from HQ Business Centers:

✔ 24-hour-a-day access to your own private office or suite of offices

✔ Telephone answering service using the name of your business and greeting of your choice

✔ Full-time receptionist to greet your clients and visitors

✔ Use of conference rooms

✔ Secretarial services

✔ Photocopy and fax service

✔ Voice-mail and toll-free phone service

✔ Computer services

✔ Mailroom services

✔ Kitchen facilities and coffee mess

✔ Building directory listing

✔ Janitorial services

Many executive suites also provide travel booking, business meeting planning and coordination, and other business services on a pay-as-you-go basis. One thing that is particularly neat about HQ Business Centers — especially if you travel much as a part of your work — is that all full-time clients get eight free hours of office or conference room usage each month at *any* HQ Business Center — anywhere in the world. So the next time you're on a business trip to San Francisco, Toronto, or Paris, you can set up shop in the local HQ Business Center.

Other office options

Another way to achieve the same goal as using an executive suite, and save some money at the same time, is to sublease an office or offices from a business such as a legal, CPA, or real estate office that has vacant space to fill. The setup is much the same as for an executive suite: You use a common receptionist and telephone service, and you share kitchen, mailroom, and other facilities — probably even the organization's copying equipment and computer network. However, you most likely have to provide your own furniture, computer, and other equipment.

For those of you who spend more than a little time on the road (or in the air), one of the best deals going for short-term office space is available in almost every major airport around the world. The big airlines — American, United, and others — have established clubs in these airports that offer a variety of facilities and services for the busy traveler. For example, at American Airlines Admiral's Club, not only can you check in for your next flight and partake of complimentary coffee, newspapers, and magazines, but you also have full use of telephones, offices, conference rooms, computers, fax machines, and other services, all for a very modest annual membership fee. These offices are also great for meeting associates and clients from multiple locations for up to three or four hours. You simply fly in, meet, and fly out.

Part V

Marketing Your Business

The 5th Wave   By Rich Tennant

Gesundheit.

In this part . . .

*I*t's one thing to have a great idea, but it's another thing altogether to attract the attention (and money!) of the clients that you need to make your consulting business take off. In this part, we present strategies for publicizing your business and building business with new clients and through referrals.

Chapter 20

Getting the Word Out: Promoting Your Business

*P*romotion is informing your potential clients that you have a product or service that they need. Unfortunately, very few products sell themselves. Most products — including consulting services — need to be promoted in order to sell in quantities sufficient to maintain a business. Although some consultants exist strictly through word-of-mouth advertising and referrals, an element of promotion is still involved when the client-to-be contacts you, the consultant, and then you *sell* the client on the wisdom of having you do the proposed work. You promote yourself by using various channels of communication to inform and to persuade prospective clients.

You can promote your firm and its products and services in four main ways:

✔ **Personal selling:** Personal selling is promotion by person-to-person communications between representatives of your business and your prospective clients. Methods include telemarketing, personal meetings, and proposal presentations.

✔ **Public relations and publicity:** Public relations involves promotion by communications that create favorable public images of your business and your products or services. Publicity entails promotion by creating nonpaid organizational messages in the media through press releases, media kits, television interviews, and other communication materials.

✔ **Advertising:** Advertising is promotion through paid, nonpersonal channels of mass communication, such as newspapers, direct mail, radio, and television.

✔ **Sales promotion:** Sales promotions are short-term promotional techniques used to stimulate an immediate purchase of your product or service. Such techniques include discount coupons, product samples, and contests.

Some consultants use a mix of all four categories of promotional techniques, and others pick and choose from the list. We suggest that you develop a mix of techniques from each key promotional category. Experiment with different combinations of techniques and measure the results. What works best for you and your business depends on the nature of the consulting you do and the buying habits of your target market.

For example, if you conduct termite inspections and consult with homeowners on how best to prevent and treat termite infestations, you probably want to advertise your business — perhaps in the Yellow Pages and in local newspapers, or by direct mail to homes in escrow — and also employ sales promotions, such as discount coupons or free offers. However, if you are a political consultant who advises political candidates on how best to raise money for their campaigns, you probably want to rely on personal selling, public relations, and publicity to promote your business. For some reason, most political consultants don't use buy-one-get-one-free coupons or give away free samples to promote their services.

One thing to keep in mind: You have to weigh the cost of promoting your products or services against the benefits. Buying a big display ad in the Yellow Pages may be an expensive proposition, but if it works, it's worth it. The key is to discover what works for your particular consulting business and then to use it to your best advantage. The best way is to experiment and then measure your results. How? One of the most effective methods is to ask your clients how they found out about you. For example, if you are running an expensive Yellow Pages ad but a survey of your clients tells you that none of them came to you as a result of the ad, that might indicate that your valuable promotional budget could be better spent elsewhere.

In this chapter, we review each of the four ways of promoting your business and its products and services, and we look closely at the many different promotional methods that consultants use. Although the listings are quite comprehensive, you can promote your business in other ways. Be creative and try something new!

Personal Selling

Consulting is built on relationships, and personal selling is the cornerstone of many consultants' promotional efforts. *Networking* — or building contacts with new clients through personal selling and referrals from current clients or associates — is a very effective way for you to promote your consulting business. Some kinds of consultants — legal and medical consultants, for example — primarily use personal selling to find qualified prospects.

Here are some of the ways that consultants promote their services through personal selling:

- **Face-to-face meetings:** There's nothing like a good old-fashioned, one-on-one meeting with a client to promote your business and its products or services. The advantages are endless: You can tailor your message to the individual client with whom you are meeting, gauge his or her reaction in real time, and then adapt your message to address any concerns that your client may express. In these days of "technology this" and "technology that," people seem to find the human touch very comforting.

- **Telephone calls:** If you can't meet with someone in person, you can use the telephone to promote your business. If you have new information of interest to your clients or just want to keep in touch, most clients will welcome your call. Although you miss the nonverbal cues that you pick up in a personal meeting, you can call far more clients in a day than you can meet with in person.

- **Letters and notes:** Keep in touch with your clients and your highest-potential prospective clients by occasionally writing them a personal letter or note. Your clients will appreciate that you took the time to keep in touch, and they're much more likely to remember you when they need to hire a consultant. If you can include a newspaper or magazine clipping or brochure highlighting your business or products or something they may be interested in professionally or personally, so much the better.

- **Computer bulletin boards and affinity groups:** All the major online services — America Online, CompuServe, and The Microsoft Network — have established bulletin boards for members of a wide variety of affinity groups to communicate with one another. You can find bulletin boards for small-business owners, scriptwriters, engineers, doctors, and just about every other profession you can imagine. Savvy clients search these boards for talented consultants to do work for them. For example, Peter has received several unsolicited requests to perform consulting work because of his presence within professional bulletin boards on America Online.

✓ **Association memberships:** Most industries have trade groups and other associations that you can join for a nominal annual fee. These associations offer opportunities to promote your business by networking with other members and potential clients at events including regular meetings, conferences, trade shows, and more. Locally based groups, such as the chamber of commerce, offer the same kinds of opportunities, but with a much broader membership base.

✓ **Speeches:** Giving speeches — before community groups, clients, or groups of your peers — is a great way to network with potential clients or with firms that may offer you subcontracting possibilities. You may even pick up the attention of the print or broadcast media. Not only do you enhance your personal credibility and image by making speeches, but you also may generate numerous qualified leads.

✓ **Seminars and workshops:** Many consultants find great success in promoting their businesses by offering seminars and workshops — often for free — to prospective clients. For example, stockbrokers love to drum up business by offering personal finance seminars to people who are interested in learning how to better handle their finances. A certain number of attendees then naturally turn to the broker for help in executing and managing their personal stock transactions.

✓ **Social events:** A heck of a lot of business is done informally at cocktail parties, golf tournaments, and other social events. Picture this conversation: "What do you do for a living?" "I'm a chiropractor." "Oh, you are? I've had this kink in my neck for weeks. Is there anything you can do for it?" Although you should usually avoid making a sales pitch at the event — hand out your business card instead and approach your prospect during normal business hours — you can certainly be ready to respond if you're asked to share your opinions. Many consultants seek invitations to social events simply for the opportunity to meet prospective clients.

✓ **Telemarketing:** Although many people cringe when the phone rings at dinner time, telemarketing *must* work or the telemarketers would stop doing it. Telemarketing can be an effective way to drum up business if you can reach your intended market. Random phone calls do little to bring you qualified prospects.

✓ **Community events:** Community events — everything from block parties to park dedications to museum openings — are great ways to network with members of the community who may need your services. Be sure to bring plenty of business cards to hand out to your new friends and acquaintances!

Personal selling adds a human touch to your promotional efforts. Because consulting is so dependent on the care and maintenance of personal relationships, most consultants discover that personal selling techniques are the most effective way to promote their products and services. Make sure that you make it a big part of *your* marketing mix.

Public Relations and Publicity

Public relations and publicity are the fine art of building and enhancing your public image through a variety of carefully crafted techniques, all aimed at getting a positive message about your business and its products and services into a variety of media outlets. Whether you just won the Nobel Prize or you're simply volunteering your time to help a good cause in your community, public relations and publicity make sure that you're not the only one who knows what you have done.

Here are some proven ways to ensure that you get your 15 minutes of fame:

- **Press releases and media kits:** If you're serious about getting a publicity campaign off the ground, you need to send out press releases and media kits to a list of media outlets that have the greatest probability of reaching your prospects. *Media kits* — folders that include a photo, biography, and information of interest to readers, listeners, or viewers — are a definite must if you want to line up print, radio, and television interviews.

- **Articles and books:** Writing articles or books on your field of expertise is a great way to both build your credibility and get your name in front of a wide range of potential clients. Many trade journals and association magazines are particularly hungry for articles written from an insider's perspective. They probably won't pay you for your efforts, but you reap some free publicity. Just make sure that the publications that you write for have a large readership of your target prospects.

  Writing a book can make you an instant expert in the eyes of the media and gain you entry for interviews and other opportunities to get your word out.

- **Web pages:** The Internet — particularly the World Wide Web — has exploded as an opportunity for promoting your services and products. A Web page can be a showcase of your business and the unique skills and expertise that you offer your clients. (See *Creating Web Pages For Dummies,* written by Bud Smith and Arthur Bebak and published by IDG Books Worldwide, Inc., for more information about creating your own Web page.)

- **Newsletters:** Newsletters are a particularly effective way to generate favorable publicity for your business *and* keep your clients informed about the latest happenings and innovations in your field and in your consulting practice. Not only can you keep in touch with your current clients, but you also can reach out to new ones.

Bob reaches out to a very focused group of clients, potential clients, and media outlets with his monthly newsletter, *Rewarding Employees*. As a special thanks to his loyal subscribers, he recently sent each one a personally autographed copy of one of his books.

✔ **Media interviews and talk shows:** The various media — newspapers, magazines, radio, television, and now the Internet — have an insatiable appetite for interviewing interesting, informative, and entertaining people. You can either approach the media directly with story ideas or hire a publicist to take care of the heavy lifting for you. Every media outlet that you may want to target is looking for one thing: a personality who is entertaining to an established audience. If you are entertaining, informative, and engaging, you should have no problem getting the attention you desire. What do you have to offer?

✔ **Community service:** By offering your services to nonprofit community organizations for free, you are helping them obtain the kinds of services that they might not otherwise be able to afford. You also have the opportunity to network with other businesspeople who often inhabit the boards and leadership of these types of organizations.

✔ **Independent surveys:** Some consultants are very successful in garnering tons of publicity by conducting surveys and then publishing the results in a press release. If the results are newsworthy, the media may pick up your study (and the name of your business) and distribute it nationwide.

✔ **Sponsorships:** By sponsoring an event in your community — perhaps a charity fundraiser or a job fair — you help create a positive public image for your business in the community and have the opportunity to draw media focus to your efforts. Imagine the value of explaining on camera to your local television news shows why your event is so important to the community and why you feel so strongly that you should sponsor it.

✔ **Awards and honors:** Many consultants seek professional awards and honors, not only for the prestige that they bestow upon the recipients but also for the value of the publicity that they generate.

Successful consultants (and other businesspeople, for that matter) pay close attention to their public image and are always on the alert for new ways to get their message out to the public through the media. Don't forget: If *you* don't create your public image, you may not end up with the one you want.

Cindy Kazan knows how to get the word out for her clients

Cindy Kazan (phone 414-352-3535, e-mail ckprwiz@execpc.com) is president of Communi-K, Inc. — a publicity and public relations firm located in Milwaukee, Wisconsin. After graduate school, Cindy went to Arthur Andersen & Co., where she held a position as an internal consultant in the world headquarters division, focusing primarily in state and local tax. She left Arthur Andersen & Co. to become the marketing director for a law firm and then, when she had her first child, decided to start her own firm. Cindy started out with some subcontracting work and has built her business into the highly successful firm that it is today. We took some time out of Cindy's busy day to talk with her about the importance of publicity and promotion to consultants.

Consulting For Dummies: How do you like the change from working for a large consulting firm such as Arthur Andersen to having your own firm?

Cindy Kazan: I find it to be great in most respects. It's challenging and at the same time very rewarding because you're working for yourself versus for other people. On the other hand, it can be difficult. There's no one next to me to say, "Hey, what do you think about this?" That camaraderie and input from other people make being on my own a little more challenging. I have really had to learn to be extremely independent and to be confident. I have to think that what I'm doing is the best because I *don't* have anybody to bounce it off of.

CFD: So the positives outweigh the negatives?

Kazan: Let me put it this way: I would never go back to a big firm as long as I live. I find that I am *much* more productive. My office is in my home — I work all hours of the day and night.

But I wouldn't trade that for the world. I can balance my business life and my personal life much more so than I think you can if you're working for someone else.

CFD: It's amazing how much more motivated you can be when you work for yourself. When you know that everything that you do is going to contribute to your own success, that makes all the difference in the world.

Kazan: Exactly. And it was different for me. When I went out on my own, it wasn't like, "Oh, I've got to put food on the table." It was more like, "Oh, I think this will be a fun thing to do in my spare time while I'm with my kids." And I wanted to still keep alert — in the loop. The success I've had has almost come in spite of myself. So it wasn't like so many other people who go out on their own and have all the pressures. *I* didn't, and I was fortunate in that respect.

CFD: How important is publicity and promotion to consultants?

Kazan: I think I find that, because I'm working with providers of services or small firms, they need to find a cost-effective way of getting their message out. I try to work with materials that they already have. They've written articles, or at least they have the foundation of some articles, and so we're able to use that in our efforts. By placing articles in the right trade journals, it gives my clients the third-party endorsement that *their* prospective clients look for. Placing targeted articles is much more effective than buying advertisements because, if you get into the right publication, it promotes them so much better. The right people are reading it, and they say, "If this publication believes in this person enough

(continued)

(continued)

to publish their article" — which is 90 percent of what I do, draft and place articles — "then that's somebody I want to talk to."

CFD: So does placing an article usually lead directly to sales?

Kazan: No, placing an article isn't going to get them business. However, it's going to help lay the foundation to promote my clients in many different ways. Placing articles and using reprints is just one small part of an overall plan for promotions. My clients still have to have their collateral pieces, they still have to have their client references, etc. But they're seeing the value of having published articles as part of that overall package, and it's a very cost-effective way of doing it.

CFD: What do you feel is the most effective way for consultants to promote their services?

Kazan: The most effective thing to do is to have a very specific objective in mind — what does the client want to do? Then I help them figure out who they want to talk to and how best to get their message across to the selected audience. So many of the clients I work with started out by saying, "I want to be on *Oprah*," or "I want to be in *The Wall Street Journal.*" Yeah, it would be great, and it's a nice ego trip, but that's not what's going to help them. So the most important thing is for them to decide *what* do I want to say, *who* do I want to say it to, and *how* can I get the best results the fastest. I really help my clients take it down to a very specific level. If it's somebody who's talking to human resources people, then you want to be in the human resources trade publications. My clients have seen how this works to their benefit. If they can get in there and if they can get in there at the right time, this helps them far more than having their name brought up in *The Wall Street Journal.* They're able to get a much broader message across to the people who need to have it.

CFD: So you're really targeting an audience instead of doing the good old shotgun approach that probably misses 99.9 percent of its targets.

Kazan: Exactly. I think another big thing is managing people's expectations. I think that's the most important role a consultant plays. If a client comes to you and says that he wants to get on *Oprah,* the chances of that are slim to none. They have to know that going into it. However, if you promise you're going to do it and you don't deliver, chances are you're going to get fired. Managing expectations has to start with the first telephone conversation. If you can't do that up front, then you're never going to be successful.

CFD: How important is timing in the publicity and promotion process?

Kazan: *Very* important. A new client had a really, really bad experience with somebody else. When I came in with my approach, she said, "That's exactly what I'm looking for." I don't know if she would have caught on to it as quickly had she not had the bad experience before that. The other guy used more of a shotgun approach — let's just send out hundreds of letters and see who responds. Because of that catastrophe — she spent a *lot* of money needlessly — I was at the right place at the right time. She needed somebody, she needed somebody who could work right away, and she needed somebody with a targeted approach. Timing is a *lot* of it.

CFD: What advice would you offer someone who is new to consulting?

Kazan: The most important thing to do is to get the right client to start — not someone too big and not someone too small. Someone you know you can do a good job for. Next, work hard to get some really good results right away. Nothing sells yourself to the next client as well as the results you have already had. You don't want to start out doing too many things at one time. Start out small and build on that. That's the best route to success.

CFD: And then you can grow your business as your reputation grows.

Kazan: Right. Focus on what *you* do well. I share clients with a couple of different people.

One in particular will call me up and say, "Hey, listen, I work on radio and TV, and I know you work on print. Why don't we work on a client together?" If you stick with what you do best, you're going to be better at it in the long run. You can't be all things to all people.

Advertising

For many businesses, advertising is necessary for survival. For other businesses — including many different types of consultants — advertising is an effective adjunct to their primary sources of qualified prospects. For example, although stockbrokers and real estate agents depend on referrals from satisfied clients as their primary source of new client leads, advertising is an important supplement to this source, *and* it helps build their image in the community at the same time.

The best thing about advertising is that you control the message that your clients-to-be receive and when and where they receive it. You can send your message to the public in a shotgun fashion — gaining exposure to a huge number of people, some of whom may be interested in what you have to sell — or you can direct it with rifle-sharp accuracy to only those potential clients who are your best prospects.

Advertising may or may not be for you. However, it can be a powerful part of your overall marketing mix, and you shouldn't write it off too quickly. Here are some of the most common forms of advertising available to you:

- **Newspaper and magazine advertisements:** Newspaper and magazine advertising can be an effective way for certain kinds of consultants to promote their services. One thing is for sure: You get your message out to a lot of potential readers, although your message may be of little interest to most of them. Although a newspaper may not be the best place for an aerospace consultant to advertise, it may be a great place for a home audio and video consultant to advertise — especially in the weekly television guide. The wide variety of narrowly focused special interest magazines on the market today — as well as trade journals and association magazines — can make magazine advertising a particularly effective way to reach your targeted audience.

Note: Newspapers have a very short shelf life — one day — whereas magazines tend to hang around for weeks and even months. Your message, therefore, may have a greater chance of being noticed in a magazine unless you run newspaper ads on a daily basis.

✔ **Direct mail:** Direct mail is the mailing of advertisements in the form of letters, flyers, brochures, coupon books, or other offers to your prospective clients. This is one of the best ways for consultants of all sorts to reach a large audience of qualified prospects. The real beauty of direct mail is that you can target your mailing with extraordinary precision. If, for example, you make your living as an advertising consultant, you can buy mailing lists from magazines and associations whose subscribers and members contain a high percentage of individuals who likely would be interested in receiving your message. The mailing lists — complete with names and addresses — are available on diskette, CD-ROM, or preprinted mailing labels.

If you can profile your clients, a mail list house, for a midest fee, can produce a list of other clients whose characteristics match those of your clients. For consultants, customized mailing lists are both effective and efficient. And besides attracting *new* clients, direct mail can also help you keep in touch with *existing* clients.

✔ **Yellow Pages and other directories:** The Yellow Pages and industry-specific directories, such as those published by the American Institute of Architects (AIA), are a fantastic way to reach qualified prospects. Most professional and industry associations list member firms in their directories for free. If you have a business phone line, you earn a simple telephone listing in your local Yellow Pages telephone directory. However, if you want to buy a display advertisement, be prepared to pay a *lot* of money for this particularly effective form of advertising. Not only do readers of these publications have a need when they pick up a directory, but they also are usually ready to buy in the very near future.

✔ **The Internet:** For those of you who are already online, you probably have noticed that advertising on the Internet has exploded over the past couple years. As members of America Online, both of us receive at least ten or more unsolicited e-mail advertisements every day for a wide variety of incredible get-rich-quick opportunities *(right!).* Regardless, mass mailing of e-mail messages to prospective clients remains the most effective way for most consultants to advertise their services over the Internet. Many online companies can provide you with thousands and thousands of potential leads for less than $100.

As you may already know from reading your own Internet e-mail in-box, unsolicited, mass-mailed advertisements can be *very* annoying to recipients. How many get-rich-quick schemes and lowest-rate-in-the-world long-distance phone ads can you tolerate before you are ready to unplug your computer once and for all? Mass mail at your own risk! If you do decide to use the Internet to advertise your consulting business, choose your recipients very carefully.

✔ **Radio and television advertisements:** As with newspaper and magazine advertisements, radio and television advertisements can reach a large audience; everybody has at least one radio or television at home or at work. Your message, however, may be of interest to only a very narrow market. Cable television — with boutique channels such as The Weather Channel, MTV, The Cable News Network, Nickelodeon, Bravo!, and more — and radio stations that specialize in news, talk shows, and different music formats offer you the opportunity to aim your message at specific demographic groups. However, the relatively high cost of running ads in these media outlets and the complexity and expense of putting together a quality advertisement make running radio and television advertisements a daunting task for most consultants.

✔ **Outdoor advertising:** Unless your last name is Goodyear and you're in the tire consulting business, sticking an advertisement on the side of a blimp or on a billboard is probably not the best way to drum up business. However, if you're an immigration consultant who advises people on their legal rights when they are threatened with deportation, advertising in buses and subways and on street benches may work. For the rest of you, at least you know that outdoor advertising is always an option should you choose to pursue it.

Make sure that you consider advertising when you develop your marketing plan. It's one of the best ways to get the exact message you want to send to your most likely prospective clients.

Sales Promotion

What do you do if you want to try to get a potential client to buy your product or service *right now* or at least keep your name and phone number handy for the time when he or she needs you? Independent consultants use sales promotions — coupons, imprinted coffee mugs, free samples, and the like — to fulfill this task. Many sales promotions are fun and exciting for your clients, and they help to generate excitement about your business and its products.

Sales promotions come in all kinds and all flavors, so you surely can find something that fits your business and its clients. Consider some of these options:

✔ **Business cards:** Business cards are probably the ultimate low-cost way to promote your business. For less than $50 (even less if you print your own on a laser printer like Peter does), you can have a box of 500 cards printed to your exact specifications. Once you have them, use them. Hand them out at parties, give them to your clients, staple them to proposals and reports, and always carry extras when you're out in the field. Some consultants print messages on the backs of their business cards, such as The Rules of Negotiating or other tips that may be valuable to prospective clients. If you have employees, give them business cards, too.

✔ **Brochures and sales materials:** If you are actively selling your product or service to others, then you probably have already developed your own promotional brochures and sales materials. They're easy to design and inexpensive to have professionally printed. If you haven't gotten on board yet, you're missing out on a great opportunity to promote your business. Few clients are ready to hire you immediately; most would prefer to look over your promotional literature first. Of course, your brochures and sales materials should be as attractive and inviting as possible.

✔ **Discount coupons:** Discount coupons are a time-honored tradition for promoting consumer goods and certain kinds of services, such as automobile maintenance and carpet cleaning. There are a number of ways to distribute them to your targeted clients: through newspaper or magazine advertisements, through direct mail, or even via the Internet. Depending on what kind of consulting you do, discount coupons may be worth a try.

✔ **Advertising specialties:** How could we live without coffee mugs, pens, pencils, refrigerator magnets, calendars, and more — all bearing the name of your business and your phone number or Internet address? Handing out inexpensive and useful imprinted specialties can help you keep your name in front of your clients year-round.

✔ **Contests and prizes:** There's nothing like a good contest with some good prizes to get everyone excited about what you have to say. A real estate agent in our area gathers lists of potential clients and promotes his business at the same time by running periodic contests in a local newspaper. The contests are keyed to Valentine's Day, the Fourth of July, and other important dates. To enter, people fill out a brief entry form (that just happens to include questions about whether they are planning to sell or buy a home in the near future) and submit it by a certain date. Winners receive a free dinner for two at a local restaurant.

✔ **Free samples:** Everyone loves to get something for free. Offer free samples — a free home inspection, a free newsletter, a free Web page — in exchange for trying your product or listening to your sales pitch.

Now that you've had the opportunity to review many of the different ways to promote your business, you need to develop a marketing plan that incorporates your selected mix of the approaches and techniques. All these approaches must be integrated to present and reinforce the professional image you are trying to project. Don't forget to closely monitor the results of your promotional efforts and to fine-tune your approach based on your market feedback.

Chapter 21

Building Business with New Clients

• •

• •

*A*ttracting potential clients to your business is a definite must if you expect to sell them on your product or service. (Chapter 20 details the kinds of things that you need to do to bring potential clients to your door.) Now that they're at your door — or on the phone, in your mailbox, or on electronic mail — what do you do next?

The next step is to convince your clients that they need to do business with your consulting firm. Or rather, that you — and perhaps only you — can best help them with their needs. So much so that your business has the clear edge over all your competitors.

In this chapter, we explore exactly what you need to do after you get the attention of prospective clients. We tell you about the importance of the personal introduction and the significance of quickly establishing good rapport and a firm basis of trust and goodwill. We walk you through the process of making a pitch to your clients and then following up — and we talk about the importance of keeping your commitments.

The Personal Introduction

In many ways, the personal introduction of a prospective client to your business is probably one of the most critical points in the process of selling your services. Blow it here, and you probably won't have to worry about seeing *that* client again. However, if you make the right impression (and we're *sure* you will!), you'll have a client for life — or at least as long as the checks don't bounce!

We know that you're not necessarily in business to make friends. You're in business to make money. But you have to remember that business involves *much* more than just dollars and cents (or pounds, pence, marks, yen, or whatever your monetary persuasion). Consulting is first and foremost a *social* activity. Not person-to-machine, not client-to-faceless bureaucracy. We're talking human being to human being. One on one.

In the sections that follow, we consider the things that go into this most important beginning phase of your consulting relationships: the personal introduction.

First impressions count!

Depending on the size and nature of your organization, the first experience that a potential client has with your consulting business may be anything from speaking to your answering machine or receptionist to visiting your Web page to meeting you personally through a mutual acquaintance. We can't emphasize enough the importance of a potential client's first experience with your business — in many cases, it may be your only opportunity to sell that client on the benefits of working with your organization. Consider these two scenarios:

- ✔ **Scenario A:** The client of your dreams calls the long-distance phone number that you advertised in your Internet e-mail solicitation broadcast last week to 100,000 potential clients nationwide. Your answering machine picks up, "Hi, this is the Acme Consulting Group. Sorry, we can't take your call right now, but leave a message and we'll get back to you as soon as we can." The client of your dreams leaves a brief message expressing his urgent need and asks you to return the call as soon as possible. Unfortunately, you are halfway across the country at the time, and you don't get the call until you return home several days later. When you finally return the call, the client of your dreams has already found someone who can meet his urgent schedule.

- ✔ **Scenario B:** One of your best current clients refers the client of your dreams to you. When the prospective client drops by your office unannounced, she is warmly greeted by your receptionist — who offers a cup of coffee or soda — and is steered to the waiting area while you are paged. Because you *always* have time to meet a new client, you drop everything and come out to the waiting area to greet your client-to-be. After you take her on a brief tour of the architectural models of some of your most involved and successful projects and then review her needs and make a rough pricing estimate, your new client asks how soon you can start.

What kind of initial impression does *your* organization make with your clients?

There's never been a valid excuse for sloppy service — and there still isn't one today. What's more, in these days of satellite telephones, nationwide telephone paging, personal digital assistants, Internet e-mail, and more, you have less of an excuse than ever before to be hard to reach — even if you're a one-person organization. If you can't get your introduction right, why should a client trust you to get *anything* right?

Peter remembers the time he called a large insurance firm to get advice on a business transaction. Instead of a real-live receptionist, Peter got a voice-mail system that presented him with six — count 'em, *six* — different dialing options. That wasn't so bad in and of itself, but when Peter got to the option he wanted — the next to last option, of course — and punched the number into his phone, he was quickly and efficiently cast into the River Styx of voice-mail hell. "All telephone attendants are busy right now. Your call is important to us. [*You*, however, apparently are not.] Please continue to hold while we serve other callers."

After listening to the message — over and over again — for five full minutes, Peter decided to try to escape. Pressing 0 on his phone, Peter was greeted with a curt "I'm sorry, but that is not a valid system option." "*Here's* a valid system option," Peter thought to himself as he slammed down the phone and then called another insurance firm (coincidentally, a *smaller,* local brokerage), where a *live* person answered and then quickly transferred his call to an agent who took the call and answered the question. Mission accomplished!

If you want a quick reality check on the first impressions that your organization is making with your clients, pretend that *you* are a new client and do the following:

✔ **Call your business and see what happens.** Does someone answer the phone on the first few rings, or does it take a while for someone to pick up the phone? Is the initial greeting upbeat and cheery, or is it the kind of greeting that makes you feel like the receptionist would rather be doing something — anything — else than taking the call? If the receptionist is out, does another employee pick up the phone quickly and courteously? Do you end up in voice-mail hell with no chance of escape?

✔ **Take a close look at your facilities.** If you're a freelance advertising copywriter, your clients may not be surprised (or disappointed) to visit an office that is located in a spare bedroom of your home. However, if you're a tax accountant, your clients may prefer to see that you have a real office in a real office building with a real employee or two — indicating that your practice is financially stable and viable.

✔ **Take a close look at your marketing materials and work output.** Are your company brochures and other marketing materials of high quality, or do they look like something your third-grade kid knocked off at school one day? Are your letters and work samples laser-printed on high-quality paper, or are you still using an antique 9-pin dot-matrix printer that's a few pins short of a full set? Would *you* pay your hard-earned dollars for your products?

✔ **Take a close look at yourself.** It probably goes without saying that you should be well groomed and dressed appropriately for the kind of consulting you do. Although your clients may expect their investment advisers to wear pin-striped suits, the same clients might expect their computer consultants to be dressed in polo shirts and khakis.

Seriously consider the answers to these questions and then make any changes that you need to make to ensure that all your clients and prospective clients have a positive first impression of you and your organization. Don't forget: You have only *one* chance to make a first impression!

Ask and listen

The best professional salespeople know that their primary responsibility is to help potential clients find the best solutions to their needs. This means asking questions and then listening — *really* listening — to the answers.

You have no doubt dealt with salespeople who have their own agendas and have little time to hear about yours. Before you can get out even one word, they launch into a prepackaged speech about whatever they have to sell. And if you *do* manage to get a word or two in edgewise, your word is quickly ignored as the canned speech continues, and continues, and continues.

How does that make you feel? Like trying to find another salesperson? Exactly!

In his book *Selling For Dummies* (published by IDG Books Worldwide, Inc.), master salesperson Tom Hopkins presents a very useful rule:

> *Listen twice as much as you talk and you'll succeed in persuading others nearly every time.*

Think about why this is true:

▶ *Everyone* **likes to be listened to.** Not only does listening show respect, but it also makes the speaker feel important. However, good listening skills go *way* beyond simply stroking a client's ego.

▶ **Good listening helps you do *your* job better.** Why? Because when you listen, you *hear* exactly what your clients want, and you can respond with the exact answers that your clients need.

The simple fact is that you can't possibly understand what your potential clients need unless you give them the opportunity to *tell* you. And you can't possibly *hear* what your client is telling you unless you take the time to listen! To make sure that you both ask clients the right questions *and* listen to their answers, we have developed the following four steps to effective asking and listening:

1. **Ask open-ended questions that define the boundaries of the opportunity.** When you first meet potential clients, you really have no idea what their needs are, how extensive those needs are, and what addressing them will require. Therefore, your first task is to ask the kinds of open-ended questions that help you define the big picture, the rough boundaries of their opportunities, and thereby the rough boundaries of your solutions. For example, you might ask, "What results do you want to see come out of this management training?" or "Exactly what can our firm do for you?"

Avoid asking questions that might introduce an element of trepidation into your relationship. Questions along the lines of, "Do you realize how incredibly expensive it's going to be to straighten out this mess?" or "Who's the incompetent jerk responsible for running this department?" are to be avoided at all costs.

2. **Use active silence.** When it comes to listening, silence is golden — not the disinterested silence that comes from having more pressing matters on your mind *(Yikes! My foursome tees off in 45 minutes!),* but the active silence that tells your clients that you're involved in what they have to say and are interested, thinking, and putting your all into understanding their issues and perspectives. When your clients appear to have ended a thought and seem ready for you to respond, first prod them to give you deeper understanding with a nod of the head or by asking "Is that all, or is there more?" before you launch into *your* side of the discussion.

3. **Ask clarifying questions.** Clarifying questions take you from the big picture to the little picture and help you to refine your understanding of your clients' opportunities. For example, asking, "Do you really want a full review of your entire quality assurance system, or do you think that a random sampling of products might accomplish the same goal?" is a good way to help define the extent of the effort required to accomplish a task.

4. Confirm your understandings. An important part of the process of asking questions and listening to their answers is periodically confirming your understandings with your clients. For example, you might say, "Now here's what I'm hearing that you would like me to do . . ." or "Correct me if I'm wrong, but I believe that what you would like me to do is to create a Web site for your firm that illustrates and explains all your products and then to update it on a regular basis — am I right?"

Never forget the golden rule of consulting: *listen before you leap!* You'll have plenty of time to do plenty of talking after you land your client. For now, content yourself with asking a few questions to help draw your client out, and listen, listen, and listen some more.

Tell them about yourself

Just who do you think you are? What makes you such an expert?

Your clients want the best service that their money can buy. Your job is to give it to them. However, before you get the opportunity to do so, you have to *prove* that you've got the right stuff. And just how can you do that? Here are a few ideas to get things rolling. You don't want to overwhelm your potential clients at this point in the process — you just want to set the stage for your relationship.

✔ **Related experience:** Of the firms you've worked with, whose needs were most like those of your client-to-be? How large or small were the firms, and what was your part in the project's success? Why will this experience help you deal with your prospective client's needs?

✔ **Personal credentials:** What are your *personal* credentials for doing the job that your client needs to get done? What firms have you worked for and with? What college and professional degrees do you have? What major projects have you been personally responsible for, and what are the quantifiable measures of their success?

✔ **Company credentials:** Who are the key clients of your business? What do you do for them, and how long have they been associated with your company? What are some of your business's most prominent successes, and what was your role in making things happen?

Green Light or Red?

You have now reached your first critical intersection in building business with new clients — do you go forward, or do you tell your potential clients to look elsewhere?

What? Tell your clients to look elsewhere? Did we temporarily lose our marbles, perhaps? Are we a few cards short of a full deck? No. It may seem nuts — after all, why would anyone turn away a paying client? In the real world of consulting, a wide variety of good reasons for turning down work exist.

Consider these reasons, for example:

- **Not your thing:** Although the temptation to try to conquer every single problem that lands on your doorstep often arises, you may run across one or two problems that someone else is better able to deal with. If that's the case, don't be afraid to refer your client to another associate or another consultant or, absent that option, just say thanks but no thanks.

- **Previous commitments:** If you're already fully booked with other clients, you don't do *anyone* any favors by taking on even more clients. Your current clients suffer because their work is put on hold as you get new clients online, your new clients suffer because you have to put them off until you can get around to their projects. Finally, *you* suffer as you try to juggle all these different clients and priorities.

- **Goals unaligned:** After reviewing the opportunity, you may feel *very* strongly that your client should approach things one way, but the client may insist on a completely different approach — one that you find ineffective, incompetent, or unethical. If this is the case, and you can't bring your client around to your point of view, simply walk away from the opportunity — you'll find plenty more fish in the sea.

- **No chemistry:** Although part of being an effective consultant is the ability to get along and work with an incredibly wide range and diversity of clients, sometimes your personalities just don't mesh, and it may be best for the project that someone else take it on. Part of the introduction process is getting to know each other. Make sure that you do whatever you can to get a feeling for what working with this particular client will be like.

- **Insufficient client resources:** After meeting with your clients, it may quickly become apparent that they are not interested in paying the kind of fees that you charge. You have to make enough money to support your business, and you shouldn't be ashamed to charge clients a fee that reflects the high quality of service that they receive. If you don't stick to your fees at the beginning of your relationship with a new client, it's unlikely that you will ever get those fees — no matter *how* well you perform.

- **Inadequate client commitment:** Occasionally, you'll be approached by clients who don't *really* want you to solve their problems; they merely need to show someone — a boss or management in general — that they are doing *something* to justify their existence. When that kind of client comes through your door, *run!* Not only will you be frustrated when the client brushes aside or shelves your recommendations, but your reputation can be potentially tarnished due to your "failure" to turn things around.

Regardless of the reason you decide to veto a particular project, try to refer the client to someone who may be better able to take on the opportunity. Successful consultants maintain extensive networks of associates who can pitch in to help on particularly large or complex projects.

So is the light green or is the light red? Only you can decide.

Getting to Know You

Because of the nature of person-to-person interactions, every consulting relationship involves a certain amount of chemistry. If the chemistry is good, a consulting relationship can be long-lasting and beneficial to all. If the chemistry is bad — like a high-school lab experiment careening out of control — you can count the length of the relationship in nanoseconds instead of years.

So how do you build the foundation for a stable and mutually beneficial relationship? We'll let you in on a little secret: It's not rocket science. Just as in your nonbusiness relationships (you *do* have at least one or two non-business relationships, right?), consulting relationships are built on trust and on an honest desire to help one another. Sure, every consultant has something to sell, whether it's dragging a company kicking and screaming through a long-range planning process, conveying a lifetime of expertise in finding underground oil deposits, or setting up a company's Web page. But the best consulting relationships come first from a place of wanting to share your unique skills and expertise to help someone who needs them.

In this section, we consider some techniques to help you establish a good relationships with your potential clients. We discuss how to build rapport with your clients-to-be, get your clients what they need, and build a firm foundation of trust to carry your relationship forward into the future.

Establishing rapport

Before you enter into a business relationship with prospective clients, you have to establish some degree of rapport with them. *Rapport* is the connectedness that individuals in a relationship feel for one another. Rapport comes from shared experiences. A shared experience can be as simple as a shared joke or as complex as a common lifelong interest. In some cases, a relationship is established between people instantly; in other cases, a relationship never really blooms. If rapport doesn't develop between the parties of a relationship, you can bet that the relationship won't last.

When you're the client, it really doesn't matter whether you're an introvert, an extrovert, or something in between. However, when you are a consultant and are on the selling side of the equation, you definitely have to take on the personality of an extrovert — whether you feel like one or not.

Two ways exist to be comfortable initiating new relationships: Either you developed this skill as you were growing up, or you can learn it now.

We both grew up in homes where our families were transferred from one place to another every few years. Although this lifestyle did disrupt more than a few friendships as we grew up, all the moving around *did* teach us how to feel comfortable with all kinds of people. Whether it was the suburbs of Washington, D.C.; a small town 100 miles south of Atlanta, Georgia; or Paris, France; we learned how to adjust to new circumstances and make friends quickly with an incredibly diverse range of people around the world.

Fortunately, if you weren't lucky enough to learn the art of establishing instant rapport when you were growing up, it's not too late to learn how:

- **Be friendly.** Everyone likes people who are friendly and who seem genuinely interested in them. When you take the first step to reach out to someone, they'll likely reach back.

- **Assess your client's personality.** Does your client want to chat and socialize for a bit before getting down to business, or does he or she want to skip all that and keep business at the very top of the agenda? If your client is oriented to socializing first, allow plenty of time for getting to know one another before getting down to business. However, if your client is the kind of person who wants to forgo social pleasantries and get right to business, do that.

- **Find something in common with your client.** Do you share a common interest or hobby with your client — perhaps ice fishing, playing Bach fugues on the harpsichord, or collecting bottle caps? Common interests can break the ice between you and a client faster than a Russian icebreaker at 30 knots. You never know until you ask, so ask!

- **Be sincere and down to earth.** Don't try to pretend to be someone you're not. Just relax, be sincere, and, above all, be yourself.

Helping them get what they want

Helping your clients get what they want is really your number one job, and you have to be particularly vigilant to avoid letting *your* needs take priority over *their* needs. It's not uncommon for a consulting business to develop certain assessment or training tools or products and to then feel a lot of pressure to make clients fit these tools or products — even if it means pushing the clients into a box that really doesn't fit.

For example, a business that conducts long-range planning sessions with the top management teams of for-profit corporations may have developed an assessment model that works great in the private sector. When a local nonprofit agency asks for help in *its* long-range planning, the consulting business decides to apply its standard for profit assessment model to the nonprofit organization — despite the fact that the fundamental nature of the organizations is quite different. Although this tactic makes perfect sense from the consulting practice's cost perspective (why spend the money to adapt the assessment tools for a one-off project, after all) it may make no sense at all from the perspective of getting the best results. In a case like this, if the consultant is unwilling to take the time or spend the money to tailor its approach to the needs of the client, it would really be better for all concerned to refer the work to someone else.

Some consultants allow their egos to get bigger than the side of a barn. When you're selling yourself or your business as an expert in a particular field, it's hard not to start believing your own sales pitch. Although nothing is inherently wrong with letting your ego show from time to time, you should do so only if it doesn't interfere with your client relationships or with giving your clients the best advice possible at all times. If you see that ego is starting to get in the way — either with you or with an associate — step back for a moment and take a close look at what your clients really need. Then push that big bad ego out of the way, if only for a few moments, to determine whether what you're offering is really what your clients need. If it is, great! You're on the right track. If it's not, go back to the drawing board and come up with an approach that *does* meet your clients' needs.

On the flip side of this coin, you may need to tell your clients things that they just don't want to hear but that reflect the truth of a situation. For example, while speaking with your client about a problem he's having with the response rate for direct-mail advertising, you may quickly realize that the problem is the poor quality of the advertising piece that the client's firm is sending out. Even if your client disagrees vigorously (after all, he created the ad personally and *knows* what works and what doesn't) you have to call it like you see it. To do any less would be to do a disservice both to you and to your client. A good consulting relationship is built on trust, and part of building trust is being honest with your clients — even if occasionally the truth hurts.

Building a foundation of trust

Although many things go into making a good consulting relationship, trust is probably the most important factor of all. Trust is the cement that holds a relationship together. Without it, a relationship quickly falls apart — crumbling into little bits and pieces before your very eyes.

So how do you build trust in a consulting relationship? At this early phase of the consulting relationship, doing the kinds of things that set the stage for the development of a strong, long-term relationship is most important. Here are some quick and easy ways to build trust with your clients:

- ✔ **Make commitments and keep commitments.** One of the easiest ways to build trust in a relationship is to make commitments and then keep them. If, for example, you tell a client that you will be available at 3:00 p.m. on Wednesday for a conference call, then, when you're ready and waiting for the call at 3:00 on Wednesday, you're sending a message to your client that you can be trusted. Whether the commitments that you keep are big or small, they add up to increased trust. Make commitments and then keep them.

- ✔ **Give your honest opinion.** If your clients have a problem, tell them that they have a problem. Sometimes you may be tempted to sugarcoat problems in the hopes that your clients will find them easier to swallow. However, this tactic can backfire when your clients finally realize (and most eventually *will* realize) the full extent of their problems and wonder why you kept them in the dark. Trust is built on honesty. Be honest with your clients.

- ✔ **Keep secrets.** When you are hired as a consultant, you may have access to some of the organization's most important information and secrets. *Never* disclose this confidential information outside your business or outside the circle of individuals with whom the client designates for you to work. From confidential payroll information to new product strategies to the rumor that the president of the firm is an alcoholic, your silence is crucial. Not only can leaking confidential information destroy the trust you have worked so hard to build, but it can also expose you to an expensive lawsuit. Keep secrets secret, and you prove your trustworthiness every day.

- ✔ **Do great work.** When you do a great job for your clients, you demonstrate that you value their work and their organizations and that you can be trusted with taking on even more important responsibilities in the future. Do great work, and the trust that you have established with your clients continues to build.

Meeting Clients

It's very likely that your first contact with a potential client will not be in person but will be by phone, e-mail, letter, or other mode of communication. However, after you get past the initial introductions and find a clearly mutual interest to proceed, you have to take the relationship to the next step, which usually means a face-to-face meeting. Don't get us wrong — we're not saying that you have to fly across the country for a meeting whenever a prospect calls. Your decision to meet face-to-face with a client depends on many factors. But, as we have said before, consulting is a people thing. Although you can establish and carry on a long-distance business relationship with your phone company or with a mail-order bookstore for years without a face-to-face meeting, consulting is a different animal.

Consulting is different because it is very much a *personal* service. As a personal service, consulting depends on person-to-person interaction for its success. Think about it: Would you entrust the financial viability of a business that you spent your lifetime to create and build to someone whom you have only just met through an online chat room? We don't think so!

Steve Dente and Signature Software

As the owner of San Diego, California-based Signature Software, Steve Dente (stevensdente@msn.com) does software programming and custom application consulting for a wide variety of firms — from small companies that don't have their own software development teams to larger companies with specific needs that Steve can fulfill more cost-effectively than their own in-house staffs can. According to Steve, his work ranges from industry-specific, in-house development programs to shrink-wrapped products for the general public. We interviewed Steve to get his perspective on finding and keeping new customers.

Consulting For Dummies: How do you find your clients?

Steve Dente: Almost all have come from networking with other programmers and other companies in the industry.

CFD: Let's consider both of those avenues. So how do you network with other programmers?

Dente: I belong to programmer groups, which include independent consulting programmers *and* programmers who work for large and small companies. When they get a call to do a program and they're too busy to do it, they'll

pass the work on to someone else in the group. We all know what each one of us is best at, so if they hear of a job that requires certain skills, they'll recruit one of us for it.

CFD: So if you have a job that *you* need some help on, then you give one of the members of your group a call, and vice versa?

Dente: Right. And also, each of the programming language groups maintains Web sites on the Internet where companies can post needs or you can offer your services. For example, I am a member of discussion and programmer groups at a number of Web sites.

CFD: You said that there were two ways that you network, the first with other programmers and the second directly with businesses. How do you pursue networking directly with businesses?

Dente: The companies that I consult for hire me because I am involved as a geologist in the mineral business. So having knowledge of that business and being able to write software programs as well gives me a unique expertise to write industry-specific software for gems and minerals.

CFD: What is a typical consulting job for you in the gem and mineral industry?

Dente: The last one I did was for a large American mining company. I wrote a program that helps them sort and track the cutting, [calculate] the yield results, and organize the pricing of their sapphires.

CFD: How do you break the ice with a new client? How do you tell them about yourself and convince them to hire you?

Dente: Well, normally you talk about who you know in the business and what your potential client's company is doing in the market. In other words, you show an understanding of what their business is. I often send them samples of programs I've done before.

I think if you show people that you understand the general nature of their business, that you also have insight into how other people are doing business, and that you understand what their problem is — and you can present the outline of a solution — then the rest takes care of itself.

It's all a matter of developing a relationship and gaining a level of comfort with the client. If you can convince a customer that you understand the problem and have insight into a solution, then *that* becomes the area of conversation. The terms of the contract and the finances then become pretty easy to deal with.

CFD: So the money becomes secondary?

Dente: Yes! The money pretty much takes care of itself; it's not the main issue. That's the way I like to work.

CFD: When you meet with clients, do you meet with them at your office, or do you go out to see them at their offices, or someplace in between?

Dente: Most of my consulting jobs are initiated over the telephone and, because the problem is theirs, I usually go to their site. In the last year, I have called on clients throughout Southern California, New York, Montana, Korea, China, Sri Lanka, and Thailand. The field of geology is international in nature, and I have contacts in all these places.

CFD: So why do these firms hire you instead of another programmer?

Dente: In general, programmers are programmers, and business people are business people. I'm in the unique position of having spent 20 years in the gem field as a geologist, and then becoming a programmer as well, just out of my personal interest. That gives me a businessperson's insight to programming, which is useful. A lot of times, programmers know how to write code, but they don't know how to solve business problems. My level of consulting is multilevel and multifaceted instead of just a limited skill set.

CFD: What advice would you give to new consultants to establish and develop their businesses?

Dente: You can advertise all you want, but advertising is the *least* effective way for consultants to get clients. Your last client is your best source of the new client. And your current client list generates your new client list. So the best thing is to maintain a good rapport with your clients, provide them a quality service, and effect a solution to their problems. Business is the maintenance of relationships. And consulting in particular depends on relationships because what you're selling is yourself — your skill set and your services.

CFD: Right. You're not selling a can of soup, are you? You're selling yourself.

Dente: That's right. So, how well you work with them, how well you listen to them, and how well you gain insight into their needs results in how happy your clients are with you. This then results in more work — both with that particular client, as well as referrals to other people *they* network with.

Virtual or real?

The world is a big place. We understand that the potential rewards of a business relationship don't always justify the expense of setting up a one-on-one meeting. And we also understand that the Internet, e-mail, voice-mail, cellular phones, and all those other nifty technologies make it easier than ever to communicate with anyone you want, anytime you want. But despite all these great innovations, *nothing* can replace the power of a face-to-face meeting.

Meetings put a face on a distant voice on the phone or on the typed meanderings of an e-mail message. Meetings breathe humanity into the digital bits and bytes that flow through the phone lines from your office to your client's office. When you're sitting before your client — in living color — ignoring your message is a *lot* harder than when it arrives by mail, phone, fax, or computer. And getting your message across is a *lot* easier.

Not convinced? Check out this story.

A couple of years ago, Peter's literary agent called him with some good news — he had met a woman who was looking for someone to ghostwrite a book for her. The potential client had built a very successful company around a series of seminars that she presented around the country. She hoped that a book distilling the essence of her seminars would be useful for furthering her goals — both by having something to sell to participants in her seminars and for reaching a wider audience through distribution in bookstores. Although she was a gifted communicator, she just didn't have the time to run her business, conduct seminars, *and* write a book at the same time. Armed with her name and phone number, Peter made the call.

Unfortunately, although Peter's client-to-be was interested in discussing the project with him, she let Peter know that she had already pretty much decided to contract with a writer with whom she had already met and discussed the project. Hmmm . . . what to do? In a last-ditch effort to save the project, Peter suggested that they get together over coffee the next morning anyway, and that he would pick up the tab. What would it hurt to spend a little time discussing the project? His client agreed, and the stage was set.

When Peter and his client met, they felt an instant rapport, a connectedness that just wasn't evident when they talked on the phone the day before. Despite the fact that Peter's client was 99 percent certain that she already knew who was going to write her book, what was supposed to be a 15- or 20-minute cup of coffee and chitchat became a two-hour discussion of personal philosophy, vision, and project goals. Peter's client called later that evening to tell him that she had selected him to do the project.

If there is a lesson to learn here, it's that you can never underestimate the power of face-to-face meetings. The meeting sparked a new level of communication that was absent in their phone conversation the preceding day. As a result, Peter was able to persuade his client that he would do a better job on the project than the writer she had already selected. When Peter confirmed that he could meet her budget and schedule to boot, the deal was sealed.

One more thing: Scientists and other smart people have determined that some 85 percent of communication when people meet with one another is nonverbal — you know, facial expressions, tapping of toes, crossing of arms, and sighs of boredom, or edge-of-the-chair excitement indicating rapt attention and interest. When you communicate with a client over the phone, through the mail, or via a computer, you end up with only 15 percent of the message, and you lose the other 85 percent that you can't see. Of course, this is also true for the messages that you send to your clients. So if you can't meet in person, make sure that you're especially careful to get your *entire* message across.

Despite our attempts to fill in some of this communication gap with cute voice-mail messages ("You have reached the desk of the great and powerful Oz — ignore that man behind the curtain!") or the ubiquitous usage of those pesky emoticons in e-mail messages (you know, these things :-), :-(, and worse), nothing has yet replaced the emotional power of the personal meeting and, at least until we all have access to full-body videoconferencing worldwide, it's likely that nothing ever will!

Weighing the costs versus the benefits

The question is not *should* you meet with a prospective client. The question is: *Do the benefits of meeting outweigh the costs?* For example, at a cost of a cup of coffee and 20 miles worth of gas, the benefit of Peter's meeting with his ghostwriting client far outweighed the cost. However, if the client lived in New York — 3,000 miles away — the relative advantage of the benefits to be gained over the costs would not have been so clear and compelling. When you consider your options, take the time to weigh the potential benefits of a face-to-face meeting with your potential clients against the costs.

In the following sections, we present some of the things to consider when you decide whether to meet with a prospective client. If the pluses outweigh the minuses, pack your bags and get going!

The travel experience
Plus: You may get to visit some interesting new places and meet some interesting new people.

Minus: You may get stuck in the airport in a blizzard and your bags may get lost. Also, airplane food is pretty bad news unless you can talk a flight attendant into bringing you a few crumbs from the first-class cabin.

Net Result: Make the trip if the potential benefit outweighs the cost of the trip, but bring your own food supplies for the airplane flight. A laptop computer loaded with the game Myst is a compelling bonus.

Time

Plus: You can catch up on your work and return phone calls while you wait for the snowplows to clear the airport runways.

Minus: Due to a special government regulation, airports are inherently boring places to be. Especially if the airline loses your bags. You'll probably want to do anything *but* work as you wait in the airport bar for your oft-delayed flight.

Net Result: Your time is worth money. Do the benefits of the trip equal or exceed the opportunity cost of staying home? If not, cancel that reservation — right now!

Cost

Plus: Travel costs are generally tax deductible. Unfortunately, the costs that are the most fun are generally *not* tax deductible.

Minus: Could cost a *lot* of money, especially if the client is a long way away or if you have to travel on short notice. Furthermore, airlines don't reimburse you for the full amount of your loss when they lose your bags.

Net Result: The money you make on the deal should at least meet or exceed the amount of money that you spend trying to get it. Don't forget to add in the cost of replacing your lost luggage.

Future work

Plus: This meeting may lead to a long and fruitful consulting relationship that allows you to get your kids through college and step up from that '68 Volkswagen you've been driving since college.

Minus: This meeting may turn out to be a complete waste of both your time and your client's time.

Net Result: You don't know until you give it a try. When in doubt, consult with your nearest psychic.

Whom to meet?

In most cases, the best person to meet with is the one who can decide whether or not to hire you or your firm. Why? Because if you're dealing with people who don't have the authority to hire you, you may be wasting your time. However, the next best thing to meeting with the person who can make the decision is to meet with the people who can favorably *influence* the person who makes the decision.

Who are some of the people you should meet with? Before you schedule your next meeting with your clients-to-be, make sure you see how they stack up according to the following list:

- ✔ **The big cheese:** Also known as the fearless leader, the omnipotent one, the big kahuna, or simply the boss. Whether this person owns the company or is beholden to the company's shareholders, this man or woman usually has unlimited spending authority and can hire you so fast your head will spin. Not only that but, after you're hired, the big cheese can clear-cut a path through the organization's obstacles for you, making it *much* easier to get your job done.

- ✔ **The executive assistant:** Also known as the power behind the throne, the great organizer, the all-knowing and all-seeing one, or simply the boss's secretary. Because they have the ear of the big cheese, executive assistants wield tremendous power in their organizations. If you can't get to the big cheese, the executive assistant is definitely a close second in priority.

- ✔ **Middle management:** Also known as chief bottle washers, VPs, corporate overhead, or simply the management team. Though these individuals don't have the unbridled authority of those in the big cheese category, most have some amount of financial authority and can hire you after filling out a small mountain's worth of internal forms and paperwork or after doing the proper amount of begging with the big cheese. Because these folks are busy creating the obstacles that you are being hired to identify and correct, don't expect them to clear organizational obstacles out of your path.

- ✔ **Employee committees:** Also known as a thorn in the side of management, manager-free zones, or simply the folks who really make things happen. In these days of self-managed work teams and employee empowerment, employee committees have gained a large measure of power and authority within their organizations. Many control their own budgets and can decide whether or not to contract for your services. Although convincing a committee of multiple individuals to hire you is harder than convincing just one person, your time working with employee committees can be time well spent.

So how do you get to the right person or group in an organization? After you select your target, simply pick up the phone and call. In our experience, you save a lot of time and money by sidestepping staff and using your phone to go directly to the person or group in charge. E-mail is also a great tool for getting to the right person. We have found that, in many cases, a person who won't return a phone call for days or weeks (or ever!) will reply to an e-mail in minutes. You may have to spend a little time with the receptionist or other employees in doing some research on who's who in the organization, but, after you find out, be deliberate and assertive in your efforts to contact the right people.

Where to meet?

You have the option of meeting at your place, the client's place, or somewhere in between. The selection depends greatly on the nature of your business, on whether you're traveling a great distance for the meeting, and on your client's time constraints. Consider the pluses and minuses of each option.

- **Your place:** Meeting at your place may make the most sense if you have a place to meet. Another reason to do so is that your business may require you to demonstrate a product that is not easy to carry around. For example, a firm that provides custom computer hardware and software solutions on large office servers and networks may have a difficult time lugging the appropriate equipment to a client's site for a demonstration. In such cases, bringing the client to your site, where the equipment is already installed, configured, and up and running, makes more sense.

  The upside of a meeting at your place is that the cost of transportation is not an issue. The downside of meeting at your place may be that your office is more virtual than real; in fact, your office may be in a closet in the corner of your bedroom. Hmmm . . . that won't do, will it? If you think that the sight of your office might leave a negative impression with your clients, suggest that you go to them instead.

- **Their place:** This is often the preferred choice — especially if your client-to-be is too busy to get away from the office or if you need to meet with more than one or two people at a time. The advantages are that your clients are on their own turf, and they are probably more comfortable meeting with you there than in an unfamiliar setting. The disadvantages include clients who answer their phone every time it rings or who spend time chatting with everyone who walks through the door.

- **In between:** Think of a comfortable coffeehouse or a favorite restaurant for lunch or dinner. Pluses: The location is neutral, and you get the opportunity to get away from the moment-to-moment demands of a busy office. Minuses? You may accidentally insult your client when you comment on the evils of caffeine.

Most busy clients prefer for you to meet them at their office. So where you meet with a particular client really depends on whether you can effectively demonstrate a solution to your client's problem at his or her site and whether the cost of getting to your customer does not exceed the expected financial benefits of doing business. When in doubt, err on the side of going out of your way to meet your client at the place of his or her choosing.

When to meet?

Should you try to set up a meeting as soon as possible — strike while the iron is hot, as it were — or should you take things slow and easy? Although some people say that good things come to those who wait, this is not necessarily the case when it comes to consulting. The truth is that consulting is a very competitive field, and the more appropriate adage is likely, "You snooze, you lose."

When you press for immediate meetings with prospective clients, you not only impress them with your obvious interest in meeting their needs, but you also help to ensure that your firm is selected before other consultants have an opportunity to get their foot in the door.

So what is the correct answer to the question of when to meet? Now! Not enough time or not enough notice to meet today? Then set up a meeting for first thing tomorrow. The point is, the sooner you get your meeting scheduled, the better chance you have of landing the deal.

Follow-Through Is Everything!

Despite successfully making it through all the hurdles of getting to know new clients and winning their trust and confidence, many consultants ultimately lose their deals when they fail to follow through with their clients. Though you may prefer to think of consulting as the art of performing the services in which you're expert, the one thing that makes the world of consulting go around is ultimately your ability to sell yourself to the people and organizations who can afford to pay your bills.

If you can't sell yourself, you can't sell your services. It's that simple.

After you make your sales pitch, the next step is to set up a system of follow-through with your prospective client. As a consultant, you find that many of your prospects are very busy people, and it is easy for them to lose your proposal amongst all the other priorities that they are charged with juggling. The purpose of follow-through is to keep your proposal fresh in your client's mind and make sure that he or she doesn't forget about you.

Bob has his system of client follow-through down pat. Whenever he meets prospective clients for his services, he puts them on the mailing list for his newsletter, *Rewarding Employees.* The newsletter, which is published monthly and sent to more than 2,000 clients and clients-to-be, provides its readers with an enormous amount of useful information about employee rewards and reward programs. Not only do Bob's clients learn something useful, but they also are reminded that Bob offers a wide variety of reward-oriented products and services.

However, don't forget the number-one rule of following up with your clients: Don't be a pest. Proper follow-through walks a fine line between an occasional reminder that keeps your name in mind and a full-court press that makes you more trouble than you're worth. Be sensitive to the needs of your clients when you decide on your follow-through strategy. Although every situation is different, you can't go wrong by applying the follow-through techniques presented in this section.

Setting a date for the next step

If you don't have an appointment calendar, a daily planner, or a personal digital assistant to keep track of your appointments, stop right now. Do not pass go or collect your $200 until you go out and buy one. You have one? Great! You're all set.

What is the next step in selling yourself to your client? Another meeting? A technical demonstration? Mailing or faxing a copy of a journal article that you authored? A phone call to check to see whether you are going to be selected to do the proposed job? Until you land your consulting job, make sure that you always decide on what step is required next to get you closer to your goal, and set a date and time for its completion.

Whatever the next step is — no matter how trivial — make a note of it in your calendar. If the event is set for a definite time, make sure that you make a point of recording the time, too. The point is, you don't want to take the chance of forgetting what you need to do to land your consulting job. Two of the key tests that you have to pass for your clients are punctuality and reliability. If you say that you'll call to follow up at 9:00 a.m. on September 30, then you'd better be dialing the number at 8:59 a.m. on the 30th of September.

The fine art of the thank-you note

A thank-you note can do wonders to get you planted squarely in the middle of your client's good graces. Just as a post-interview thank-you letter makes a positive impression on a company that is hiring a new employee, a sincere thank-you note makes a positive impression on the individuals who decide whether you get a contract for your services.

Writing good thank-you notes is an art. They should be sincere and from your heart, and they should leave the reader with a positive impression of both you and your business. Whenever you write a thank-you note, make sure that it does the following three things:

- ✔ Personally thanks your client for her time and interest

- ✔ Firmly expresses your interest in doing the proposed work for your client

- ✔ Includes any additional information that the client may need to make a decision in your favor

So when should you take the time to thank a potential client? Consider sending a thank-you note whenever you find yourself in the following situations:

- ✔ **You want to thank a client for agreeing to meet with you at some future time.** This thank-you note also serves to confirm the date and time of your meeting.

- ✔ **You want to thank a client for having taken time to meet with you.** Not only do you get to express your sincere thanks to your client, but you also get to reiterate the many compelling reasons for selecting you or your consulting business.

- ✔ **You want to thank a client for the business.** After you're hired, a thank-you note expressing your gratitude is certainly in order.

Of course, you may feel that a thank-you note is appropriate at other times. If so, follow your instincts. You don't have to write a book — all it takes is jotting down a couple of sincere sentences of thanks and then dropping your note in the mail. When in doubt, send it out!

Following up via letter, phone, or e-mail

The medium that you select to follow up with your clients is not as important as making sure that you do follow up. Each possible way of following up with clients has its pluses and minuses, and which one you choose depends on your style of doing business and on what seems to work best with a particular client. You always have the flexibility of selecting one method or a combination of methods of follow-up. Ultimately, the decision is up to you.

Consider the advantages and disadvantages of several media for client follow-up:

✔ **Letter:** You can easily hand-write or type up a letter anytime or any-place. Although a personal letter delivered by messenger, by overnight delivery, or by mail is the most impressive to potential clients, you can also send it via fax. On the plus side, letters are convenient and effective. On the minus side, letters can get lost in the shuffle of busy executives.

✔ **Phone:** The most personal form of follow-through besides a face-to-face meeting is a personal phone call. When you phone your clients, you demonstrate that their business is important to you and that you are very interested in winning it. On the plus side, you can make a phone call from anywhere, most anytime you like. And with voice-mail, you can leave an extensive message for your clients even when they are on the phone or away on business or vacation. On the minus side, playing phone tag over a prolonged period of time or getting lost in voice-mail hell is certainly not unheard of.

✔ **Electronic mail:** Computer e-mail is a bit less personal than either a letter or a phone call, but, when used properly, it can still be quite effective. On the plus side, e-mail offers the ultimate in flexibility and convenience. On the minus side, if you get just one letter or number wrong in the address, your message can end up in Vladivostok instead of Toronto.

Here's a sample e-mail thank-you note to help get your creative juices flowing:

```
To: ElwoodHayes@bigbiz.com
Cc:
Subject: Thank you!

Just a note to thank you for taking the time to speak with
me about the companywide performance assessment that you
would like to conduct next fiscal year. We are very inter-
ested in working with you to complete this important task.
As you have seen, my company has more than 15 years of
experience in successfully completing performance assess-
ments for a wide variety of Fortune 500 firms. Each of
these firms has been tremendously satisfied with the re-
sults, and I have no doubt in my mind that we can do the
same for you.

I will call you next week to see where we go from here.

Sincerely,

Debbie Fritsch
```

However you decide to thank your clients for their time, you need to keep one key rule in mind: Be sure to *thank* them. Not only do you leave a positive impression in their minds that may help you land the deal, but you'll also be remembered for future opportunities even if you don't do business this time.

Moving On

In the process of selling your services to potential clients, you have to decide which ones have the greatest potential of doing business with you or your firm and which ones have the least potential. Although being able to put your all into pursuing every single lead that you get might be nice, it just isn't realistic from a cost perspective.

Following through with clients takes both time and money — and *lots* of it. Because both time *and* money are available in limited amounts for most consultants, the wise thing to do is to split your client list into two pieces, active and inactive, and put most of your resources into the former. Consider the differences between active and inactive clients:

✔ **Active clients** are the clients who have shown a definite interest in hiring you or your firm. Because they are the most probable source of future work, they should get most of your attention. Make sure that you place them on a schedule of regular follow-up communication — phone calls, e-mails, letters, product brochures, newsletters, and more — from your firm that keeps you and your services in their mind.

> ✔ **Inactive clients** may have once expressed an interest in your business, but your repeated attempts over a prolonged period of time (six months or more, depending on your own criteria) have failed to land a deal. You should downgrade such clients from active to inactive status and also decrease the amount of resources you devote to them. A good way to keep in touch with inactive clients is to add them to the mailing list for your firm's newsletter. For the minimal cost of printing and postage, you keep open the possibility of doing business in the future.

In our experience, considering both active clients and inactive clients as potential clients is always wise. You never know when a client who has been inactive for months or even years will suddenly spring to life and want to hire you for an important job. We have seen this happen time and time again. Never *burn* bridges with your clients. Always *build* bridges with your clients. After all, in consulting, it's not always *what* you know, but *who* you know — and what they think about you — that can make the difference between success and failure.

Chapter 22

Building Business through Referrals

• •

In This Chapter

▶ Approaching different sources of referrals

▶ Greasing the skids

▶ Obtaining quality referrals

▶ Following through with your referrals and your clients

• •

*E*very consulting business needs new clients to thrive and to grow. Building your business is an activity that should never stop. Sure, you have to attend to your current clients and your current projects (after all, your best bet for new business is repeat business from your current clients), but you always should be looking down the road — a month, six months, a year into the future — for new clients. You need new clients to fill in the inevitable gaps between the projects that you do for your current clients *and* to grow your business over time.

Just as there are many different ways to drive a car from Calgary to Atlanta, there are many different ways to bring new clients into your business. You can place advertisements and hope that your clients-to-be see them and decide to contact you; you can go door-to-door and sell your services personally; you can run a contest or give away free samples and gather leads that way; or you can choose any one of an almost unlimited number of different approaches for attracting new clients.

However, there is another way to get new clients — a way by which some consultants derive almost all their new business but that others overlook entirely. This way of building your business is through referrals. *Referrals* are prospects sent to you by someone outside your own business. For example, say you're a successful nutrition consultant. If your clients are happy with the work you do for them (they *are* happy, right?), they are bound to want to tell their friends about their positive experiences. When your clients' friends call you as a result, *those* are referrals. Referrals are a fantastic way to obtain new clients, and you should not overlook this method.

The benefits of referrals to your business are many. Here are 181 words explaining why referrals are such a good thing for you:

- ✔ **Referrals are a major source of new business for many consultants.** Although some consultants depend on referrals to identify almost all their new business leads, others may not have tapped very deep into this vast resource. You can increase the number and quality of your referrals easily by following the advice in this chapter.

- ✔ **Referrals are easier to close than other kinds of prospects.** Because the people who send you referrals have most likely already told the referrals what you do and what a great job you do, your referrals come to you to some extent presold. The hard part of attracting their attention and getting them to listen to what you have to say has already been accomplished.

- ✔ **Referrals cost less to market than other kinds of prospects.** Because referrals are sent to you by other people, you don't have to spend any of your promotional budget to get their attention. And because they are presold, convincing them to buy your product or services doesn't take you as much time as convincing a prospect who was not referred to you.

In this chapter, we help you determine *who* are the best sources of referrals for your business, and we consider the importance of keeping your current clients happy with the work that you are doing for them and the way that you do it. We look into the very best ways to get referrals and then tell you what to do with them once you have them.

Deciding Whom to Approach for Referrals

Referrals can come from anyone at any time. Although your best source of referrals is most likely your many current, happy clients, referrals can pop into your life from the least expected places at the least expected times. Of course, like anything else in business (and in life, for that matter), you can greatly improve your chances of getting referrals by making a conscious effort to seek them.

You have two choices: You can either choose to wait for people to make referrals to you or your business, or you can actively work for them.

Assuming that you have made the decision to seek referrals, whom should you approach for them? Although you can approach almost anyone, the following sources of referrals are likely your best bets:

✔ **Current clients:** Your current clients are without a doubt your best source of referrals. Not only do they know the quality of your work on a firsthand basis, but they are often your biggest fans and boosters. And when your clients are out looking for new clients for you, your own marketing and promotion efforts are multiplied many times. The best approach with your clients is a direct one. Simply tell them that you would be happy to service any associates who may also need your services. The best time to make the approach is after you complete a project successfully for your client. Be sure to take care of your current clients first, and they'll be sure to take care of you.

✔ **Other consultants:** Consulting can be a very cyclical business. One week you have hardly anything to do; the next week you're so busy you don't know how you're going to get your work done. The fact is, other consultants are in much the same situation. Many consultants, when temporarily overwhelmed with business, contract out some of their work to individuals and firms that they know and trust. Doing so enables them to get the work done on time without having to hire permanent employees. Some consultants actually refer their clients to other consultants when they are already booked up. By getting to know other consultants — and helping them get to know you — you can pick up referrals that help you get through your slow times.

✔ **Business associates:** During the course of a typical business day, you probably interact with a number of business associates — perhaps your accountant, a clerk at your favorite office supply store, or even your mail carrier. Do *they* know about the products and services that you offer? If not, you have another opportunity to bring an entirely new group of referral opportunities to your business. Your attorney and accountant can be terrific sources of referrals because they're likely plugged in to your local business community. You just need to get them the information so that they know.

✔ **Family and friends:** Unless you just recently arrived from another planet or galaxy, you have lots of family and friends who also can be a great source of referrals. Be sure to remind them periodically of what you do for a living and invite them to tell *their* families and friends. Keep them up-to-date by mailing them copies of newspaper or magazine articles about your business and by sending them copies of your brochures or other sales materials.

How you find referrals is really up to you. If you are more comfortable waiting for your contacts to make referrals to you and would really rather not push them in that direction yourself, then that's what you should do. However, if you want to enjoy the benefits of a greatly enhanced quantity and quality of business referrals, take a close look at the people with whom you are acquainted and do business, and ask yourself whether they would be good sources of referrals. You may be surprised by how many of your clients, friends, and other associates are more than happy to refer new clients to you, if only you ask them to do so.

Setting the Stage with Current Clients

Because your current clients are your most likely source for referral business, you want to focus your efforts on them before you explore the other possibilities, such as the guy who drives your local ice cream truck or the gal who walks by your office every morning at 8 a.m. You can do a number of things to set the stage with your clients for referrals. Here are some ways that you can help to motivate your clients to keep those referrals coming:

- ✔ **Do great work.** We've said it before, and we'll say it again. One of the best ways to keep your clients happy is to do great work for them. If you do, they'll probably be so happy that they'll want to tell all their associates about the great job you did.

  A couple of months ago, a house painter did a job for Peter's next-door neighbor. The painter did such a great job for such a great price that Peter immediately hired him to paint some rooms in his house. When Peter recommended him to another neighbor, *she* hired the painter to do some work for her. This went on and on until the painter — who was completely unknown to anyone in the neighborhood only a few weeks before — had done work for almost everyone on the street.

- ✔ **Do your work on budget and on time.** What are two things that your clients hope they'll never hear from you? That you're going to be late and that the project is going to cost more than you originally estimated. One of the best ways to keep your clients happy and ensure that you are on the top of their list of referrals is to do your work at the price you originally agreed on and on time. Of course, few clients will fault you if *they* do something to make you go over cost or deliver your results late. But even if they do something that creates a problem for you, do everything *you* can to keep things on track. You'll be a hero!

- ✔ **Keep your clients well informed.** When you are working on projects for your clients, you can earn their everlasting and undying affection by taking the time to keep them informed about your progress and notifying them if you encounter problems or difficulties that require their attention.

- ✔ **Be reliable and dependable.** If anything turns off a client, it's your being unreliable. If you promise your clients that you are going to do something, then they expect you to do as you have promised —

nothing less and nothing more. If you're reliable and dependable, you'll have more business — and more referrals — than you can imagine. However, if you aren't, you'll have plenty of spare time on your hands to do other things (maybe look for a new way to make money, for a start!).

✔ **Be flexible.** In any business, change is usually the rule and not the exception. It seems that if you're not changing, you're not going *anywhere*. The best consultants are able to quickly adapt their approaches, schedules, and project staffing when required by their clients.

✔ **Thank your clients for their referrals.** Be sure to thank your clients whenever they refer you to a prospective client — whether or not you end up doing business with the prospect. This gesture of gratitude demonstrates to your clients that you appreciate their assistance.

Your good work sets the stage for more work with the same clients *and* for your clients to refer others to you. Do everything you can to keep your current clients happy with the work you do for them, and you'll be busier than you can imagine.

How to Get Referrals

You can either wait for your associates and acquaintances to refer new clients to you, or you can actively seek them. Referrals are a great thing for any business to have because they are much easier to sell and cost less to obtain. You can increase the number and quality of your referrals by pursuing them through a variety of different techniques.

The following sections describe a few different approaches for you to try in your quest for new clients.

Use the direct approach

Why beat around the bush if you can ask your clients and acquaintances *directly* to send you referrals? Although there are other ways to get referrals, often the direct approach works best. Simply tell your clients that you would like them to refer any of their acquaintances and business associates to you if they need services of the sort that you offer. You can do this in person or by telephone, letter, e-mail, or fax. Figure 22-1, shown on the next page, presents an example of a letter soliciting referrals from a client directly.

October 25, 199x

Ms. Sara Blanc
Blanc & Associates
1330 Del Mar Avenue
Del Mar, CA 92014

Dear Sara:

I'm pleased to let you know that we successfully completed the redesign of the Laurel Canyon aqueduct, and we finished the project a week early. I have you to thank for helping us cut through wads of red tape at City Hall, and I am personally very proud of the partnership that we developed during the course of the project.

I look forward to our next project. Until then, if you know people who need the services of a good civil engineering consultant, I hope you'll send them my way. I'll be sure to make sure that they get the best service possible for the best price possible.

Thanks again for your help.

Best wishes,

John Adesanwo

Keep in touch with your clients

How's the old saying go? Out of sight, out of mind? Everyone today is incredibly busy, doing more with less and doing it more quickly and with less time to think about it than ever. If you don't keep in touch with your clients, your clients will soon forget you as they turn their attention to the crisis of the day. When you are between jobs with your clients, drop by their offices to say hello every once in a while, or send them a note or a newspaper or magazine clipping that they might find interesting.

Reward your clients for referrals

You should always reward your clients when they refer business to you. The reward you select depends on the kind of consulting you do; it can range from a simple thank-you note all the way to a commission based on a percentage of the fee that the referral pays you. At a minimum, call your client and thank him or her personally. As an extra show of thanks, you can send a gift of nominal value — say, a coffee mug with your name and telephone number printed on it, or a nice flower arrangement — or you can extend your client a discount on your next job. In some cases — especially for a particularly valuable referral — you may want to pay your client a cash finder's fee (a flat amount) or a commission (an amount that varies depending on the size of the fee that you bill the client) for his or her consideration.

Build a contact database

How many different clients and potential clients do you meet every year? 15? 150? 1,500? The problem is, after you meet with more than a few people, forgetting the personal details about each one is easy. This is where a contact database earns its weight in gold over and over again. After you set it up, you can target your referral efforts to specific clients with great precision. At a minimum, your contact database should include your contact's name and title, company name and address, telephone and fax numbers, business needs, personal interests, and any other information that you believe will help you in your efforts.

Make referrals yourself

Here's an important lesson that can help you both in business and in your everyday life: *What goes around comes around.* What does that have to do with getting referrals? A lot. Just as you hope that your clients will refer you to *their* associates, you can refer them to *your* associates. Say you're a travel consultant and are doing work for an accounting firm. If an acquaintance tells you that he is looking for a good accountant, then it only makes sense to refer your acquaintance to the accounting firm for which you are doing work — assuming, of course, that it is a quality firm. It's really quite simple: The more referrals you make, the more referrals you'll receive.

Following Up on the Referral

After you receive a referral, you need to follow up on it to determine whether you have a qualified prospect or just a dead end. Leads are kind of like a loaf of bread sitting on your kitchen shelf. The longer your leads sit on a shelf — while you take no action to follow up on them — the more stale they become. Eventually, when they start to grow green hair, you have to throw them in the trash.

Referrals are an important part of your new business and your future. Do the following to ensure that you'll have plenty of referrals far into the future:

- **Follow up with your referrals.** Whenever you get a referral from a client, friend, or acquaintance, be sure to follow up *immediately*. Get on the telephone and return the call — right now! Nothing is more embarrassing to a client who has made a referral than to hear that you never returned the call or responded to the message. You can bet that *that* client won't bother making any more referrals to you!

  When you reach the referral, provide a brief summary of what you offer and then press for a face-to-face meeting to define the problem. Respect your referrals *and* your clients by responding to referrals quickly. Even if you can't help, you at least leave the door open for future referrals from your clients and also for future business with the referral you couldn't help out at this time.

- **Follow up with your clients.** Keep your clients in the loop about how the work with their referrals is going. They'll appreciate the update, and the communication helps to remind them that you're ready, willing, and available for additional assignments.

  Try an approach like this:

  You: "I just wanted to thank you for sending me the referral for Text2000 Corporation — I landed a nice job with them as a result."

  Client: "No problem. You do such great work for us, I thought I should share the wealth. I have a lot of business associates who are in desperate need of someone who is smart and experienced and has been around the block a few times. Keep your eyes open — I'll be sending more business your way soon."

  You: "Fantastic. I always have room to accommodate a few more great clients like you. I'll make sure that we treat them just as well as we treat you."

Part VI
The Part of Tens

"ANNUITIES? EQUITY INCOME? TAX-FREE MUNICIPALS? I SAY WE STICK THE MONEY IN THE GROUND LIKE ALWAYS AND THEN FEED THIS CONSULTANT TO THE SHARKS."

In this part . . .

These short chapters are packed with quick ideas that can help you become a better consultant. Read them whenever you have an extra minute or two.

Chapter 23

Ten Ways to Use the Internet to Market Your Services

*T*alk about wide-open, unlimited opportunity! As more and more people and organizations go online every day, the Internet is becoming an increasingly valuable way to market your services. Although no one knows whether the huge amount of money being pumped into Internet marketing will really pay off in the long run, you can get your message onto the Internet with relative ease for little money. However, the Internet is *so* huge that getting lost or frittering away your marketing dollars on dead-ends is easy.

By focusing your efforts on a number of proven strategies, you can find many ways to use the Internet to your advantage. If you want to multiply your Internet marketing muscle on an exponential basis, give these ideas a try.

Create a Web page

In case you haven't noticed, just about every organization in the world has established a home page on the World Wide Web. From the Vatican to Coca-Cola to your neighborhood bagel shop, many organizations include Web pages as an essential part of their marketing mix. Web pages are so popular because they are a very inexpensive way to get a message out to clients anywhere in the world. It doesn't matter what time or what day of the week it is or whether it's a holiday. Your Web page stands ready to inform your clients 24 hours a day, 7 days a week, rain or shine.

If you want to try one out for little or no cost, you can build your own page at some of the popular online services, such as America Online, or *Inc.* magazine (`http://www.inc.com`), or through your Internet service provider.

What is really essential to understand is that providing the same information as a catalog isn't the answer. Creating value (a new way of doing business, receiving knowledge, and so on) is what determines money well spent.

If you *really* get serious about your Web page, you can easily find and hire an Internet consultant to build and maintain it for you for a very reasonable price. Check with your Internet service provider or local computer magazines or newspapers.

Get noticed!

After you establish a presence on the Internet, you need to get noticed. With the emergence of powerful Internet search programs and directories such as Yahoo! and AltaVista, your clients can easily find you by simply typing in a key word that describes what they are looking for. However, if you want Yahoo! and the like to find you, you'll have a much better chance if you register with them first.

Register your site with the most popular search engines and directories as soon as you establish your site. You can either go directly to each site and submit your home page address yourself, or you can have someone else do it. *Inc.* magazine (`http://www.inc.com`) will submit your Web page address to six of the most popular search engines for free. You can also hire firms to place your address with a wide variety of search engines for a nominal fee. If you really want to get noticed, Submit It! (`http://www.submit-it.com`) will register your page with more than 300 different search engines and directories for very little money.

Build and trade links

Part of the fun of surfing the Web is happening across hypertext links to other Web pages. So when you're reading an article on breeders of Great Dane dogs, you can click on the highlighted text **Canadian Breeders** to be cybersent to the home page of an association of Canadian Great Dane Breeders. You can include links to other Web pages within your own home page. Similarly, other Web pages can contain links to your home page.

When you build your home page, consider what Internet resources would be of value to your clients. For example, if you do investment consulting, your clients might enjoy linking to *The Wall Street Journal,* to an investment club in Miami, or to an Internet service offering free stock quotes. Build those links into your Web page and then ask the *Webmaster* (the person who maintains the site) at each site to include links to *your* site within *that* page. If you are persistent, you can build up quite a network of free links to your home page.

Do targeted e-mail mass mailings

Using Internet e-mail, your advertising message can be sent to thousands of recipients worldwide in mere seconds. No printing and folding brochures, no licking stamps, and no standing in line at the post office. Sounds great, doesn't it? It is, with one caveat: Spamming your clients-to-be is a *big* no-no! The temptation to send an unsolicited message to 100,000, or 500,000, or even 1 million or more recipients for some ridiculously low price can be overwhelming. However, if you choose to take this route, you're sure to generate far more ill will than sales. The best approach is to develop a list of potential clients who *want* your message, and who will be receptive to getting it. Do this by offering clients and visitors to your Web site the opportunity to join your mailing list, or by purchasing managed mailing lists from reputable firms such as IDG Communications List Services.

Get involved in bulletin boards

All the major online services offer bulletin boards where a wide variety of business people and professionals can "talk" to one another by posting messages for others with similar interests. This is a *great* way to network with other consultants in your field — to ask questions, give advice, and get emotional support or a quick shot of energy. It's also a pretty good way to meet potential clients who go to the boards to find experienced consultants.

When Peter was first getting serious about starting his consulting business in writing, he used to hang out at the America Online writers' board — he even sponsored a discussion group on ghostwriting for a time. As a result of this association, he met several other writers — some of whom he collaborated with on writing projects — and he received several writing jobs from clients looking for a good writer. If you aren't associated with one of the large online services, you can still do much the same thing through Internet newsgroups, Internet mailing lists, and Internet Relay Chat.

Advertise your Internet address

If you have a Web page or an e-mail address, plaster it anywhere and everywhere you can. Use it on your business card, your stationery, your advertisements, your report covers, and everything else you give and send to potential clients. If you have an e-mail address, great! If you have a Web page address, even better! The point is to make it easy for potential clients to communicate with you.

One note of caution: After you establish an e-mail address, try to stick with it. Not only is updating your address on all your stuff a pain in the neck, but you may not get mail that's sent to your old address. The problem is that when you cancel your original address and switch to a new address, few online services or Internet service providers will forward mail to your new address.

You have one of two choices: Either establish an e-mail account and stick with it or establish a "permanent" forwarding address, such as the one offered by the Stanford Alumni Association. As a free service, the Alumni Association creates a permanent forwarding address for students and alumni of the university. So no matter what online service Peter uses to get his e-mail — currently America Online — any mail sent to `bizzwriter` `@alumni.stanford.org` is immediately forwarded to Peter's America Online in-box. A number of organizations, such as Bigfoot (`http://` `www.bigfoot.com`) or StarMail (`http://www.starmail.com`), can also get you set up with a permanent forwarding address for little or no cost.

Establish your own Web domain name

You have undoubtedly noticed that the Web addresses of most big organizations incorporate the name of the organization within them. For example, if you want to find Nike's home page, you can simply type in `http://` `www.nike.com` and within seconds find yourself at Nike's front door. If the Internet becomes the incredibly earth-shattering marketing monster that everyone seems to think it will become, then claiming your domain name now is a definite must in your online marketing plan. Then when your future clients are trying to find you online, they can simply type in: `http://` `www.yourname.com` instead of some gobbledygook like `http://` `www.earthlink.net.useraccounts/html/yourname`. To establish your own Web domain name, check with your friendly, local Internet service provider or simply do a Yahoo! search (`http://www.yahoo.com`) on the term "domain name" to obtain a long list of organizations that will be more than happy to set one up for you (for a price, of course).

Become a system operator for an online service forum

Many consultants have found success in expanding their marketing efforts to the Internet by signing on as system operators or moderators for related forums located in the big online services such as America Online, CompuServe, and the Microsoft Network. For example, self-employment experts Paul and Sarah Edwards can be found online at CompuServe in the

Working at Home Forum (you CompuServe fans can type keyword **GO WORK**). This online forum makes for a great marketing supplement to the many books that the couple has written and many public appearances that the Edwardses make each year. You can do it, too! The major online services are always looking for talented people to lend their expertise to their forums. Simply contact the online service of your choice and let them know what you have to offer.

Affiliate with a consultant referral service

An easy way to get your feet wet in Internet marketing without investing much time or money is to join a consultant referral service that already has a presence on the Internet. For example, the Expert Marketplace (`http://www.expert-market.com/em`), which describes itself as "the industry resource for technical and consulting services," maintains a searchable database of more than 214,000 consultants and consulting firms. If you belong to an industry association — for example, the Association of Professional Consultants (`http://www.consultapc.org`) — your association may offer a free Internet referral service to its members.

Set up a mailing list

Whether it's called a listserv, a discussion list, or a mail reflector, an Internet mailing list can be an important way to get your information into the hands of potential clients. Here's how it works: Your client "subscribes" to your mailing list, and then e-mail messages sent to a central address are forwarded to *everyone* on your list. You can run your list in one of two ways: either as a *discussion* list, where anyone can post messages that are then redistributed to everyone else on the list, or as an *announcement* list, where only messages that *you* post are redistributed to everyone else on your list.

If you're using your mailing list primarily for marketing purposes, an announcement list is probably your best bet. With this form of list, you can easily broadcast newsletters, press releases, and other marketing information to your prospective clients. If you're Internet savvy, you can set up the list yourself through your Internet service provider. Otherwise, many firms will be happy to do it for you for a nominal fee. Check with your Internet service provider or find an Internet Mailing List Provider by pointing your browser to `http://www.catalog.com/vivian/`.

Chapter 24

The Ten Biggest Mistakes a Consultant Can Make

*E*veryone makes mistakes, consultants included. Making mistakes is particularly easy when you are just starting out in your own business. However, the biggest mistake of all is not learning from your mistakes. Review the list that follows, and perhaps you won't have to learn your lessons the hard way — that is, over and over and over.

Not listening

More than many other kinds of business, consulting is *very* much a people business. Your ability to determine the best solutions for an organization depends on your ability to communicate effectively with your clients. Although talking to your clients is certainly important, being a good listener is even *more* important. Your clients probably know what they want, and they often tell you exactly what is wrong within their organizations. By listening to them, you learn far more in a much shorter amount of time than you could any other way. When you are meeting with your clients, make it a point to listen far more than you talk. And check what you heard by trying to explain it back to the client.

Failing to establish rapport

Consulting is very much a one-to-one, person-to-person kind of business. Your ability to land lucrative consulting jobs — and then to be successful in performing them — is based, to a large degree, on the rapport that you establish with your clients. When clients hire you, they are placing a lot of trust in your ability to get the job done — correctly, on time, and at the price on which you agreed. Establishing rapport with your clients builds a bridge that allows trust to grow. Work hard at establishing strong social — cordial "hi-how-are-the-kids" kinds of interactions — and professional relationships with your clients. Allow time to get to know them and for them to know you.

Letting your ego get in the way

It's okay to be confident in your ability to get the job done. It's okay to insist that things be done a certain way to protect the integrity of your work or to maintain your high ethical standards. It's even okay to argue your point in an attempt to sway your client. What's *not* okay is for you to let your ego get in the way of your common sense and your ability to listen to what your client is telling you. If you find yourself dominating all the discussions with your clients, or if you are too busy listening to yourself to listen to your clients, then step back for a moment and assess what's going on. If your ego is getting in the way of your ability to communicate, stop talking and listen for a while. You may be surprised at what you learn.

Being inflexible

Nothing kills a consulting business quicker than being inflexible. Although inflexibility may have served you well when you worked in a large, bureaucratic organization, it just doesn't cut it when you're out on your own. First, flexibility is one of the main reasons that organizations hire consultants in the first place. Consultants are often able to get things done much more quickly than can a larger organization burdened by its rules, procedures, and policies. Second, when an organization has a problem, it has a problem *right now.* If you can't respond to the organization's needs immediately, someone else will. Be flexible and responsive to your customers' needs. Your ability to respond quickly is a major competitive advantage. Don't give it up.

Overpricing your services

Many organizations are generally familiar with the standard market prices for the services you offer. Chances are that they may have used the services of other consultants before you happened upon them, or they took the time to survey other firms before they contacted you. In economics, a fundamental rule exists: The higher your price, the less demand there will be for your services. Though charging a high fee for your services may be exciting (and profitable), if your price is *too* high, you may not get enough business to support yourself. When you price your services, keep an eye on the rates that other consultants in your field charge. If your prices are significantly higher than average, you must be able to demonstrate the advantages that your clients will receive as a result. The only way that you can price your services above the market (and still get any business) is to convince your clients that you are the best person for the job — period!

Underpricing your services

Underpricing your services presents a couple of major problems. First and most obvious, if your price is too low, then your business will not be profitable and will grind to a screeching halt before too long, and you'll become a charity case. After you establish a rate with a client, your client will expect to pay that rate in the future, and changing the rate later will be difficult. Second, because of your "too-good-to-be-true" rates, you may be swamped with business. That might sound great, but the problem is that if you're swamped with unprofitable business, then you have no time to take on *profitable* business. When you price your services, make sure that you determine your costs of doing business and then build in a reasonable profit. And take the time to find out what your competitors charge for similar work. No client will ever tell you that you are charging too *little*.

Pricing caveats: Pricing is tricky and requires some serious thought. Remember that *prices* are set by the marketplace; *costs* are set by you. Profit is the difference. If you fail to manage your costs — for example, by taking a suite when a single office will suffice — you are throwing away your profits. Frequently, clients are concerned about consultants overrunning the budget. You can price the project on a *not-to-exceed* basis, which increases your chances of getting the contract. However, you should not agree to a lot of costly client-initiated changes after the project is under way. You should also earn extra profit if you complete the project significantly under the not-to-exceed ceiling.

Having only one primary client

Just as diversifying a stock portfolio is a wise decision, diversifying your business is also a wise decision. This means that you should work toward securing a number of clients instead of just one. If you depend on just one client for all your business, what would happen to you if that client went out of business or decided to bring your function in house? Ironically, the larger the client, the less the need you seem to have to find other clients, which is part of the seduction.

Diversifying your business also means taking on different kinds of jobs related to your chosen field. For example, instead of just performing Internet consulting for retailers of musical instruments, perhaps you could diversify your client base to include rock bands. By diversifying, you reduce your financial risks of losing a client, and you increase your opportunities by introducing new clients to your business.

Turning down work

Some consultants make the mistake of turning down small jobs because they don't think that small jobs are worth their time — whether they are profitable or not. The problem is that you never know when a small job may lead to much larger, long-term assignments. When hiring consultants, many organizations prefer to test the waters first by giving out small assignments and then evaluating the performance of those consultants. If you do a good job on the small assignment, then you'll get the opportunity to work on larger assignments. Do your best to *never* turn down work unless doing so will stretch you so thin that the quality of your work will suffer.

Taking current clients for granted

When you're constantly worried about bringing in future business, you naturally focus on your new clients and neglect the clients you already have. This is a potentially fatal error for your practice. Not only do your current clients pay your current bills, but they are generally your best source for future business, both through future orders and through referrals. Although you should always work at marketing for future clients, don't forget your most important clients: the ones you have *now* who are paying your bills.

Failing to market for future business

You can easily get so involved in your current work — especially if you have lots of it — that you forget to spend sufficient time developing leads for future business. This is another potentially fatal error for your practice. Although your current clients pay your current bills, you need *future* clients to pay your future bills and to grow. Treat your current clients like gold (and don't neglect them, for heaven's sake), but set aside a certain portion of each workday — anywhere from one-third to one-half of your time — prospecting for future clients.

Chapter 25

Ten Tips for a Winning Proposal

In This Chapter
▶ Highlighting your qualifications
▶ Adding a personal touch

Although you may occasionally be lucky enough to win a consulting job based only on an oral presentation, in most cases you need to submit a written proposal to prospective clients before they will hire you. A proposal can be anything from a one-page e-mail message to a more formal letter proposal to a multivolume tabbed, perforated, and indexed extravaganza. Because proposals are so important to the financial well-being of your business, they deserve your utmost attention and care. This chapter gives you ten tips to help you create winning proposals.

Don't assume that your clients know that you can do the best job

One easy mistake that you can make when developing and submitting a proposal is to assume that your client already knows everything about you. This assumption is especially problematic when you and your client have an ongoing business relationship and you take your relationship for granted. If you believe that you can do the best job for your client, be sure to prove it in your proposal. Write your proposals assuming that the intended reader knows little about you or your practice. Be very clear about your experience, and tailor your proposal to the exact needs of your client. This is another reason why listening to your client is critical. To tailor your proposal to your client's needs, you need to have heard them first.

Help your client develop the specs for the job

Salespeople have known for eons that if they can help you develop the specification for the product you want to buy, then you are more likely to buy the product from them. Why? Because they define your problem in ways they can address. Few of your clients are expert in your area of technical specialty — that's why they hired you. The wealth of knowledge and experience that you possess can save your clients time and money in trying to figure out how to describe their problem and what needs to be done to fix it. Volunteer your services freely — and for free — when asked; that small investment of time will undoubtedly pay off in a big way down the road.

Learn about your competition

If you're competing with other firms for the same business (and what firm *isn't* competing with other firms for the same business?), you have to become very familiar with your competition. However, not only do you need to know how many competitors you have and who they are, you must also become knowledgeable about your competitors' pluses and minuses relative to your own business if you expect to survive and prosper. Ask your clients what they like and dislike about your competitors. Read national business magazines and newspapers in addition to your local business press. Subscribe to industry journals and attend conferences and expositions. Research your competitors through the Internet. Get to know your competition inside and out.

Hint: Set up a file folder for each competitor. When you get some information or an article about a competitor, file it. If you review the file every six months or so, you'll see a picture begin to emerge.

Talk through the proposal with your client first

Before you submit your proposal, talk through your concepts with your client. Drop in for a visit, or make a phone call, or send an e-mail to communicate your ideas. Although you may be certain that your proposed approach is the right one for the particular situation, you may be surprised to find out that your client doesn't agree. Discovering this *before* you submit your proposal is better than finding out after you submit your proposal. Not only that, but whether or not you get the work, you begin to develop a relationship and rapport that make you a welcome bidder in the future.

Submit your proposal in person

Mailing or overnighting a proposal to a client is *okay*. Your client will most likely get it on time, and everyone will be happy. Delivering your proposal in person, however, is much better. Why? Because you not only ensure that the proposal is delivered promptly and accurately, but you also demonstrate to your client that his or her business is important to you. Delivering a proposal in person also allows you to answer your client's questions on the spot and to leave a good parting impression. Unless the cost is prohibitive, always deliver proposals in person.

Be prepared to answer every question

When you develop and submit a proposal to a prospective client, you must be prepared to answer any question that the client may ask you. This requires you to know *what* you wrote in your proposal (don't laugh; we both have met with consultants who hadn't read their own proposals). By knowing what's in your proposal, you are prepared to address your clients' needs and concerns with thoughtful responses tailored to their specific situations. Don't forget: *You* are the expert. Don't be unprepared when your clients expect you to act like one!

Sell your qualifications

Whether you are proposing a team approach to solving a client's problem or selling your individual expertise, itemize and highlight your qualifications in your proposal. Individually, what qualifications directly relate to the work that a client needs done? As a team, how can your group best obtain the desired results? Include resumes of anyone who will be working on the project. The resumes should be complete but written to highlight the experience that is most directly applicable to the job at hand. Because your clients will be working closely with you and any other team members that you bring to the project, they will be *very* interested in the qualifications of the individuals you present. Make your qualifications a major focus of your proposal.

Include stellar references

If you were going to hire someone to advise you in some aspect of your business — say, a certified public accountant to help you do your taxes — wouldn't you prefer to hire someone who had years of experience and a list of satisfied clients about half the size of your phone book? Your ability to show prospective clients in a proposal that you have an established and successful track record in your field goes a long way to prove that you can do the proposed work. A successful track record can directly result in your being hired for a job; this is especially the case when clients you have worked for in the past are in the same line of business as your prospective client. Make a point to include the names of your best clients in your proposal — *after* getting their permission to do so. Asking satisfied clients to call new clients on your behalf is often a good idea.

Be flexible on terms

When you're looking for new work, be as easy to work with as possible. The terms and conditions of your proposal should allow for changes based on additional input from your client. For example, your client may prefer that you complete the project in six months instead of nine. No one answer covers *all* situations, and anticipating your client's every need in your proposals is extremely difficult. The solution is to build lots of flexibility into your proposal so that you can tailor your approach to your client's exact requirements after you learn them. If, for example, you believe that a comfortable completion date would be June 30 but that you could finish the project as soon as May 31 if you had to, use the completion date of June 30 in your proposal to allow room to move if requested by your client.

Be proactive in follow-up

After you deliver your proposal to your prospective client, setting up a definite time and process for follow-up is important. First, call your client within two days after you deliver the proposal to ask whether you can answer any questions and when the client expects to make a decision. When the decision date arrives, call your client again to ask whether he or she has made a decision. Continue with this approach until your client makes a decision. If the decision is favorable, congratulations! If it's not, ask what you can do to win the business. A new approach? A tighter schedule? An extended payment plan? Whether you win or lose a job, be sure to ask your prospective clients what led to their decision and what you can do to improve your proposals in the future. Then fine-tune your approach accordingly.

Chapter 26

Ten Tips for Negotiating a Great Contract

. . . .

In This Chapter
▶ Working out a contract that pleases both parties
▶ Setting reasonable limits

. . . .

Contracts are very important to consultants. Not only do they tell you exactly what you are going to do for your client, but they also tell you exactly what your client is going to do for you. In other words, contracts communicate *expectations*. Usually, this means that you do work or provide a service or product for your client, and in exchange your client compensates you in the form of good old-fashioned cash. So how do you ensure that you get the money and other terms and conditions that you need and desire in your contracts? You do so through negotiation — *effective* negotiation. This chapter gives you ten tips that are guaranteed to help you negotiate a winning contract.

Be patient

Great things come to those who are willing to wait — as long as you don't wait *too* long! When you are negotiating contracts and other agreements, patience truly is a virtue. In our experience, if you are too hasty in trying to make a deal happen, you may not get the terms and conditions that you desire. Be patient and take the time to allow your negotiation to unfold. You can and should be interested in moving forward in your negotiations, but you certainly don't have to allow yourself to be pushed into a contract that is unfavorable to your own interests. Be patiently persistent, following up when you say you will.

Be prepared

Preparation is key to getting a great contract. In fact, the extent of your success probably will relate directly to the extent that you are prepared for working through the ins and outs of your deal. Lack of preparation can put you at a tremendous disadvantage when you are negotiating a contract. The more you know about your clients — their needs, their motivations, and their limits — the better you can respond and suggest alternatives that benefit both parties. Take the time to study and learn all you can about your clients *before* you begin negotiating — it's definitely worth your time.

Know your limits

How do you know whether your contract is a good one or a bad one? We're sorry, but that's not something we can tell you — you have to figure that out for yourself. You can figure it out by determining what your limits are and then making sure that you don't exceed them when you finalize your contract terms. For example, by reviewing the elements that make up what it costs you to do business and adding in a comfortable amount as profit, you may determine that your clients need to pay $45 an hour for you to meet your goals. This being the case, you know that if you accept a job for $30 an hour, there's no way that you're going to achieve your goals. Similarly, if there is no possible way that you can perform a service for your clients in a quality manner within a two-week time frame, then you have to draw a line at the point at which you *can* perform the job well — perhaps two or three months.

Don't give up too much too soon

A general rule in the art of negotiation says that the party who makes the first concession is the party that loses the negotiation. Although *we* don't subscribe to this old view of win-lose negotiation, many people out there in the real world would like to make *you* the loser in any contract that they negotiate with you. A great contract results when *both* parties are willing to make concessions that preserve the balance of equity and lead to a win-win outcome. When you give up too much too soon — for example, by giving up a large piece of your hourly billing rate as soon as you are asked to make a concession — you put yourself at a tremendous disadvantage in the negotiation, and you invite the other party to take advantage of you. Never be too anxious to give up your positions — especially when the other party is making few or no concessions. Every concession you make should be answered by an equal concession from the other party. Your mutual objective is a win-win contract.

Clearly define the boundaries of your job

Great contracts precisely and clearly define the exact tasks that you agree to carry out. Why? Because if you don't define what you're going to do, how do you know whether you've done what you said you would? One of the most confounding mistakes you can make in a contract is not clearly defining what you're going to do for your fee. This mistake can result in unlimited amounts of uncertainty, misunderstanding, bad will — and often additional work as you attempt to live up to your *client's* expectation of the job to be done. In the best case, you get lucky, and your client accepts whatever it is that you *think* you should have done. In the worst case, your client rejects your work because it doesn't meet his or her expectations, and you don't get paid. You don't want to learn this lesson more than once!

Don't be afraid to say no

You can use two very powerful words in negotiating any deal: *yes* and *no.* Although most people find that saying yes is very easy, saying no is usually much more difficult. That's because most people want to be agreeable and, being peaceable folks, want to avoid conflict if they possibly can. However, if you want to get a *great* contract, you have to learn to stand your ground and say no when it becomes necessary. You have to fight the seduction of closing the contract if the terms make it a bad or undoable contract. For example, if a prospective client tells you that all you have to do is cut your usual fee in half and you've got a deal, just say *no!* If your client wants you to do twice the amount of work with no increase in fee, just say *no!* If the IRS asks you to send more money, just say *no!* (Well, maybe you'd better say *let's talk* to that one.)

Listen more than you talk

If you're talking, you're not listening. And if you're not listening, you're missing out on the cues — verbal and nonverbal — that can tell you if your client needs additional information or has questions that must be answered before the deal can be finalized. Don't leave listening to chance — be an active listener. This means to stop talking and then *really* listen to what your client has to say. If you don't understand a point, ask for clarification. And if your client isn't listening to *you,* find ways to get his or her attention, such as by asking your client questions or by making what you have to say more interesting.

Leave room to negotiate

Both you and your clients need room to maneuver to get a great contract; that arrangement is just good business sense. No one likes to negotiate a contract with someone who is unwilling to compromise or consider alternatives that benefit both parties. If you start out with your *best* deal, you don't have the flexibility that you need to compromise with your client — and your client won't be very happy with that. When you offer to do work for a client, give yourself plenty of room to make amendments to your terms — and for your client to make amendments, too. The result is a win-win contract that makes both of you happy.

Be prepared with alternatives

We're sorry to be the ones to inform you, but sometimes you just don't get what you want — perhaps not on the first time you try, or the second, or even the third. Having alternatives ready is important in case your client doesn't accept your initial position. For example, you might offer to create an extensive Web site for your client for $2,500. If your client balks at that price, you can offer a less extensive version for $1,500. Of course, these alternatives should be well thought out in advance, and they should be consistent with the limits you have set for yourself. Show your clients the trade-offs they can choose and let them select what they want. The goal is to always keep the deal alive — even when your client doesn't accept your initial position and even when you don't find your client's counteroffer acceptable. In this situation, the objective is to just keep talking. If you just keep talking, chances are that you'll eventually reach an agreement that pleases you both.

Confirm spoken understandings in writing

Even if you're the best of friends with a client and your relationship is professional beyond reproach, confirming your spoken understandings and agreements in writing is always a good idea. Over time, forgetting all the details of an agreement — even the simplest one — is simply too easy. For example, although you may remember agreeing to deliver a draft report on March 1, your client may remember that you agreed to deliver the draft report on February 1. Or you may have thought that you agreed to a fee of $40 an hour, but your client may insist that you agreed to do the job for $30 an hour. The best solution to prevent such misunderstandings is to confirm all your verbal understandings in writing — preferably in your contract.

Chapter 27

Ten Effective Marketing Strategies for New Business

• •

In This Chapter

▶ Trying different approaches

▶ Getting the word out

• •

Marketing is a wonderful thing. Part of your job as a consultant is to do a great job for your current clients. However, attracting and signing future work with new clients is equally important. Although you can approach your marketing in a haphazard, fly-by-the-seat-of-your-pants fashion, the *best* marketing comes from identifying your target clients and then strategizing how best to reach them. What do they read? Where are they? What do they like to do? Before you develop your marketing plan, review the following marketing strategies.

Choose your targets

Before you do anything else, your first task when developing your marketing plan is to identify your target clients. As you choose your targets, you should always have two questions in mind:

✔ Who are your clients?

✔ How can they best be reached?

The answers to these questions help you select the best ways to get the message to your targeted audience. If you are a political consultant, then you know that your target clients are people who are running for elected office or thinking about running for elected office. You know that sticking an advertisement on the bulletin board at your local supermarket won't generate any new clients. However, getting interviewed in a local newspaper or a national publication, such as *USA Today,* may lead to *lots* of business.

Discover what works

Good marketing is a state of constant experimentation to discover what works and what doesn't work. Your goal is to learn from your experimentation, build on what works, and discard the strategies that don't work. When you develop plans for marketing your business, first identify every possible way to get your message out to your targeted audience; then start trying them out. You can try one approach at a time or several at once — it all depends on your budget and how much time you can devote to tracking the results. What is the response from your direct mailing campaign? Good? Then try it again with a somewhat wider distribution. How did the newspaper ad fare? Not well? Then drop it. Keep fine-tuning your marketing campaign and trying new things. To determine what works, you must set up criteria in advance to judge the effectiveness of the technique. For example, each newspaper advertisement should generate ten prospects, of which two can be converted to clients.

Use client success stories

Nothing breeds success like success. As you successfully complete jobs for your clients, you automatically create a pool of client success stories that you can draw from to publicize your firm. And the more work you do, the larger the pool grows. The beauty of using success stories for publicity is that potential clients get an idea of the kind of work you do; at the same time, the success stories build a positive impression of your abilities and expertise. Use client success stories whenever you can: in proposals, advertisements, newsletters, speeches, seminars, and so forth. Even better, ask your clients if you can get an endorsement or testimonial from their organization for use in your publicity materials. Whichever way you decide to use client success stories, be sure to get your clients' permission first if you plan to use their names.

Encourage word-of-mouth referrals

Some of the best marketing you can get is from your satisfied clients. And it's free! Encourage your clients to tell their friends and business associates about your business. You can encourage this word-of-mouth advertising by meeting or exceeding your commitments, being reliable, doing great work, and asking for referrals. Give your clients extra business cards, brochures, and other promotional materials to pass on to other potential clients. You can thank your clients for referring you to others by sending a thank-you note or by giving them a nominal reward, such as a free subscription to your newsletter or a copy of a report on industry trends — or a finder's fee!

Become a media animal

If you want to get prospective clients' attention, you have to be relentless in your campaign to get their attention. Depending on the nature of your consulting business, you have to select the media outlets that are most effective in getting your message to your clients and then bombard them with newsworthy materials. If you're serious about getting publicity, get on the phone, write letters, send e-mail, make personal visits — in short, do whatever it takes to land an interview, place an article, or end up on the 5 o'clock news. Don't take no for an answer. Keep pushing until you get the attention you want. Of course, positive media is the best media. You certainly don't want to find a *60 Minutes* news team in your office waiting to interview you!

Hire a good public relations person

Good public relations people are definitely worth their weight in gold. If you're a media novice and you try to approach the media on your own, you can waste a lot of time. Public relations experts already know how the system works, which media outlets are best to tell your story, and the most effective ways to convince the people in power to take time to listen. Not only can public relations specialists line up media opportunities, but many are happy to create your press kits, press releases, biographies, brochures, and other marketing materials. Be sure you know what *your* PR person will provide to you. To keep things affordable, you can hire the person on an hourly basis and authorize specific tasks as the need arises, or you can specify a retainer arrangement that provides you with a constant level of service for a set fee every month. The choice is up to you and your budget.

Start a newsletter

Newsletters are great publicity tools for *every* kind of consulting business. Not only are they an inexpensive and effective way to target *potential* clients, but they are also effective for retaining and developing new business with *current* clients, who typically want to be on the inside track about what you're doing. Newsletters also add to your credibility. The heart and soul of most consulting newsletters are stories describing the numerous successful projects that the firm has undertaken. These success stories make terrific publicity — both for your firm and for the firms that you serve. Typical newsletters also contain statements of the owner's vision for the firm and its clients, letters to the editor, tips on how to improve a certain aspect of your business, and general industry news. And although subscriptions to some newsletters are free, others — particularly those produced by popular management consultants, such as Tom Peters and Peter Senge — can run in the hundreds of dollars per year. And if you e-mail your newsletters, the money you earn is all profit!

Offer free samples

Countless businesses have found offering free samples to be a highly effective way to secure new clients. What better way to show your potential clients the value of your service than to let them try it at no risk and no obligation? Depending on the exact nature of your business, you can offer a free needs analysis, inspection, initial use, product sample, or other such avenue for letting your clients get a taste of what you offer. Some consultants — financial planners, investment counselors, and so on — offer free public information sessions. These sessions include a short program of investment advice and an overview of the services that their firms provide. A freelance ad copywriter might send prospective clients samples of his or her work clipped from the local newspaper. What do *you* have to offer to *your* clients to get their future business?

Be responsive to media

Newspapers, television, radio, and magazines are among the quickest and most effective ways to reach a wide audience of potential clients. Whenever the media wants to talk to *you,* you should always drop everything and run, don't walk, to the phone. Unless you just gave birth to quintuplets, you usually can't get media attention without spending a lot of time, money, and effort; therefore, when the media is ready for you, you need to be ready for it. Go out of your way to be responsive to the needs, deadlines, and opportunities of media outlets.

Help clients even if you can't do the work

From time to time, you'll get requests from clients to do work that is outside your firm's focus or experience. Instead of just telling your clients that they need to go elsewhere, do everything you can to help connect them to someone who *can* get the work done. Why pass on perfectly good clients to someone else? One, because what goes around comes around, and the firms to which you pass your clients just might return the favor someday. Two, because the client may need your services in the future, and he or she will be grateful that you helped out in his or her time of need. This is an opportunity to begin to build a long-term relationship with a prospective client. And you establish a network of future partners — both on the delivery side and on the client side.

Chapter 28

Ten Ways to Build Business with a Client

. . . .

In This Chapter
▶ Delighting your clients
▶ Asking your clients to help you build your business

. . . .

*Y*our current clients are your best friends. You should love, honor, and cherish them until death do you part. Your current clients are the source of the revenue that keeps your lights lit, your computer humming, and the finance company from repossessing your car. In addition, if you are successful at building long-term relationships, your clients are your absolute *best* source of future business — both through additional business and through referrals. You can significantly improve your odds of building business with your current clients by heeding the advice in this chapter.

Always be on time and within budget

In our experience, dependability is a particularly important quality for consultants to possess. This quality mean doing *what* you promised to do, *when* you promised to do it, and for the *price* you agreed to. A lot of people make a lot of promises, but few actually live up to the standards they set for themselves. Being on time and within budget sets you apart from the individuals who promise the moon but then deliver too little too late. If your clients can't depend on you to do what you promised to do, then before long, they will start looking for someone they can depend on. Set realistic time and budget goals when you negotiate your contract, and then do whatever it takes to achieve them. Better yet, deliver more than you promise! When you deliver more than the client expects and than you promised, you create client delight. And client delight gives you a client for life.

Anticipate your clients' needs (and suggest ways to address them)

When you're working on a job for a particular client, you often see other things that need fixing, too. This situation is like taking your car to a repair shop to get a tune-up, only to find that you need your entire engine replaced. So how can you anticipate your clients' needs? One of the best ways is to keep up on emerging industry trends — by reading business magazines, newspapers, and industry journals; by attending conferences; and by learning through your experience with your other clients. By anticipating your clients' needs, you can bring solutions to your clients before they even know that they need them.

As a consultant, you are in the enviable position of having a clear view of the inner workings of the organization, as well as having the ear of the organization's management. As you work, keep your eyes and ears open to other needs that your client may have. After you identify these needs, talk to your client about them and submit a proposal with your suggested solution. Your client will appreciate your advice, and you will appreciate the additional business that your attention to your client's needs generates.

Be easy to work with

Who would you rather hire: an individual who complains every time you give him or her an assignment to do, or one who is eager to please? Your clients will ask themselves the same question when they decide whether to send more business your way. As a consultant, you're selling more than your products or services — you're selling yourself. You have to offer more than great work; you also have to be easy to work with. Displaying arrogance and throwing temper tantrums are not the ways to turn your clients into long-term partners. Go out of your way to please your clients: Take their phone calls immediately, be responsive to their requests, meet them at *their* offices whenever possible, and maintain the pleasant and agreeable personality of a person *you* would want to work with. This way, you make it easy for your clients to say yes rather than no.

Keep in touch

What's the old saying — "Out of sight, out of mind"? If you let your clients forget about you, you're going to be an awfully lonely consultant. After you establish working relationships with your clients, keep in touch with them. Make a phone call, or send a letter, or drop in on your clients from time to time. How about lunch? Keep them abreast of your latest successes and up-to-date on new services that you add to your repertoire. Offer to help them solve a difficult organizational or technical problem. Above all, don't let your clients fall off your active list of contacts. Schedule regular contacts with both active and inactive (the ones you want to reactivate) clients into your time-management system. Keeping established communication channels open is much easier than establishing new communication channels with new customers.

Be honest and ethical

You should always maintain the highest standards of honesty and ethics in all your business practices. Doing so not only makes it easier for you to sleep at night, but it also builds a strong foundation of trust between you and your clients upon which to build future business. Ethical lapses and breaches of confidentiality can spell disaster for your client relationships. Make a point of setting the highest standards of conduct — both for yourself *and* for your employees. You have only *one* reputation; build and enhance it.

Give more than you promise

A rule in consulting is to always give your client more than you promised. Finding consultants who do exactly what they say they will do, when they say they will do it, can sometimes be difficult. It's simple: When you keep your promises, you have a happy client. But if you want to elevate your client to a new plateau of excitement — the kind of excitement that generates unsolicited testimonials and referrals — then give a little more. Deliver your report a few days early or include an extra set of data for no extra charge. We can guarantee that if you give more than you promise, your clients will come back for more.

A brother of one of our business associates was in the painting contracting business, focusing on painting the homes of the elderly. He was very patient with his clients in selecting colors and would stop to socialize with them as his crew painted. About three weeks after the end of a job, he would return unasked to do any touch-up work that was required. About two months later, he would stop by to do another touch-up, and frequently he would bring a small bouquet of flowers or a bottle of wine or fresh preserves. His clients loved him and overwhelmed him with work. He knew how to create customer delight.

Ask for testimonials and referrals

Clients *like* being bragged about! If you can showcase them as a positive example, such a testimonial can not only leverage additional business with new clients but also strengthen the bond you have with your existing clients. Testimonials are a critical ingredient in your new client proposals: Not only do they lend credibility to your words, but they also give your proposals *life*. Some consultants have found success by featuring their clients in their advertising. For example, if you are a makeup consultant, before-and-after photographs of your most successful clients are an important way for you to show new clients what results they can expect.

Referrals are one of the most important ways for you to get new business from your current clients. Don't be shy; give your clients extra business cards and brochures to give out to their friends and business associates. And don't forget to thank them — a personal note or spoken word of thanks is usually sufficient — whenever you get a new client as a result.

Offer incentives

As you develop a long-term relationship with a client, offering financial incentives to help develop more business can often pay off. For example, you can offer a standing discount of 10 percent to your best customers, or you can give them an occasional free premium. Last year, for example, to thank his loyal newsletter subscribers for their business, Bob sent each one a free autographed copy of his book *The Perfect Letter*.

Educate your clients

Are your clients aware of every service that you offer? Probably not. For example, perhaps you specialize in conducting home inspections for clients who are buying real estate, and you run an ad in the Yellow Pages for that business. When a client hires you to do a home inspection, he or she may not be aware that you *also* do quality carpentry work at very reasonable rates. Your job is to educate your clients about the *full* range of services that you offer. And after you educate your clients, remind them from time to time about the other kinds of work you can do for them. With repeat customers, your marketing materials are the number-one focus of interactions with you and your staff. Your goal is to make them more intelligent consumers of your products and services to effectively manage their expectations.

Do great work

We shouldn't have to tell you that doing great work is what consulting is all about. Your clients hire you because they expect great work, and you went into business for yourself because you were convinced that you could deliver great work. Always do the best job you possibly can, even if you occasionally have to spend more time on a job than you anticipated. Great work creates, maintains, and enhances your reputation as a professional consultant. And delivering great work is one of the best ways to build future business with your current clients.

Index

FOR DUMMIES®

A world of resources to help you grow

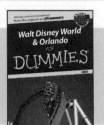